THE ASIAN KITCHEN

Savor the authentic flavors of dishes from all parts of Asia—
from the spicy satays of Indonesia to the fragrant spring rolls of Saigon.

Compiled by Kong Foong Ling
Forewords by Cheong Liew and Ming Tsai
Photos by Luca Invernizzi Tettoni

PERIPLUS EDITIONS
Singapore • Hong Kong • Indonesia

Published by Periplus Editions (HK) Ltd.,
with editorial offices at 6 Joo Seng Road #06-01
Singapore 368357.

ISBN-10: 0-7946-0498-6
ISBN-13: 978-0-7946-0498-1

Food photography
Food photography by Luca Invernizzi Tettoni,
except as noted below:
Masano Kawana: 112–115
Heinz von Holzen: 72–87, 94–107, 176–187

Location photography
Doan Duc Minh 170; Jean Léo Dugast/Photobank 22;
Michael Freeman/Photobank 89; Jill Gocher 9 [fish-
ing boys], 66, 68, 117; Tim Hall 171, 173;
Heinz von Holzen 9 [Balinese procession], 69, 90,
91, 93, 174; Catherine Karnow 172; Masano
Kawana 108, 109, 111; Leong Ka Tai: 34;
Shin Kimura 18; Kal Muller 67; Eric Oey 88;
Photobank 6, 8 [Japanese girl], 32, 92 [tea ceremony],
137, 139, 153, 154; Dominic Sansoni 144, 145, 147;
Luca Invernizzi Tettoni 8 [tea house], 9 [banana leaf
restaurant], 23, 25, 30, 31, 33, 48, 49, 50, 51,
52, 53, 116, 118, 120, 152, 155, 156;
Sonny Yabao 136.

Printed in Singapore

10 09 08 07
6 5 4 3 2 1

Distributors

North America,   Tuttle Publishing
Latin America   364 Innovation Drive
& Europe   North Clarendon, VT 05759-9436
                     Tel: 1 (802) 773-8930
                     Fax: 1 (802) 773-6993
                     info@tuttlepublishing.com
                     www.tuttlepublishing.com

Asia Pacific   Berkeley Books Pte. Ltd.
                     130 Joo Seng Road, #06-01,
                     Singapore 368357
                     Tel: (65) 6280-3320
                     Fax: (65) 6280-6290
                     inquiries@periplus.com.sg
                     www.periplus.com

CONTE

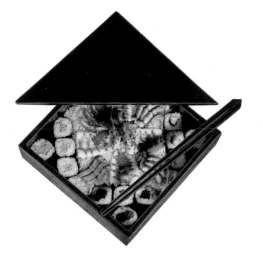

NTS

Authenticity and Tradition

Courtesy of Alan Richardson

Whether you're sweating out a spicy curry from India or Sri Lanka, delighting in flavorful grilled meats from Korea or Vietnam, or marveling at the intricate delicacy of a Japanese or Thai meal, Asian food—with its delightfully heady mix of flavors, smells and colors—has plenty to offer the dedicated foodie.

Asian cuisine is so much more than just food—steeped as it is in social and cultural lore. The region's recipes and cooking methods have developed over many centuries and now, thanks to globalization and migration, Asia's time-honored cooking traditions and fabled dishes have made their way to all corners of the globe. Asian ingredients that were once hard to come by are readily available in supermarkets worldwide as well as from Asian grocers and online merchants, and more people than ever before are eating Asian food on a regular basis.

At my restaurant, Blue Ginger, and in my cookbooks, I strive to properly blend the flavors of the East with those of the West. My feeling is that in order to successfully combine the two cuisines, one must first learn the proper and traditional methods of preparation for each region. *The Asian Kitchen* thoroughly and expertly presents the entire spectrum of the Asian culinary landscape, from Burma to Vietnam. For those who lack the time or resources to travel to Asia, this book brings the region to you, all without leaving your own kitchen.

Peace and Good Eating!

Ming Tsai

New Inspiration from The East

I recall sitting in a vine-covered courtyard in Adelaide, South Australia, some 30 years ago and meditating on what modern Australian cuisine would be like in the future. I remember thinking of the vast resources of food knowledge which abound to the north of us on the Asian continent, and the relative accessibility of it all to young Australian chefs who travel there to gain firsthand information about the best ways of preparing Asian dishes.

The Asian knowledge of fish and seafood preparations, for example, is peerless—from knife skills to stir-frying, oil poaching, steaming and multi-step boiling, deep-frying and then steaming—which is another way of braising. Asian methods of grilling after marinating in spices and yogurt, and the appreciation for spice mixtures and the subtle fragrances of a particular spice in combination with various foods—the knowledge and learning of all this is truly without end!

Foods and recipes from Asia have today become an integral part of the Australian diet and it is hard to imagine a restaurant menu or meal without some Asian influences. Herb and spice combinations from Thailand and Indochina add fragrance and excitement to our salads. The dry spice cooking of India provides a wealth of flavors and subtle aromas. The wet spice cooking of Southeast Asia provides aromatic bouquets mingled with the sweetness of creamy coconut. The aquaculture cuisine of Japan teaches us to respect the quality of fresh fish and appreciate raw fish, revealing its true taste. And the traditional food science and philosophy of China provides the basis for many of our cooking skills and a better appreciation of food generally.

To know how to cook, one must first learn how to eat! From many Asian traditions, we learn that eating is not only the basis of good living but also of good health, and that certain foods act as preventative medicines. I am so glad that after 30 years, the food traditions of Asia have so profoundly influenced the modern international cuisines of today. And I welcome the publication of *The Asian Kitchen* which presents a wealth of authentic recipes and dishes as they are prepared and served today in Asia. At the Grange Restaurant at Hilton Adelaide, I am continually striving to perfect the combination of traditional Asian food cultures represented in this book with our contemporary dining world in Australia.

Cheong Liew

The Essential Flavors of Asia

From roadside hawker stalls in the small villages to the food courts in shopping malls in the large cities, the five-star restaurants and the joys of home-cooking, food is an all-consuming passion in Asia.

There is so much good food in Asia that the first-time traveler cannot help but be enchanted. It often comes as a surprise to people unfamiliar with Asian cultures how much the joy of living of most Asian peoples centers around the preparation, sharing, and discussion of food. As a chef once said, food in Asia is an exercise in tradition, in aesthetics, mutual caring, and moral lessons.

Even out of Asia, it is hard to find a place on earth with food that has not been touched by some aspect of Asian cooking, be it in the form of ingredients, cooking methods or presentation. From elegant New York brasseries to stylish Sydney restaurants, Asian food has come a long way since the American take on Chinese food, *chop suey*, or soupy, flavorless curries made with lots of curry powder and nothing else. These days, modern cooks around the world use fresh coriander leaves (cilantro) with the same confidence as rosemary; add lemongrass and kaffir limes to their tomato broths; and, with their family and friends, want to eat their food spicier and spicier.

Chopsticks are placed alongside the trinity of spoon–fork–knife in Western-style restaurants—if indeed such a category still holds—that now serve roast lamb and tandoori chicken on the same menu. And just as kids in some Asian countries are demanding cornflakes and milk for breakfast, some people in the West are trading in their breakfast cereals for steaming bowls of noodles or plain rice with *miso* soup and pickles. The popularity and pervasiveness of Asian food, particularly in the West, has never been higher.

But in order to cook Asian food—any food—properly, you need to understand the origins of the particular cuisine. You also need to know the best way of getting the most out of your ingredients. As many good cooks will tell you, if you do the basics properly, the rest will follow. Once you understand why a certain ingredient is tempered with another or used in conjunction with something else, you can then play and let your imagination (and taste-buds) take you to new taste sensations.

Let *The Asian Kitchen* be your guide through a diverse selection of cuisine from China, India,

Burma (Myanmar), Sri Lanka, Japan, Korea, Indonesia, Malaysia, Singapore, Philippines, Thailand, and Vietnam. Because the countries covered here encompass a diverse geography and climate, from the temperate to the tropical, all the cuisines are quite distinct, despite the similarity in cooking techniques and some ingredients. All, however, emphasize freshness and flavor; in Asia, they believe that good eating is essential to good living.

Many of the popular favorites from each country are represented here: the gorgeous red and green curries of Thailand, invigorating Vietnamese *pho*, fluffy Indian breads, cleansing *sushi* and *sashimi* from Japan, and incendiary *laksa* and noodle soups from Malaysia and Singapore. There are simple dishes that require just a little cooking and no complicated techniques, making them ideal for day-to-day use in the home. For the confident cook, there are more complex dishes that are guaranteed to impress family and friends at your next dinner party or Sunday lunch, and taste delicious too! Most of the dishes are readily adapted to a Western-style table, and hints and tips have been included as to how best to serve them.

Common to the tables of all these countries is grain, which holds pride of place during a meal, as distinct from the Western table where the meat component or main course is the height of the meal. In most tropical countries located on or near the equator such as Malaysia, Singapore, Philippines, and Indonesia, plain steamed rice is the staple. However, be warned: there is rice and there is rice, and they are not always interchangeable. The Chinese prefer the fragrant long-grain jasmine rice, the Japanese a starchier short-grain variety. The Thais and Indonesians often serve glutinous rice to mop up their curries. The Indians favor the basmati. As you venture above the equator, preference is frequently given to wheat, which may be served in the form of noodles, buns, or pancakes.

Another characteristic of Asian food is its dependence on the humble soybean and its by-products. Tofu (beancurd), soy sauce, tofu skin and bean paste sauces are used in dishes from China to Indonesia, with a little tweaking to local tastes.

And then there is the noodle... whether it be flat, round, dried, fresh, or is made of egg, buckwheat, mung bean, potato starch, wheat or ground rice, the Chinese love affair with noodles has left its mark on other Asian cuisines. The machines and factories have taken over from the hand-pulled noodles that the Chinese were particularly famous for, but there is no denying the versatility of the end product. In Asia they are stir-fried or pan-fried, or used in soups, salads, and spring rolls, or eaten with a sauce. They can be eaten as part of a meal or be a meal in a bowl, eaten at all times of the day, from breakfast to supper.

Asian cooks demand—and receive—the very best there is on offer from their local markets and suppliers, a hangover from their agricultural heritage perhaps, or because supermarkets were few and far between until recently. The ingredients have to be of the freshest quality: the vegetables just picked, the fish just out of the water, the chicken just caught. This ingredient is then quickly cooked, usually in a simple manner that would allow the essence of the produce to shine through.

Please do not be wary of the foreignness of some of the ingredients used in this book; remember that the now-ubiquitous ginger and green onions (scallions) had to start somewhere too! Most of the ingredients called for in *The Asian Kitchen* are readily available from your local Asian grocery store, and it is worth your while searching out a good one and befriending the people who run it—they will be a rich source of advice and hints on how best to prepare your purchases. Many Asian food stores these days have an extensive range of fresh greens and vegetables, and they do not have to be used only in the Asian way.

Try to use the best of what's in season and don't be afraid to experiment. For instance, there is no reason why you can't serve Chinese broccoli in place of conventional broccoli with your next leg of lamb, or use coconut milk instead of milk to make a crème caramel, or serve steamed baby *bok choy* instead of green beans with a traditional roast chicken. You may also like to try smearing tandoori paste over a rack of lamb for a change of pace, or baste the next chicken you roast with green curry paste, and serve it with roast potatoes and a crisp green salad. The recipes are meant to be a guide and not a constraint! Frequently, ingredients may be substituted for each other without compromising on authenticity—just make sure you do try the recipe as it is set out at least once though. If you are attempting a recipe for the first time, it is very important that you read the recipe all the way through to the end to make sure you have the right equipment and ingredients to hand. With much Asian cooking, the time-consuming work is in the preparation. After the ingredients have been cleaned, chopped and sliced, the cooking

Below: The men in this Chinese tea-house have gathered to gossip as much as to drink tea. *Right:* Like modern Japanese culture, Japanese food is a striking blend of the old and the new.

process itself is usually fairly simple and straightforward.

A comprehensive, illustrated glossary (see pages 10–19) has been included to help you demystify and use some of the knobbly tubers and jars of brown stuff you may find in food stores. There is also a chapter on cooking implements and a few simple techniques to help you prepare Asian food. Despite the advent of modern methods and gizmos in Asian kitchens, some traditional implements are still regarded as irreplaceable. Not all kitchens, for instance, have cookers complete with an oven, as most cooking is done on the top of a stove. Many Asian kitchens are functional rather than aesthetic, with meals cooked over an open fire. In urban areas, gas rings fuelled by LPG are increasingly used.

Measurements in this book are given in volume as far as possible. A conversion guide has been included on page 188 for your conve-

Top, main picture: This Balinese ritual should help ensure a plentiful crop of rice. *Above:* In Indonesia, you're never too young to contribute to the family dinner table. *Right:* An array of succulent offerings at a Singaporean banana-leaf restaurant.

Western-style dinner, where the dishes come out sequentially (as opposed to all at once). The recipes in this book have been structured with this in mind, into categories such as appetizers, soups, salads, main courses, and desserts for ease of use. You may need to increase the quantities of the main dishes slightly if you are not planning to serve rice or bread with the meal. A number of suggested menus— for family meals, dinner parties etc— are included in each chapter to help you plan your meals.

Most diners in Asian countries drink tea throughout a meal. Spirits are also popular, especially at formal dinners and banquets. But there's no reason why you can't drink your favorite red or white wine if you are eating Asian food—with some judicious tasting you will soon find out which goes best with what.

We hope *The Asian Kitchen* will inspire you, with its pictures, words and delicious recipes, to prepare these luscious dishes at home. It will also let you gain a better understanding of the wonderful cuisines of the region and give you many years of happy eating. And don't forget to have fun in the kitchen!

nience. Unless otherwise stated, these recipes will serve four to six people as part of a shared meal of two to three dishes with rice.

The Asian table is a communal table. All dishes, with the exception of dessert, are usually presented at once and served with rice. Diners help themselves to whatever they want and to as much as they desire. There will usually be a soup, followed by or accompanied with one or two meat dishes and a vegetable dish. Dessert, especially in a domestic situation, is almost always sliced fresh seasonal fruit.

Of course you may like to serve a series of Asian dishes for a

Asian celery

Annatto seeds

Asafoetida

Asian eggplants

Asian Ingredients

Most of the ingredients called for in this book are readily found at Chinese or Asian grocery stores and well-stocked supermarkets.

Baby anchovies, dried

Bamboo shoots

Banana blossom

Banana leaves

AGAR-AGAR A setting agent derived from seaweed which hardens without refrigeration and is used for cakes and desserts. It comes in long strands or in powder form; 1 teaspoon of powder sets 1–1^1/2 cups liquid. To use, sprinkle powdered agar-agar over liquid and bring it gently to a boil, stirring until dissolved.

ANNATTO SEEDS The dark reddish-brown seeds of the "lipstick plant" and are commonly used as a coloring agent. Usually the seeds are fried in oil to extract their brick red color, then discarded. Commonly available where Caribbean foods are sold.

ASAFOETIDA A strong-smelling brown tree resin. Known in India as *hing*, it adds an oniony flavor to cooked foods and is believed to aid digestion. Often used in lentil dishes, it is sold in a box or tin as a solid lump, or in the form of powder.

ASAM GELUGUR The Malay name for the sweet-sour garcinia fruit that resembles a dried apple. Dried slices of the fruit are used in some Malay and Nonya dishes and tamarind may be used as a substitute.

ASIAN CELERY The celery used in Asia is much smaller than the Western variety, with slender stems and particularly pungent leaves. Often known as "Chinese celery" and used as a herb rather than vegetable, it is added to soups, rice dishes and stir-fries. Substitute regular celery leaves or Italian parsley.

ASIAN EGGPLANTS Known also as aubergine or brinjal, this vegetable is much smaller and thinner throughout Asia than its Western counterpart. Japanese eggplants are often no more than about 4–8 in (10–20 cm) long. The Thais also use a rather bitter pea-sized eggplant and the apple variety. Use slender Asian or Japanese eggplants for all recipes in this book—they are less bit-

ter and have a better texture. They do not need salting before use.

AZUKI BEANS Small red beans that are sold dried and need to be soaked before using. *Azuki* beans are cooked, sweetened and sometimes mashed into a paste to make desserts. Cooked, sweetened red beans are readily available canned in Asian supermarkets.

BABY ANCHOVIES, DRIED Also known as *ikan bilis*, these are tiny whitebait fish ranging from 1–2 in (2–5 cm) in length. They are usually sold in Asia—salted and sun-dried. Remove the head and black intestinal tract before using. If possible, buy them split, cleaned and ready for use. Ikan bilis are usually quite salty, so taste any dish using ikan bilis before adding more salt. They are used as a seasoning or deep-fried with chilies and peanuts to make a crunchy side dish or appetizer.

BANGKUANG See JICAMA.

BAMBOO SHOOTS The fresh shoots of the bamboo plant that makes an excellent vegetable. Fresh shoots taste better than canned, but must be peeled, sliced and simmered in water for about 30 minutes before using. Ready-to-use sliced bamboo shoots, packed in water, can be found in the refrigerated produce section of some supermarkets and are convenient and easy to use. Canned bamboo shoots should be boiled for 5 minutes to reduce any metallic flavor before using. Both fresh and canned bamboo shoots are increasingly available in many supermarkets.

BANANA BLOSSOM The unopened male flowers of the banana plant—a purple-red inflorescence tinged with yellow at the base which hangs at the end of a clump of developing bananas. Tasting like artichokes, the hearts of these flowers, which have been stripped off their purple petals, are a popular salad ingredient

Bonito flakes

Carambola

Dried red chilies

Finger-length red chilies

Bird's-eye chilies

Candlenuts

in some Southeast Asian cuisines, especially in Vietnam. Fresh, canned and dried banana blossoms can often be found in specialty stores outside Asia, particularly those stocking Vietnamese and Thai ingredients. Choose a firm, large blossom with an even color and check that the outer petals are not wilted. To prepare the blossom for cooking, remove the coarse outer petals to reveal the creamy white heart. Quarter the heart lengthwise with an oiled stainless steel knife to avoid the sticky sap from clinging to it. If not cooking immediately, soak in cold water or rub with lemon or lime juice to avoid discoloration. Simmer the cut heart in plenty of lightly salted water until tender, about 15 to 20 minutes. Drain, cool then pull out and discard the hard filaments inside each cluster of yellow stamens as they have an unpleasant texture.

BANANA LEAVES infuse a delicate flavor and aroma to foods. They are often used as wrappers when steaming or grilling dishes, or as little trays to hold food when cooking. Soften them in boiling water before use to prevent them from cracking when wrapping foods. Fresh banana leaves are sometimes sold in Hispanic or Asian markets, but frozen banana leaves are more readily available. If banana leaves are not available, aluminum foil can be used, though it does not impart the subtle flavors that banana leaves do.

Thai basil (*horapa*)

Lemon basil (*mangklak*)

Holy basil (*kaprow*)

BASIL This is often used as a seasoning and garnish in Thai cooking, and there are several types. The most commonly used basil is known as **Thai basil** or *horapa* and is fairly similar to European or American sweet basil. It is used liberally as a seasoning and sprigs of it are often added to platters of fresh raw vegetables. **Lemon basil** or *manglak* is similar to horapa but paler and with a distinctive lemony fragrance. It is used in soups and salads. **Holy basil**, known in Thailand as *kraprow*, has a fragrance redolent of cloves. Its taste is sharp and hot and it is mainly used in spicy stir-fries. Basil is known as *daun selasih* or *kemangi* in Indonesia. Thai basils are commonly available in Asian food stores and many supermarkets, but sweet basil makes an acceptable substitute.

BELIMBING WULUH See CARAMBOLA.

BESAN A pale yellow flour which has been finely ground from *channa dal* (Bengal gram) or the yellow split pea. It is sometimes referred to as chickpea flour, Bengal gram flour or simply gram flour. It is commonly found in Asian food stores and some health food stores.

BLACK BEANS, SALTED Also called fermented black beans or Chinese black beans. They are soybeans that have been fermented and preserved in salt, hence their strong, salty flavor. Mainly used to season a number of dishes, especially fish, beef and chicken, they are sold in packets or cans and can be kept for several months if stored in the refrigerator. Soak in warm water for 30 minutes before using, to remove excess salt.

BLACK CHINESE VINEGAR Made from rice, wheat and millet or sorghum. The best black vinegars are well-aged and have a complex, smoky flavor similar to balsamic, which may be substituted. Chinese cooks add black vinegar sparingly to sauces, dips and when braising meats.

BLACK MOSS FUNGUS A fine, hair-like fungus valued in Chinese cooking. Soak in warm water until pliable before using.

BOK CHOY A highly nutritious variety of cabbage with long, crisp stalks and spinach-like leaves. It has a clean, slightly peppery flavor and is a wonderful addition to soups and stir-fries. It is available in most well-stocked supermarkets.

BONITO FLAKES, DRIED This—along with dried kelp (*konbu*)—are the essential ingredients for making Basic Dashi Stock (page 94). The shavings of bonito fish are available in small plastic packets of varying sizes. The larger ones are used to make dashi soup stock whereas the finer ones are used as a garnish. They are readily available in Japanese food stores as well as many supermarkets.

BURDOCK ROOT is a long, brown and stick-like root that can measure up to 25 in (60 cm) in length. It is sold as a whole root, or halved. It should be put into water immediately after scraping off the skin to stop it from discoloring. Nutritious and enjoyed for its texture, fresh burdock is often available in Japanese stores and Asian supermarkets. Canned burdock can be used as a substitute.

CANDLENUT A waxy, cream-colored nut similar in size and texture to macadamia nut, which can be used as a substitute, although less-expensive raw almonds or cashews will also do. Candlenuts are never eaten raw or on their own, but are chopped, ground and cooked with seasonings and added to curries and spice mixes for flavor and texture. They go rancid quickly because of their high oil content, so buy in small quantities and keep refrigerated.

CARAMBOLA A pale-green acidic fruit about 2–3 in (5–8 cm) long that grows in clusters. A relative of the starfruit, it is used whole or sliced to give a sour tang to soups, curries, fish dishes and *sambals*. Sour grapefruit juice or tamarind juice are good substitutes.

CARDAMOM PODS Used to flavor curries and desserts—giving foods a heady, sweet scent. The fibrous, straw-colored pods enclose 15–20 pungent, black seeds. Whole pods are bruised lightly with a cleaver or a pestle before use. Try not to use ground cardamom as it is virtually flavorless compared to the whole pods.

CAROM *Carum ajowan* comes from the same family as cumin and parsley. Known as carom or bishop's weed in the West, it is called *ajwain* in India. The seeds are similar in appearance and flavor to caraway seeds. If unavailable, substitue dried thyme.

| Chinese broccoli (kailan) | Chinese (Napa) cabbage | Chinese chives | Chrysanthemum leaves |

CHILIES Many different varieties of chilies are used in Asia. The flavor of fresh and dried chilies is different, so be sure to use the type specified in the recipes. **Finger-length green** and **red chilies** are usually moderately hot. Red chilies are often dried and ground to make **chili flakes** and **ground red pepper**. The main types of chilies used in Southeast Asia are the finger-length red or green chili, tiny but fiery-hot **bird's-eye chilies** (which may be red, green or yellowy-orange) and **dried red chilies**. Cut or break dried chilies into pieces and soak in hot water for about 10 minutes to soften before grinding or blending. If you want to reduce the heat without losing flavor, discard some or all of the seeds. Be careful to wash your hands thoroughly after handling chilies—use rubber gloves if possible. **Chili oil** is made from dried chilies or chili powder steeped in oil and is used to enliven many Sichuan dishes. **Chili paste** consists of ground fresh or dried chilies, sometimes mixed with vinegar and garlic and sold in jars. Sichuan chili paste is made from dried chilies, soaked and ground with a touch of oil. **Chili sauce** is made by mixing ground chilies with water and seasoning the mixture with salt, sugar and vinegar or lime juice. It is available bottled and in jars.

CHINESE BROCCOLI Also known as *kailan* or Chinese kale, it has long, narrow stems and leaves, and small edible flowers. The stems are the tastiest part while the leaves are slightly bitter and are often discarded. Chinese broccoli is available fresh in Asian markets. Substitute broccoli stems, *bok choy* or broccolini.

CHINESE CABBAGE Also known as Napa cabbage, it has tightly packed white stems and pale green leaves with a mild, delicate taste and is a good source of minerals such as calcium, potassium and iron. Chinese cabbage is the basic ingredient in kimchi and is also commonly used in many soups.

CHIRONJI NUTS Small brownish nuts that look a little like large sunflower seeds, they are sometimes ground together with other nuts, such as cashews or almonds, or with white poppy seeds to enrich the sauces of some dishes. The flavor is similar to that of hazelnuts, although they are perhaps best substituted with a mixture of hazelnuts and almonds.

CHIVES, CHINESE Also known as garlic chives, with a garlic flavor and aroma. Unlike the Western chives, which have rounded stems, Chinese chives have long, thin stems and resemble flat spring onions. They can be found in Asian markets and many gourmet produce markets. Regular Western chives are an acceptable substitute.

CHOY SUM Also know as *Chinese flowering cabbage*, this is a leafy green vegetable with crisp crunchy stems. Available in supermarkets in Asia, it is now increasingly available in Western countries too. Substitute any other leafy greens.

CHRYSANTHEMUM LEAVES These are the tender edible leaves of the giant chrysanthemum plant. The serrated leaves have a slightly bitter, grassy flavor. They are often used as a garnish and a flavoring in Korean soups. A more commonly available variety, garland Chrysanthemum, also known by its Chinese name *tung ho*, are sold in bunches often with the roots attached. Store refrigerated and wrapped in paper. Substitute Chinese celery leaves or watercress.

CINNAMON True cinnamon comes from the fragrant bark of a tree native to Sri Lanka, and is lighter in color, thinner and more expensive than cassia bark, which is often sold as cinnamon. Powdered cinnamon is not a substitute.

CLOUD EAR FUNGUS Also known as wood fungus, this crinkly greyish-brown dried fungus swells to many times its original size after soaking in warm water for a few minutes. They have little flavor but are prized for their texture.

CLOVES A small, brown, nail-shaped spice that emits a floral, spicy fragrance. Used in spice blends.

CORIANDER An indispensable herb and spice in Thai cooking. **Coriander seeds** are roasted and then ground in spice pastes. **Coriander roots** are used in the same way, while **coriander leaves** (also known as cilantro or Chinese parsley) are used as a herb and a garnish.

CUMIN Pale brown to black fragrant seeds that look similar to caraway. Frequently partnered with coriander in spice mixtures and curry pastes.

CURRY LEAVES Sprigs of these small, dark green leaves with a distinctive fragrance are often used in Indian curries. A sprig is about 8–12 individual leaves. Dried curry leaves are milder. There is no good substitute.

CURRY POWDER A commercial blend of Indian spices which typically contains turmeric, coriander, chilies, cumin, mustard, ginger, fenugreek, garlic, cloves, salt and any number of other spices. Curry powders are often blended with water to a stiff paste before being fried. For maximum freshness, store in a jar in the freezer.

| Cloud ear fungus | Coriander leaves (cilantro), with roots attached | Curry leaves | Daikon radish |

Dried shrimp

Dried chinese sausages

Dried rice paper wrappers

Dried shrimp paste

DAIKON RADISH is a large white radish which can grow to a length of 15 in (40 cm), with a diameter of about 3 in (8 cm). Choose firm, heavy and unblemished daikons. Widely used in Japanese cooking, the fresh root is often served finely grated and eaten with soy sauce. Pickled daikon radish is yellow or white in color, and sold vacuum-packed and in jars.

Channa dal   Masoor dal   Mung dal

Tur dal   Urad dal or blackgram dal

DAL Also "*dhal*". Dal refers to a wide variety of dried split peas and beans. Several kinds are used in these recipes. **Channa dal** or **Bengal gram** resembles a yellow split pea but is smaller; yellow split peas may be used as a substitute. Channa dal is also ground to make **channa flour** (besan). **Masoor dal** are skinned and split masoor lentils. They're salmon-colored, cook quickly, and turn golden and mushy when cooked. **Mung dal** is the split version of the bean used to make bean sprouts. It is pale yellow, slightly elongated and is popular in northern Indian cooking. **Tur dal** (also **tuvar** or **arhar dal**) is a pale yellow lentil which is smaller than channa dal. **Urad dal** or **blackgram dal** is sold either with its black skin on or husked, when it becomes creamy white in color.

DASHI A stock made from dried kelp and dried *bonito* flakes, the basis of Japanese soups and sauces. Instant *dashi* granules (*dashi-no-moto*) are sold in glass jars in Japanese stores.

DRIED CHINESE SAUSAGES Also known as *lap cheong*, these are thin, sweet Chinese pork sausages delicately perfumed with rose-flavored wine. They are used as an ingredient in stir-fries or braised dishes rather than being eaten on their own like European sausages. Sold in pairs, they keep almost indefinitely without refrigeration. Substitute sweet Italian sausage.

DRIED MANGO POWDER Also known as *amchoor*, it is used to give a sour tang to some Indian dishes. It is ground from dried unripe green mangoes. If unavailable, use a squeeze of lemon juice.

DRIED RICE PAPER WRAPPERS Made from a batter of rice flour, water and salt, then steamed and dried in the sun on bamboo racks, which leaves a crosshatch imprint. Used to wrap a wide variety of

spring rolls, dried rice paper wrappers must be moistened before using. Available in many Asian food markets, they will keep for many months if stored in a cool dark place.

DRIED SHRIMP A popular Asian ingredient, particularly for sauces and sambals. They are tiny, orange-colored saltwater shrimp that have been dried in the sun. They come in different sizes and the really small ones have their heads and tails still attached. Look for dried shrimp that are pink and plump, avoiding any with a grayish appearance. The better quality ones are bright orange in color and shelled. Dried shrimp will keep for several months. They should be soaked in warm water for 5 minutes to soften slightly before use.

DRIED SHRIMP PASTE Known variously as *kapee, trasi,* and *belachan*. A dense mixture of fermented ground shrimp with a very strong odor that may be offensive to some. It is sold in dried blocks that range in color from caramel to dark brown. It should be roasted before use—either wrapped in foil and dry-roasted in a wok or skillet, or toasted over a gas flame on the end of a fork or back of spoon —to enhance its flavor and kill bacteria. In some recipes, it is ground with the rest of the ingredients and fried in oil without roasting.

FENNEL Similar in appearance to cumin although slightly longer and fatter. Fennel has a sweet fragrance that is similar to aniseed. The seeds are used whole or ground.

FENUGREEK SEEDS An almost square, hard, yellowish-brown seed. The seeds are strongly flavored and are often used in southern Indian dishes and in pickles.

FISH SAUCE This is the ubiquitous Thai and Vietnamese condiment used in almost every dish, just as salt or soy sauce are used in other cuisines. Made from salted, fermented fish or shrimp, it has a very pungent, salty flavor in its pure form. Fish sauce is often combined with other ingredients such as sugar, garlic and lime juice to make the various dipping sauces known as *nuoc mam cham*. Use sparingly and always look for a quality brand for a better flavor. Refrigerate after opening.

FIVE SPICE POWDER A blend of ground dried spices containing cinnamon, cloves, fennel, Sichuan pepper and ginger. It is sold in small packets in the spice section in most supermarkets.

GARAM MASALA An Indian blend of powdered spices, usually including cinnamon, cardamon, cloves, fennel and black pepper. Pre-blended *garam masala* can be bought from any store specializing in spices. Store in an airtight jar away from heat or sunlight.

GHEE The rich, delicious clarified butter oil used as the main oil in Indian cooking. It is made by removing the milk solids from butter, and is therefore known as "clarified butter oil." It keeps well at room temperature. Substitute vegetable oil or butter.

GINSENG A highly prized medicinal root believed to have rejuvenating properties. It is widely cultivated in Korea and used extensively in Korean cooking. As aged ginseng root is very expensive, substitute cheaper, vacuum-packed white ginseng (similar in taste to parsnips). Another alternative is to use dried ginseng root shavings and strings, available from Asian food stores and apothecaries.

GREEN PEPPER, JAPANESE Japanese green peppers are much

Ginseng

Jackfruit

Jicama (bangkuang)

Kaffir lime and leaves

smaller, and are not spicy. They have a milder flavor than Western bell peppers (capsicum). Generally, 8 Japanese green peppers are equivalent to 1 large bell pepper.

GREEN ONIONS Also known as scallions, they have slender stalks with dark green leaves and white bases. They are sliced and sprinkled generously on soups and other dishes as a garnish.

HOISIN SAUCE Also called Peking sauce, it is a sweet dark brown sauce made from soybeans, garlic, sugar and various spices. It is commonly used as a dipping sauce for pork and duck dishes, and as a flavoring in stews. The bottled sauce keeps indefinitely if stored in the refrigerator.

IKAN BILIS See BABY ANCHOVIES, DRIED.

JACKFRUIT A large, green fruit with a tough, knobbly skin. The segmented flesh is sweet and perfumed when ripe. In Vietnam, the young jackfruit is used like a vegetable in cooking. Readily available fresh in Southeast Asia, it can be purchased canned in the West.

JAGGERY A crude sugar popular in Sri Lankan cookery most commonly made from cane sugar and the sap of coconut or palmyrah palms. Southeast Asian palm sugar makes an acceptable substitute, or use dark brown sugar.

JICAMA Also known as *bangkuang* or *singkamas*. A crunchy mild tuber with a white flesh and beige skin that peels off easily. It is excellent eaten raw or cooked. Substitute daikon radish.

KAFFIR LIME These are small limes with a very rough and intensely fragrant skin, but virtually no juice. The skin or rind is often grated and used as a seasoning. Fragrant kaffir lime leaves are added whole to soups and curries or finely shredded and added to salads or deep-fried fish cakes, giving a wonderful tangy taste to these dishes. They are available frozen or dried in Asian food stores; frozen leaves are much more flavorful than dried ones.

KALE See CHINESE BROCCOLI.

KAILAN See CHINESE BROCCOLI.

KANGKUNG See WATER SPINACH.

KELP See SEAWEED.

KENCUR *Kencur* has a unique, camphor-like flavor and should be used sparingly. It must be rinsed and the skin scraped off before using. Dried *kencur* should be soaked in boiling water for 30 minutes to soften before use. If using ground *kencur*, substitute $^1/2$–1 teaspoon of the powder for 1 in ($2^1/2$ cm) of the fresh root. Try to use the fresh root whenever possible as it is more fragrant.

KINOME The leaves have a decorative appearance and a distinctive

taste that makes them a popular garnish during the warmer months. They are readily available in Japanese stores and can be kept refrigerated for about a week. Sprigs of watercress make an acceptable substitute but the flavor is different.

KRACHAI is a rhizome widely cultivated in Thailand, also known as Chinese keys or sometimes referred to as "Thai ginger." It gives a subtle spicy flavor to dishes and goes well with seafood. Fresh *krachai* is beige in color and looks like a bunch of baby carrots or turnips. Buy smooth and firm ones. Store in a paper bag in the refrigerator for up to a few weeks. Preserved *krachai* is sold in jars either whole or cut into strips.

KRUPUK SHRIMP CRACKERS These are dried wafers made from bits of shrimp, fish, vegetables and nuts mixed with various types of flour to make a very popular snack in Indonesia and parts of Southeast Asia. They must be thoroughly dried in the sun or in an oven set on very low before deep-frying in very hot oil for a few seconds, when they puff up spectacularly and become crispy. Once cooked, store in an airtight container.

LAKSA LEAF See VIETNAMESE MINT.

LEMONGRASS This is a fragrant, lemony stalk that is either bruised and used whole in soups or curries, or sliced and ground as part of a basic spice mix. It is usually sold in bunches of 3–4 stems in supermarkets. The tough outer layers should be peeled away and only the inner part of the thick lower third of the stem is used. Always slice the stem before grinding to get a smooth paste.

LOOFAH A type of gourd with a woody, earthy flavor often used in Vietnamese soups. Any type of squash may be used as a substitute.

LOTUS ROOT Lotus root has a delicious crunchy texture and a beautiful lacy pattern when sliced crosswise. The large roots are sold fresh in Asian grocery stores, often wrapped in dried mud to keep them moist and are also available frozen and pre-sliced in plastic packets, or canned. Its seeds are used fresh for sweets or dried in stews. Soak dried **lotus nuts** in boiling water for 1 hour, then peeled, and the bitter green core in the middle of the seed removed and discarded. Canned lotus nuts normally have this bitter core removed.

MACE The lacy orange-red covering or aril of the nutmeg seed. It is often sold in the form of dried blades and is also available in powdered form.

MINT LEAVES One of the most common herb used in salads. Mint grown in Southeast Asia has a very intense flavor, the closest equivalent elsewhere being spearmint although regular mint leaves may also be used.

Krachai

Krupuk shrimp crackers

Lemongrass

Loofah gourd

Lotus root

Mace

Mustard seeds (black and yellow)

MIOGA is a pretty, pale pink ginger bud with green tips. Although it is a member of the ginger family, mioga is not spicy, unlike most gingers. Only its flower and bud are eaten. The buds are very fragrant when thinly sliced and are used as a garnish, in salads or made into vinegar pickles.

MIRIN is a type of sweetened rice wine sold in bottles in Japanese stores. It is used only for cooking—the alcohol dissipates through cooking. Use 1 teaspoon sugar added to 2 teaspoons sake as a substitute for 1 tablespoon mirin.

MISO is a protein-rich, salty paste made of fermented soy beans. It has a distinctive aroma and flavor, and is a very important ingredient in Japanese cuisine. Miso must be kept refrigerated and is sold in plastic packs or tubs in the refrigerated section of Asian food stores. It comes in different grades, varieties and colors and the taste ranges from very salty to mild to sweet. The word "miso" used in this book refers to the common brown miso used for soups and sauces and which is easily available in well-stocked supermarkets. White miso is actually a light yellow paste, light in flavor and is one of the least salty varieties. White miso is good for both soups and dressings. Red miso is reddish brown in color, with an emphatic flavor, and is used for winter soups and stews. Other varieties include inaka miso or country miso, which is sweeter and grainier and can be eaten as a dip with fresh vegetables.

MITSUBA A member of the parsley family, both the stems and leaves of this decorative herb, are used in Japanese cuisine—in soups, salads and fried foods. Parsley makes an acceptable substitute, although the flavor of *mitsuba* is more like celery.

MORNING GLORY See WATER SPINACH.

MUNG BEANS Small green beans that reveal a yellow interior when the skins are removed (split). Mung beans are often used in desserts and appetizers. They can be found in well-stocked supermarkets and health food stores.

MUSTARD OIL A vegetable oil infused with ground mustard seeds and used for cooking as well as preserving. It is particularly pop**MUSTARD SEEDS** Both yellow and brownish-black mustard seeds are used in Indian cuisine. Brown-black mustard seeds are more common in southern Indian cuisine as they impart a nutty flavor to dishes. Try to use the type specified.

NIGELLA Often incorrectly referred to as onion seeds, these small, black seeds are known as *kalonji* in India. Omit if not available. If specified for Indian breads, substitute black sesame seeds.

NORI See SEAWEED.

NUTMEG A spice native to the Moluccan islands of Indonesia, the nutmeg is actually the seed of a fleshy fruit, and is covered by a lacy red membrane known as mace. Store whole nutmegs in a glass jar. Whole nutmeg should always be freshly grated before using.

OIL, COOKING Blended vegetable oils (never olive oil) are used by Chinese cooks for frying. Peanut oil is sometimes specified for its distinctive flavor.

OKRA Also known as ladies' fingers and is a variety of banana. It is a green, ridged vegetable ranging from $2^{1}/2$–8 in (7–20 cm) in length. Okra has long been popular in India and Southeast Asia as a vegetable.

ORANGE PEEL, DRIED Dried orange peel is added to slow-cooked dishes for flavor. Although usually available in Chinese stores, fresh peel can be used as a substitute.

OYSTER SAUCE A flavorful soy-based sauce made with oyster extract; a Cantonese specialty. A vegetarian version is available, and is sometimes sold as "mushroom oyster sauce" or "oyster-flavored sauce." If you do not like monosodium glutamate, choose your brand carefully as most are laden with this additive. Oyster sauce is available in most supermarkets. Mushroom sauce or a combination of fish sauce and soy sauce is a good substitute although the flavor will not be the same.

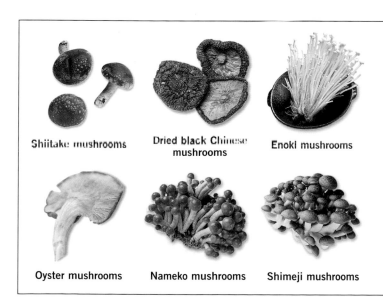

Shiitake mushrooms

Dried black Chinese mushrooms

Enoki mushrooms

Oyster mushrooms

Nameko mushrooms

Shimeji mushrooms

MUSHROOMS They are grown commercially, though the wild mushroom season is eagerly awaited in Japan, as fresh wild mushrooms are highly sought after. Fresh **shiitake mushrooms** have an excellent flavor. **Dried black Chinese mushrooms** are similar to shiitake mushrooms but must be soaked in water before use. **Enoki mushrooms** or golden mushrooms are clusters of slender cream-colored stalks with tiny caps, and are sometimes available fresh and canned—the tough end of the stems must be discarded before use. Fresh **oyster mushrooms** (*maitake*) are also sold in cans. **Nameko mushrooms** have a slippery texture and attractive reddish brown caps; as their season is short, they are more commonly found in jars or cans. Although rather similar to nameko mushrooms in terms of size and shape, **shimeji mushrooms** lack their slippery texture. See also CLOUD EAR FUNGUS.

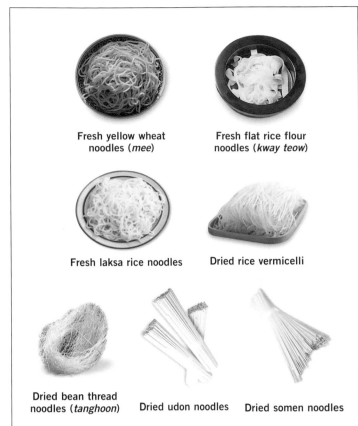

Fresh yellow wheat noodles (*mee*)

Fresh flat rice flour noodles (*kway teow*)

Fresh laksa rice noodles

Dried rice vermicelli

Dried bean thread noodles (*tanghoon*)

Dried udon noodles

Dried somen noodles

NOODLES Both fresh and dried noodles made from either wheat flour, rice flour or mung bean flour are used in Asian cooking. The most popular types are **fresh yellow wheat noodles** or "Hokkien" noodles, spaghetti-like noodles made from flour and egg; **dried wheat flour noodles** (not shown), plunged into boiling water to soften; fresh flat **rice flour noodles**, ribbon-like noodles about 1 cm (¹/2 in) wide, used in soups or fried; **fresh** laksa **noodles**, which look like white spaghetti; **dried rice vermicelli** which are very fine rice threads that must be plunged into hot water to soften before use; and **dried bean thread noodles**, generally used in soups and sometimes referred to as "glass", "cellophane" or "transparent" noodles. In Japan the wheat noodle, **udon**, comes in various widths and is either flat or round. Packets of dried *udon*, whitish-beige in color, are readily available in Japanese stores. **Somen** are also made from wheat, but are very fine and white in color. **Soba** are made from buckwheat flour, and are sometimes flavored with green tea. **Shirataki** noodles are made from *konnyaku* starch and they can be replaced with cellophane or glass noodles, which are made from mung bean flour. Soak them in warm or hot water until they swell and become transparent.

PALM SUGAR Made from the sap of the various palm fruits. It is usually sold as a solid block or cylinder of sugar. It varies in color from gold to light brown and has a faint caramel taste. It is used

to make Palm Sugar Syrup (page 73). To measure, hard palm sugar should be shaved, grated or melted in a microwave oven. Substitute dark brown sugar or maple syrup.

PANDANUS LEAF A fragrant member of the *pandanus* or screwpine family, pandan leaf is used to wrap seasoned morsels of chicken or pork, and added to various cakes and desserts. Pandanus leaves impart a subtle fragrance and a green hue to a range of Indonesian dishes. They are usually tied in a knot and then added to a liquid recipe. Bottled pandanus extract can be substituted in desserts, but if fresh or dried pandanus leaves are not available, omit them from savory dishes. Vanilla essence may be substituted in dessert recipes.

PLUM SAUCE A piquant reddish-brown condiment made from plums, vinegar and sugar. Sold in jars or cans in Chinese stores.

POLYGONUM LEAVES See VIETNAMESE MINT.

POMELO A citrus somewhat similar to grapefruit, the pomelo is drier, sweeter and has a much thicker and tougher peel. It is eaten as a fruit or broken up for salads. Grapefruit may be used as a substitute.

POPPY SEEDS These tiny white seeds are prized for their delicate nutty flavor and used as a thickening agent. Soak in warm water for 10–15 minutes, then ground. Substitute cashews or almonds.

RED DATES Valued for their medicinal properties as well as their prune-like flavor, these are added to soups. Soak in boiling water for 1 hour to soften before use.

RICE WINE Wine made from fermented rice used in cooking. Wine from Shaoxing, generally considered the best, is available from Chinese food stores. Substitute Japanese sake, *mirin* or dry sherry.

ROCK SUGAR Crystallized cane sugar, sold in chunks in boxes. Added to Chinese red-braised dishes, desserts and drinks.

SAFFRON The world's most expensive spice. The dried strands should be allowed to infuse in warm milk before being added to rice and dessert dishes. Store saffron in the freezer as it loses its fragrance quickly, and never buy powdered saffron if you want the true aroma of this spice.

SAGO PEARLS Dried beads of sago starch obtained by grinding the pith of the sago palm tree to a paste and then pressing it through a sieve. The pearls are glutinous, with little taste and are used in Asian desserts. Sago pearls must be rinsed in water and drained to remove excess starch before use. They are sold in various sizes and colors. Available in plastic packets in grocery stores.

SAKE Besides being popular as a drink, sake is an important ingredient in Japanese cooking. Available in many different qualities in liquor stores or in supermarkets, it is also sold as cooking sake in Asian supermarkets. Keep refrigerated after opening. Chinese rice wine or very dry sherry are alternatives.

SALAM LEAF A subtly flavored leaf of a member of the cassia family—used in the same way bay leaves are used in Western cooking—to add a complex earthy fragrance to dishes. If unavailable, omit them from the recipe altogether. Do not substi-

Whole nutmegs

Palm sugar

Pandanus leaf

Salted fish, dried

Pomelo

Saffron strands

Salam leaves

Sato-imo potatoes

tute bay leaves as the flavor is totally different.

SALTED FISH, DRIED Used as a seasoning or condiment in Asia. It is necessary to soak in water before use.

SALTED (PICKLED) MUSTARD CABBAGE Also known as *kiam chye*, this is slightly sour and extremely salty. Various types of heavily salted cabbage are used in some Chinese and Nonya dishes; the most common is made from mustard cabbage. Soak in fresh water for at least 15 minutes to remove excess salt, repeating if necessary.

SALTED BLACK BEANS Salty and with a distinctive tang, these are often lightly pounded before being used to season fish, noodle or vegetable dishes. Varieties packed in China are sometimes labelled "Yellow Bean Sauce". Mash slightly before using. Sichuan brands contain additional chili. Keeps indefinitely on the shelf. Japanese miso is similar and may be substituted.

SATO-IMO POTATO Also known as taro potato or small baby yam, the *sato-imo* potato has a fine creamy texture when well cooked and a subtle, mildly sweet flavor that is slightly different from that of Western potatoes. If *sato-imo* potatoes are not available, use the alternatives given in the recipes in this book.

SCALLIONS See GREEN ONIONS.

SEAWEED Used extensively in Japan. Dark green **dried kelp** or **konbu** is an essential ingredient in Basic Dashi Stock (page 94). It has a dark brown color, often with whitish patches of salt and is sold in strips or small folded sheets. Wipe with a damp cloth but do not soak before using. When cooked, it expands into smooth, green sheets which are discarded before serving. Other varieties include small squares of **salted dried kelp** (*shio-kobu*), and **nori**, also referred to as laver, is dried and sold in very thin, dark green sheets of varying sizes. Nori is also available as thinly shredded strips or flakes, both of which are used as a garnish served with rice. **Wakame** is a type of seaweed with a pleasant chewy texture and subtle flavor. It is often used in soups and salads. Wakame is sold either dried (it looks like a mass of large crinkly green-black tea leaves) or in salted form in plastic bags. Reconstitute dried seaweed by soaking in water before use. The salted version should be rinsed thoroughly before use.

SESAME SEEDS Both black and white sesame seeds, the latter more common, are used in Japanese cooking. White sesame seeds are

toasted and crushed to make a paste; if you don't want to do this yourself, you can buy either a Chinese or Japanese brand of sesame paste. Smooth peanut butter makes a good substitute. Middle-Eastern *tahini,* which is slightly bitter, has a different flavor, as the sesame seeds have not been toasted before grinding; add a bit of sugar if you are using *tahini* as a substitute.

SESAME OIL Extracted from roasted (darker oil) or raw (lighter oil) sesame seeds. It is used as a seasoning and never for stir-fries as high heat turns it bitter.

SEVEN-SPICE POWDER Seven-spice chili powder (*shichimi*) is a mixture of several different spices and flavors. It contains *sansho,* ground chilies, hemp seeds, dried orange peel, flakes of nori, white sesame seeds and white poppy seeds. *Shichimi togarashi,* a similar but spicier condiment, consists of several types of chilies and spices. Both are available in small bottles in Japanese stores.

SHALLOTS, ASIAN Small, round and pinkish-purple, shallots add a sweet oniony flavor and a hint of garlic to countless dishes. They are also sliced, deep-fried and used as a garnish. Indonesian shallots are smaller and milder than those found in many Western countries.

SHISO LEAVES The leaves have an attractive dark green color, sometimes with reddish veins, and are widely used in Japanese cooking either as an ingredient or a garnish. It is a member of the mint family, and the leaves have a hint of basil and spearmint flavor. They are crisp-fried as tempura, used to garnish sushi, or minced and added to rice served with sashimi. Decorative sprigs of **shiso flowers** are sometimes used as a garnish.

SHRIMP PASTE, BLACK A black, pungent, molasses-like seasoning also known as *hay koh*. Made of fermented shrimp, salt, sugar and thickeners, it is used as a sauce or a dip. It is sometimes labeled as *petis* and is unrelated to *belachan*. Usually sold in jars or plastic tubs, it is commonly added to *rojak*, a fruit and vegetable salad, and Penang *laksa*.

SICHUAN PEPPERCORNS Not really pepper, but a round, reddish-brown berry with a pronounced fragrance and acidic flavor, it is used primarily in Sichuan cuisine and as an ingredient in five spice powder. It is also known as prickly ash or *fagara*, and is often sold powdered under the Japanese name *sansho.*

SOUR PLUMS Salty pickled plums (*umeboshi*) are very popular with

Salted (pickled) mustard cabbage

Konbu seaweed (left), Wakame seaweed (top) and Nori seaweed (bottom)

Asian red shallots

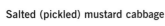

Shiso leaves

Sichuan peppercorns

Sour plums

Star anise pods

plain rice for breakfast in Japan, as they are believed to aid digestion. These dull-red plums are available in jars, and should be refrigerated after opening.

STAR ANISE An 8-pointed dried pod encasing shiny black seeds with a strong aniseed flavor. The whole spice is usually used when cooking and is discarded before serving. Whole star anise keeps for a year in an airtight container.

STARFRUIT A star-shaped fruit, eaten raw and finely sliced. Young starfruit has a tart taste and is often served on the Vietnamese vegetable platter as a complement to grilled or fried foods.

Regular or light soy sauce | Dark soy sauce | Sweet black soy sauce | Thick sweet soy sauce (kecap manis)

SOY SAUCE A very important condiment in Asian cooking. It is a brown liquid made by fermenting boiled soybeans and roasted wheat or barley. Asian countries such as China, Korea and Japan produce a number of varieties ranging in color from light to dark and in texture from thin to thick. Chinese **dark soy sauce** is extremely dark and thick. It has a much richer flavor and color due to the addition of molasses. **Light** or **regular soy sauce** is thinner, lighter in color and saltier and is the type most commonly used as a table condiment as well as for cooking. **Sweet black sauce** is a thick fragrant sauce used in marinades and sauces. Sweet black soy sauce is not widely available in the West but can be approximated by adding 1/2 teaspoon brown sugar to 1 tablespoon of dark soy sauce. Hoisin sauce also makes a good substitute. Another type of soy sauce, **tamari**, is black and has a slightly smoky, full-bodied flavor that comes from the addition of wheat. Tamari is available in most Japanese stores and well-stocked supermarkets.

In Indonesia, **thick sweet soy sauce** (*kecap manis*) is most frequently used as a condiment. It is much sweeter and thicker than normal soy sauce. It has palm sugar and cane sugar molasses added.

SUGAR CANE Fresh sugar cane juice—extracted from the stalks by a crushing machine—is a very popular drink in Vietnam. In addition to the familiar uses of sugar cane, the peeled stalks are also used as skewers in cooking.

TAMARIND A fruit that is often sold dried, still encased inside its long narrow tree pod. The pulp is more often sold in jars and packets already shelled, but still containing some fibers and seeds. It is used as a souring agent in many dishes. To obtain **Tamarind Juice**, mash 1 part tamarind pulp in 2 parts warm water and strain to obtain the juice, discarding the seeds and fibers. If using already cleaned tamarind pulp, slightly reduce the amounts called for in the recipes. The dried pulp keeps indefinitely in an airtight container.

TAPIOCA The root of this plant (also known as cassava) and the tender green leaves are both eaten, though the leaves have to be cooked for at least an hour to remove the mild toxins. The root is grated and mixed with coconut and sugar to make sweetmeats. Fermented tapioca root is added to some desserts, while the dried root is made into small balls and used in the same way as pearl sago. Substitute spinach or water spinach for tapioca leaves.

TAPIOCA STARCH Used as a thickening agent, and sometimes in the making of fresh rice papers. Combined with rice flour, it adds a translucent sheen and chewiness to pastries. Available in many Asian food markets. Cornstarch may be used as a substitute.

TEMPEH Fermented soybean cakes, a Javanese creation, made of compressed, lightly fermented soybeans with a delicious nutty flavor. They can be fried, steamed or baked and are a rich source

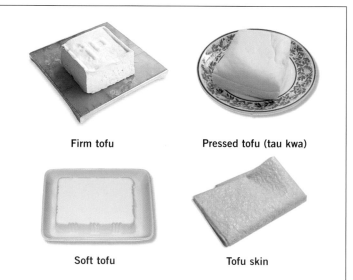

Firm tofu | Pressed tofu (tau kwa)

Soft tofu | Tofu skin

TOFU Tofu or bean curd comes in various form. **Soft tofu** is silky and smooth but difficult to cook because it falls apart. **Firm tofu** holds its shape well when cut or cooked and has a strong, slightly sour taste. **Pressed tofu** (often confusingly labeled as firm tofu) is a type of firm tofu with much of the moisture extracted and is therefore much firmer in texture and excellent for stir-fries. Refrigerate fresh tofu enclosed in a plastic container submerged in water. **Dried tofu skin** is the dried skin that forms on top of boiling soy milk; it is dried and sold in sheets as a wrapper.

Starfruits

Tempeh

Turmeric root

Vietnamese mint (laksa leaf)

of protein, riboflavin, calcium and iron. They are low in cholesterol and sodium and are increasingly popular with health enthusiasts. They are sold in most health food stores and Asian specialty shops—plain, marinated or smoked. Look for them in the refrigerator or freezer section.

TURMERIC Also known as *kunyit*, turmeric is a root similar to ginger but with a bright yellow to orange color and a strong woody flavor. Turmeric has antiseptic and astringent qualities, and stains permanently, so scrub your knife blade, hands and chopping board immediately after handling. Purchase fresh turmeric root as needed as the flavor fades after a few days. Substitute 1 teaspoon ground turmeric for 1 in (2^1/2 cm) of the fresh root. Turmeric leaves are used as a herb, particularly in Sumatra. There is no substitute.

VIETNAMESE MINT Also known as laksa leaves, polygonum or *daun kesum*, they are traditionally added to spicy soup dishes. The spear-shaped leaves will wilt quickly once they are plucked from the stem. They have an intense fragrance reminiscent of lemon with a hint of eucalyptus. There is no real substitute, but a mixture of spearmint and coriander leaves or basil does approximate its flavor and fragrance.

VINEGAR Black, red and white Chinese vinegars are all made from rice, and as the flavor differs, be sure to use the type specified. **Red vinegar** has a distinctive tang. **Black Chinese vinegar** is made from rice, wheat and millet or sorghum. The best black vinegars are well-aged and have a complex, smoky flavor similar to balsamic, which may be substituted. Chinese cooks add black vinegar sparingly to sauces, dips and when braising meats. Balsamic vinegar is a good substitute. **Japanese rice vinegar** is fermented from rice and is less acidic than malt or wine vinegars. It has a mild and pleasant fragrance. Slightly diluted cider vinegar or a good quality Chinese rice vinegar, slightly diluted, can be used as substitutes. **White vinegar** is made from glutinous rice and has a mild, sweet flavor. It is colorless and is one of the definitive ingredients used in sweet and sour sauce. Substitute Japanese rice vinegar or white wine vinegar.

WASABI Wasabi is a pungent root similar in taste to ginger and hot mustard. It is sold fresh, as a prepared paste, or in dried powdered form. Fresh wasabi root should be peeled and grated from the stem top down and should be used within 1–2 days of cutting before it loses its freshness and pungency. The powdered variety may be cheaper, but it is actually powdered horseradish colored green with mustard added. Wasabi paste can be made from the powder or the root. Real wasabi is more expensive but has a more potent flavor.

WATER CHESTNUTS Small, acorn-shaped roots with a brown leathery skin on the outside and a crisp, juicy-sweet flesh inside. Their crisp texture and sweet flavor make them ideal in salads, stir-fried vegetable dishes and desserts. Fresh water chestnuts can be found packed in water in the refrigerator sections of some supermarkets. Chunks of fresh jicama are a good substitute, although canned water chestnuts are also widely available.

WATER SPINACH A nutritious, leafy vegetable also known as morning glory, water convolvulus or *kangkung*. The leaves and tender tips are often stir-fried. *Bok choy* or spinach make good substitutes.

WHITE FUNGUS Also known as *white woodears*, it has a crunchy texture and a slightly sweet flavor. It is sold dried and must be soaked in water before using. White fungus is prized for its texture as well as its health-giving properties.

WILD GINGER BUDS The pink buds of wild ginger plants, also known as torch ginger or *bunga kanta* in Malaysia and Singapore. They are highly aromatic and lend a subtle but distinct fragrance to dishes of Malay and Nonya origin.

YUNNAN HAM A smoked salted ham used mainly as a seasoning. It is sold in tins.

YUZU ORANGE Oranges with a unique fragrance—reminiscent of lemons, mandarin oranges and limes—which give ponzu sauce its distinctive flavor. The essence of yuzu is sold in little bottles. Substitute a very fresh lemon.

YOGURT This is often vigorously stirred (use a hand-held mixer) to ensure the liquid whey is reincorporated with the curds; this is referred to as **whipped yogurt**. Some Indian dishes call for a solid yogurt called **hung yogurt**. The thicker curd is desired for its firm texture. You can obtain this by simply pouring off the liquid whey if it has already separated, or by placing it in a muslin cloth or paper-lined coffee filter and setting it over a jar or hanging it over the kitchen sink. The whey, or liquid, will drop out and leave behind the yogurt solids.

Water chestnuts

Water spinach

Wild ginger bud

Wasabi

The traditional open hearth or *irori* is virtually a museum piece in Japan today

Rice cooling tub (*hangiri*) and wooden rice paddle (*shamoji*)

A bamboo rolling mat is indispensable in a Japanese kitchen.

Granite mortar and pestle used for grinding spice pastes.

The Asian Kitchen

You do not need a range of exotic implements to cook Asian food. Perhaps that is the most surprising aspect of Asian cooking—that often sophisticated food is prepared with so few utensils! Most of the implements found in the average Western kitchen can be adapted for use in Asian cooking, although several items, such as a wok or rice cooker, will make the preparation and cooking of certain dishes much easier. Far more time is usually spent on the preparation of the ingredients, which have to be peeled, chopped, grated, ground, and blended before the cooking begins. You should be able to obtain most of the implements mentioned here from Asian grocery stores.

Cooking Implements

Perhaps the most essential ingredient in the Asian kitchen is the **wok**—known as a *kuali* in Malaysia and Indonesia—a deep, curved pan traditionally made of cast iron and used for just about everything except cooking rice: stir-frying, deep-frying, braising, making sauces, steaming, and so on. The shape of the wok distributes the heat evenly, while its sloping sides ensure that food falls back into the pan and not over the edge during stir-frying. It's also practical for deep-frying, requiring less oil than a conventional saucepan or skillet. It allows just the right amount of evaporation for many dishes which begin with a large amount of liquid and finish with a thick sauce. When choosing a wok, avoid aluminum or Teflon-coated types; a heavy cast-iron wok that won't tip over easily is preferable, or best of all, a non-stick alloy that will

not scratch when metal scoops are used.

A wok should be "seasoned" before its first use so that food will not stick. Wash the inside of the wok with warm soapy water but do not use a scouring pad. Rinse with fresh water and dry thoroughly. Put some oil on a paper towel and wipe the inside of the wok. Repeat until the paper towel comes away clean. Chinese cooks always heat the wok before adding oil to be sure that it is dry and the oil will not splatter. After cooking, never clean your wok with detergent or harsh abrasives; just rinse it with warm water and wipe dry. Remember to buy a lid for your wok—invaluable for when you want to steam food and for finishing off dishes.

In India, the **kadai**, a large wok-like utensil, is used for frying and stir-frying. The *kadai* is made of iron, brass or aluminum, and slightly deeper than a wok, but the latter makes an excellent substitute. For rice and curries, a flat-lidded, straight-sided pan known as a **degchi** is used, but a good heavy-based pot will do.

To partner your wok, a **frying spatula**, as well as a **perforated ladle** for lifting out deep-fried food, are useful. Chinese cooks use a round-edged spatula for tossing stir-fried ingredients in the wok. Indonesian cooks use an assortment of wooden or coconut husk spoons for stirring.

Other useful utensils include a **wire mesh basket** on a long handle, good for scooping out deep-fried food or boiled noodles. Chinese cooks also use a pair of long wooden **chopsticks** for turning over food during deep-frying, although this requires a certain dexterity, only acquired with practice. You may be happier with tongs.

The multi-purpose stainless steel wok

Electric rice cooker

Electric Blender

Extremely high heat is needed when stir-frying food in a wok, and many electric cookers cannot achieve the ideal heat. Malaysian cooks—especially Chinese—insist on at least one gas fire, often with a double ring of gas jets. If you are using an old-style electric cooker which cannot reach a very high heat nor be reduced in temperature quickly, you should consider investing in a gas-fired ring to be used with your wok.

Almost any **saucepan** can be used for cooking Asian dishes, but take care to choose one that has a non-reactive lining, since many dishes contain acid such as tamarind or lime juice. Non-stick saucepans are ideal for Asian food as they avoid the problem of spices sticking on the bottom and allow you to use less oil when frying. **Claypots** of various shapes and sizes, with a sandy outside and a glazed interior, are used for slow cooking and for making soups and stocks. These are attractive and inexpensive, but any type of saucepan can be used.

Rice was usually cooked in an aluminum or a stainless steel saucepan, although most homes in the cities now boast an electric **rice cooker**—a great boon if you eat rice fairly often. It's foolproof, produces dry fluffy rice every time, and also keeps rice warm for latecomers. Alternatively, use a heavy saucepan with a firm-fitting lid.

Steaming is a healthy method of cooking in Asia, and a multi-tiered **bamboo steamer** with a plaited cover to absorb any moisture (unlike a metal cover where moisture condenses and falls on the food) is invaluable. If you are using a multi-tiered metal steamer, put a tea towel under the lid to prevent moisture from dripping back onto the food. The steaming basket is placed inside a wok on a trivet above boiling water. Chinese stores also sell perforated metal disks that sit inside a wok above the water level; these are useful for steaming a single plate of food. Cover the wok with a lid and keep the water level topped up and at a gentle simmer during steaming.

Just as indispensable as a wok is the **cleaver**, which comes with either a heavy rectangular blade about 3–4 in (8–10 cm) deep, ideal for cutting through bones, or a lighter weight blade for chopping, slicing, mincing, bruising garlic cloves and scooping up food on the flat edge to carry to the pan. A cleaver does the work of a whole battery of knives in a Western kitchen. You will also need a strong chopping board.

In addition to the usual knives found in any kitchen, a useful implement used by traditional Asian cooks is a narrow, double-bladed knife for carving vegetables into decorative shapes, and slicing fruit and vegetables thinly for the various rolls and wraps.

If the thump-thump of the stone, granite or porcelain **mortar** and **pestle** is not for you, blenders, food processors, and coffee grinders make light work of the pounding, grinding, and blending of spices and seeds. It's essential that all the ingredients to be made into a paste be finely chopped before blending. Whether using a mortar and pestle, blender or food processor, the principle is to grind or blend the toughest ingredients first, adding softer and wetter ingredients towards the end. First grind any dried spices or nuts until fine, then add hard ingredients such as chopped-up lemongrass and galangal. Pound or process until fine, then add softer rhizomes such as fresh turmeric and ginger, soaked dried chilies and sliced fresh chilies. When these are minced, add the ingredients that are full of moisture, such as chopped shallots and garlic, and soft shrimp paste.

If you are using a food processor or blender, you will probably need to add just a little liquid to keep the blades turning. If the spice blend is to be fried, add a little of the specified amount of cooking oil. If it is to be cooked in coconut milk, add some of this. While processing, you will probably need to stop the machine frequently to scrape down the sides. Continue until you have a fine paste.

Some cooks add water rather than the cooking medium to the blender; this means that the spice mixture will need to be cooked for a longer period of time before adding the other ingredients, to allow the water to evaporate and the mixture to fry rather than stew.

The multi-purpose **banana leaf** is often used in Southeast Asia to wrap food in for grilling, steaming, or placing directly onto hot coals. If you are able to obtain banana leaf, wipe it clean and cut to the required size. Hold it directly over a gas flame or plunge in boiling water until it softens before wrapping the food. aluminum foil is generally recommended as a substitute, but for a texture that is closer to that obtained by using the leaf, wrap food in greaseproof paper first, then in the foil.

In Japan, **bamboo baskets** are used for draining noodles (a colander or sieve makes an adequate substitute). **Bamboo mats**, available in speciality Asian stores, are useful for rolling rice inside wrappers of seaweed, rolling up Japanese omelets and for squeezing

Square omelet pan

Flat grater (left) and fish scaler (right)

Thai wooden mortar and pestle

Bamboo steamer basket and lid

Korean octogonal lacquered platter with nine compartments (*Gujeolpan*)

Kimchi urn

the liquid out of cooked vegetables.

The **Japanese grater**, usually made of porcelain or bamboo, is perfect for grating ginger or horseradish, since it breaks down the fiber beautifully.

Indian and Sri Lankan breads are rolled out with a wooden rolling pin on a flat circular stone slab or wooden board, and cooked on a heavy iron griddle or **tawa**. A heavy cast-iron skillet or griddle makes a good substitute.

Coconut graters are essential in Asian countries. They are sometimes available in Western countries.

Cooking Techniques

The general cooking techniques used in Asian cookery are not too different from those used in the West.

The most common cooking method is probably **stir-frying**, which is fast cooking over a high heat in oil, usually in a wok. Evenly sliced ingredients are tossed about constantly; contact with the heat from the sides as well as the bottom of the wok means that food cooks very rapidly, sealing in the juices and flavor. Timing is absolutely crucial to the success of stir-frying, so chop all ingredients, measure all the seasonings, and have the garnishes and serving dishes at hand before starting.

Deep-frying involves cooking food by immersing it totally in heated oil. For best results, cook the food in small amounts so that the temperature of the oil does not drop too much. The optimum temperature for deep-frying is 375–400°F (190–200°C). Properly deep-fried food is not greasy at all—usually the result is a crisp exterior and a moist, succulent interior. Drain well on paper towels before serving.

Steaming is a cooking technique much prized by the Chinese and Japanese. The gentle cooking is an excellent method for showcasing the freshness of the produce, since all the natural flavors are retained. Make sure the water level in your steamer or wok is always topped up when you're steaming.

Grilling is another popular cooking technique, and it is hard to imagine Indonesia, Malaysia, and Singapore without their variations on satay, or Vietnam without its sugar-cane prawns. The meat to be grilled is placed on skewers (remember to soak the skewers in water

beforehand to prevent them from burning). Most of the dishes in this book can be cooked under a domestic grill or over a barbecue. Baste with some of the marinade as you cook. In Korea, where grilled marinated beef is a national dish, many families have their own table-top grill on which to cook *bulgogi* and *galbi* ribs.

Braising involves cooking food over a low heat in flavored liquid for a long time, and is ideal for tougher cuts of meat and some vegetables. To **red braise** meat is to cook it in dark and regular soy sauces, star anise or fivespice powder, Chinese cooking wine, and sugar.

Poaching is carried out in water or stock that is barely simmering. The liquid should only just cover the meat which must be fished out as soon as it is ready.

To **blanch**, bring a pot of water to a rolling boil and immerse the food—usually vegetables—in small batches. Cook until they are tender but still crisp.

Many Indian, Sri Lankan, Indonesian, Malaysian, and Thai dishes involve the use of spices, and as each spice takes a different amount of time to release its flavor and aroma, it is important to follow the correct order given when adding spices to the pan. Many spices need to be **dry-roasted** before use. It is best to do this in a heavy cast-iron pan without oil. Watch the heat carefully, shaking frequently so that the spices do not catch. For maximum flavor and aroma, buy whole spices and grind them just before cooking.

When cooking with coconut milk, it is important to prevent it from curdling or breaking apart. Stir the milk frequently, lifting it up with a large spoon or ladle and pouring it back into the saucepan or wok while it is coming to the boil. Once the coconut milk is simmering, be sure never to cover the pan. Thick coconut milk is sometimes added at the final stages of cooking to thicken and enrich the flavor of the dish. Stir constantly while heating but do not allow to boil.

Cooking rice is a subject that often arouses controversy, and if you have a reliable method, stick with it. Whatever method is used, first wash the rice thoroughly to remove any impurities and excess starch until the water runs clear. The absorbency of rice depends on the variety of rice and its age, with older rice absorbing more liquid. Cooking times depend on the type and weight of your saucepan, and the heat of your cooker.

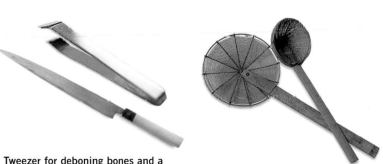

Tweezer for deboning bones and a long, thin filleting knife

Long-handled scoops

Wire mesh basket and frying spatulas and scoop

"Full of flavor, healthful, sometimes hauntingly similar to neighboring cuisines, at other times dramatically different, the food of Burma is not difficult to prepare at home."

BURMA

The undiscovered treasures of this land of gold and gems are its culinary delicacies.

Burma, "The Land of Gold" of ancient Indian and Chinese manuscripts, has one of the Asia's least known cuisines. This is more a result of the country's long period of self-imposed isolation than the intrinsic quality of the food itself. However, as Burma—or Myanmar as it is now officially called—opens its doors to visitors and international business, more people are discovering its intriguingly different cuisine.

The Land and its People

Burma's beginning dates back some 2,500 years, when Tibeto-Burman-speaking people moved from Tibet and Yunnan into the northern part of the country. Kingdoms rose and fell over the centuries, many different tribes arrived and established themselves. The British gained control over the country little by little, annexing it to British India in stages, until the last king was dethroned in 1886. Burma regained its independence in 1946, becoming a socialist republic in 1974. In 1979, the ruling authorities changed the name to Myanmar.

Although religion and tribal customs influence the cuisine of the people of this polyglot land—in which today's specialists have identified 67 separate indigenous groups—it is perhaps the terrain and climate, which have had the greatest effect on regional cuisines. These factors determine the basic produce and therefore influence the dishes prepared by the people living in each area. The Burmese tend to classify their country into three broad areas: what used to be referred to as "Lower Burma," the humid Ayeyarwady delta around Yangon, and the land stretching far south into the Isthmus of Kra, "Middle Burma," the central zone around Mandalay, ringed by mountain ranges and thus the driest area in all of Southeast Asia, and "Upcountry," the mountainous regions which include the Shan Plateau and Shan Hills to the east, the Chin Hills to the west and the ranges frequented by the Kachin tribe to the far north.

The long southern coastal strip of "Lower Burma," Tanintharyi, is washed by the waters of the Andaman Sea and shares a border with

Thailand. This region is rich in all kinds of seafood, which is understandably preferred to meat or poultry. While people in other areas of Myanmar eat freshwater fish caught in the rivers, lakes and irrigation canals, this coastal region offers a cornucopia of marine fish, crabs, squid, shrimp, lobsters, oysters, and shellfish.

Flowing in a general north-south direction for some 1,349 miles, the life-giving Ayeyarwady rises in the mountains of the far north, then branches into a maze of rivers and creeks that make up the delta—about 168 miles at its widest. This is the rice granary of the nation. Rice is the staple crop in Myanmar and is consumed not only for the main meals of the day but for snacks as well. It is eaten boiled, steamed and parched; in the form of dough or noodles; drunk as wine or distilled as spirits. A combined coastal length of about 1,492 miles and a network of rivers, irrigation channels and estuaries, particularly in the Ayeyarwady delta region, yields a dazzling array of fresh- and saltwater fish, lobsters, shrimp and crabs. The Ayeyarwady delta supplies the bulk of freshwater fish, sold fresh, dried, fermented or made into the all-important *ngapi*, a dried fish or dried shrimp paste (similar to Thai *kapi*, Malaysian *belachan* and Indonesian *trasi*).

Mandalay, where the last king of Burma ruled, is the cultural heart of the fiercely hot, dry plains of central Myanmar. Irrigation has made it possible to expand agriculture from dry rice (which depended on seasonal rain for its growth) to include crops such as peanut, sorghum, sesame, corn and many types of bean and lentil. Various fermented bean or lentil sauces and pastes are used as seasonings in this region, rather than the fermented fish and shrimp products typical of the south. Not having access to fresh seafood, the people of the central plains generally eat freshwater fish, with the occasional dish of pork or beef.

The most populated "upcountry" area of Myanmar is the Shan Plateau, a region of mountain ranges and wide fertile valleys with a mean altitude of 3,443 feet above sea level, adjoining China, Laos and Thailand. A wide variety of food is grown here: rice, wheat, soybeans, sugar cane, niger seed, sunflowers, maize, and peanuts; and vegetables including potatoes, cabbage, cucumber, cauliflower, celery, eggplant, hops, kale, kholrabi, lettuce, mustard, rape, roselle, tomatoes, and chayote. Soups from this region are more likely to be based on beef or pork stock than made with fish or dried shrimp. The soups are not as clear as those found elsewhere in Myanmar, as they are often thickened with powdered soybean. One example of this is the Shan version of Burmese noodles (*kyaukswe*), which is based on pork in a soup thickened with powdered soybean, rather than made with chicken and coconut milk as in the rest of the country.

A Unique Cuisine Evolves

Poised between two culinary giants, India and China, and inspired by the ingredients and styles of Southeast Asia, the cuisine of Myanmar has developed a unique personality of its own. China has had a marked impact on the food of Southeast Asia, including that of Myanmar. Noodles made from wheat, rice and mung peas are perhaps the most noticeable legacy of China. In Myanmar, these are found in noodle soups like *mohinga*, a spicy, fish-based dish with sliced banana heart that is virtually the national dish. Another widely available dish is chicken in spicy coconut gravy, *ohn-no kyaukswe*, which includes either wheat, rice or mung pea ("transparent") noodles.

The Indian influence on Myanmar food is seen in the widespread use of ingredients such as chickpeas, coriander seeds, cumin, and turmeric. But whereas Indian cuisine relies on a complex blending of spices, Burmese food uses only a few dried spices, adding extra flavor with many fresh seasonings and condiments.

The food of Myanmar has, perhaps, more in common with its Southeast Asian neighbors, Laos and Thailand, than with India. The use of fermented shrimp and fish products such as dried paste, fermented fish in liquid, and clear fish sauce has parallels in both Laos and Thailand, where these ingredients largely replace salt and give a characteristic flavor to many dishes. The sour fruit of the tamarind tree, most commonly used in the form of a dried pulp, is often preferred to vinegar or lime juice in many Burmese dishes.

Coconut milk, so prevalent in the cuisine of Southeast Asia, is also used in many Burmese dishes and for sweetmeats, while agar agar—a setting agent from seaweed—is also popular in Burmese desserts and drinks.

At the Burmese Table

Breakfast in Myanmar is traditionally a light repast of fried rice, or yesterday's rice warmed up, served with boiled garden peas and green tea. Many delicious alternatives are now becoming popular though. Breakfast today could take the form of steamed glutinous rice topped with roasted sesame seeds and fish or vegetable fritters; smoked dried fish; *mohinga*, thin rice noodles in fish soup; or *ohn-no kyaukswe*, wheat flour noodles in chicken and coconut gravy. Rice gruel garnished with chunks of fried Chinese dough sticks might be gulped down, as might *naan*, flat bread fresh from the *tandoor* oven, with either boiled garden pea salad or lamb bone soup. Alternatively, a steaming chickpea broth or a chicken curry might provide the morning's sustenance.

The main meal is not served in courses as in the West. All the dishes, soups, condiments and vegetable dips are arranged in the middle, with a large bowl of rice for second helpings placed on the side. Meat and fish dishes are usually prepared in the form of curries, with fish dishes being much more popular in the lands bordering the lower reaches of the Ayeyarwady River and the delta region, while upcountry palates are partial to beans and pulses and their various by-products. Most curries are prepared with a thin gravy, which is then drizzled over the rice, mixed in and eaten with the fish or vegetables and fish preserve.

Soup is almost always served during the course of a meal and helps wash down the rice. It may be a *hingga*, meaning hot peppery soup, or a *hincho*, a slightly milder concoction. The soup is usually a clear broth with leaves, buds or slices of fruit. On more formal occasions, a thicker broth of fish and vegetables is served with rice noodles. Vegetable and fruit salads are very popular. Some of the heavier salads, such as a rice-based "salad," can be eaten either as snacks between meals or as meals in themselves.

No meal would be considered complete without the condiment *ngapi*, or to use its full name, *ngapi-seinsa*: fish, or sometimes shrimp, boiled and garnished with crushed garlic, toasted dried chilies and chili powder.

After a meal, fruits such as banana, mango, pomelo, and durian are usually eaten in lieu of cooked desserts, which tend to be eaten as snacks throughout the day. As a special treat, *lephet*, or fermented tea leaf salad, might be served. The main ingredient of this unusual salad is fermented tea leaves; these are then mixed with, or accompanied by, peanuts, roasted sesame seeds, fried garlic, coconut, and ginger slices, and so on. Though it may seem unusual to serve a savory dish after the main meal, this is when *lephet* is often eaten; though you may find it served as a first course in Burmese restaurants in the West.

SUGGESTED MENUS

Family meals

For a simple yet satisfying family meal, try serving with steamed white rice and a Fish Sauce Dip (page 28):

• Rice Noodle Fish Soup (page 29);
• Tossed Noodle Salad (page 28);
• Fish in Tamarind Sauce (page 30);
• Fresh fruits such as mango or papaya,

Dinner parties

For a fun Burmese-style dinner party, serve:
• Pumpkin Basil Soup (page 28),
• Grilled Eggplant Salad (page 28);
• Burmese Crab Curry (page 30);
• Pork and Mango Curry (page 30).
• Semolina Cake with Coconut and Sesame (page 31).

Finger food

The following snacks and appetizers may be eaten throughout the day, even as desserts:
• Tea Leaf Salad (page 28), which is also served after a meal in Burma;
• Rice Pancakes (page 31).

A melting pot menu

Enjoy a culinary tour of Asia at your dining table with:
• Grilled Shrimp on a Sugar Cane Skewer (page 178) from Vietnam as an appetizer;
• Pork and Mango Curry (page 30) from Burma and Fried Shrimp with Sweet and Sour Sauce (page 159) from Thailand with plain rice;
• Coconut Mango Pudding (page 135) from Malaysia for dessert.

THE ESSENTIAL FLAVORS OF BURMESE COOKING

Indispensable to the Myanmar pantry are **garlic**, **ginger**, and **cilantro leaves (coriander)**. A good supply of **fresh jasmine rice** is a must and **glutinous rice** would be useful for some dishes. Flavorings you'll need include **fish sauce**, **soy sauce**, and **sesame oil**. **Fresh chilies** and **dried chili flakes** are a common addition to dishes as are **dried shrimp** and **dried shrimp paste**. **Fermented tea leaves** are easily found at all Burmese foodstores and come ready packed with all the extras making for a great instant Burmese snack.

While Burma has long been renowned for its natural beauty, its culinary treasures have remained a well-kept secret until recently. The country has absorbed the culinary influences of its neighbors to make its food even more unique.

Fish Sauce Dip

1 cup (250ml) water
1 tablespoon preserved fish paste
1/4 teaspoon ground turmeric
2 dried red chilies, soaked
2 bird's-eye chilies
1 tablespoon dried shrimp, soaked
2 cloves garlic

Bring the water, fish paste and turmeric to a boil, simmer until reduce by half. Strain and discard the solids. Pound the remaining ingredients in a mortar and mix with the fish stock. Serve with raw vegetables.

Pumpkin Basil Soup

1 tablespoon oil
3 cloves garlic, coarsely chopped
1 pumpkin, peeled, deseeded and cubed
4 cups (1 liter) chicken stock
Salt and pepper to taste
1/2 cup (20 g) chopped Thai basil (horapa) leaves (substitute with European basil)

Heat the oil in a pan and lightly stir-fry the garlic for 5 minutes till fragrant. Add the pumpkin

and chicken stock to the pan and bring to a boil. Cover and simmer for 20 minutes till the pumpkin is tender. Transfer to a blender and process till smooth. Return the soup to the pan and add salt and pepper to taste. Add the chopped fresh basil just before serving.

Daikon Salad

This refreshing salad can be eaten as a starter or accompaniment to curries and rice.

3 tablespoons rice vinegar
1 teaspoon salt
1 tablespoon sugar
1 daikon radish (about 1 lb/500 g), peeled and finely sliced
1 small onion, sliced
9 cloves garlic, finely chopped
3 tablespoons peanut oil
2 tablespoons peanuts
1 tablespoon toasted sesame seeds
1 teaspoon fish sauce
2 tablespoons chopped coriander leaves (cilantro)

Mix the rice vinegar, salt, and sugar in a salad bowl and whisk till the salt and sugar are dissolved. Add the radish, toss and chill for 15 minutes. Soak the sliced onion in cold water for 5 minutes. Drain. Fry the chopped garlic in oil over high heat till golden, remove with a slotted spoon and drain on paper towels. (Discard the oil or retain for use in another dish). Dry-roast the peanuts in a pan, cool and grind

finely. When ready to serve, remove the radish mixture from the refrigerator and drain any excess liquid. Add the remaining ingredients and toss well.

Grilled Eggplant Salad

2 large Asian eggplants
2 tablespoons oil
2 tablespoons finely sliced onion, soaked in water
6 cloves garlic, sliced
2 tablespoons chopped roasted peanuts
1 tablespoon toasted sesame seeds
2 bird's-eye chilies, finely sliced
2 teaspoons fish sauce
2 tablespoons chopped coriander leaves (cilantro)

Grill the eggplants over a charcoal flame till the skin is lightly charred; or bake under a grill (broil) till soft. Cool, discard the skin and mash the flesh. Heat the oil in a wok, add the garlic and deep-fry till crisp. Remove with a slotted spoon and retain the oil.

Place the eggplant, onion, garlic, peanuts, sesame, chili, and fish sauce in a salad bowl. Add 1 teaspoon of the garlic-infused oil and mix well. Garnish with the coriander leaves.

Tea Leaf Salad

Lephet is part of Burmese social culture. It is served to welcome guests, as a peace offering after an argument, as a snack, as a palate cleanser after a meal, and even as a stimulant to ward off sleep during all-night Burmese opera. Instant packaged *Lephet Thoke* is now readily available from Burmese shops.

4 tablespoons *lephet* (fermented tea leaves)
3 cloves garlic, sliced and deep-fried till crisp
1 bird's-eye chili, finely chopped
2 tablespoons dried shrimp, soaked and blended to a powdery fluff
2 tablespoons roasted peanuts
1 tablespoon toasted sesame seeds
2 teaspoons lime juice
2 teaspoons fish sauce
1 tablespoon peanut oil

Grilled Eggplant Salad

Traditionally, *lephet* is served in a lacquer container with different compartments for each ingredient. Diners then choose their ingredients and, using only the thumb and first two fingers of the right hand, delicately serve themselves. Finger bowls would be provided.

Today, most Burmese combine all the ingredients in a bowl and mix them thoroughly as with a conventional salad.

Tossed Noodle Salad

4 small potatoes, peeled and cubed
2 cakes firm tofu
1/4 cup (60 ml) oil
1/2 cup (50 g) cooked rice
1 red finger-length chili, chopped
7 oz (200 g) fresh egg noodles, blanched
3 oz (90 g) dried glass noodles, boiled 3 minutes
1 cup (50 g) shredded cabbage
1 cup (50 g) bean sprouts, blanched
1 cup (150 g) grated green papaya
1 medium tomato, chopped
1 small cucumber, peeled and shredded

Garnishes
2 tablespoons peanut oil
1 medium onion, finely sliced
12 cloves garlic, finely sliced
2 tablespoons chili flakes
2 tablespoons tamarind pulp soaked in 1/2 cup (125 ml) water, mashed and strained to obtain the juice
3 bird's-eye chilies, finely sliced
4 tablespoons dried shrimp, soaked and grounded to a powdery puff
1 teaspoon sugar syrup

Pumpkin Basil Soup

4 tablespoons roasted pea flour
4 tablespoons fish sauce
1/2 cup (25 g) chopped coriander
  leaves (cilantro)

Boil the potatoes till done. Drain the tofu cakes and dry with paper towels. Slice each one in half then cut each half into 9 pieces to yield 36 cubes. Heat the oil, deep-fry the tofu over medium-high heat for 5 minutes till golden on all sides. Remove with a slotted spoon and set aside. Knead the chilies into the cooked rice to color it.

To prepare the Garnishes, heat the oil in a pan and fry the onion and garlic till crisp. Remove and set aside, retain the oil. Stir-fry the chili flakes by spooning the retained hot oil onto the chili flakes in a separate bowl and set aside (if the chili flakes are placed directly into very hot oil, they will burn immediately). Add the bird's-eye chili and sugar syrup to the tamarind juice and set aside.

To serve, arrange all the main ingredients on a large plate. Place each of the Garnishes in individual bowls. Take a small handful of each item from the main ingredients. Then sprinkle on a little of each of the garnishes and mix thoroughly by hand.

Rice Noodle Fish Soup

Stock
1 whole catfish (about 2 lbs/1 kg)
5 stalks lemongrass, tender inner
  part of bottom third only, bruised
1 teaspoon ground turmeric
4 tablespoons fish sauce
8 cups (2 liters) water

Soup
3/4 cup (150 g) uncooked rice,
  dry-roasted till light brown and
  ground to a powder
12 cups (3 liters) water
4 dried chilies
1 medium onion, roughly chopped
3 cloves garlic, minced
1 teaspoon ground ginger
2 tablespoons coarsely ground
  lemongrass, tender inner part of
  bottom third only
1/2 cup (125 ml) peanut oil
1/2 teaspoon ground turmeric
11/2 teaspoons salt
1 teaspoon ground black pepper
3 tablespoons fish sauce
12 whole shallots, peeled

7 oz (200 g) banana stem, sliced
  1 in (21/2 cm) thick (optional)

Garnishes
10 oz (300 g) dried rice vermicelli,
  soaked for 2 minutes, boiled for
  21/2 minutes, drained and tossed
  with a little peanut oil
4 hard-boiled eggs, peeled and
  quartered
1 small onion, finely sliced and
  fried with a pinch of turmeric
  till crisp
Split-pea Crackers (recipe on this
  page), crumbled
Fried Fish Cakes (recipe on
  this page)
3 green onions (scallions), sliced
1/2 cup (25 g) chopped coriander
  leaves (cilantro)
4 limes, quartered
Fish sauce
Chili flakes

To make the Stock, boil all the ingredients in a pot. Reduce the heat, cover and cook for 20 minutes. Remove the fish, flake the flesh and set aside. Strain the Stock and discard the solids.

To make the Soup, add the rice powder to the water, stir and set aside. Blend the chilies, onion, garlic, ginger and lemongrass to a paste. Heat the oil in a pan and stir-fry the chili paste with the turmeric till fragrant.

Stir in the fish, then add the salt, pepper, fish sauce, and whole shallots and continue to cook for 5 minutes. Add the banana stem, Stock, and rice powder water. Bring to a boil, stirring to prevent lumps forming. Boil for 15 minutes, reduce the heat and simmer for 20 minutes.

Arrange all the Garnishes on the table, add a little of each to a bowl. Add a drop or two of the fish sauce and chili flakes to taste.

Fried Fish Cakes

1 lb (500 g) fresh white fish fillets
  (cod, seabass, flounder)
1 clove garlic
1 teaspoon ground ginger
1/4 teaspoon ground turmeric
1/4 teaspoon salt
1/2 teaspoon chili flakes
Water to moisten fingers
1 cup (250 ml) oil

Fillet the fish, flake the flesh and transfer to a mortar. Add the garlic and ginger and pound to a paste. Add the turmeric, salt

and chili flakes and continue to pound for 10–15 minutes.

Roll the mixture into 3-in (7-cm) long "sausages", moistening your fingers whilst shaping. Heat the oil in a pan, add several of the "fish sausages" at a time (not too many as they expand). Deep-fry for 5 minutes till golden brown. Remove and drain on paper towels.

Split-pea Crackers

5 tablespoons rice flour
2 cups (500 ml) water
1/2 cup (100 g) dried yellow split-
  peas, soaked overnight
1/4 teaspoon salt
1 cup (250 ml) oil

Add the rice flour to the water and stir well. Stir in the split-peas and salt.

Heat the oil for deep-frying. Spoon 1 tablespoon of the mixture into the oil and deep-fry till crisp. Deep-fry several crackers at the same time. Drain on paper towels and cool. Crumble by hand if required.

Rice Noodle Fish Soup

Burmese Crab Curry

The natural sweetness of the crab and onion is complemented by the sour tang of tamarind and the aroma of *garam masala*.

3 lbs (1¹/₃ kgs) whole live crabs
4 cups (1 liter) water for boiling the crabs
4 dried red chilies, soaked
3 tablespoons chopped onion
2 whole cloves garlic
2 tablespoons oil
¹/₄ teaspoon ground turmeric
1 tablespoon fish sauce
2 teaspoons tamarind pulp soaked in 2 tablespoons water, mashed and strained to obtain the juice
1 teaspoon *garam masala*
1 cup (250 ml) water

Plunge the live crabs into about 4 cups (1 liter) of boiling water for 3 minutes, then drain. Clean the crabs and discard the spongy grey matter. Use a cleaver to chop the crabs into large pieces; smash the claws lightly with the side of a cleaver to allow the flavors to penetrate.

Drain the chilies and transfer to a blender, add the onion and garlic and blend to a paste. Heat the oil in a pan, stir-fry the chili paste for 4 minutes till fragrant. Stir in the turmeric and fry for 1 minute. Add the crabs and fish sauce and mix thoroughly. Cover and cook over a medium heat for 5 minutes, stirring occasionally. Add the tamarind juice, *garam masala*, and water to the crabs, bring to a boil and simmer for 10 minutes.

Pork and Mango Curry

The sourness of this pork curry depends on the mango used. Serve with plain rice, a vegetable dish and salad.

1 lb (500 g) pork loin, cubed
1 tablespoon fish sauce
2 tablespoons oil
3 tablespoons minced onion
2 cloves garlic, minced
1 teaspoon ground ginger
3 dried red chilies, soaked and ground
1¹/₂ tablespoons peeled and shredded young (unripe) mango
1 teaspoon salt
1¹/₄ cups (310 ml) water

Marinate the pork in the fish sauce for 10 minutes. Heat the oil in a pan and stir-fry the onion and garlic for 5 minutes till fragrant. Add the ginger and chili and continue to fry for 2 minutes. Stir in the pork, mango and salt and mix well. Cover and cook over low heat for 20 minutes, stirring occasionally. Add the water and simmer over low heat for 20–25 minutes.

Coconut Noodles

1 lb (500 g) boneless chicken, cubed
6 tablespoons fish sauce
¹/₄ cup (60 ml) oil
3 tablespoons ground onion
1 tablespoon ground garlic
¹/₂ tablespoon ground ginger
¹/₂ teaspoon ground turmeric
1 tablespoon chili flakes

Pork and Mango Curry

¹/₂ cup (60 g) chickpea flour
1 cup (250 ml) water
7 cups (1³/₄ liters) chicken stock
1¹/₃ cups (330 ml) coconut milk

Garnish
4 hard-boiled eggs, peeled and sliced
1 medium onion, soaked and finely sliced
¹/₂ cup (25 g) chopped coriander leaves (cilantro)
2 limes, quartered
1 lb (500 g) fresh egg noodles, blanched in boiling water
12 oz (375 g) fresh egg noodles, deep-fried in 1 cup (250 ml) oil till crisp, drained on paper towels, cooled and crumbled by hand into bite-sized pieces
7 tablespoons chili flakes
Fish sauce

Burmese Crab Curry

Marinate the chicken with the fish sauce for at least 15 minutes. Heat the oil in a large pan, stir-fry the onion, garlic, ginger, and turmeric for 5 minutes. Stir in the chicken and chili flakes. Cover and cook over medium-low heat for 10 minutes. Stir occasionally to prevent the chicken sticking to the pan. Meanwhile, add the chickpea flour to the water and whisk to remove any lumps.

Add the chicken stock to the pan and bring to a boil. Reduce the heat, add the chickpea flour paste, cover and simmer for a further 10 minutes. Add the coconut milk and continue to simmer for 30–40 minutes, stir-

ring occasionally, till the sauce thickens slightly.

Arrange each Garnish item on a separate plate around a central bowl of chicken and coconut soup. To serve, take a portion of the fresh noodles, add a little of each Garnish (a dash of fish sauce if desired) and a generous helping of soup.

Fish in Tamarind Sauce

1¹/₂ lbs (750 g) fish fillets
¹/₂ teaspoon salt
1 cup (250 ml) water
2 tablespoons fish sauce
2 tablespoons tamarind pulp soaked in ¹/₂ cup (125 ml) water, mashed and strained to obtain the juice
3 tablespoons oil
1 tablespoon sugar
2 tablespoons minced onion
1 clove garlic, ground
1 teaspoon chili flakes
¹/₂ cup (25 g) chopped coriander leaves (cilantro)

Rub the fish with the salt and allow to marinate for 10 minutes. Transfer to a pan, add the water and fish sauce, cover and simmer for 6–8 minutes. Heat the oil in a separate pan and stir-fry the onion and garlic till fragrant. Stir in the sugar and chili. Add the fish and mix well. Add the tamarind juice, cover and cook for 10 minutes. Garnish with the coriander leaves.

Chicken Curry

Chicken Curry

1 chicken, cut into 8 pieces
3 dried red chilies, soaked and ground
3 tablespoons finely sliced onion
1 small tomato, deseeded and chopped
1 tablespoon sliced green chili
1/4 cup (60 ml) peanut oil
1 teaspoon dried shrimp paste
1 cup (250 ml) water
1/4 cup (60 ml) chopped coriander leaves (cilantro)

Marinade
1 tablespoon fish sauce
1 teaspoon salt
1/4 teaspoon ground turmeric
1 teaspoon ground ginger
3 cloves garlic, minced

Mix the Marinade, combine with the chicken and set aside. Heat the oil and stir-fry the chili paste and onions for 5 minutes till fragrant. Stir in the dried shrimp paste.

Add the tomato, green chili, and chicken, cover and cook for 5 minutes. Stir occasionally to prevent the chicken from sticking. Add the water, cover and cook over moderately low heat for 30 minutes till the chicken is done. Garnish with the saw-leaf herb or coriander leaves.

Shrimp Curry

Use fresh large shrimp for this curry. Serve this with plain rice and stir-fried vegetables.

1 lb (500 g) fresh large shrimp, shelled and cleaned
1 tablespoon fish sauce
1/3 cup (80 ml) oil
2 tablespoons minced onion
3 cloves garlic, minced
1/4 teaspoon ground turmeric
1 tablespoon dried chili flakes
2 small tomatoes, cut in wedges
1 green finger-length chili, halved lengthwise
1/2 teaspoon salt

2 tablespoons chopped coriander leaves (cilantro)

Marinate the shrimp in the fish sauce for at least 15 minutes. Heat the oil in a pan and stir-fry the onion and garlic for 5 minutes till fragrant. Stir in the turmeric. Lower the heat and add the chili flakes, tomato, green chili and salt. Cook for 6–8 minutes stirring to a paste. Add the shrimp and coriander leaves and cook for another 3–4 minutes, stirring frequently, till the shrimp are done.

Rice Pancakes

These deliciously light rice flour crêpes can be filled with a variety of different ingredients.

2 1/4 cups (300 g) rice flour
2 1/2 cups (625 ml) cold water
1 teaspoon salt
1/4 teaspoon baking soda
1 teaspoon finely chopped ginger
2 tablespoons peanut oil
1/2 cup (100 g) fresh or frozen green peas
3 green onions (scallions), sliced

Mix the rice flour, water, salt, baking soda and ginger in a bowl. Place a frying pan over medium heat and pour 4–5 tablespoons of the rice paste into it. Lightly brush the pancake with a little oil and sprinkle on the peas and green onions. Fry for 3–4 minutes till the underside is crisp. Fold in half and fry for 1 minute on each side.

Rice Pancakes

Semolina Cake with Coconut and Sesame

1 1/2 cups (250 g) semolina flour
2 1/2 cups (625 ml) coconut milk
2 1/2 cups (625 ml) water
2 1/2 cups (500 g) sugar
2 teaspoons salt
2 eggs, beaten
1/2 cup (125 ml) oil, heated
2 tablespoons white poppy seeds
1/2 cup (80 g) raisins

Preheat the oven to 400°F (200°C). Dry-roast the semolina in a pan over low heat till reddish brown, then cool. In a saucepan, add the roasted semolina, coconut milk, water, sugar, salt, eggs and hot oil. Bring to a boil and cook over medium-low heat for 20 minutes till the mixture comes away from the sides of the pan, stirring continuously. If the mixture begins to stick, add a teaspoon of oil. Before the end of cooking, add the raisins and mix well.

Transfer the mixture to a lightly oiled round baking tray 12 in (30 cm) in diameter and 3 in (7 1/2 cm) deep. Smooth the surface with a metal spoon or cake knife and sprinkle the poppy seeds on the surface. Bake on medium shelf for 15 minutes. Remove from the oven and set aside for several hours to cool. Cut the cake in the baking tray and arrange the slices on a serving plate.

"An ancient Chinese proverb says, 'To the ruler, people are heaven; to the people, food is heaven.'"

CHINA

**An ancient and inventive cuisine, known for its huge
diversity and loved all over the world.**

Left: Three generations sit
down to a meal in the
courtyard of an old house
in Fujian province, in
Southern China.

Right: Steamed dumplings
are popular in most regions
of China and connoisseurs
can recognize their provin-
cial origin by their stuffing
and accompanying sauces.

**From a country whose usual greeting is "*Chi fan
le mei you*?"—Have you eaten?—you can expect
nothing less than a passionate devotion to food.
Chinese food is known the world over, thanks to
the peripatetic nature of its people, but the
success of its food hinges on much the same
things: fresh ingredients and the balance of
flavors. The next time you go to an Asian market,
observe: the Chinese shoppers are likely to be the
ones who prod the fish, inspect entire bunches of
vegetables, and accept and reject a batch of
shrimp based on the kick in their legs.**

While the array of seasonings and sauces used
by Chinese cooks is not vast, every dish must meet
three major criteria: appearance, fragrance, and
flavor. The Chinese also prize texture and the
health-giving properties of food.

An old Chinese proverb says, "To the ruler,
people are heaven; to the people, food is heaven."
This is no truer than in China, where gastronomy
is a part of everyday life.

The Making of a Cuisine

So large is China, and the geographic and climactic
variations so diverse, that you can travel through
the country and never have the same dish served in
exactly the same way twice. The paradox of Chinese
food is that it is one borne of hardship and frequent
poverty: this is, after all, a country that houses 22
percent of the world's population and has only
seven percent of the world's arable land.

There is much debate and confusion about
how many regional cuisines there are, but most
gourmets agree that at least four major Chinese
regional styles exist: Cantonese, centered on southern Guangdong province and Hong Kong;
Sichuan, based on the cooking of this western
province's two largest cities, Chengdu and
Chongqing; Hunan, the cooking of eastern
China—Jiangsu, Zhejiang, and Shanghai; and
Beijing or "Northern" food, with its major inspiration from the coastal province of Shandong. Some
would add a fifth cuisine from the southeastern
coastal province of Fujian.

All regions use various forms of ginger, garlic, green onions, soy sauce, vinegar, sugar, sesame oil, and bean paste, but combine them in highly distinctive ways. What distinguishes these regional styles is not only their cooking methods but also the particular types and combinations of basic ingredients.

The southern school of cooking was the cuisine taken to the West by Chinese migrants—egg rolls, *dim sum, chow mein,* sweet and sour pork, *chop suey,* and fortune cookies. With the exception of the last two, which were American inventions, the other dishes are orthodox Cantonese creations.

Cantonese food is characterized by its extraordinary range and the freshness of its ingredients, a light touch with sauces, and the readiness of its cooks to incorporate "exotic" imported flavorings

Smiling Shanghai children enjoying a snack. Each region has its own special array of morsels for when the next meal is just too far away.

such as lemon, curry, and Worcestershire sauce. Cantonese chefs excel in preparing roasted and barbecued meats (duck, goose, chicken, and pork), and *dim sum*—snacks taken with tea for either breakfast or lunch. *Dim sum* can be sweet, salty, steamed, fried, baked, boiled or stewed, each served in their own individual bamboo steamer or plate. To eat *dim sum* is to "*yum cha*" or drink tea. In traditional *yum cha* establishments, restaurant staff walk around the room pushing a cart or carrying a tray offering their tasty morsels. *Dim sum* restaurants are important institutions where the locals go to discuss business, read newspapers and socialize.

The home of spicy food, Sichuan, is a landlocked province with remarkably fertile soil and a population of over 100 million. The taste for piquant food is sometimes explained by Sichuan's climate. The fertile agricultural basin is covered with clouds much of the year and there is enough rain to permit two crops of rice in many places. Strong spices provide a pick-me-up in cold and humid weather, and

make a useful preservative. The most popular spices are chilies and Sichuan peppercorns (prickly ash), tempered with sugar, salt, and vinegar. Despite the province's incendiary reputation, many of the famous dishes are not spicy at all, for example, the famous camphor- and tea-smoked duck, made by smoking a steamed duck over a mixture of tea and camphor leaves. But it is the mouth burners that have made Sichuan's name known all over the world, dishes like *ma po tofu* (spicy stir-fried tofu)—stewed tofu and ground meat in a hot sauce and *gung bao ji ding* (gung bao chicken)—chicken with dried chilies.

When the Grand Canal was built in the Sui dynasty AD 581–618, it gave rise to several great commercial cities at its southern terminus, including Huaian and Yangzhou, after which this regional cuisine (Hunan) is named. Its location on the lower reaches of the Yangtze River in China's "land of fish and rice" gave it an advantage in terms of agricultural products, and it was renowned for seafood such as fish, shrimp, eel, and crab, which were shipped up the canal to the imperial court in Beijing. Hunan cuisine is not well known outside of China, perhaps because it rejects all extremes and strives for the "Middle Way". Freshness *(xian)* is a very important concept in the food of this region, but *xian* means more than just fresh. For a dish of steamed fish to be described as *xian,* the fish must have been swimming in the tank one hour ago, it must exude its own natural flavor, and must be tender yet slightly chewy. *Xian* also implies that the natural flavor of the original ingredients should always take precedence over the sauce. Some of the best known dishes from this region are steamed or stewed and require less heat and a longer cooking time, for instance chicken with chestnuts, the glorious pork steamed in lotus leaves, duck with a stuffing made from eight ingredients, and the evocatively named "lion head" meatballs.

The cuisine of Beijing has perhaps been subjected to more outside influences than any other major cuisine in China. First came the once-nomadic Mongols, who made Beijing their capital during the Yuan dynasty (1279–1368). They brought with them mutton, the chief ingredient in Mongolian hot pot, one of Beijing's most popular dishes in the autumn and winter. The Manchus, as the rulers of the Qing dynasty (1644–1911), introduced numerous ways of cooking pork. As the capital of China for the last eight centuries, Beijing became the home of government officials who brought their chefs with them when they came from the wealthy southern provinces. But the most important influence comes from nearby Shandong province, which has a pedigree that goes back to the days of Confucius C. 550 BC. Shandong cuisine features the seafood found along China's eastern seaboard: scallops and squid, both dry and fresh, sea cucumber, conch, crabs, and shark's fins, often teamed with the flavors of raw leek and garlic.

Beijing's most famous dish, Peking duck, owes as much to the culinary traditions of other parts of China as to the capital itself. The method of roasting the duck is drawn from Hunan cuisine, while the pancakes, raw leek, and salty sauce that accompany the meat are typical of Shandong.

Beijing is also famous for its steamed and boiled dumplings *(jiaozi)*, which are filled with a mixture of pork and cabbage or leeks, or a combination of eggs and vegetables.

The Food of the People

The proliferation of refrigerators in China today is making inroads on an institution that for centuries has been an essential part of daily life: shopping in the local food market. Many housewives and househusbands go to the market two or three times a day. In some state-run offices in Beijing, half-hour rest periods are allotted to enable its employees to shop for fresh produce.

In addition to fresh food markets, there are shops selling a huge variety of prepared and packaged food. Along with food markets, most cities have areas where snack foods are sold in stand-up or sit-down stalls. Breakfast may be a fried egg wrapped in a pancake; an "elephant ear" plate-sized piece of fried bread; noodles; congee (rice gruel) or beancurd jelly accompanied by a deep-fried cruller *(you tiao)*; or a slice of cake and a jar of milk. Lunch or dinner could be noodles from a food stall or careful preparation of the just-bought produce from the market.

Every region has its own particular snacks, very often sold on the street. Snack food is very inexpensive and includes such regional specialties as Beijing's boiled tripe with fresh coriander leaves (cilantro), fried starch sausage with garlic, sour bean soup, and boiled pork and

leek dumplings *(jiaozi)*. Shanghai is known for its steamed *baozi* dumplings, sweet glutinous rice with eight sweetmeats *(babaofan)* and yeasty sweetened wine lees (the sediment of the wine left after fermentation). Sichuan is noted for spicy *dan dan* noodles, dumplings in hot sauce, and beancurd jelly *(dou hua)*, while Cantonese *dim sum* is a cuisine unto itself.

The average urban family eats its main meal of the day in the evening. This meal usually consists of a staple such as rice or noodles, one or two fried dishes, at least one of which contains meat or fish, and a soup. Northerners eat more wheat than rice, in the form of steamed buns or noodles, which are fried or simmered in stock.

Beer regularly accompanies meals at home; stronger spirits are reserved for special occasions. The whole family gets involved in the business of shopping and cooking, and friends or relatives may be invited to join in the feast.

Western foods have made tentative inroads into the 6000-year-old bastion of Chinese cuisine, but fast-food outlets succeed mainly because of their novelty and location in Chinese tourist cities.

China's Ancient Gourmet Culture

As the Son of Heaven, the emperor of China enjoyed a status so elevated above the common mortal that it is difficult to conceive of the awe in which he was held and the power that he enjoyed. There are no dining rooms in the Forbidden City; tables would be set up before the emperor wherever he decided to eat. Every meal was a banquet of approximately 100 dishes. These included 60 or 70 dishes from the

Esoteric and often extremely expensive ingredients such as shark's fin, dried scallops and dried oysters go into some of China's prized dishes.

imperial kitchens, and a few dozen more served by the chief concubines from their own kitchens. Many of the dishes served to the emperor were made purely for their visual appeal, and were placed far away from the reach of the imperial chopsticks. These leftovers were spirited out of the palace to be sold to gourmets eager to "dine with the emperor."

From the palace, this gourmet culture filtered down to the private homes of the rich and powerful and to the restaurants where the privileged entertained. Banquets are important social and commercial events in China today and many high officials attend banquets five or six nights a week. Almost any event can supply the reason for a banquet: the completion (or non-completion) of a business deal, wedding, graduation, trip abroad, return from a trip abroad, promotion, moving house and so on. One can also give a banquet to save or give "face" in the case of some unpleasant situation or mishap.

Some of the best restaurants in China today are the pre–1949 enterprises that have managed to survive by virtue of the quality of their cooking and by their location. One example is Fangshan Restaurant in Beihai Park in Beijing, set in a former imperial palace on the shores of an artificial lake, where many of the recipes are taken from the late-Qing dynasty Forbidden City. Fangshan is renowned for its Manchu-Chinese Banquet, a three-day dining extravaganza that consists of over 100 different dishes, a souvenir of Qing dynasty court banquets. At another famous restaurant, Listening to the Orioles Pavilion, in the gardens of the famed Summer Palace (known to the Chinese as *Yi He Yuan*), dinners for 10 at around $1000 per table are reputedly not uncommon.

The Chinese Kitchen and Table

Rice is essential to a Chinese meal. This is particularly true in South China, although this division is not hard and fast. One reason the Grand Canal was built in the sixth century was to transport rice from the fertile Yangtze delta region to the imperial granaries in the relatively dry North. And since the Ming dynasty (1368–1644), an annual crop of short-grain rice has been grown in the suburbs of

This child seems to be eating with more gusto than finesse. You may need some practice before becoming adept with chopsticks.

Beijing, originally for the palace and today for the military leadership. Numerous varieties of rice are produced in China, supplemented by the more expensive Thai rice which is available at urban markets throughout the country. Southerners seem to prefer long-grain rice, which is less sticky than other varieties and has strong "wood" overtones when steaming hot.

The basic Chinese diet and means of food preparation were in place about 6000 years ago, although many imported ingredients entered the Chinese larder and new cooking methods were adopted. From the earliest times, the Chinese have divided their foodstuffs into two general categories: *fan* (cooked rice and staple grain dishes) and *cai* (cooked meat and vegetable dishes). A balanced mixture of grain and cooked dishes has been the ideal of a Chinese meal since time immemorial. Further balances were sought between the *yin* (cooling) and *yang* (heating) qualities of the foods served. The notion of food as both preventative and curative medicine is deeply embedded in the Chinese psyche.

The specific proportion of grain and cooked dishes on a menu depends on the economic status of the diners and the status of the occasion. The grander the occasion, the more cooked dishes and less grain. Even today, this tradition is maintained at banquets, where a small symbolic bowl of plain steamed rice is served after an extensive selection of dishes.

Rice is served steamed, fried (after boiling) or made into noodles by grinding raw rice into rice flour. It is also cooked with a lot of water to produce congee or *zhou* (rice gruel), a popular breakfast food and late-night snack eaten with savory side dishes. Rice is eaten by raising the bowl to the mouth and shoveling the grains in with the chopsticks in a rapid fanning motion.

The Chinese table is a shared table. The average meal would comprise three to four *cai, fan,* and a soup, served at once, to be shared between the diners who help themselves. The *cai* dishes should each have a different main ingredient, perhaps one meat, one fish, and one vegetable. Each dish should complement the other in terms of taste, texture and flavor, and the total effect appeal to both the eye and the tongue.

When cooking Chinese food, prepare all the ingredients and have them ready before you start cooking as trying to juggle a hot wok and chop a chicken at the same time inevitably leads to catastrophe!

Tea is drunk before and after a meal, but rarely during a meal. The most famous of clear-spirits drunk "straight up" in small handle-less cups or glasses during a meal is Maotai, made in the south-west province of Guizhou.

Chinese meals are socially important events, and special menus are presented for weddings and birthdays; important festivals also have their traditional dishes and snacks.

Finally, some tips on etiquette. Don't point with your chopsticks and don't stick them into your rice bowl and leave them standing up or crossed. Don't use your chopsticks to explore the contents of a dish—locate the morsel you want with your eyes and go for it with your chopsticks without touching any other pieces.

If you wish to take a drink of wine at a formal dinner, you must first toast another diner, regardless of whether he or she responds by drinking. If you are toasted and don't wish to drink, simply touch your lips to the edge of the wine glass to acknowledge the courtesy.

It is incumbent upon the host to urge the guests to eat and drink to their fill. This means ordering more food than necessary and keeping an eye out for idle chopsticks. It is polite to serve the guest of honor the best morsels, such as the cheek of the fish, using a pair of serving or "public" chopsticks or with the back end of one's chopsticks. And remember, all food is communal and to be shared.

SUGGESTED MENUS

Family meals

For simple family meals, try serving with steamed jasmine rice:

• Corn and Crab Chowder (page 41);
• Bamboo Shoots with Mushrooms (page 44);
• Sliced fresh fruit.

Alternatively, you could offer:
• Steamed Tofu with Pork (page 38);
• Black Pepper Beef (page 44);
• Sliced fresh fruit

Dinner parties

For a dinner party that is guaranteed to impress, present a selection of appetizers and two main dishes served with noodles instead of rice, such as.

• Marinated Sliced Beef (page 39), Carrot and Radish Rolls (page 38) and Shrimp and Crab Tofu Skin Rolls (page 38);
• Steamed Whole Fish (page 44) or Sweet and Sour Pork (page 46) and Gung Bao Chicken (page 45);
• Stir-fried Noodles (page 42);
• Candied Apples (page 47).

One-pot meals

Many of the noodle soup dishes here are meals-in-a-bowl, and make an ideal lunch or supper. In China, dishes such as the following are often eaten for breakfast and in-between meals:

• Spicy Sichuan Noodles (page 41);
• Chilled Summer Noodles (page 41).

A melting pot menu

For a festive culinary tour around Asia:
• Hot & Sour Soup (page 40) from China;
• the ubiquitous but always delicious Classic Hainanese Chicken Rice from Malaysia/Singapore (page 129);
• Chinese Broccoli with Crispy Pork or Bacon (page 162) from Thailand served with rice;
• Chilled Almond Jelly with Longans (from Malaysia/Singapore) (page 135).

THE ESSENTIAL FLAVORS OF CHINESE COOKING

Indispensable to the Chinese pantry are **garlic**, **ginger**, and **green onions**. A good supply of **fresh jasmine rice** and **dried egg noodles** is also a must. Flavorings you'll need include **soy sauce**, **rice wine or sake**, **sesame oil,** and **chili sauce**. **Bamboo shoots** and **tofu** are a common addition to everything from stir-fries to one-pot braises. **Rock sugar** is frequently used in red-braised dishes. **Sesame paste** is mixed into dipping sauces, and **Sichuan peppercorns** add a subtle heat to dishes.

Chili Oil

3/4 cup (175 ml) peanut oil
1 tablespoon Sichuan peppercorns
2 dried chilies, sliced

Heat the wok and add the oil, peppercorns and chilies. Cook over low heat for 10 minutes. Allow to cool, then store in a covered jar for 2–3 days. Strain and discard the peppercorns and chilies. Store the oil in a tightly sealed jar and keep in a cool place for up to 6 months.

Sichuan Pepper Oil

2 tablespoons Sichuan peppercorns
3/4 cup (175 ml) peanut oil

Stir-fry the peppercorns in a dry wok until fragrant. Add the oil and cook over low heat for 10 minutes. Allow to cool, then store in a covered jar for 2–3 days. Strain and discard the peppercorns. Store the oil in a tightly sealed jar and keep in a cool place for up to 6 months.

Gourmet Soup Stock

1 lb (500 g) pork ribs, blanched
12 oz (375 g) chicken pieces, blanched
12 oz (375 g) duck pieces, blanched
12 oz (375 g) smoked ham hock
2 green onions (scallions), coarsely chopped
2 in (5 cm) ginger, sliced
1/4 cup (60 ml) rice wine or sake
20 cups (5 liters) water

Combine all the ingredients and simmer, uncovered, for 2 hours. Strain stock through cheesecloth.

Ginger Garlic Sauce (bottom), Chili Garlic Dip (top right) and sliced chilies in soy sauce (top left, no recipe)

Basic Chicken Stock

3 lbs (1 1/2 kgs) chicken bones or 1/2 chicken
2 in (5 cm) ginger, sliced
3 green onions (scallions) or shallots
1 celery stalk, leaves attached, roughly chopped
1 teaspoon peppercorns
10 cups (2 1/2 liters) water

Combine all the ingredients in a large stock pot and bring to a boil over high heat. Reduce the heat and simmer for 1 hour. Discard the solids and strain the stock through a fine sieve. The stock can be frozen for up to 3 months.

Ginger Garlic Sauce

4 in (10 cm) ginger, peeled and sliced
6 cloves garlic
1 teaspoon salt
1 teaspoon sugar
1 teaspoon sesame oil
1 tablespoon oil

Process the ginger and garlic in a food processor until fine. Combine with the remaining ingredients and store in a covered jar. Shake just before serving.

Ginger Soy Dip

2 tablespoons grated ginger
2 teaspoons soy sauce
1 tablespoon finely sliced green onions (scallions)
1/2 teaspoon sugar
2 tablespoons peanut oil
1/2 tablespoon sesame oil

Combine the ginger, soy sauce, green onion, and sugar. Heat both oils in a small saucepan together until they smoke, then pour over the ginger mixture and stir. Serve immediately with steamed chicken or fish.

Black Vinegar Dip

3 in (8 cm) ginger, peeled and cut into thin shreds
3 tablespoons black Chinese vinegar

Combine the ginger and vinegar together. Serve with dumplings and other dim sum dishes.

Chili Garlic Dip

5 red finger-length chilies
3 cloves garlic
3 tablespoons white vinegar
1 teaspoon sugar
1/2 teaspoon salt

Process all the ingredients in a food processor until smooth. Store refrigerated in a dry, covered jar. Serve with steamed poultry or rice.

Sesame Sauce

4 tablespoons sesame seeds
4 tablespoons Basic Chicken Stock or water (recipe on this page)
1/2 teaspoon sesame oil
1/2 teaspoon salt
1/2 teaspoon sugar

Heat a dry skillet gently over low heat and dry-roast the sesame seeds for 1 to 2 minutes.

Place the sesame seeds in a spice grinder or food processor with the Chicken Stock or water and grind to a paste. Mix in the remaining ingredients and serve with any seafood dish.

Pickled Garlic

1 cup (250 ml) water
2 bulbs garlic cloves, skins left on
1/2 cup (125 ml) white vinegar
1 1/2 tablespoons sugar
1/2 teaspoon salt
1 small bay leaf

Bring the water to a boil in a large saucepan. Add the garlic and the remaining ingredients and set aside to cool.

Place the garlic in a dry, glass jar, top with the liquid and leave to marinate for 1 day before using. Drain and serve as an accompaniment or appetizer.

Tofu Skin Spring Rolls

3–4 sheets dried tofu skin
6 oz (180 g) shrimp, peeled and deveined
5 fresh or canned water chestuts, peeled and drained
4 sprigs fresh coriander leaves (cilantro)
3 cloves garlic
1/2 teaspoon salt
1 cup (125 g) cooked crabmeat
2 green onions (scallions), sliced
Oil for deep-frying

Soak the tofu skin in hot water until pliable. Cut the skin into ten, 5-in (12-cm) square pieces and set aside.

Combine the shrimp, water chestnut, coriander leaves, garlic, and salt in a food processor and pulse until blended. Stir in the crabmeat and sliced green onion.

Spread 2 to 3 tablespoons of the filling across the center of a piece of tofu skin. Fold the skin over the filling, fold the sides in, then fold over to seal the filling in. Repeat until all the filling is used up.

Heat the oil in a wok over high heat. Fry the rolls, a few at a time, until crisp and golden, about 2 minutes per side. Drain on paper towels and repeat until all the rolls are fried. Serve immediately with Chili Garlic Dip and Black Vinegar Dip (both recipes on this page.)

Carrot and Radish Rolls

3/4 cup (75 g) shredded carrot
2 1/2 oz (75 g) daikon radish, peeled and thinly sliced, lengthwise
3 teaspoons sugar
2 teaspoons white rice vinegar
2 teaspoons sesame oil
1/2 teaspoon salt

Blanch the carrot and radish separately in a little boiling water. Drain well and pat dry with paper towels. Place the slices of radish flat on a board and put some shredded carrot crosswise in the center of each. Roll up to enclose the carrot, then cut each roll on the diagonal into 1/2-in (1-cm) pieces.

Arrange on a plate. Combine all the remaining ingredients, mixing until the sugar dissolves. Pour over the rolls and serve.

Steamed Tofu with Pork

1 lb (500 g) tofu
3 teaspoons cornstarch
4 oz (125 g) ground lean pork
3 dried black Chinese mushrooms, soaked and finely chopped
2 teaspoons chicken stock powder
1/2 teaspoon salt
1 teaspoon sugar
1 1/2 cups leafy greens (spinach or *bok choy*), blanched

Steamed Tofu with Pork

1 teaspoon rice wine or sake
1/2 cup (125 ml) Basic Chicken
Stock (page 38)

Cut the tofu into squares about
3 x 1 1/2 in (8 x 4 cm) thick. Use
a teaspoon to scoop out some of
the tofu from the center to make
a hole for the pork filling.

Combine 1 teaspoon corn-
starch with all the other ingredients, except the leafy greens and
stock, mixing well. Stuff this into
the tofu and steam over high heat
for 4 minutes.

While the tofu is steaming,
cook the greens in the Chicken
Stock. Drain, keeping the stock.
Arrange the greens on a plate.
Blend the remaining 2 teaspoons
cornstarch with water and thick-
en the stock. Pour over the vegetables, arrange the cooked tofu
on top and serve.

> For the stuffing, ground chicken
> or beef works as well as pork.
> For a vegetarian variation, use
> soaked, chopped vermicelli.

Steamed Vegetable Dumplings with Black Vinegar Sauce

Tender parcels of stir-fried vegetables served with a hot and
tangy sauce.

Filling
1 tablespoon oil
4 cloves garlic, minced
1 tablespoon grated ginger
6 dried black Chinese mushrooms,
soaked in warm water for 10 minutes, stems discarded and caps diced
1 teaspoon sesame oil
2 teaspoons soy sauce
2 cups (250 g) shredded Chinese
(Napa) cabbage
1/2 cup (100 g) water chestnuts,
diced

2 cups (250 g) grated carrot
2 green onions (scallions), finely
sliced
40 round wonton wrappers, 4 in
(10 cm) across

Black Vinegar Sauce
2 tablespoons soy sauce
2 tablespoons chili oil
4 tablespoons black Chinese vinegar
1/2 teaspoon sesame seeds
1 green onion (scallion), thinly sliced

To make the Filling, heat the oil
in a wok over medium heat. Add
the garlic, ginger, mushrooms,
sesame oil, and soy sauce, and
stir-fry for 1 to 2 minutes. Add
the carrot, cabbage, water chestnuts, and green onion, stir-fry
for 2 to 3 minutes until the
vegetables soften, then remove
from the heat. Place the vegetables in a bowl, draining any
liquid before using.

Place a wonton wrapper on a
clean, dry surface. Place 1/2
tablespoon of the Filling in the
center of a wrapper, gather the
edges around the Filling to form
a pouch, then press the edges of
the wrapper firmly to seal. Set
aside and repeat with the
remaining wonton skins and
Filling. Arrange all the wontons
on a lightly-oiled plate and
steam covered in a bamboo
steamer for 10 minutes.

Prepare the Black Vinegar
Sauce by combining the soy
sauce, chili oil, and black vinegar in a small bowl, then sprinkle with sesame seeds and green
onion. Remove the wontons
from the steamer and serve with
the Black Vinegar Sauce.

> White Peking wonton wrappers,
> sold in some Asian markets, give
> these wontons a chewy texture
> and make a nice presentation.

Pork Dumplings with Soy Sauce Dip

Dumplings are a favorite snack
in most of China, from Beijing
in the north to Shanghai on the
east coast, from the southern
province of Guangdong to
Sichuan in the far west. The
fillings differ from one area to
another, as well as according to
season. In summer in Beijing,
the basic pork stuffing might be
seasoned with fresh dill or
chopped Chinese chives. The
dumplings may be steamed,
fried, boiled, served in soup (like
the famous Cantonese wonton
soup), or, as in this Sichuan version, bathed in a tangy sauce.

Filling
8 oz (250 g) ground pork
1 egg, lightly beaten
1 1/2 teaspoons grated ginger
2 tablespoons rice wine or sake
1 teaspoon salt
1/4 teaspoon ground white pepper
25 wonton wrappers

Soy Sauce Dip
1 clove garlic, minced
4 tablespoons soy sauce
1 tablespoon chili oil
1/2 teaspoon sugar
1/4 teaspoon ground cinnamon
2 green onions (scallions), sliced

To make the Filling, combine all
the ingredients, except for the
wonton wrappers, and mix well.

Place a teaspoonful of the
Filling in the center of a wonton

Pork Dumplings with Soy Sauce Dip

wrapper and use a fingertip
dipped in water to moisten the
edge of the wonton wrapper.
Fold the wrapper in half to
make a semi-circle, then press
firmly to enclose the Filling,
making sure there are no air
pockets inside the wonton.
Repeat until all the Filling is
used up.

Carefully lower the dump-
lings into a pot of boiling water
with a strainer or slotted spoon.
Simmer for 2 to 3 minutes and
drain.

To prepare 4 servings, place
1/4 teaspoon garlic, 1 tablespoon
soy sauce, 1/4 teaspoon chili oil,
a pinch of sugar, and a pinch of
cinnamon in the bottom of 4
bowls. Divide the boiled dumplings among the bowls and garnish with sliced green onions.

Marinated Sliced Beef

14 oz (400 g) topside beef
Water as required
2 tablespoons rice wine or sake
2 teaspoons salt
4 bay leaves

Put the beef in a pan with
sufficient water to cover. Add all
the other ingredients and simmer, covered, until the beef is
tender. Turn the meat from time
to time and add a little more
water if it dries up. Allow to
cool. To serve, slice the beef
thinly and arrange on a plate.
Serve with a dipping sauce.

Crispy Shrimp Toast

Classic Egg Rolls

An all-time favorite, these golden egg rolls are filled with crunchy vegetables and savory pork. Accompanied with fragrant Jasmine tea, they make the perfect snack.

3 teaspoons cornstarch
1 teaspoon soy sauce
8 oz (250 g) ground pork or diced ham or bacon
2 tablespoons oil
1/2 cup (90 g) thinly slivered cooked bamboo shoots
2 carrots, peeled and grated
2 cups (180 g) thinly sliced Chinese (Napa) cabbage
2 green onions (scallions), sliced
2 cups (100 g) fresh bean sprouts
1 teaspoon salt
1/4 teaspoon pepper
20 spring roll wrappers
1 egg, beaten
Oil for deep-frying
Plum sauce, to serve
Hot Chinese or English mustard, to serve

Blend 1 teaspoon of the cornstarch with the soy sauce and combine with the pork. Set aside.

Heat the oil in a wok over medium-high heat and stir-fry the pork until it changes color, about 3 minutes. Add the bamboo shoots and grated carrot and stir-fry for 2 minutes.

Add the cabbage and stir-fry for about 2 minutes, or until the cabbage is soft but still crisp. Remove from the heat and stir in the green onions, bean sprouts, salt, and pepper. Drain the filling before using.

Lay a spring roll wrapper on a flat surface, with a corner facing you. Spoon 2 tablespoons of the filling onto the wrapper, about 2 in (5 cm) from the bottom corner. Shape the filling into a long, narrow strip.

Fold the bottom corner up and over the filling, and roll once, away from you. Dab a bit of egg on the left and right corners and fold each in, pressing to seal. Dab the top corner with a bit of egg and roll, sealing the egg roll. Repeat until all the wrappers and filling are used up.

Heat the oil in a wok over high heat until almost smoking. Add 5 egg rolls at a time and fry until crisp and golden, about 3 minutes. Remove the egg rolls with a slotted spoon and drain on paper towels. Serve with plum sauce and mustard.

Crispy Shrimp Toast

This version includes whole shrimp in addition to the shrimp paste, and the bread can also be cut into disks with a cookie cutter to obtain the shape shown in the photo.

4 slices lightly toasted white bread
12 oz (350 g) fresh shrimp, peeled and deveined
2 cloves garlic
1 tablespoon grated ginger
1 teaspoon sugar
1/2 teaspoon salt
1 egg white
1/2 teaspoon sesame oil
2 green onions (scallions), sliced
1 egg, beaten
1/2 cup (30 g) unseasoned breadcrumbs
Oil for deep-frying

Dipping Sauce
1/4 cup (60 g) sugar
3/4 cup (180 ml) rice vinegar
1/4 cup water
1 red finger-length chili, deseeded and sliced
2 green onions (scallions), thinly sliced

To make the Dipping Sauce, combine the sugar, vinegar, and water in a small pan and stir over low heat until the sugar dissolves. Remove from the heat and stir in the chili and green onions. Set aside.

Remove the crusts from the bread and cut each piece diagonally into 4 triangles, or use a cookie cutter to cut out circles.

Set aside 12 shrimp. Place the remaining shrimp, garlic, ginger, sugar, salt, egg white, and sesame oil into a blender and process until smooth. Stir in the green onions.

Spread a tablespoon of the shrimp paste on each piece of bread and place a reserved shrimp on top. Brush the shrimp paste with beaten egg and sprinkle with breadcrumbs.

Heat the oil in a wok over medium-high heat. Fry the bread pieces a few at a time until crisp and golden, about 1 minute per side. Remove with a slotted spoon and drain on paper towels. Serve hot with the Dipping Sauce.

Restorative and satisfying, Chinese soups are usually drunk throughout a meal.

Hot and Sour Soup

This tangy Sichuan favorite combines tofu and dried mushrooms, but you can modify it by adding cooked shrimp, chicken or pork. Chili oil makes a nice condiment for this soup, and a touch of black Chinese vinegar or balsamic vinegar may be added for extra zing.

4 cups (1 liter) Basic Chicken Stock (page 38)
1 teaspoon salt
1 teaspoon sugar
1/2 tablespoon grated ginger
1/2 cup (100 g) fresh or frozen green peas
1 large tomato, diced
8 oz (250 g) soft tofu, diced
4 large fresh shiitake mushrooms, diced; or 4 dried black Chinese mushrooms, soaked in warm water, stems discarded, and caps diced
2 dried wood ear mushrooms, soaked in water and thinly sliced (optional)
2 tablespoons soy sauce
2 tablespoons black Chinese vinegar

Chilled Summer Noodles

1 teaspoon sesame oil
1/2 teaspoon freshly ground black
  pepper
1/2 teaspoon ground Sichuan
  peppercorns or *sansho* pepper
2 eggs, beaten
2 tablespoons cornstarch blended
  with 2 tablespoons water
4 green onions (scallions), sliced
Pinch of ground white pepper
Chili oil, to serve (optional)
Black Chinese vinegar, to serve

Bring the stock to a boil in a
large pot. Add the salt, sugar,
ginger, peas, tomato, tofu, and
mushrooms. Return to a boil
and simmer for 3 minutes.

Add the soy sauce, vinegar,
sesame oil, black pepper, and
Sichuan pepper, and stir. Slowly
drizzle the beaten eggs into the
soup and let sit for 1 minute. Do
not stir.

Stir the cornstarch mixture,
then pour it slowly into the simmering soup while stirring gently. Keep stirring until the soup
thickens. Simmer for 1 more
minute, then turn off the heat.

Serve hot, garnished with
green onions and white pepper.
Add a few drops of chili oil and
black Chinese vinegar, if desired.

Corn and Crab Chowder

A comforting homestyle soup
that can be made with fresh or
frozen corn kernels, or with
canned cream-style corn for a
thicker consistency.

1 tablespoon oil
1 tablespoon rice wine or sake
2 thin slices of ginger
4 cups (1 liter) vegetable or chicken
  stock
5 dried black Chinese mushrooms,
  soaked in water for 20 minutes,
  stems discarded, and caps diced;
  or 8 button mushrooms, diced
1 small carrot, peeled and diced
1 cup (250 g) fresh or frozen sweet
  corn kernels, or 1 can (12 oz/350 g)
  cream style corn
2 tablespoons fresh or frozen
  green peas
1/2 cup (60 g) cooked crab meat, or
  minced chicken
3 tablespoons cornstarch blended
  with 3 tablespoons water
1/4 teaspoon freshly ground black
  pepper
1 teaspoon sesame oil

Heat the oil in a wok over medium-
high heat, then add the rice wine
and ginger, letting it sizzle before
adding the stock. Bring to a boil.

Add the mushrooms and
carrot, simmer for 5 minutes,
then add the corn, peas, crab
meat, and salt. Simmer for
another 5 minutes.

Stir in the cornstarch mixture, stirring until the soup
thickens. Season with pepper
and sesame oil before serving.

Chilled Summer Noodles

If you've always eaten noodles
piping hot, this dish might seem
a little surprising. However, chilled
noodles are a popular summer
dish in China as well as in neighboring Japan. This dish is quick
and easy to prepare and makes a
nice lunch. Try to get fresh wheat
noodles for this dish—they are
available in most supermarkets.

8 oz (250 g) dried or 14 oz (400 g)
  fresh wheat noodles
1 cup (50 g) fresh bean sprouts
Green onions (scallions), sliced, to
  garnish

Sauce
2 1/2 tablespoons grated ginger

Spicy Sichuan Noodles

5 large cloves of garlic, crushed
1 tablespoon sesame paste or
  peanut butter
1/2 tablespoon oil
3 tablespoons soy sauce
2 teaspoons sugar
2 teaspoons black Chinese vinegar
1/2 tablespoon sesame oil
1 teaspoon chili oil

To make the Sauce, combine the
ingredients and mix well.
Alternatively, you may serve all
the ingredients in small sauces as
shown and allow each person to
mix their own sauce at the table.

Cook the noodles according
to the package directions, then
drain well. Combine the noodles
with the Sauce and bean
sprouts, tossing gently. Take care
not to break the bean sprouts.

Garnish with the green onion
and serve immediately, or chill
and serve later.

Spicy Sichuan Noodles

This spicy Sichuan favorite is
often sold at street-side stalls and
by mobile vendors, known as
hawkers

1/2 tablespoon Sichuan peppercorns
1 1/2 tablespoons peanut oil
1 teaspoon oil
8 oz (250 g) ground pork
2 cups (500 ml) Basic Chicken Stock
  (page 38)
1/2 cup (125 g) preserved salted
  radish (*chye poh*) or spicy Sichuan

Pickles (*zha cai*), diced
4 tablespoons soy sauce
1 1/2 tablespoons black Chinese
  vinegar
1 tablespoon minced garlic
2 teaspoons sesame oil
1 teaspoon chili oil
1/4 teaspoon ground white pepper
1 lb (500 g) fresh wheat noodles or
  8 oz (250 g) dried wheat noodles
4 green onions (scallions), finely
  sliced, to garnish

Heat a wok over low heat and
dry-fry the Sichuan peppercorns
for 2 to 3 minutes until fragrant.
Add the peanut oil and cook
over low heat for 10 minutes to
infuse it with the flavor of the
peppercorns. Cool, then strain
the oil, discarding the pepper
corns. Set aside.

Heat the oil in a wok over
high heat and stir-fry the pork
for 2 to 3 minutes, or until
cooked. Set aside.

Combine the Sichuan pep-
percorn oil, Chicken Stock, preserved radish, soy sauce, black
vinegar, garlic, sesame oil,
chili oil and white pepper in a
saucepan. Keep warm over
medium heat.

Bring a pot of water to a boil
and cook the noodles. Fresh
noodles will take about 2 minutes
to cook, dried noodles about 4
minutes. Drain the noodles, divide
among 4 large soup bowls and
pour in the hot broth. Top with
the pork and garnish with green
onion. Serve immediately.

Stir-fried Noodles

Very fine, fresh wheat noodles, like angel hair pasta, are used for this dish, popular in the southern coastal province of Fujian. The shrimp stock accents this dish with the wonderful taste of the sea.

10 oz (300 g) fresh shrimp
1 cup (250 ml) water
1 lb (500 g) fresh noodles or 10 oz (300 g) dried rice vermicelli or wheat noodles
2 tablespoons oil
4 shallots, thinly sliced
13 cloves garlic, minced
4 oz (120 g) ground pork
2 cups (500 g) slivered cooked bamboo shoots
1 carrot, peeled and cut into matchsticks
4 dried black Chinese mushrooms, soaked in hot water for 20 minutes, stems discarded, and caps diced
1/4 cup (60 g) coarsely chopped Chinese chives
2 tablespoons rice wine or sake
Pinch of salt and freshly ground black pepper

Peel the shrimp. Place the heads and shells in a small saucepan with the water and bring to a boil. Reduce the heat and simmer for 10 minutes. Mash the shells, then strain and reserve the broth, discarding the shells.

Blanch the noodles in boiling water for 1 minute. Drain and set aside.

Heat the oil in a wok over medium-high heat. Add the shallots and fry until golden brown, about 3 to 4 minutes. Drain, remove the shallots from the wok and set aside. Reserve the oil in the wok.

Add the garlic to the wok and stir-fry for 30 seconds. Add the shrimp, pork, bamboo shoots, carrot, mushrooms and chives. Stir-fry until the pork and shrimp change color, about 3 to 4 minutes. Pour in 1/2 cup (125 ml) of the reserved shrimp stock, then add the rice wine, salt, and pepper, and simmer uncovered for 5 minutes, stirring occasionally.

Add the blanched noodles and stir-fry for 3 minutes. Mix well and serve.

Classic Fried Rice

This dish can be made with just about any meat and vegetable leftovers you have on hand. A sliced red chili or bits of bell pepper or asparagus add a wonderful zing.

4 cups (500 g) cooked rice, cooled to room temperature or in the refrigerator
3 teaspoons oil
2 eggs, lightly beaten
8 fresh medium shrimp, peeled, deveined, and diced
1/2 cup (60 g) thinly sliced chicken or pork
2 dried Chinese sausages (*lap cheong*), thinly sliced diagonally
4 green onions (scallions), thinly sliced
1 red finger-length chili, deseeded and minced (optional)
1/4 teaspoon salt
1/2 cup (40 g) diced bell pepper or asparagus or green peas or sliced cabbage

Break up the rice grains with a fork, or with your hands, and set aside.

Heat 1 teaspoon of oil in a wok. Pour in the beaten eggs and cook until set. Break the omelet into small pieces with a spatula, then remove from the wok and set aside.

Heat the remaining oil over high heat in the wok and stir-fry the remaining ingredients, except for the rice and salt, for 2 minutes. Add the rice and salt and stir-fry for another 4 to 5 minutes, turning constantly to brown the rice. Add the fried egg and serve hot.

> If you don't have Chinese sausages, any kind of sausage, ham or bacon can be substituted.

Stir-fried Eggplant (top) and Stir-fried Vegetables (bottom)

Stir-fried Eggplant

This dish provides a wonderful aromatic blend of flavors. The traditional recipe uses ground pork, but you may substitute diced black Chinese mushrooms for a vegetarian version.

10 oz (300 g) Asian eggplants, cut into strips
2 teaspoons salt
1/2 cup (125 ml) oil
6 cloves garlic, minced
3 tablespoons grated ginger
1/2 cup (100 g) lean ground pork or diced black Chinese mushroom caps
2 teaspoons chili paste
1 teaspoon salted soybeans, mashed
Green onions (scallions), sliced
Fresh coriander leaves (cilantro), minced

Sauce
2 teaspoons soy sauce
2 teaspoons rice wine or sake
1 teaspoon sesame oil
1 teaspoon black Chinese vinegar
1 tablespoon sugar
1/2 teaspoon freshly ground black pepper
2 tablespoons water

To make the Sauce, combine the ingredients, then set aside.

Sprinkle the eggplant with the salt and let it sit for 10 minutes. Drain away any liquid,

Classic Fried Rice

then rub off any remaining salt from the eggplant. Squeeze the eggplant to extract any additional liquid.

Heat the oil in a wok over high heat until the oil is very hot, then stir-fry the eggplant for 3 to 4 minutes. Turn off the heat, remove the eggplant from the wok and drain on a plate lined with paper towels. Set aside.

Discard all but 1 tablespoon of the oil, and stir-fry the garlic and ginger over high heat for 1 minute until fragrant. Add the pork and continue to stir-fry for 2 minutes. Add the chili paste and salted soybeans and continue to stir-fry.

Stir in the Sauce, then add the eggplant and stir-fry until everything is evenly coated with the Sauce. Cover and simmer for 3 to 4 minutes, or until heated through. Garnish with the green onion and fresh coriander leaves.

Stir-fried Vegetables

Whatever vegetables you have on hand can be substituted for this quick and easy stir-fry.

2 teaspoons oil
1 cup (80 g) fresh snowpeas, ends trimmed
Pinch of salt
1/2 teaspoon sugar
8 dried black Chinese mushrooms, soaked in 1/2 cup (125 ml) hot water for 15 minutes, stems discarded and caps sliced; liquid reserved
3/4 cup (120 g) cooked bamboo shoots, sliced
1/2 tablespoon grated ginger
2 tablespoons rice wine or sake
1/2 teaspoon mushroom oyster sauce
1/2 teaspoon sesame oil
1/4 teaspoon soy sauce
Pinch of ground white pepper

Heat the oil in a wok over medium-high heat and stir-fry the snow peas with the salt and sugar for 30 seconds. Add the mushrooms, bamboo shoots, 1/4 cup (60 ml) of the reserved mushroom liquid, and the remaining ingredients. Simmer for 2 minutes, then serve.

Hoisin-glazed Green Beans

Tender-crisp green beans bathed in a sweet and spicy sauce—an irresistable combination!

1 tablespoon oil
1 tablespoon minced garlic
12 oz (350 g) green beans, ends trimmed, halved
3 tablespoons hoisin sauce
1 1/2 tablespoons soy sauce
1 teaspoon sesame oil
2 teaspoons Chili Garlic Dip (page 38), or 1 red finger-length chili, minced

Heat the oil in a wok over high heat until smoking. Add the garlic, stir-fry for 1 minute, then gently slide the beans into the wok and stir-fry for 2 minutes.

Stir in the hoisin sauce, soy sauce, sesame oil, and Chili Garlic Dip. Continue to stir-fry for 1 to 2 minutes until the beans are cooked and tender-crisp.

> This recipe is excellent with long beans or French green beans. Leave the beans to cook covered over medium heat for an additional 2 to 3 minutes if you prefer a softer texture.

Stir-fried Chinese Broccoli with Beef

Bite-sized pieces of Chinese broccoli and succulent beef, stir-fried in a delicious mushroom oyster sauce.

8 oz (250 g) beef, thinly sliced
1 tablespoon oil
1/2 in (1 cm) ginger, thinly sliced
1 tablespoon minced garlic
12 oz (350 g) Chinese broccoli (kailan), cut into bite-sized pieces, stems separated from the leaves
1/2 tablespoon mushroom oyster sauce

Marinade
3 teaspoons soy sauce
2 teaspoons mushroom oyster sauce
1/2 teaspoon freshly ground black pepper
1 teaspoon sugar
2 teaspoons rice wine or sake
1 teaspoon cornstarch

Mix all the Marinade ingredients together and combine with the beef. Marinate for 30 minutes, or overnight.

Hoisin-glazed Green Beans

Heat 1/2 tablespoon of the oil in a wok over high heat and stir-fry the ginger for 30 seconds, then discard the ginger. Add the beef to the wok and stir-fry for about 1 minute until the beef changes color, then remove the beef from the wok and set aside.

Add the remaining oil to the wok, stir-fry the garlic for 30 seconds over high heat, then add the broccoli stems and stir-fry for 1 minute. Add the broccoli leaves to the wok and continue to stir-fry.

Stir in the mushroom oyster sauce and continue to cook for 1 minute, then return the beef to the wok, stir, heat through, and serve.

Spicy Stir-fried Tofu

This is a classic Sichuan dish. Ground beef or dried shrimp may be substituted for the pork in this dish, however the dominant ingredient is tofu laced with pungent Sichuan seasonings. A vegetarian version can be made where the meat is omitted altogether, and substituted with fresh shiitake or dried black Chinese mushrooms.

2 tablespoons salted black beans
1 lb (500 g) firm tofu
2 tablespoons oil
6 oz (180 g) ground pork
1 tablespoon grated ginger
4 tablespoons minced spicy Sichuan pickles (zha cai—optional)
2 cloves garlic, minced
4 green onions (scallions), thinly sliced
2 tablespoons hot chili paste
1/2 cup (125 ml) Basic Chicken Stock (page 38)
1 tablespoon soy sauce
2 teaspoons cornstarch, blended with 2 teaspoons water
1/2 teaspoon ground Sichuan peppercorns

Cover the black beans with water and leave to soak for 10 minutes. Drain, then mash slightly with a fork. Set aside.

Drain the tofu, place it between 2 plates, and top with a weight for 10 minutes. Drain any additional liquid, then dice the tofu and set it aside.

Heat the oil in a wok over medium-high heat and stir-fry the black beans and pork until the meat is completely browned, about 3 minutes. Add the ginger, Sichuan pickles (if using), garlic, chili paste, and half of the green onions. Stir-fry for another 2 minutes, then add the Chicken Stock and tofu. Simmer for 5 minutes.

Add the soy sauce, then pour in the cornstarch mixture and stir until the sauce thickens. Sprinkle with Sichuan pepper and green onion.

> For a vegetarian version, substitute 6 fresh shiitake or 8 dried black Chinese mushrooms. If using fresh mushrooms, discard the stems and dice the caps. If using dried black Chinese mushrooms, soak them in warm water for 15 minutes to soften, then drain, discard the stems, and dice the caps. Add the mushrooms in place of the meat.

Bamboo Shoots with Mushrooms

12-oz (375-g) can bamboo shoots
2 teaspoons oil
1 teaspoon rice wine or sake
1 heaped teaspoon very finely
  chopped or crushed garlic
10 dried black Chinese mushrooms,
  soaked in warm water, drained
1 teaspoon chicken stock powder
1 teaspoon sugar
1/2 teaspoon salt

Drain the canned bamboo shoots, then simmer them in boiling water for 5 minutes, drain and slice coarsely.

Heat the oil in a wok and stir-fry the garlic and mushrooms until fragrant. Add the bamboo shoots and all the seasonings and stir-fry for 1–2 minutes. Serve immediately.

Steamed Whole Fish

1 fresh pomfret, pompano, butter
  fish or plaice, about 1 3/4 lbs (750 g)
1/2 cup (100 g) salted mustard
  cabbage (kiam chye), soaked and
  finely sliced
2 sour salted plums (available in jars)
1 red finger-length chili, deseeded
  and finely shredded
3-in (8-cm) celery stalk, finely
  shredded
1 green onion (scallion), chopped in
  lengths
3 in (8 cm) ginger, cut into very fine
  shreds
1 cake firm tofu, sliced
1 dried black Chinese mushroom,
  soaked and finely sliced
2 teaspoons chicken stock powder
1/2 teaspoon sugar
1/4 teaspoon salt
Coriander leaves (cilantro),
  to garnish

Clean the fish inside and out and wipe dry. Place the fish in a heatproof dish and arrange all the ingredients on top of the fish. Sprinkle with the stock powder, sugar and salt and put inside a large steamer. Steam over high heat for about 8 minutes, until the fish is cooked. Take care not to overcook for optimum texture and flavor. Garnish with coriander leaves.

Crispy Fried Fish

The Chinese believe that freshwater fish from lakes, rivers and fish ponds are more delicate in flavor and texture than fish from the sea. Although this recipe calls for freshwater fish, fine-textured ocean fish such as perch, grouper, bream or snapper can be used also.

1 fresh fish, 1 1/2–2 lbs (3/4–1 kg),
  cleaned and scaled
3 in (8 cm) ginger, finely sliced
1 green onion (scallion), chopped
1 teaspoon ground white pepper
1/2 cup (125 ml) rice wine or sake
2 tablespoons cornstarch
Oil for deep-frying
1 green onion (scallion), finely sliced

Sauce
1–2 tablespoons chili paste
1 1/2 teaspoons finely chopped garlic
1 1/2 teaspoons finely chopped ginger
1 1/2 teaspoons white rice vinegar
1 teaspoon sugar
1/2 teaspoon salt

3/4 cup (185 ml) Basic Chicken
  Stock (page 38)
2 teaspoons cornstarch, blended
  with water
1 green onion (scallion), finely sliced

Cut 4 or 5 deep diagonal slashes on each side of the fish to help it cook more quickly. Marinate the fish for 15 minutes with the ginger, chopped green onion, pepper, and rice wine. Drain the fish and scrape off any pieces of the marinade. Dry thoroughly.

Heat a wok and add the oil. When the oil is hot, sprinkle the fish on both sides with cornstarch, shaking it to remove any excess. Carefully lower the fish into the oil and cook, over moderate heat, for about 5–8 minutes until golden brown and cooked through. Drain and keep warm on a serving dish.

Discard all but 1 teaspoon of the frying oil. To prepare the Sauce, stir-fry the chili paste, garlic and ginger for a few seconds until fragrant, then add all the other ingredients, except the cornstarch. Simmer for 2 minutes, then thicken with the cornstarch. Pour the Sauce over the fish and garnish with the green onion. Serve immediately.

Black Pepper Beef

Black Pepper Beef

Simple and quick to prepare, this dish tastes like a flavor-enhanced version of black pepper steak, with Sichuan peppercorns adding a distinctive difference.

1 lb (500 g) beef fillet, trimmed and
  cut into bite-sized cubes
4 tablespoons rice wine or sake
1/2 teaspoon salt
1/4 teaspoon ground white pepper
2 teaspoons oil
4 cloves garlic, minced
2 teaspoons coarsely ground black
  peppercorns
1 teaspoon crushed Sichuan
  peppercorns
4 teaspoons oyster sauce
4 teaspoons soy sauce
2 teaspoons sesame oil
6 lettuce leaves, shredded
2 red finger-length chilies, sliced

Place the beef in a bowl and add the rice wine, salt, and white pepper. Mix and set aside for 10 minutes.

Heat the oil in a wok over high heat and stir-fry the beef until browned on all sides, about 3 minutes. Lower the heat to medium-high, then add the garlic, and stir-fry for 30 seconds. Add the remaining ingredients, except the lettuce and chilies, and stir-fry for 1 minute, mixing well.

Serve the beef on a bed of shredded lettuce, surrounded by sliced red chilies.

Steamed Whole Fish

Black Bean Chicken

Tender chicken and crisp snow peas simmered in a flavorful, salty black bean sauce.

2 skinless chicken breast fillets (1 lb/ 500 g), cut into strips
$1/2$ tablespoon grated ginger
$1/2$ tablespoon cornstarch, blended with 1 tablespoon rice wine or sake
2 tablespoons oil
4 shallots, diced
1 clove garlic, minced
2 tablespoons black bean and garlic sauce, or $1/3$ cup (20 g) salted black beans, soaked and mashed
$1/2$ cup (125 ml) Basic Chicken Stock (page 38)
$1^1/2$ teaspoons sugar
1 cup (80 g) snow peas (optional)

Combine the chicken strips with the ginger and cornstarch mixture, and leave to marinate for 10 minutes.

Heat the oil in a wok over medium-high heat. When the oil is hot, add the shallots and garlic, and stir-fry for 30 seconds. Add the black bean and garlic sauce (or salted black beans) and stir-fry for another 30 seconds.

Add the chicken, chicken stock, and sugar and bring to a boil. Reduce the heat to low and simmer for 3 minutes. Add the snow peas, if using, and cook for another 2 minutes, or until the snow peas have softened.

If using whole salted black beans, soak the beans in enough hot water to cover for 30 minutes. Rinse, drain, then roughly mash the beans.

Gung Bao Chicken

Dried chilies, Sichuan peppercorns, peanuts and garlic give this popular dish an intense flavor and spice.

2 tablespoons oil
3-4 dried chilies, deseeded and cut into small pieces
10 Sichuan peppercorns
1 in ($2^1/2$ cm) ginger, thinly sliced
1 lb (500 g) boneless, skinless chicken breast, cut into bite-sized pieces
4 green onions (scallions), sliced into short lengths
$1/4$ cup (30 g) dry-roasted, unsalted peanuts (optional)

Black Bean Chicken

6-10 cloves garlic, peeled

Sauce
$2/3$ cup (150 ml) Basic Chicken Stock (page 38)
2 tablespoons soy sauce
2 tablespoons rice wine or sake
$3/4$ teaspoon black Chinese vinegar
2 teaspoons sesame oil
2 teaspoons sugar
$1^1/2$ teaspoons cornstarch

Make the Sauce by combining the Chicken Stock, soy sauce, rice wine, black vinegar, sesame oil, sugar, and cornstarch in a small bowl. Set aside.

Heat the oil in a wok over high heat until very hot. Add the dried chilies and stir-fry for 30 seconds, or until they are almost black and start to smoke. Remove the chilies and set aside. Add the Sichuan peppercorns and garlic cloves to the wok and stir-fry for 1 minute. Add the ginger and stir-fry for another 30 seconds. Add the chicken to the wok and stir-fry for 3 to 4 minutes, or until it completely changes color.

Add the green onion and the Sauce. Mix well. Reduce the heat and simmer for 2 minutes, stirring continuously. Stir in the peanuts, if using, and garnish with green onion.

Twice-cooked Pork with Bell Peppers

Sweet red and green peppers add color and a contrasting texture to this quick recipe, where pork is flavored with salted black beans, chili, and hoisin sauce. "Twice-cooked" refers to the use of previously cooked leftover pork, however, fresh meat may be used also. Cooking the pork several times removes all the moisture and gives the meat a chewy texture.

8 oz (250 g) cooked or uncooked pork, thinly sliced
1 tablespoon oil

1 large red bell pepper, sliced
1 large green bell pepper, sliced
2–3 teaspoons chili paste
1 heaped tablespoon salted black beans, soaked, drained, and slightly mashed
1 teaspoon hoisin sauce
2 cloves garlic, minced
1 tablespoon grated ginger
2 teaspoons soy sauce
2 teaspoons sugar
$1/4$ teaspoon ground white pepper
1 green onion (scallion), coarsely chopped

If using uncooked pork, heat 1 teaspoon of oil in a wok over high heat and lightly stir-fry the pork until it is cooked. Remove the pork from the wok and set aside.

Heat the oil in a wok over medium-high heat, then add the

Gung Bao Chicken

peppers and stir-fry for 2 minutes. Add the sliced pork and stir-fry for 1 minute. Remove the pork and peppers from the wok and set it aside aside.

Add the chili paste to the wok and stir-fry for 30 seconds, then add the remaining ingredients and stir-fry for 1 minute, mixing thoroughly. Return the pork and peppers to the wok, stir to heat through and serve.

Stir-fried Shrimp with Chili Sauce

This easy stir-fry can also be made with fresh lobster meat for a wonderful indulgence.

1^{1}/2 lbs (750 g) fresh large shrimp, peeled and deveined or 8 oz (250 g) fresh lobster meat
1 teaspoon cornstarch, blended with ^{1}/4 cup (60 ml) water
1 egg white
^{1}/2 teaspoon plus a pinch of sugar
^{1}/2 teaspoon salt
2 tablespoons oil
^{3}/4 cup (50 g) snow peas, sliced
4 cloves garlic, minced
^{1}/2 tablespoon grated ginger
^{1}/2 tablespoon soy sauce
1 tablespoon rice wine or sake
1 tablespoon Basic Chicken Stock (page 38)
^{1}/2 tablespoon chili bean paste
2 tablespoons tomato ketchup

Season the shrimp or lobster with the cornstarch mixture, egg white, ^{1}/2 teaspoon sugar, and ^{1}/4 teaspoon salt. Massage the shrimp or lobster gently, mixing well. Set aside.

Heat 1 tablespoon of oil in a wok until very hot, then add the snow peas, ^{1}/4 teaspoon salt, and a pinch of sugar. Stir-fry for 1 minute, then remove from the heat and set aside.

Heat the remaining oil in a wok until very hot, then stir-fry the shrimp or lobster for 1 minute. Add the garlic and ginger, stirring to mix thoroughly. Add the soy sauce, rice wine, Chicken Stock, chili bean paste, and tomato ketchup. Continue to stir-fry until the shrimp or lobster is cooked, then serve.

Sweet and Sour Pork

This sweet and tangy sauce is best made with Chinese rice vinegar, but distilled cider vinegar will work as well. This recipe makes sweet and sour sauce the traditional way, where the sauce is translucent and thin. Modern versions of this recipe often include a thick sauce and a variety of other vegetables as well. You can add carrots, onions, or any other of your vegetable favorites. If canned pineapple is

Stir-fried Shrimp with Chili Sauce

used, the syrup may be substituted for the sugar and water called for in the Sauce below.

1 lb (500 g) boneless pork, cut into bite-sized cubes
1 tablespoon cornstarch
Oil for deep-frying
1 tablespoon minced garlic
1 tablespoon minced ginger
1 green or red bell pepper, diced
2 green onions (scallions), sliced into lengths
1 cup (100 g) fresh or canned pineapple chunks

Batter
^{3}/4 cup (100 g) flour
^{3}/4 cup (100 g) cornstarch
2 teaspoons baking powder
^{1}/4 teaspoon salt
1 cup (250 ml) water
1^{1}/2 teaspoons oil

Sauce
^{1}/2 cup (125 ml) Chinese white vinegar or cider vinegar
^{1}/2 teaspoon salt
2 tablespoons tomato ketchup
1 tablespoon soy sauce
^{1}/2 cup (125 g) sugar
1^{1}/2 tablespoons cornstarch, blended with ^{3}/4 cup (175 ml) water

To make the Batter, combine the flour, cornstarch, baking powder, and salt in a large bowl. Gradually pour in the water, mixing with a fork until smooth. Add the oil and mix well. Set aside.

Whisk together all the Sauce ingredients and set aside.

Combine the pork with the cornstarch. Heat the oil in a wok until it just starts to smoke. Working in small batches, use tongs to dip the pork in the Batter, then into the wok. Deep-fry the pork for a few seconds until it is a light brown, then remove from the wok and drain on paper towels. Use a slotted spoon to discard any batter from the wok. Repeat until all the pork has been battered and fried.

Return all the pork to the wok and deep-fry a second time, this time for about 3 minutes, or until golden brown. This step is optional, but it removes the remaining moisture from the pork and makes it crispy and chewy—similar to what you get in a Chinese restaurant. Discard the oil and return the wok to the stove over high heat.

Stir-fry the garlic and ginger for 30 seconds, add the bell pepper, and continue to stir-fry for 1 minute. Add the green onion, pineapple chunks, and Sauce, mix well and bring to a boil. Pour over the pork and serve with rice.

A splatter screen for covering the wok comes in handy when the pork is returned to the pan for additional frying.

Sweet and Sour Pork

Banana Fritters

The most popular Chinese dessert is a platter of sliced, fresh fruits. For more formal banquets one of the desserts in this section may be served; however, these are more commonly eaten as snacks.

Banana Fritters

Sweet bananas that have been lightly battered, fried until golden, and drizzled with honey. An irresistable snack or a sweet ending to a Chinese meal.

7 large firm bananas, or 15 small finger bananas, peeled
Oil for deep-frying
Honey (optional)

Batter
1 cup (125 g) all-purpose flour
2 tablespoons milk
3/4 tablespoon butter
1 tablespoon superfine (caster) sugar
1/2 cup (125 ml) water

To make the Batter, combine the flour, milk, butter, and sugar. Gradually add the water, mixing thoroughly until a smooth batter is formed.

Halve the large bananas if necessary, then dip all the bananas in the Batter, coating well.

Heat the oil in a deep saucepan or a small pot until very hot. Test the oil with a wooden chopstick or a dry wooden spoon; if the oil sizzles, it is ready to be used. Deep-fry the bananas, a few at a time, for 3 minutes until browned on all sides. Drain on paper towels and if desired, serve drizzled with honey.

Candied Apples

Apples, crisp Asian pears, or even ripe bananas can be used for this delightful dessert. It is important that everything is laid out in preparation so that the final stages of cooking can be done quickly.

2 large green apples
Juice of 1 lemon
1 cup (250 ml) oil
Cooking spray

Batter
1 cup (125 g) all-purpose flour
2 tablespoons cornstarch
1 teaspoon baking soda
1 egg, lightly beaten
1/2–3/4 cup (125–175 ml) water

Syrup
1 cup (200 g) sugar
1/4 cup (60 ml) water

Peel, core and slice the apples into eight wedges. Place the slices in a large bowl and toss with the lemon juice. Set aside.

Prepare the Batter by combining the ingredients in a bowl, adding enough water to achieve the consistency of thick cream.

To make the Syrup, heat the sugar and water in a saucepan over medium heat. Once the sugar dissolves, increase the heat to high and bring to a boil without stirring. Continue boiling until the mixture turns to a golden syrup, about 8 to 10 minutes.

While the sugar is boiling, fill a large bowl about half way with ice cubes and fill with cold water. Once the sugar has turned to a syrup, place the saucepan of Syrup in the bowl of iced water for a few seconds to cool. Set the saucepan back on the stove over low heat and keep warm.

Heat the oil in a wok over medium-high heat. While the oil is heating, coat a serving dish with cooking spray. Dip slices of apple, a few at a time, into the Batter and deep-fry for about 30 seconds on each side, or until golden brown. Remove the apple slices with a slotted spoon and drain on a plate lined with paper towels.

Dip the fried apple slices into the Syrup with kitchen tongs coated with cooking spray. Coat in the Syrup, then drop the slices into the iced water. Remove immediately, then place the slices on the greased serving dish. Repeat until all the slices are fried and candied, then serve.

Once boiling, it is very important not to stir the Syrup until it reaches the appropriate consistency. Stirring will break the sugar crystals and the syrup will not properly set.

Candied Apples

"Cooking and eating Indian cuisine is a discovery of the culture, the richly varied history and the spicy treasures of this fascinating land."

INDIA

Three thousand years of tradition and culture are reflected in the cuisine of the subcontinent.

Left: The ultimate in Indian dining, an elegantly laid antique table set with *thalis* of Rajasthani food, while attentive retainers hover nearby.

Right: One of the peaceful canals that criss-cross the southern state of Kerala.

India is a vast and ancient land, with a recorded history that dates back over three thousand years. It is divided into many provinces that stretch from the snowy mountains of Kashmir to the southern tip of verdant Kerala, from the harsh arid deserts of Rajasthan in the west across to the remote tribal region of Assam along the Burmese border. Thus India has it all—from palm-fringed beaches to desert, and bustling cities to small one-ox towns.

This is also the land that gave rise to two of the world's major religions, Buddhism and Hinduism, and produced Jainism and Sikhism. Caste, too, plays its role in influencing the food of the people.

With all these differences Indian cuisine may seem undefinable, but there are enough common strands that combine to form a thrilling and exciting tapestry.

The Land and its People

Located in southern Asia, India ranges from the Himalayas in the north to the great Gangetic plain with its immense and sacred waters, to the lush tropical splendor of Kerala in the south. With its considerable land area—it is the seventh largest country in the world—India naturally encompasses four defined seasons.

In the cooler north and in the Gangetic plain of the middle and eastern part of India, rice and wheat are the main staples; while in the deserts of Rajasthan and Gujarat, it is millet and corn. Rice is also a basic food in the eastern belt of India, where its large and fertile alluvial lands make it an ideal rice-growing region. Along the coastal area of Kerala, fish and meat are the basic foods in the people's diet.

Spices, the foundation of Indian cooking, are widely cultivated according to region. Cardamom, cloves and peppers are harvested mainly in the south, while Rajasthan, Kashmir, and Gujarat are known for their chilies and turmeric. One of the

Above: Nutmegs being weighed in the wholesale spice market of Cochin.
Right: A southern Indian *thali* with an array of vegetables, pickle, soup, rice, bread, banana, and dessert.

three types: those which needed expulsion, those which were absorbed into the flesh, and those which were transformed into thought or mind. The last were the finest and rarest of foods and referred to as *manas*. The term *prasad* was used for food left over from offerings to the gods, food which was considered nectar, left no trace, and which maintained man's spirituality.

Food was classified into different categories: cereals, legumes, vegetables, fruit, spices, milk products, animal meats, and alcoholic beverages. This was the time when ghee or clarified butter emerged as a popular cooking medium because of its associations with purity, as it was used in religious sacrifices and offerings. Most traditional Indian cooking in the north still uses cholesterol-high ghee, although modern Indians have switched to cooking oil.

Ancient food habits were altered by religion and trade, through occupation and invasion, with Indian cuisines becoming more varied and vibrant. Religion was a major influence in changing food habits, with Buddhism and Jainism starting the first indigenous movements which challenged Hindu practices. Abstinence, austerity and simplicity were the tenets of changes which questioned, among other things, the eating of meat. Jainism underlined the importance of innocent foods and vegetarianism was born. Sikhism followed to reaffirm simplicity, with tobacco and alcohol becoming inscribed targets.

Geography also plays a role in what is served. In Gujarat, *nasto* is made from Bengal gram flour (*besan*) mixed with an assortment of spices and fried. *Chevda* or beaten rice is fried and mixed with salt, spices, almonds, raisins, and peanuts. The Parsis brought with them a strong meat-eating tradition and a love of egg dishes, raisins, nuts, butter and cream. They inevitably absorbed Gujarati influences and a hybrid cuisine developed. One of the most famous of these dishes is the Parsi fish steamed in banana-leaf packets. Another is *dhansak*, a one-pot meal that combines several types

glorious sights of Kashmir is the fields of purple-blue crocuses, source of the world's most expensive spice, saffron.

Islam has been in India since the 8th century, but it was not until the 16th century that the Muslims gained control over large parts of India. The Mughal dynasties, which ruled various independent states of pre–Independence India, upstaged the mainstream Hindu culture and cuisine significantly.

Besides the Muslims and Hindus, Jewish settlers also came to Kerala in AD 7, bringing with them the notion of kosher meat. The Christians settled here during the fourth century AD. Zoroastrians came and settled in large numbers when they were hounded out of Persia as far back as AD 850. Parsis, as they are now known, settled largely in Gujarat.

Besides the British, other Europeans who established themselves in India were the Portuguese, who remained largely in Goa, north of Kerala, from the 16th century until after Indian independence from the British.

The Making of a Cuisine

The Vedas, ancient historical and religious texts dating from 1700–1500 BC, set the framework for what is broadly known as Hindu culture. They record the civilization of the Aryans or nomadic tribes from the upper Urals, who traveled as far east as India on one side and as far west as Ireland on the other. Most Hindu food practices were influenced by the Aryans, beginning in the north and the northwest of India and gradually spreading all over the country.

The Aryans did not treat food simply as a means to physical sustenance but saw it as part of a cosmic circle, their dictum being that "food that man eats and his universe must be in harmony." Food, they believed, can be grouped into

of *dal* with spices, meat, and vegetables.

New flavors, rich relishes, meats with cream and butter sauces, dates, nuts, and delectable sweets were the hallmarks of Mughal cuisine, which is widely known and famed for its exotic non-vegetarian food.

Finally, the period of British colonial rule in India—the Raj—has left an indelible mark on both the food and eating practices of this country. In middle-class homes, the dining table replaced the kitchen floor and porcelain, the banana leaf. Cutlery was introduced.

The blending of eastern spices into "western" food began at this time, and some of these "crossings" have endured to this day: kedgeree (a rice and lentil mixture, known as *kichidee* in India), mulligatawny soup (literally, pepper water or *mooloogoo thani*), and the ubiquitous curry. Curry is a catch-all term used initially by the Raj to refer to any sauced dish of spicy meat, fish or vegetables and is probably a corruption of the Tamil word for sauce "*kari*."

The Food of the People

In temperate Kashmir, tucked into the Himalayas, the food is characterized by a subtle blend of fragrant spices, richness and pungency. Some of the most popular dishes include lamb marinated in yogurt; mutton simmered in milk and scented with nutmeg; and rich meat curries.

In the Ganges, plain rice is usually accompanied by vegetables stir-fried with spices, *dal*, unleavened bread, plain yogurt, and a sweet. Chutneys and pickles are commonplace.

Bengali cuisine is considered elaborate and refined: Bengal being the only place in India where food is served in individual courses, the sequence of which is based on ancient beliefs relating to the aiding of the digestive process. Fish plays a large part in this cuisine, as do rice, *dal*, and chutney.

In the south, where rice is the staple, it appears in many guises: steamed, puffed, made into paper-thin crêpes known as *dosai* (page 57) or steamed to form *idli*, which are served with a variety of chutneys, vegetables and light *dal* broths known as *sambar*.

In Karnataka, the central southern state, the basic meal consists of vegetables which accompany *dosai*, *idli* or steamed rice. Popular southern vegetables include eggplants and bitter gourd, and lots of relishes are served to punctuate a meal.

Goans are known for their use of vinegar and kokum fruit (other Indians add sourness with tamarind, lime juice or dried mango powder), and, of course, for their love of fiery chilies. Classic examples of Goan dishes include the pork curry *vindaloo*, which gets its name from the Portuguese words for vinegar and garlic, and *sorpotel*, a sour hot curry of pork, liver, and pig's blood.

We can't leave the food of the people without making mention of the food of the Raj. The culinary fusion has yielded piquant dishes that pay homage to their roots; the spiced chutneys and curries of today have their humble beginnings in the Indian kitchen.

The Indian Table and Kitchen

At the heart of Indian cuisine is spice—carefully overlaid, one on the other, into dishes, with care. The use of spices in India was recorded in Sanskrit texts three thousand years ago.

Walk into an Indian home at meal time or into a good Indian restaurant and you will be engulfed by a wave of heavenly aromas. So great was the importance of spices for seasoning, as preservatives and as medicine that the search for their source pushed the Europeans into the Age of Exploration in the 15th century.

The Indian kitchen's range of spices is hard to beat in terms of

Offerings of coconut, bananas, flowers and incense on display at a market stall in a typical southern Indian village.

variety, color and aroma—from the sweetness of cumin and coriander to the pungency of *asafoetida* and turmeric. In a culinary sense, "spices" as used in India embraces dried seeds, berries, bark, rhizomes, flowers, leaves, and chilies. These may be used dried or fresh, come in the form of pods or seeds, be roasted, ground or put into hot oil to expel their flavors. Certain spices are used whole, others always ground; some are used only with meat, since they would overpower more delicate seafood and vegetable dishes. Some, such as cardamom, saffron, and cinnamon, are also used for desserts.

Any combination of spices is referred to as a *masala*. The most widely used is *garam masala*, a fragrant combination of cinnamon, cloves, black pepper, and cardamom, with the optional addition of nutmeg, mace, and saffron in northern regions. The spices are then combined with fresh rhizomes and leaves such as ginger, garlic, turmeric, garlic, mint, and chilies.

The medicinal properties of spices are always taken into account when food is prepared, as well as the interaction of each spice with the natural properties of a particular vegetable or *dal*.

The Indian kitchen is a place of surprising simplicity: it has a stove, often heated by charcoal, and a few implements such as the *kadai* (a wok-like utensil), straight-sided pots, and pans.

The house guest is looked on as a visiting god in India, and treated with attendant respect. By and large, home food is influenced by such factors as climate, nutritional balance and religion, and is usually simple fare, where rice, bread, and *dal* constitute the core of the meal. Each region and household then adds its distinctive touch with the vegetables, meat and fish, and the palate teasers: the pickles, *pappadums*, *raita*, or chutneys.

All Indian food is served with either rice or bread, or both. In the cooler north, breads are commonplace; in the south, rice is the staple. Food is generally served on a banana leaf or a stainless steel *thali*. Washing the hands before meals is an important ritual, since Indians generally use their fingers to eat and the meal is eaten squat-

The richness of Mughal cuisine—the food of emperors—has seen its popularity spread throughout India and the rest of the world.

ting down, usually on the kitchen floor. A small straw mat is placed for sitting and the *thali* or banana leaf is laid in front of the mat, either on the floor or on a low stool.

Families eat together, except for the mother or wife who serves the meal. In middle-class homes, this role is taken over by the household help. The family usually sits in a straight line and the women of the household serve and refill the *thali* repeatedly.

The *thali* contains all the courses of the meal, but there is usually an order in which the food is eaten. The first mouthfuls of rice are eaten with ghee or chutney and spicy additives. *Dal* is served with a variety of dry-cooked vegetables seasoned with different spices and garnishes. Pappadums and relishes are replenished, as are the *dal* and rice. The best portions of fish and meat are always offered to the guest. *Roti* or unleavened bread, *puri* (deep-fried bread puffs) and *paratha* (flaky fried flatbreads) are common in the north and eaten with *dal* and vegetables.

The sweet, which is milk-based, completes the meal, although in the south it is followed by rice with curds or buttermilk which are believed to soothe the stomach after a spicy meal.

A very Indian end to a meal is the betel leaf and its seasonings or *paan*. The leaf is chewed along with a slice of areca nut, a dab of slaked lime and a smear of *katha* paste (another wood extract). The betel quid can mean many things: hospitality, moral and legal commitment, a digestive, and a fitting end to the remarkable hospitality displayed during a meal.

Many of the curries in this chapter store very well—indeed many people believe that curries taste better the day after they are made, since the flavors are allowed to mature. You may wish to double the quantities of whatever you're making and freeze a batch in an airtight container—very convenient for quick meals and if unexpected guests turn up!

If properly stored, many of the condiments will keep for up to a month in the refrigerator. Just make sure you use a clean, dry spoon when taking any from the jar and seal the top with a thin film of vegetable oil before refrigerating. However, it is worthwhile roasting and grinding spices for the *garam masala* as you need it, as ground spices lose their aroma very quickly.

SUGGESTED MENUS

A family meal

What's so good about this menu, apart from how delicious everything is, is that most of it can be cooked ahead and served at room temperature if you like.
• Vegetable Samosas (page 56) and some Pakora (Batter Coated Vegetables (page 56);
• Spiced Chickpea Stew (page 60) and Chicken Tikka (page 61) with a fresh green salad and a selection of breads (or just one type);
• fresh fruit with Indian Kulfi Ice Cream (page 65).

A dinner party

For a dinner party that mixes the familiar with the more exotic, serve the following foods:
• Mulligatawny Soup (page 58);
• Paneer Cheese Skewers (page 59) and skewered pieces of Tandoori Chicken (page 62); with these you should serve a selection of raitas and chutneys (page 54) (you may wish to buy the latter if you do not want to make your own);
• Gulab Jamun (page 65)

A regional menu

For a gastronomic tour around the country, offer curries from the different regions in India:
• Lemon Rice (page 58) and some bread (the Deep-fried Bread Puffs [page 56] are particularly elegant);
• Potatoes in Yogurt (page 59), Mild Chicken Curry (page 61), some Goan Pork Vindaloo (page 63), and Creamy Shrimp Curry (page 62);
• Gulab Jamun (page 65)

A melting pot menu

An all-Asian menu:
• from Indonesia, Classic Gado Gado (page 76), accompanied by Crispy Peanut Wafers (page 73);
• Curried Crabs (page 62) served with lots of plain rice or, for a change, *Dosai* (page 57);
• Red Ruby Chestnuts in Sweet Coconut Cream (page 169).

THE ESSENTIAL FLAVORS OF INDIAN COOKING

Spices are the backbone of Indian cooking, so buy the freshest you can to roast and grind—**cardamom**, **cumin**, **nutmeg**, **cinnamon**, **fennel seeds**, and **fenugreek**—as you need. **Chilies**, dried and fresh, are pounded and sliced into cooking pastes with **garlic**, **onions**, and **ginger**. **Lentils** and **beans**, **breads** and **basmati rice** are eaten with curries. **Saffron** and **turmeric** are used to add flavor and color to dishes. **Yogurt** is not only used in both sweet and savory dishes but is also the main ingredient in *lassi*, a popular drink.

Sweet Mango Chutney

1 lb (500 g) ripe mangoes, peeled
   and pitted, flesh diced
2 tablespoons grated ginger
1 cup (250 g) sugar
2 teaspoons salt
1 1/2 teaspoons ground red pepper
1 teaspoon Garam Masala Spice Mix
   (recipe on this page)
5 tablespoons lime juice

Place the mango and ginger into
a saucepan and cook for 8–10
minutes over low heat until most
of the juice has evaporated.

Add the sugar, salt, red pepper, Garam Masala Spic Mix and
lime juice, and cook over low
heat until the sugar dissolves
and the chutney thickens.

Cool thoroughly before storing in clean sterilized jars. The
chutney can be eaten the next
day, but is best served a week
later. It can be stored in the
refrigerator for up to 3 months.

Mint Coriander Chutney

1 cup (50 g) coriander leaves
   (cilantro)
1/2 cup (25 g) mint leaves
2 green finger-length chilies, sliced
1/2 in (1 cm) ginger
3 cloves garlic
2 tablespoons yogurt
1 teaspoon sugar
1/2 teaspoon ground red pepper
1/2 teaspoon salt
1 teaspoon Chaat Masala Spice Mix
   (recipe on this page)
1/2 teaspoon lemon juice

Place all the ingredients in a
blender and process until
smooth. Serve with snacks or
tandoori dishes.

Sweet Date Chutney

3/4 cup (200 g) tamarind pulp
3 cups (750 ml) hot water
10 dates, stones removed (optional)
2 teaspoons ground red pepper
2 tablespoons grated ginger
1/2 teaspoon nigella seeds (kalonji)
1/2 teaspoon fennel seeds
2 teaspoons cumin seeds
1 cup (120 g) shaved palm sugar or
   dark brown sugar
2 teaspoons sugar, or more to taste
1/2 teaspoon salt, or more to taste

Place the tamarind pulp and hot
water in a saucepan. Mash and
strain the pulp to obtain the liquid. Add the dates, if using, and
simmer over low heat for 30
minutes. Strain to remove the
seeds and fiber.

Dry-roast the nigella, fennel
and cumin seeds in a nonstick
wok or skillet for 1 to 2 minutes,
until fragrant. Grind the seeds
to a powder in a blender or mortar and pestle.

Return the strained juice to
the saucepan and add the red
pepper, ginger and the ground
spices. Cook over low heat for
10 minutes, then add the palm
sugar and stir until dissolved.
Add the sugar and salt and mix
thoroughly. Serve with appetizers or simple vegetable dishes for
extra tang. Will keep in the
refrigerator for about 1 week.

Tomato Chutney

2 tablespoons oil
1 1/2 teaspoons black mustard seeds
1 teaspoon nigella seeds (kalonji)
10 curry leaves
2 pinches of asafoetida powder
2 teaspoons crushed garlic
1 1/2 teaspoons grated ginger

3–4 green finger-length chilies, slit
   lengthwise and deseeded
1 can (1 lb/500 g) peeled whole
   tomatoes, drained; or 4 medium
   tomatoes, blanched and peeled
1 teaspoon ground turmeric
2 teaspoons ground red pepper
4 teaspoons sugar
1/2 teaspoon salt

Heat the oil in a wok or skillet
and fry the mustard and nigella
seeds, curry leaves and asafoetida until the spices crackle.

Add the garlic and ginger,
stir-fry gently for a few minutes,
then add the chilies and tomatoes and cook until the tomatoes turn pulpy.

Add the turmeric, red pepper
and sugar and stir until the
sugar dissolves. Add the salt and
serve hot. This chutney keeps
for 3 to 4 days refrigerated, if
stored in a covered jar.

Garam Masala Spice Mix

1/2 cup (75 g) cumin seeds
2 tablespoons coriander seeds
3 small cinnamon sticks
10–12 green cardamom pods,
   bruised
4–5 black cardamom pods, bruised
10 cloves
1/2 nutmeg, broken
3–4 blades mace
1 tablespoon black peppercorns
4 whole star anise
5 bay leaves

Dry-roast all the spices in a nonstick wok or skillet and heat
over a very low fire, stirring the
spices continuously for 2 to 3
minutes until fragrant. Allow to
cool, then grind to a powder in
a blender or a mortar and pestle. Store in an airtight bottle (if
stored in the freezer, spices keep
fresh almost indefinitely).

While the freshly prepared
spice mixture is more flavorful,
pre-blended Garam Masala
Spice Mix can also be found in
Asian food stores.

Chaat Masala Spice Mix

1 tablespoon cumin seeds
1 tablespoon black peppercorns
5 cloves
1/2 tablespoon dried mint leaves
1/4 teaspoon carom seeds (ajwain)
1/4 teaspoon asafoetida powder
1 tablespoon rock salt
2 1/2 tablespoons dried mango
   powder (amchoor)
1 teaspoon ground ginger
1 teaspoon ground red pepper
1/4 teaspoon cream of tartar
2 teaspoons salt

Dry-roast the first seven ingredients in a nonstick skillet and
heat gently, stirring for 2 to 3
minutes until fragrant.

Remove from the heat, add
the salt and grind to a powder
in a blender or mortar and
pestle while still warm. Mix in
the remaining ingredients and
allow to cool. Store tightly
bottled. This salty, sour Chaat
Masala (the approximate trans-
lation of the name is "finger
licking"!) is sprinkled over
cooked food for additional flavor.

Mint Cucumber Raita

1/2 cup (25 g) mint leaves
1/2 cup (25 g) coriander leaves
   (cilantro)
1 baby cucumber, diced
2 teaspoons grated ginger
1 teaspoon minced green chilies
1 cup (250 g) plain yogurt
1/4 teaspoon salt
1/4 teaspoon ground black pepper

Mince the mint and coriander
leaves and combine with the
cucumber, ginger and green
chilies.

Whisk the yogurt in a bowl,
add the mint mixture, salt and
pepper and mix well. Serve as
an accompaniment to any
Indian meal.

Mint Coriander Chutney

Paneer Cheese

4 cups (1 liter) fresh milk
1 tablespoon of lemon juice or
  1 tablespoon white vinegar

Bring the milk slowly to a boil in a heavy-bottomed saucepan, stirring occasionally. Remove from the heat and stir in the lemon juice while the milk is still hot, stirring vigorously until the milk starts to curdle.

Strain through a muslin or cheesecloth until all the whey or liquid has drained off. The curds left are known as chenna. Knead the curds lightly until smooth.

Wrap the curds in the muslin or cheesecloth, then shape it into an oblong or a square. Wrap tightly and place it under a heavy weight for 1 to 2 hours to compress it.

Remove the weight and cut the paneer into the desired shape. Paneer can be kept for 3 to 4 days if stored in an airtight container in the refrigerator.

Clockwise from top right: Lemon Mango Pickles (no recipe), Mixed Vegetable Pickles, and Onion Pickles

Onion Pickles

1/2 cup (125 ml) mustard oil or
  vegetable oil
2 tablespoons black mustard seeds
1 teaspoon ground red pepper
1/2 teaspoon ground turmeric
11/2 tablespoons white vinegar
2 tablespoons sugar
1/4 tablespoon salt
11/2 tablespoons dried mango
  powder (*amchoor*)
5–8 green finger-length chilies
15 cloves garlic, peeled
1 tablespoon grated ginger
1 tablespoon crushed garlic
1 lb (500 g) onions, peeled and sliced
2/3 cup (150 ml) lime juice

Heat the oil in a wok to smoking point, then set aside to cool.

Place the mustard seeds, red pepper, turmeric, vinegar, sugar, salt and mango powder in a blender or food processor, and grind to a paste. Add this to the oil, together with the remaining ingredients.

Stir to mix well and store in sterilized jars, covering the pickles completely with oil. Keeps 3 to 4 weeks.

Mixed Vegetable Pickles

1 medium carrot
2 medium unripe green mangoes
  (about 8 oz/250 g)
3–5 green finger-length chilies
1 cup (250 ml) mustard oil or
  vegetable oil
2 teaspoons fennel seeds
1 teaspoon nigella seeds (*kalonji*)
1 teaspoon black mustard seeds
2 teaspoons ground red pepper
2 teaspoons ground turmeric
2 teaspoons Garam Masala Spice
  Mix (page 54)
1 onion, sliced, then puréed in a
  blender
1 tablespoon grated ginger
5 cloves garlic, crushed
1 large lemon, deseeded and cut
  into wedges
3 tablespoons lime juice
11/2 tablespoons salt

Peel and cut the carrot and mango into small strips. Leave the chilies whole.

Heat the mustard oil in a wok or skillet to smoking point, then add the fennel, nigella and mustard seeds and stir-fry for 1 minute until the spices crackle.

Add the red pepper, turmeric, Garam Masala Spice Mix, onion, ginger and garlic, and continue stirring for 3 to 4 minutes. Add the vegetables and lemon wedges.

Remove from the heat and add the lime juice and salt. Stir to mix well. Place the mixture in sterilized jars, covering it completely with a layer of mustard oil in order to preserve the pickles. If necessary, add more oil which has first been heated to smoking point, then cooled. Keeps 3 to 4 months.

Clockwise from the top left: Sweet Mango Chutney, Tomato Chutney, and Sweet Date Chutney

Here are the recipes for all those tasty morsels you see at the local Indian corner store or take-away. The fried items such as *samosas* and *pakoras* are ideal for parties, and the breads are ideal for mopping up all those curry juices. And don't think that all fried foods are fatty and greasy—as long as you keep the oil hot and drain the items well, they are truly delicious and will not leave you feeling heavy.

Chapati
Unleavened Flatbreads

For the best results, *chapati* should be properly kneaded; using slow speed and a plastic blade in a food processor is an acceptable alternative to 10 to 15 minutes of hand-kneading.

2 cups (250 g) very fine whole wheat (wholemeal) flour, or plain flour
3/4 cup (175 ml) warm water
2 teaspoons softened ghee or butter

Sift the flour into a bowl, gradually adding the water and mixing together with your fingertips. The dough should be pliable, yet not too sticky. Mix in the ghee or butter. Turn the dough out onto a floured board or place in a food processor. Knead by hand for 10 to 15 minutes or process on low speed for 5 minutes. Roll the dough into a ball, cover with

a damp cloth and set aside to rest for at least 1 hour.

Knead the dough again for 3 to 4 minutes, then divide the dough into twelve balls of equal size. On a lightly floured surface, flatten the balls with your hands, then roll them out into flat circles.

Heat a nonstick skillet until very hot, place a piece of dough in the skillet and cook for 1 minute until brown spots appear underneath. Turn over and cook for 1 more minute on the other side, pressing the top of the chapati with a clean cloth to help air bubbles form and to keep the chapati light. As each chapati is cooked, wrap it in a clean cloth to keep warm. Serve with Bean and Lentil Stew (page 58) or Vegetables with Coconut (page 59).

Puri
Deep-fried Bread Puffs

Puri are a delicious alternative to chapati and exactly the same dough is used. To ensure they puff up when cooking, keep flicking the hot oil over the top while the puri are cooking.

1 quantity of Chapati dough (see recipe above)
Oil for deep-frying

Roll out the dough as for the chapati and divide into twelve

balls of equal size. On a lightly floured surface, flatten the balls with your palms, then roll them out into flat circles.

Heat plenty of oil in a wok until very hot. Place one circle of dough into the wok and immediately start flicking hot oil over the top of it with a spatula so that it swells up like a ball. This should only take a few seconds. Turn and continue to deep-fry on the other side until golden brown. Repeat with the rest of the dough. Serve immediately with a curry, such as Creamy Shrimp Curry (page 62).

Vegetable Samosas

7 tablespoons (100 g) ghee or butter
2 cups (250 g) all-purpose flour
1/2 teaspoon carom seeds (*ajwain*)
1/2 teaspoon salt
2/3 cup (150 ml) water
Oil for deep-frying

Filling
8 oz (250 g) potatoes
2 tablespoons oil
1/2 teaspoon cumin seeds
1/3 cup (50 g) fresh or frozen green peas, cooked
1/2 teaspoon salt
1 teaspoon ground coriander
1/2 teaspoon ground turmeric
1/2–1 teaspoon ground red pepper
1 green finger-length chili, deseeded and minced
1 teaspoon dried mango powder (*amchoor*)

Rub the ghee or butter into the flour until the mixture is crumbly. Mix in the carom seeds and salt, then gradually add the water to make a firm but pliable dough. Leave for 30 minutes, covered with a damp cloth.

Prepare the Filling by boiling the potatoes in a pot of salted water until tender. Cut the potatoes into small cubes. Heat the oil and stir-fry the cumin seeds in a nonstick skillet for about 1 minute until they begin to crackle. Add the remaining ingredients and continue stir-frying for 1 minute. Set aside to cool.

Roll out the pastry thinly, then cut into circles, 3 in (6 cm) in diameter. Cut each circle in half. Place a spoonful of Filling in the center of one semi-circle of pastry. Fold the two ends of the semi-circle over the Filling to form a triangle, pressing the edges together to seal firmly.

Heat the oil in a wok and deep-fry the samosas for about 5 minutes until golden brown. Serve hot with Mint Coriander Chutney (page 54).

Pakora
Batter-coated Vegetables

2 medium potatoes
1 large or 2 small Asian eggplants
1 large onion
2 cups (250 g) chickpea flour or *besan* (channa dal) flour
1 teaspoon salt
1 teaspoon ground red pepper
3/4 teaspoon baking soda
3/4 cup (175 ml) cold water
Oil for deep-frying

Peel the potatoes, halve them lengthwise, then cut in slices about 1/4 in (5 mm) thick. Do not peel the eggplant, but slice in the same thickness as the potatoes. Peel, then slice the onion in the same thickness as the potatoes. Set the vegetables aside.

Combine the chickpea flour, salt, red pepper and baking soda, mixing well. Add the cold water to make a very thick batter of coating consistency.

Dip the vegetables, one at a time, into the batter, coating thoroughly. Heat the oil in a wok until very hot and deep-fry for 5 to 6 minutes until golden brown and cooked on the inside. Drain and set aside. Serve hot.

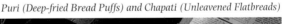

Puri (Deep-fried Bread Puffs) and Chapati (Unleavened Flatbreads)

Dosai (Southern Indian Pancakes)

Tandoori Naan
Leavened Flatbreads

The characteristic tear-drop shape of this bread is obtained by the way the dough droops as it cooks on the wall of a tandoor.

4 cups (500 g) all-purpose flour
1/2 teaspoon baking soda
1 teaspoon salt
1/2 teaspoon yeast
2 tablespoons lukewarm water
1/2 cup (125 ml) milk
1 tablespoon sugar
1 egg
4 tablespoons oil
1 teaspoon nigella seeds (*kalonji*)

Sift the flour, baking soda and salt into a mixing bowl and make a well in the center. In another bowl, mix the yeast and lukewarm water together, then add the milk, sugar, egg and 2 tablespoons of the oil. Pour this into the center of the sifted flour and knead, adding more water if necessary to form a soft dough. Add the remaining oil, knead again, then cover with a damp cloth and place in a warm, dry place for 15 minutes to allow the dough to rise.

Knead the dough again, cover and leave for another 2 to 3 hours. About half an hour before the naan is required, turn the oven to high heat. Divide the dough into eight balls and let them rest for 3 to 5 minutes.

While the dough is resting, sprinkle a baking sheet with the nigella seeds and place it in the oven to heat.

Shape each ball of dough into an elongated oval shape by flattening and stretching it. Turn on the broiler or grill, remove the baking sheet from the oven and place 2 or 3 pieces of dough onto the preheated sheet. Place the sheet several inches under the broiler and bake the naan until they are puffed up and golden brown. Serve hot.

Paratha
Flaky Fried Flatbreads

These wonderfully light breads are normally flung out in circles, like a fisherman throwing his net (*vecchu*), until paper thin. They can be hand-pulled like strudel for a similar result.

3 1/3 cups (420 g) all-purpose flour
1 teaspoon salt
3 eggs, lightly beaten
1 cup (250 ml) water
3/4 cup (180 ml) oil

Sift the flour and salt into a bowl. Make a well in the center, pour in the beaten eggs and mix together, using your fingertips. Gradually add the water and combine to make a very soft dough. Knead for 10 minutes. Divide the dough into 10 balls, cover with a damp

cloth and leave to stand for 30 minutes.

Spread out each ball on a well-oiled tabletop, flatten with the palm of your hand and pull the edges of the dough gently to stretch it out as wide and as thin as possible. Fold in half, brush the surface with oil and fold in half again. Roll each piece into a curled ball and leave to rest for 15 minutes. Flatten each ball with the palm of your hand again, then use a rolling pin to shape the dough into flat circles.

Oil a griddle or skillet and cook for 1–2 minutes, or until the bottom turns golden brown. Turn and cook on the other side for another 1–2 minutes. Serve hot with Bean and Lentil Stew (page 58) or Mild Chicken Curry (page 61).

Dosai
Southern Indian Pancakes

A southern Indian breakfast favorite, these tangy pancakes are often served with Fresh Coconut Chutney and Tomato Chutney, with a spicy dal soup on the side. They can also be stuffed with spiced potatoes to make Masala Dosai.

1 1/2 cups (300 g) uncooked long-
  grain rice
1/2 cup (220 g) white lentils (*urad dal*)
1/2 teaspoon salt
1/2 onion, halved
1 1/2 tablespoons oil

Place the rice and lentils into separate bowls, cover with water and soak overnight. Grind them separately in a blender or food processor, adding a little water if necessary to obtain a smooth consistency.

Mix the ground rice and lentils together and leave at room temperature overnight to ferment. The batter can now be refrigerated for up to 24 hours until required. Stir the batter, adding salt and sufficient water to achieve the consistency of a very thick cream.

Heat a nonstick skillet or griddle and rub with half an onion. Grease lightly with a little of the oil and pour in a ladle (1/4 cup/60 ml) of batter, smearing it quickly with the back of the ladle to form a thin pancake that is 5 to 6 in (12 to 15 cm) in diameter. Cook for 2 to 3 minutes until the bottom is golden brown and the top starts to set. Turn over and cook on the other side, then serve hot.

Paratha (Flaky Fried Flatbreads)

Lemon Rice

Lemon Rice

1¹/2 cups (300 g) uncooked Basmati
   rice, washed and drained

3 cups (750 ml) water

1 teaspoon Bengal gram (*channa
   dal*) or yellow split peas

1 tablespoon split raw cashew nuts

1 tablespoon oil

1 teaspoon black mustard seeds

Pinch of asafoetida powder

10 curry leaves

¹/2 teaspoon minced ginger

¹/2 green finger-length chili, minced

2–3 dried chilies, broken into pieces

1 teaspoon white lentils (*urad dal*)

¹/2 teaspoon ground turmeric

3 tablespoons lemon juice

1–1¹/2 teaspoons salt

1 tablespoon water

Fresh coriander leaves (cilantro),

Boil the rice in the water for 15
to 20 minutes until the grains
are just tender. Drain thoroughly and set aside.

Dry-roast the Bengal gram
and cashew nuts in a nonstick
wok for 2 to 3 minutes until
lightly toasted. Remove from
the wok and set aside.

Heat the oil in the wok and
stir-fry the mustard seeds for 1
minute until the seeds begin to
pop. Add the asafoetida, curry
leaves, ginger, chilies, Bengal
gram, cashews, lentils and

Vegetables with Coconut

Don't forget the rice and breads
when you make the recipes
here, or you'll miss out on the
wonderful flavors of the juices.
These dishes are a testament
to Indian ingenuity in blending
spices: a little more of this
and a little less of that, and
you'll end up with something
else. Enjoy!

Mulligatawny Soup

The inspiration for this Anglo-
Indian soup was southern Indian
"pepper water" or *rasam*, which
certainly did not include apple,
curry powder and chicken. This
flavorful soup is still a favorite
among Westernized middle-class
Indians, who enjoy it in their
private clubs.

2 tablespoons oil

1 teaspoon minced ginger

3 cloves garlic, crushed

1 large onion, sliced

2 tablespoons chickpea flour or *besan*

1 green apple, peeled and diced

1 teaspoon ground cumin

1 teaspoon ground coriander

¹/2 teaspoon ground turmeric

¹/2 teaspoon ground cloves

2 medium tomatoes, blanched,
   peeled and diced

1 bay leaf or 1 teaspoon thyme

1 teaspoon coarsely ground black
   pepper

1 teaspoon ground red pepper

3 cups (750 ml) chicken stock or
   2 chicken stock cubes dissolved in
   3 cups (750 ml) boiling water

¹/2 cup (125 ml) coconut cream or
   1 cup (250 ml) milk (optional)

1–2 tablespoons boiled rice (optional)

1 cup (125 g) cooked chicken,
   shredded

Lemon wedges, to serve

Heat the oil in a saucepan, add
the ginger and garlic and stir-fry
for 2 minutes. Add the onion
and stir-fry until the onion is
transparent.

Add the chickpea flour,
apple, cumin, coriander,
turmeric, cloves, tomatoes, bay
leaf, black pepper, red pepper,
chicken stock and coconut
cream. Bring to a boil, cover,
then reduce the heat to low.

Simmer for 45 minutes then
process in a blender. Add
the rice, if using, and chicken,
stir well and serve with lemon
wedges.

Bean and Lentil Stew

¹/2 cup (90 g) Black gram lentils
   (*urad dal*)

2 tablespoons (30 g) dried pinto or
   kidney beans

1 in (2¹/2 cm) ginger, sliced

1 teaspoon salt

1 tablespoon ghee or butter

1 teaspoon cumin seeds

1–2 green finger-length chilies,
   slit lengthwise

2 medium tomatoes, diced

2 teaspoons Garam Masala Spice
   Mix (page 54)

¹/2 cup (125 ml) fresh cream

Rinse and soak the Black gram
lentils and beans overnight.
Combine the lentils and beans
in a saucepan with the ginger,
salt and enough water to cover.
Bring to a boil, cover and simmer over low heat for 1 to 1¹/4
hours or until just soft.

Heat the ghee or butter in a
skillet, add the cumin seeds and
chilies and stir-fry for 1
minute until the cumin
seeds crackle. Add to the
cooked lentils and beans,
along with the diced
tomatoes and half the
Garam Masala Spice
Mix. Simmer for 10
minutes until the
tomatoes soften.

Keep aside 1
tablespoon of the
cream and stir the
rest into the lentil
stew. Stir gently to
allow the cream to heat
through then serve in
individual bowls with
a few drops of the remaining cream and a sprinkling
of the Garam Masala Spice Mix.
Serve with some Tandoori Naan
(page 57) or Paratha (page 57).

turmeric. Continue to stir-fry, then add the lemon juice, salt and water. Simmer for 2 to 3 minutes, toss in the rice and heat through. Garnish with coriander leaves and serve.

Vegetables with Coconut

2 tablespoons oil
1 teaspoon cumin seeds
1/2 teaspoon carom seeds (*ajwain*)
Pinch of asafoetida powder
1/3 cup (75 g) red lentils (*masoor dal*), soaked 4 hours in warm water, then drained
1/2 cup (75 g) diced tomatoes
1/2 cup (75 g) peeled and diced potatoes
1/2 cup (75 g) diced eggplant
1/2 cup (75 g) peeled and diced sweet potatoes
1/2 cup (75 g) peeled and diced plantain or unripe banana
2 tablespoons freshly grated or moistened unsweetened desiccated coconut

Masala
2 tablespoons coriander seeds
1 teaspoon cumin seeds
1/2 teaspoon carom seeds (*ajwain*)
2 tablespoons raw peanuts
2/3 cup (150 ml) water
4–7 green finger-length chilies, sliced
2 tablespoons roughly chopped coriander leaves (cilantro)
1 teaspoon crushed garlic
1 teaspoon minced ginger
1 tablespoon freshly grated coconut or moistened unsweetened desiccated coconut
1/2 tablespoon shaved palm sugar or dark brown sugar (optional)
1 teaspoon salt

First prepare the Masala by dry-roasting the coriander, cumin, carom and peanuts in a nonstick wok or skillet for 1 to 2 minutes, stirring until the spices crackle. Allow to cool, then place in a blender or food processor with the water and grind to a paste. Add the remaining Masala ingredients and blend or process until smooth.

Heat the oil in a wok and stir-fry the cumin, carom and asafoetida for 1 minute until the spices begin to crackle. Add the

Paneer Cheese Skewers with Tandoori and Raita (left) and Roasted Eggplant (right).

Masala paste and stir-fry for 5 minutes. Add the tomatoes and continue cooking for several minutes until the tomatoes soften.

Add the drained lentils and the prepared vegetables. Cover the wok and simmer gently over medium heat for 10 to 15 minutes until the vegetables are tender. Sprinkle with freshly grated coconut and serve.

Paneer Cheese Skewers

8 oz (250 g) Paneer Cheese (page 55)
2 green or red bell peppers
2 medium onions
2 medium tomatoes
1 cup (100 g) pineapple chunks
8 button mushrooms
Oil to brush the skewers

Marinade
3 tablespoons yogurt
1 tablespoon oil
1 tablespoon tomato paste
1 teaspoon salt
1 teaspoon ground red pepper
1 teaspoon ground coriander
1 teaspoon ground cumin

Combine all the Marinade ingredients. Cut the Paneer, peppers,

onions and tomatoes into chunks of roughly equal size, add the pineapple and mix thoroughly with the Marinade. Leave to marinate for 1 hour, then thread them onto skewers.

Cook in a hot oven, under a grill, or over a hot barbecue for 7 to 8 minutes on each side, brushing with oil and turning halfway through cooking

Roasted Eggplant

1 1/2 lb (650 g) eggplants
1 1/2 tablespoons ghee or oil
2 medium onions, diced
1 1/2 teaspoons ground coriander
2 teaspoons ground cumin
1 teaspoon ground red pepper
1 teaspoon Garam Masala Spice Mix (page 54)
3 medium tomatoes, blanched, peeled and diced
2 green chilies, deseeded and minced
1 teaspoon salt
1 tablespoon minced coriander leaves (cilantro)

Rub the eggplants with a little oil and roast under a hot grill or broiler for several minutes on each side until the skin blackens and the eggplant is soft inside.

Peel the eggplant, discard the skin, then slice and set aside.

Heat the ghee in a wok and stir-fry the onion until lightly browned. Add the coriander, cumin, red pepper and Garam Masala and stir-fry for 1 minute. Add the tomatoes and chili to the wok and continue to stir-fry for 2 to 3 minutes. Mix in the sliced eggplant and salt, and stir until dry. Sprinkle with coriander leaves.

If using large Mediterranean eggplants, it may be necessary to halve or quarter them lengthwise first before roasting, so they evenly cook through.

Potatoes in Yogurt

1 1/2 lbs (750 g) baby new potatoes, halved
3 tablespoons oil
2 onions, diced
3/4 cup (190 g) plain yogurt
4 black cardamom pods
1 teaspoon fennel seeds
1 small cinnamon stick
2 tablespoons unsalted, roasted cashew nuts or shelled melon seeds, soaked in water
1 1/2 tablespoons minced ginger
4 cloves garlic, minced

1 1/2 teaspoons ground coriander
1 teaspoon ground cumin
1 teaspoon ground turmeric
1/2 teaspoon ground red pepper
1/2 cup (125 ml) water
1 teaspoon salt

Parboil the potatoes for 7 to 10 minutes. Heat the oil in a wok and stir-fry the potatoes for about 5 minutes or until golden. Drain and set aside, leaving the oil in the wok. Stir-fry the onion in the reserved oil until browned, then remove with a slotted spoon and set aside.

Dry-roast the cardamom, fennel and cinnamon in a non-stick wok, stirring continuously for 1 to 2 minutes until the spices are fragrant. Drain the soaking cashews or melon seeds, then place in a blender with the dry-roasted spices and grind to a paste, adding 1 teaspoon of water if necessary. Set aside.

Stir-fry the ginger and garlic for 2 minutes in the wok used for frying the potatoes and onion, adding more oil if necessary. Add the coriander, cumin, turmeric and red pepper and stir for 1 minute. Leave on low heat while you whisk the yogurt.

Add the whisked yogurt, cardamom-nut paste, potatoes, water and salt. Simmer uncovered for about 10 minutes until the potatoes are tender. Stir in the browned onions and serve.

Spiced Okra (left) and Mild Chicken Curry (right)

Vegetable Pulao Rice

This dish can include additional vegetables such as green peas or small pieces of cauliflower.

1 1/2 cups (300 g) uncooked long-grain rice (preferably Basmati)
1 tablespoon ghee or butter
1 teaspoon cumin seeds
1 cinnamon stick
5 green cardamom pods, bruised
7 cloves
1 medium onion, diced
1 tablespoon yogurt
2 medium tomatoes, diced
1 cup (170g) diced, cooked potatoes
1 cup (100 g) finely sliced green beans
1 cup (120 g) diced carrot
Pinch of saffron threads, soaked in 1 tablespoon of hot milk for 15 minutes
1 teaspoon ground turmeric
1 teaspoon ground coriander
3 cups (750 ml) water
1 1/2 teaspoons salt
Fresh coriander leaves (cilantro)

Wash the rice in a pot, leave enough water to just cover the rice and soak for 30 minutes. Drain and set aside.

Heat the ghee in a wok and stir-fry the cumin, cinnamon, cardamom and cloves for 1 minute until they begin to crackle. Add the onion and stir-fry until golden, then add the yogurt, vegetables, saffron, turmeric, coriander and 1/2 cup (125 ml) of water. Cover and simmer for 3 minutes.

Add 2 1/2 cups (625 ml) of water, the drained rice and salt.

Vegetable Pulao Rice

Stir, bring to a boil, then simmer uncovered for about 10 minutes until the water is completely absorbed.

Cover the wok with a damp towel, then cover with the lid, and cook over very low heat for 5 to 10 minutes. Remove from the heat, keep covered and leave to stand for 15 to 20 minutes. Stir gently with a fork and serve garnished with coriander leaves.

Spiced Okra

12 oz (375 g) okra, washed and dried
3 tablespoons oil
1 teaspoon cumin seeds
2 green finger-length chilies, deseeded and minced
1 medium onion, diced
3/4 tablespoon minced ginger
Pinch of asafoetida powder

1 medium tomato, diced
Spice Mixture
3 teaspoons ground coriander
2 teaspoons ground turmeric
2 teaspoons ground fennel
2 teaspoons dried mango powder (amchoor)
1 teaspoon ground red pepper
1/2 teaspoon salt
2 tablespoons water

Combine the Spice Mixture ingredients. Cut the stalk off each okra and make a lengthwise slit. Fill each okra with the Spice Mixture and set aside.

Heat the oil in a wok and stir-fry the cumin seeds for 1-2 minutes until they begin to crackle and aromatic. Add the onion, chilies and ginger and stir-fry until the onion turns transparent. Stir in the asafoetida.

Add the diced tomato to the wok, simmer over low heat and stir for 5 to 10 minutes until the tomato turns pulpy. Add the stuffed okra and continue to simmer, covered, for 5 to 8 minutes or until tender and well-coated with the sauce. Serve with steamed rice.

Spiced Chicken Stew

1 cup (200 g) dried chickpeas
1 tea bag
6 cups (1 1/2 liters) water
2–3 tablespoons oil
2 medium onions, diced
2 teaspoons crushed garlic
2 tablespoons minced ginger
2 green finger-length chilies, sliced
3 medium tomatoes, diced
2 teaspoons ground coriander

1 1/2 teaspoons ground cumin
1/2 teaspoon ground turmeric
1 teaspoon ground red pepper
1 teaspoon salt
2 teaspoons minced coriander leaves (cilantro)
1/4 teaspoon Garam Masala Spice Mix (page 54)
Shredded ginger, to garnish

Soak the chickpeas for 1 hour, then drain. Discard the liquid. Place the chickpeas, tea bag and water into a pot and simmer for 30 to 45 minutes until the chickpeas are tender. Drain, reserving 1 cup (250 ml) of the cooking liquid.

Heat the oil in a wok and stir-fry the onion until golden. Add the garlic, ginger and chilies and stir-fry for 5 more minutes. Add the tomatoes, coriander, cumin, turmeric and red pepper, and stir-fry over low heat for 5 to 10 minutes until the oil separates.

Add the chickpeas, the reserved cooking liquid, salt and half the coriander leaves. Simmer uncovered for 15 to 20 minutes until the liquid has been absorbed, then add a pinch of Garam Masala Spice Mix and stir through.

Serve with the remaining Garam Masala Spice Mix, coriander leaves and ginger shreds sprinkled on top.

Mild Chicken Curry

2 medium onions, diced
4–6 cloves garlic, sliced
1 1/2 in (4 cm) ginger, sliced
1/4 cup (60 ml) water
4 1/2 tablespoons ghee or butter
4 green cardamom pods, bruised
1 black cardamom pod, bruised
1 small cinnamon stick
2 cloves
2 bay leaves
1/2 teaspoon ground cumin
1/2 teaspoon ground coriander
1 cup (250 ml) plain yogurt
1/4 teaspoon freshly grated nutmeg
1 1/2 teaspoons ground white pepper
1 1/2 lbs (750 g) boneless chicken, cut into bite-sized pieces
2 tablespoons cream
1 teaspoon salt
1 teaspoon Garam Masala Spice Mix (page 54)
1 teaspoon minced coriander leaves (cilantro)

Nut paste
3 tablespoons white poppy seeds,

3 tablespoons unsalted, shelled melon seeds, soaked in water
3 tablespoons *chironji* nuts or blanched almonds
3 tablespoons raw cashew nuts, soaked in water

To make the Nut Paste, first soak the poppy seeds in water and simmer for 30 minutes. Place the poppy seeds and the remaining ingredients in a blender or food processor and grind to a paste, adding water if necessary, then set aside.

Stir-fry the onion, garlic and ginger in a nonstick wok until the onion is transparent and very slightly browned. Place in a blender or food processor with 1/4 cup (60 ml) water and blend to a paste. Set aside.

Heat the ghee in a wok, stir-fry the cardamom, cinnamon, cloves and bay leaves for a few minutes, then add the cumin, coriander and onion paste. Continue stir-frying over very low heat, stirring continuously for 5 minutes until the oil separates. Take care that the mixture does not change color. Add the yogurt and continue to stir for 15 minutes.

Sprinkle in the nutmeg and pepper, add the chicken pieces and simmer uncovered over low heat for 10 to 15 minutes until

Chicken Tikka

the chicken is tender. Add the Nut Paste and simmer gently for 3 to 5 minutes. Mix in 1 tablespoon of the cream, salt and half of the Garam Masala Spice Mix, stirring well. Remove from the heat and serve with the remaining cream and a sprinkling of Garam Masala Spice Mix and coriander leaves.

Chicken Tikka

3 teaspoons crushed garlic
2 teaspoons grated ginger
2 teaspoons chili paste or minced fresh chilies
1 1/2 tablespoons oil
1/4 cup (60 ml) lemon juice
1 teaspoon salt
1 teaspoon Garam Masala Spice Mix (page 54)
1 lb (500 g) boneless chicken leg, cubed
1 cup (250 g) plain yogurt

Combine the garlic, ginger, chili paste, oil, lemon juice, salt, Garam Masala Spice Mix and red food coloring, if using. Rub the marinade thoroughly onto the chicken pieces. Mix with the yogurt and leave to marinate in the refrigerator for 4 hours (preferably overnight).

Thread the chicken onto skewers and brush with additional oil. Place under a very hot grill or broiler for 6–8 minutes, turning once, until cooked and golden brown. Serve with Mint Coriander Chutney (page 54), onion rings, lemon wedges and Indian bread such as Tandoori Naan (page 57).

Butter Chicken
Murgh Makhani

1 portion of cooked Tandoori Chicken (page 62)
2 cinnamon sticks
3 black cardamom pods, bruised
3 green cardamom pods, bruised
3 cloves
2 bay leaves
1 can (1 lb/500 g) peeled crushed tomatoes
2 medium onions, quartered
3/4 in (2 cm) ginger, sliced
8–10 cloves garlic
8 green finger-length chilies, sliced
8 oz (250 g) butter
2 teaspoons ground red pepper (optional)
1 tablespoon sugar
1/2 teaspoon salt
1/2 cup (125 ml) cream
1/2 teaspoon Garam Masala Spice Mix (page 54)
1 small green bell pepper, finely diced

Creamy Shrimp Curry

Cut the cooked Tandoori chicken into large pieces, leaving the bones in. Set aside.

Place the whole spices, tomatoes, onion, ginger, garlic and chilies in a pot and simmer over low heat for 10 minutes, stirring occasionally, until the tomatoes are soft and pulpy. Remove the whole spices from the pot and purée the rest of the ingredients in a blender or food processor. Strain, return the purée to the pot and add the butter, red pepper, if using, sugar and salt. Simmer over low heat until thickened.

Add half the cream and the chicken pieces and simmer for 5 minutes. Stir in all but 1 tablespoon of the remaining cream and half the Garam Masala. Mix in the bell pepper and serve sprinkled with the remaining cream and Garam Masala.

Tandoori Chicken

Murgh Tandoori

Originally from the northwest of India, food baked in a tandoor or clay oven, heated with charcoal, is very popular in restaurants all over the country. Marinated chicken cooked in a tandoor achieves an unrivaled succulence and flavor; even when using an electric or gas oven, the result is very good.

3 lbs (1½ kgs) of chicken pieces (legs and breasts)
1 tablespoon minced fresh chilies
½ teaspoon ground red pepper
¼ cup (60 ml) lemon juice
1 teaspoon salt
1 teaspoon Chaat Masala Spice Mix (page 54)
Melted butter, to baste

Marinade
2 cups (500 ml) plain yogurt
1 tablespoon minced fresh chilies (optional)
1 tablespoon crushed garlic
1 tablespoon minced ginger
1 tablespoon oil
1 tablespoon lemon juice
2 teaspoons Garam Masala Spice Mix (page 54)

Make deep cuts on the inside (if using whole chickens) and the outside of the chickens or chicken pieces, to allow the Marinade to penetrate. Combine the chili paste, red pepper, lemon juice and salt, and rub onto the chickens. Refrigerate for 30 minutes.

Make the Marinade by combining all the ingredients, then rub the Marinade onto the chickens. Save some Marinade to rub inside the chest cavity. Marinate the chickens for 3 to 4 hours or overnight.

Preheat the oven to high heat. Place the chickens on a wire rack in a roasting dish, baste with a little melted butter and roast for about 15 minutes

until the chickens are brownish-black and cooked. Alternatively, roast on a barbeque for 15 minutes. Sprinkle with Chaat Masala and serve with Mint Coriander Chutney (page 54), onion rings and lemon wedges.

Creamy Shrimp Curry

¾ in (2 cm) ginger, sliced
6 cloves garlic
½ teaspoon cumin seeds
3 tablespoons mustard or vegetable oil
1 bay leaf
4 cloves
1 small cinnamon stick
4 green cardamom pods, bruised
1 large onion, diced
4 green finger-length chilies, deseeded and minced
½ teaspoon salt
½ cup (125 ml) water
1 lb (500 g) fresh shrimp, peeled and deveined
1 cup (250 ml) thick coconut milk
½ teaspoon sugar (optional)
Minced coriander leaves (cilantro)

Place the ginger, garlic and cumin in a blender or food processor and grind to a paste.

Heat the oil in a wok and stir-fry the bay leaf, cloves, cinnamon and cardamom for 1 to 2 minutes until fragrant. Add the onion and stir-fry gently for 5 minutes before adding the green chilies and the ginger paste. Continue stirring for another 2 minutes. Add the salt and water.

Simmer uncovered for 5 minutes, then place the shrimp in the wok and simmer for another 3 minutes. Add the coconut milk and simmer gently for about 5 minutes, stirring occasionally,

until the shrimp are tender. Stir in the sugar, if using, and serve sprinkled with coriander leaves.

Curried Crabs

This dish comes from Mangalore, on the southwest coast, an area renowned for its appreciation of both fish and coconuts. This succulent curry uses coconut milk plus freshly grated coconut for a wonderfully rich sauce.

3–4 lbs (1½–2 kgs) fresh crabs
2 tablespoons oil
1 teaspoon black mustard seeds
30 curry leaves
2 bay leaves
3 green finger-length chilies, halved lengthwise
Pinch of asafoetida powder
3 medium onions, diced
3 cloves garlic, minced
½ tablespoon minced ginger
¼ teaspoon ground turmeric
1–2 teaspoons ground red pepper
3 medium tomatoes, diced
1 cup (250 ml) thick coconut milk
¼ teaspoon salt
¼ cup (20 g) freshly grated coconut (optional)

Boil the crabs in a large pot of water for 2 to 3 minutes, drain, then cool. Remove the shell of each crab by holding the bottom of the crab in one hand and using the other hand to pull the shell up and off its body. Set aside the shell and discard the feathery gills on either side of the body and any green or spongy grey matter. Rinse and scrub the shell thoroughly, then drain. Quarter the crab and crack the claws so the flavors can penetrate.

Curried Crabs

Heat the oil in a wok and stir-fry the mustard seeds until the seeds begin to pop. Add the curry leaves, bay leaves and green chilies and stir-fry gently for 1 minute. Sprinkle in the asafoetida and add the onion, garlic and ginger. Stir-fry until the onion is transparent. Stir in the turmeric and red pepper and continue stirring for 1 minute before adding the crab pieces, claws, shells and tomatoes.

Cover, and simmer for 10 minutes, stirring occasionally. Add the coconut milk and salt and bring just to a boil, stirring constantly. Mix in the freshly grated coconut, if using, and serve with plain steamed rice.

Bengali Fish Curry

1 1/2 lbs (750 g) white fish fillets
1 teaspoon salt
1 teaspoon ground turmeric
2 tablespoons minced ginger
Mustard oil or vegetable for
　deep-frying
1 large potato, cut into wedges
1 eggplant, sliced
1 large tomato, diced
1 1/2 cups (375 ml) water
2–3 green finger-length chilies, slit
　lengthwise and deseeded

Masala
1/2 teaspoon cumin seeds
1/2 teaspoon fennel seeds
1/2 teaspoon black mustard seeds
1/4 teaspoon fenugreek seeds
1/4 teaspoon nigella seeds (kalonji)

Pat the fish dry. Combine the salt, turmeric and ginger and coat the fish fillets well. Marinate for 5 minutes, then cut the fillets into large pieces.

Heat the oil in a wok and deep-fry the fish pieces for 5 to 7 minutes until golden brown and cooked through. Set the fish aside, reserving 1 tablespoon of the oil. In the same wok, stir-fry the Masala spices for 1 minute until the seeds begin to crackle. Add the potato wedges and sliced eggplant and continue to stir-fry until well-coated with the spices.

Place the potato-eggplant mixture and the water in a pot and simmer for 10 to 15 minutes, or until the vegetables are tender. Add the fish pieces and chilies and heat through. Serve with plain rice.

Goan Pork Vindaloo

This dish was once carried on sea voyages. No water is used in the preparation and the layer of fat on the top helps to seal out the air and preserve the meat. Vindaloos have traditionally been very pungent, although this recipe should cause just a gentle sweat. Choose pork that has some fat on it.

1 1/2 lbs (750 g) pork, preferably
　with some fat, cubed
4 green cardamom pods
1 small cinnamon stick
1 1/2 teaspoons mustard seeds
8 cloves garlic
2–3 teaspoons ground red pepper
4 green finger-length chilies
1 teaspoon black peppercorns
1 in (2 1/2 cm) ginger, sliced
2 teaspoons cumin seeds
1 cup (250 ml) coconut vinegar or
　1/2 cup (125 ml) white vinegar
2 medium onions, diced
1/2 teaspoon salt
1 teaspoon sugar
2 tablespoons brandy

Cut 1 tablespoon of fat from the pork and set aside.

Dry-roast the cardamom, cinnamon and mustard seeds in a nonstick wok or skillet for 1 to 2 minutes, stirring continuously until fragrant. Cool, then place in a blender or food processor with the garlic, red pepper, chilies, peppercorns, ginger, cumin seeds and vinegar, and grind to a thick paste. Coat the pork well with the paste and marinate for 30 minutes.

Fry the tablespoon of pork fat until the lard is rendered, then add the onion and stir-fry until golden brown. Add the pork (including any marinade) and salt, and simmer over low to medium heat for about 30 minutes until the pork is tender and the gravy is thick. Pour off the excess oil, then add the sugar and *feni* or brandy. Serve hot.

> If you cannot obtain coconut vinegar, use rice vinegar or cider vinegar diluted 1 part water to 4 parts vinegar.

Spicy Hot Lamb Curry

2 tablespoons oil
4 medium onions, sliced
1 teaspoon minced ginger
3 teaspoons minced fresh chilies
3 teaspoons crushed garlic
1 teaspoon ground coriander
1/2 teaspoon ground turmeric
1 1/2 lbs (750 g) boneless lamb,
　cubed
4 medium tomatoes, diced
1 teaspoon salt
1 1/2 cups (375 ml) water
3–4 whole dried chilies, fried in oil,
　to garnish
Finely shredded ginger, to garnish

Masala
1 1/2 tablespoons coriander seeds
1 1/2 teaspoons ground mace
4 cloves
2 teaspoons black peppercorns
1 cinnamon stick
3 dried red chilies, broken into pieces
1 cup (100 g) freshly grated coconut

Prepare the Masala by dry-roasting all the ingredients except the coconut in a nonstick wok over low heat, stirring continuously for 1 minute until aromatic. Cool, then grind to a powder in a blender or mortar and pestle. Add the coconut and pulse the blender a few times to mix well. Set aside.

Heat the oil in the wok and stir-fry the onion until golden brown. Add the ginger, garlic and chili paste, stirring for 1 to 2 minutes until fragrant, then add the coriander and turmeric. Continue to stir-fry for 2 to 3 minutes.

Place the lamb in the wok and stir-fry until browned. Add the Masala paste, stir for 15 minutes, then add the diced tomatoes and salt. Stir in the water and simmer over low heat for 20 to 25 minutes, stirring occasionally, until the meat is tender. Garnish with fried chilies and shredded ginger, and serve with white rice.

Goan Pork Vindaloo

Lamb Tikka Kebabs

Prepare the Biryani Rice by placing the spices and seasonings into a large pot of water and bringing to a boil. Add the long-grain rice and boil rapidly for 3 minutes until just half-cooked, then drain thoroughly. Discard the whole spices and set the Biryani Rice aside.

Heat the ghee over moderate heat in a wok or casserole dish. Stir-fry the spices for 1 to 2 minutes until they begin to crackle, then add the chilies and onion and stir-fry until the onion is lightly browned. Add the salt and the marinated meat, stir a few times, then pour the Rice over the meat. Heat the wok over moderate heat for 3 minutes, then reduce the heat to as low as possible and leave to cook for 45 minutes before serving.

Vegetarians can use firm tofu in place of the meat, but the tofu needs to be scored first before marinating. Reduce the cooking time to 15 minutes, or until the tofu is cooked.

Lamb Tikka Kebabs

2 teaspoons cumin seeds
1¹/2 lbs (750 g) boneless lamb, cubed
1¹/2 cups (375 g) plain yogurt
2¹/2 teaspoons minced fresh chilies
2 teaspoons crushed garlic
1 teaspoon grated ginger
¹/2 teaspoon ground mace
¹/2 teaspoon Garam Masala Spice Mix (page 54)
1 teaspoon salt
1¹/2 tablespoons oil
2 teaspoons lemon juice
Oil, to baste

Dry-roast the cumin seeds in a nonstick wok, stirring continuously for 1 to 2 minutes until fragrant. Allow to cool, then grind to a powder in a blender or mortar and pestle.

Prick the lamb cubes all over with a fork. Mix the ground cumin and the remaining ingredients (except the oil for basting) together and combine with the lamb, coating well. Leave to marinate in the refrigerator for a minimum of 4 hours.

Thread the meat onto skewers and cook under a very hot grill or broiler for 3 to 4 minutes. Brush the meat with oil, turn, and grill on the other side. Serve hot with Tandoori Naan (page 57).

Fragrant Lamb Biryani

1¹/2 lbs (750 g) boneless lamb, cubed
2¹/2 tablespoons ghee or butter
1 teaspoon cumin seeds
7 cloves
1 cinnamon stick
3 bay leaves
2 black cardamom pods, bruised
7 green cardamom pods, bruised
3–4 green finger-length chilies, slit lengthwise
2 medium onions, sliced
1 teaspoon salt

Marinade
1 cup (250 g) plain yogurt
¹/2 cup (125 ml) lemon juice
1 teaspoon grated ginger
2 teaspoons crushed garlic
2 teaspoons Garam Masala Spice Mix (page 54)
1¹/2 teaspoons ground coriander
2 teaspoons ground red pepper
¹/2 teaspoon ground turmeric
¹/2 cup (25 g) fresh mint leaves
¹/2 cup (25 g) fresh coriander leaves (cilantro)
¹/2 tablespoon salt

Biryani Rice
2 green cardamom pods, bruised
3 cloves
1 small cinnamon stick
1 bay leaf
1 blade of mace

A few rose petals or 2–3 drops of rose essence
2 cups (400 g) uncooked long-grain rice, soaked 1 hour and drained

To make the Marinade, combine all the ingredients. Coat the meat well and leave to marinate for at least 3 hours.

Fragrant Lamb Biryani

Sweet Rice Pudding

Desserts are eaten with much relish in India, especially among the Bengalis. Here are some of the more popular Indian treats.

Sweet Rice Pudding

A northern favorite, this rice pudding is very different from the bland version which countless children had to endure in their homes or boarding schools.

$1/2$ cup (100 g) uncooked long-grain rice, washed and drained
3 cups (750 ml) milk
2–3 green cardamom pods, bruised
2 tablespoons blanched slivered almonds
Pinch of saffron threads, soaked in 1 tablespoon hot milk for 15 minutes
1 tablespoon shelled pistachio nuts, skins removed and coarsely ground
1 tablespoon raisins (optional)
1–2 tablespoons sugar

Place the rice, milk and cardamom in a pot, bring to a boil and simmer gently for 30 to 40 minutes until the rice is soft and the grains start to break up.

Add the almonds, saffron, pistachios and raisins, if using, and simmer for 3 to 4 minutes. Add the sugar and stir until dissolved. Remove from the heat and serve—warm or chilled.

Indian Kulfi Ice Cream

4 cups (1 liter) milk
$1/4$ cup (60 g) sugar
1 tablespoon shelled pistachio nuts, skins removed and coarsely ground
1 tablespoon almonds, finely ground (optional)

Place the milk into a pot and simmer over very low heat. Stir constantly until the milk has thickened and is reduced to about 1 cup (250 ml), or until the milk is the color of the ice cream in the photo (about 1 hour). Stir the sides of the pot constantly to prevent the milk from burning, add the sugar and pistachios and allow to cool. Freeze in individual metal containers such as jelly molds.

Gulab Jamun

Fritters in Sweet Syrup

6 cups ($1^1/2$ liters) fresh milk
$1/2$ tablespoon flour
Pinch of baking soda
$1/2$ tablespoon shelled pistachio nuts, skins removed and coarsely ground
Oil for deep-frying

Homemade Chenna
$1^1/2$ cups (375 ml) fresh milk
1 teaspoon lemon juice or white vinegar

Syrup
1 cup (250 ml) water
$1/2$ cup (125 g) sugar

Bring the milk to a boil in a wide, heavy-bottomed saucepan, stirring constantly. Continue to stir over high heat until the milk changes to a dough-like consistency, about 25 minutes. Cool, then crumble the condensed milk solids.

Prepare the Homemade Chenna by bringing the milk slowly to a boil and stirring occasionally. Remove from heat and stir in the lemon juice while the milk is still hot, stirring vigorously until the milk starts to curdle. Strain through a muslin or cheesecloth until all the liquid has drained off. Knead the curds lightly until the mixture is smooth.

Make the Syrup by boiling the water and sugar together, stirring occasionally for about 10 minutes until thickened slightly. Set aside.

Mix the crumbled milk solids with the Homemade Chenna, flour, baking soda and pistachios to form a soft dough. Pinch off a piece of dough to form a small ball—to test the consistency of the mixture.

Heat the oil until moderately hot and deep-fry the small test ball; if it breaks apart, the mixture is too moist and a little more flour should be mixed into the dough. When the mixture is the correct consistency, shape the dough into bite-sized balls and deep-fry them, a few at a time, until golden brown. Drain, then place in the warm syrup. Serve warm or at room temperature.

Indian Kulfi Ice Cream (left) and Gulab Jamun (Fritters in Sweet Syrup, right)

"Silakan makan", or "please eat", are two words you will often hear in Indonesia.

INDONESIA

Just as the languages, religions and cultures of the vast Indonesian archipelago are many and varied, so too are its cuisines.

Left: Chilies, whether sold whole or ground into a paste, are an indispensable part of Indonesian cuisine.

Right: A Javanese man on his way to the market, his bike loaded with terra cotta cooking wares.

Indonesia is the world's largest archipelago, consisting of literally thousands of islands. With terrain that ranges from snow-capped mountains and lush rainforests to arid savannah, swamps and irrigated rice fields, it's hard to imagine a more appropriate national motto than "*Bhinneka Tunggal Ika*"—Unity in Diversity.

Over the past two thousand years, Buddhist, Hindu, and Muslim kingdoms rose and fell in Sumatra, Java, and Borneo, attracting merchants from China, the Middle East, and India, as well as Siam and Malacca. Their quest was spice— not surprising, since some of the archipelago's eastern isles were the original Spice Islands.

With its geographic and cultural diversity, it is to be expected that the cuisines of Indonesia are so varied. Indigenous styles have been influenced degrees over the centuries by the introduction of ingredients and cooking styles from China, India, the Middle East, and Europe.

Tanah Air: Land and Water

Stretching some 5,000 miles, Indonesia's 17,000 or so islands (home to some 220 million people) range from roughly six degrees north of the equator to 11 degrees south. Indonesia is within the so-called "Ring of Fire," the meeting point of two of the earth's tectonic plates, which gives rise to frequent seismic activity. Smoldering volcanoes periodically shower fertile ash on the land.

To a large extent, the western islands of Indonesia are lush and evergreen. While Borneo has rainforests and swampy coastlines, Java and Sumatra abound with fertile gardens, coconut groves, and paddy fields.

All of Indonesia enjoys tropical warmth and relatively high humidity, although the temperature drops significantly on the mountains. Most parts of the archipelago experience a definite dry season followed by life-giving monsoon rains. However, the eastern islands of the archipelago, especially Nusa Tenggara, the chain of islands in between

Lombok east to Timor, are often rocky and semi-arid. The dry seasons there are longer and harsher than elsewhere in Indonesia, and the land often degraded by tree felling and subsequent erosion.

Different parts of Indonesia receive their monsoon rain at different times of the year. The Maluku islands conform to the image of the lush tropics, while Irian Jaya, the western portion of the island of New Guinea, has everything from swamps to rainforest to the highest mountain east of the Himalayas, the almost 16,000-foot Mount Jaya.

The preferred staple throughout Indonesia is rice, which is grown both in irrigated paddies—where up to three crops a year can be achieved by using special strains of rice and fertilizers—and in non-irrigated fields, which depend on the monsoon rains. In areas where insufficient rainfall or unsuitable terrain make rice-growing impossible, crops such as sweet potato, tapioca (cassava or manioc), corn and sago are the staple.

The most popular accompaniment to rice is fish, which is often simply fried with a seasoning of sour tamarind, turmeric, and salt, or simmered in seasoned water or coconut milk. Although vegetables are grown throughout Indonesia, they do not always figure prominently in the diet. Some wild leaves and plants, as well as the young leaves of plants grown for their fruit or tubers, such as starfruit, papaya, sweet potatoes, and tapioca, are cooked as a vegetable. These are supplemented with water convolvulus (*kangkung*), long beans, eggplants, pumpkins, and cucumbers. Elevated areas, especially in islands with rich volcanic soil, have proved perfect for temperate-climate vegetables introduced by the Dutch.

A Culinary Tour of the Islands

Over the centuries Indonesia's cuisines, especially in the major islands, have borrowed ingredients and cooking styles from many sources. Arab and Indian traders brought their spices and sweet rose water. The Spanish were responsible for the introduction of chilies. The Chinese introduced the now-ubiquitous noodles (*mee*); soy sauce, which the Indonesians modified to suit their taste by adding sugar (*kecap manis*); mung beans; tofu and soybeans, which the Indonesians fermented to make *tempeh*.

Despite their long period as colonial rulers, the Dutch did not really have an enormous impact on the local cuisine, apart from, perhaps, the *rijstaffel*. This colonial invention is a larger-than-life

A sambal served in *daun mangkokan*, a decorative leaf used as a herb and also as a bowl in Sumatra.

adaptation of the Indonesian style of serving rice with several savory side dishes and condiments—only the Dutch modified it to a "rice table" where as many as 18 to 20 dishes might be served.

The Javanese of the sultanates of Yogyakarta and nearby Surakarta have a very refined culture. Theirs is a highly structured society where harmony depends upon consideration for others, the group being more important than the individual. Ritual events are marked by a communal feast (*selamatan*). Centerpiece of the *selamatan* may be a cone-shaped mound of yellow rice, with at least a dozen dishes accompanying, including *gudeg* (young jackfruit cooked in coconut milk); fried chicken, which had first been simmered in spiced coconut milk; fermented soybean cakes (*tempeh*) fried with shrimp and sweetened with palm sugar; red chili *sambal* and crisp shrimp wafers (*krupuk*).

Less subtle is the food of the west Sumatran region of Padang—ideal, however, if you like it hot and spicy! Most of the food in restaurants are served as a smorgasbord: portions are taken from ten to as many as twenty different dishes and carried from their display counter to the restaurant table. You help yourself to whatever you desire and pay only for what you consume. Vital to Padang food are the herbs, rhizomes and other seasonings that include chilies, ginger, garlic, shallots, galangal, turmeric, lemongrass, basil, fragrant lime and *salam* leaves, and pungent dried shrimp paste. Coconut flesh is squeezed to make the rich, creamy milk that soothes (if only slightly) the impact of much Padang food. Steaming white rice is served to counterbalance the emphatic flavors.

Sulawesi (Celebes) is renowned for its fish. *Ikan bakar*, fish roasted over charcoal and served with a variety of dipping sauces, is a regional favorite.

Feasts are commonplace in Bali, and, as the island did not turn to Islam when the rest of the nation did, pork is a popular meat.

Game from the interior highlands of the so-called wilds of Borneo include wild boar, used to make the famous roast pig *babi guling*. Many leafy greens are gathered wild, such as the young shoots of trees found in the family compound (starfruit is a favorite), or young fern tips and other edible greens found along the lanes or edges of paddy fields. Immature fruits like the jackfruit and papaya are also used as vegetables. Mature coconut is used almost daily: grated to add to vegetables, fried with seasonings to make a condiment, or the grated flesh squeezed with water to make coconut milk.

Special Indonesian *es* (ice) drinks, both refreshing and delicious, are sold at stalls and mobile carts throughout Indonesia.

Indonesia is blessed with an abundance of luscious fruit: the giant jackfruit, notorious durian, and spiky rambutan are only a few.

The Food of the People

To properly savor the diversity of Indonesian cuisine, take a walk along local streets and do as the locals do—frequent the *warung* (simple food stall). The social center of most villages and small towns, the *warung* is usually made of either woven bamboo or wood, open-fronted with dirt or cement floors, and offers everything you might need for the home—mosquito coils, laundry powder or the ubiquitous clove-scented cigarettes.

Warungs also sell a colorful array of packaged snacks, cakes, biscuits, bottles of drink and whatever fresh fruit is available that day: fresh bananas, avocados, papayas or guavas gathered from a nearby garden.

Eating out for many Indonesians is usually a necessity rather than a luxury, and basic food stalls selling cooked food at very reasonable prices are found in any large village as well as in towns and cities. Stalls are often a good source of regional favorites. You can find *soto Makassar* (a rich beef soup) and grilled fish (*ikan bakar*) along Ujung Pandang's waterfront in Southern Sulawesi. Lombok's favorite chicken, which is grilled over coals and served with a spicy sauce (*ayam taliwang*) is found at many foodstalls in the capital, Mataram, and almost any market in Bali will feature the famous roast pig (*babi guling*).

Market foodstalls often sell *nasi campur* (literally "mixed rice") with small portions of several "dishes of the day," the various vegetables, meat, poultry or fish dishes are often cooked in the regional style.

Hawkers on rumbling pushcarts, makeshift wooden contraptions resting on a couple of bicycle wheels, are also a popular sight, offering *mee bakso* (noodle and meatball soup), or bowls of shaved ice with the syrups, jellies and fruits of your choice added. Another hawker with a charcoal fire will grill satay on request.

What Westerners may consider desserts are eaten as snacks throughout the day, and may include treats such as fermented rice or cassava (*tape*), slivers of young coconut, chunks or strips of colorful jelly, sweet corn kernels or vivid green "noodles" of transparent mung bean flour.

Coffee is more popular than tea in many areas of Indonesia. Finely ground coffee is put straight into the serving glass and mixed with boiling water. The trick of drinking the coffee (known as *kopi tobruk*) without getting a mouthful of grounds is to stir it a little so that the grounds settle. Indonesians love sugar and coffee is served sweet unless one asks for it *pahit* (literally "bitter").

Stronger drinks can be found, except in conservative Islamic areas (Muslims are forbidden to drink alcohol). Two popular local brands of beer, Bintang and Anker, are made to Dutch specifications and are similar to any European lager. In many non-Muslim areas, a local brew is made from either rice or the sap of the coconut or lontar palm. Bali is noted for its *brem*, a sweetish type of rice beer. Palm wine (toddy) is made by tapping the sap that flows from the inflorescence of the coconut or lontar palm. It is enjoyed fresh the day it is gathered, or left to mature for a few days; leftovers are distilled to made a fierce *arrack*.

The Indonesian Table and Kitchen

"*Silakan makan*" is the Indonesian invitation that precedes any meal served to guests, and a phrase foreigners should wait for before beginning even as much as a snack served by their Indonesian hosts. But in countless homes throughout the archipelago, meals are usually an informal affair and often eaten alone.

The most popular staple food is rice, and Indonesians eat large quantities of it with savory side dishes and condiments. Only small amounts of savory dishes—which may include fish, poultry, meat, eggs, vegetables, tofu or *tempeh*—are eaten. Variety is preferred over quantity; a little of four or five side dishes rather than large helpings of only one or two.

Condiments are as important as savory dishes and will usually include a chili *sambal* and something to provide a crunchy contrast. This could be deep-fried *tempeh*, peanuts, deep-fried tiny anchovies (*ikan teri*), *krupuk* (wafers made of tapioca flour seasoned with anything from shrimp to melinjo nuts), a seasoned fried coconut concoction such as *serundeng* or fried peanut wafers (*rempeyek*).

The rice and accompanying dishes are normally cooked early in the day, immediately after a trip to the market. The prepared food is left in the kitchen, and members of the family help themselves to whatever they want whenever hungry, or take a container of food to the fields. Evening meals, taken at the end of the day when family members return from the fields, school or their work in the towns and cities, are often based on food left over from the main midday meal, with one or two extra dishes cooked if necessary.

As food is often served some time after it has been prepared, it is usually eaten at room temperature. Where meals are communal, the rice and all the accompanying dishes are placed in the middle of the table or on a mat on the floor for everyone to help themselves. It is considered impolite to pile one's plate with food at the first serving; there's plenty of opportunity to take more food as the meal progresses.

Indonesians traditionally eat with the right hand (the left is considered unclean by Muslims), although serving spoons are used to transfer the food to individual plates or bowls from the serving dishes. Many modern homes and almost all restaurants provide a spoon and fork, while chopsticks can be expected in Chinese restaurants.

In more affluent homes, the choice of dishes to accompany the rice is made with a view to achieving a blend of flavors and textures. If one of the savory dishes has a rich, creamy coconut-milk sauce, this will be offset by a dry dish with perhaps a sharper flavor. There may well be a pungent *sambal goreng* (food fried with a spicy chili seasoning), but this will be balanced with other mild or even sweet dishes using *kecap manis* (sweet black soy sauce) or palm sugar.

For a family celebration, food is prepared by the family involved. Larger feasts involve the whole *banjar*, or local community, the work supervised by a ritual cooking specialist, invariably a man. There is a strict division of labor along gender lines, with men being responsible for butchering the pig or turtle, grating coconuts and grinding spices. The women of the community perform the more fiddly tasks of peeling and chopping the fresh seasonings, cooking the rice and preparing the vegetables.

The Indonesian kitchen is a combination of simplicity and practicality. The gleaming modern designer kitchen is unknown to the majority of Indonesians; meals are usually cooked over a wood fire or a *kompor*, a kerosene burner.

A little known fact: despite the Moluccas's reputation as the Spice Islands—islands literally responsible for starting the Age of Exploration and for the discovery of the Americas by Christopher Columbus—cloves and nutmeg are rarely used in cooking in the Moluccas. A little grated nutmeg may be added to a rich beef soup at a pinch, but in the main, nutmeg and cloves are regarded more as medicinal plants. Nutmeg fruit, the fleshy covering of the hard nut which is used as a spice, is usually pickled and eaten as a snack.

The most widely used spice is coriander, a small round beige seed with a faintly orange flavor, commonly partnered with peppercorns and garlic to flavor food, especially in Java.

SUGGESTED MENUS

Family meals

For an easy but elegant family meal, serve the following selection of small dishes with Festive Turmeric Rice (page 77):
• Boiled Pepper Shrimp (page 74);
• Seasoned Fish Grilled in Banana Leaves (page 74);
• Asparagus in Coconut (page 81);
• Sweet Coconut Pancakes (page 87) as a sweet.

Or, you may like to consider:
• Beef Ribs Soup (page 78);
• Vegetables with Spicy Coconut Sauce (page 80) and Lemongrass Fish (page 83) with steamed rice;
• Steamed Banana Cakes (page 86) for dessert.

Dinner party (1)

Many of the dishes in this chapter make very good dinner-party nibbles:
• Seasoned Fish Grilled in Banana Leaves (page 74), Dry Spiced Beef (page 83) and Curried Lobsters (page 82);
• Chicken Simmered in Mild Coconut Gravy (page 84) or Javanese Fried Chicken (page 84) and Sweet and Spicy Fried Tempeh Strips (page 81) served with rice
• Black Rice Pudding (page 86) makes a dramatic ending.

Dinner party (2)

Other great dinner party suggestions are:
• Balinese Satay (page 74);
• Javanese Fried Chicken (page 84) and Spicy Padang Eggs (page 80) with Classic Gado Gado (page 76);
• Black Rice Pudding (page 86) completes the meal.

Salad meals

The salads in this chapter (page 76) are a vegetable lover's delight, and easy to assemble once you've prepared all the ingredients. They make an ideal lunch, served with bread or rice.

A melting pot menu

For a mixed dinner menu serve:
• Green Papaya Soup (page 79) from Indonesia;
• Spicy Jumbo Shrimp (page 183) from Vietnam and Steamed Tofu with Pork (page 38) from China;
• Sago with Honeydew and Coconut Cream from Malaysia/Singapore (page 135) makes an excellent finale.

THE ESSENTIAL FLAVORS OF INDONESIAN COOKING

For making the Indonesian *rempah*, **garlic**, **ginger**, **galangal**, **chilies,** and **dried shrimp paste** are a must. You'll also need freshly squeezed **lime juice** and *salam* **leaf**. Unique to Indonesian cuisine is the use of *tempeh*. **Coconuts**—the milk and flesh—are an integral part of Indonesian cooking, and are used in salads, curries, and desserts. **Palm sugar** is used in sweet and savory dishes. **Noodles** and **rice** are the main staples.

1–2 bird's-eye chilies
1 tablespoon oil
1 teaspoon dried shrimp paste
 (*trasi*)
1/2 teaspoon salt
Pinch of ground white pepper
1 *salam* leaf, whole
1 stalk lemongrass, tender inner part
 of bottom third only, bruised

Place the shallots, garlic, galangal, coriander seeds, turmeric, chilies, *kencur*, and dried shrimp paste in a food processor and process lightly, or grind coarsely in mortar. Heat the oil in a wok or heavy saucepan. Add the ground paste and remaining ingredients, and stir-fry for 2 minutes or until it changes color. Cool before using.

Sambal Trasi

Chili Sauce with Dried Shrimp Paste

4 red finger-length chilies, deseeded
1 tablespoon dried shrimp paste
 (*trasi*), dry-roasted (page 13)
1 tablespoon shaved palm sugar or
 dark brown sugar
1 tablespoon lime or lemon juice

Grind all the ingredients to a smooth paste in a mortar or blender. For a more fiery sambal, substitute bird's-eye chilies for the finger-length chilies.

Tomato Sambal

Spiced Roasted Coconut with Peanuts

Serundeng

1 shallot, peeled
1 clove garlic, peeled
1 teaspoon shaved palm sugar or
 dark brown sugar
1/2 teaspoon dried shrimp paste
 (*trasi*), dry-roasted (page 13)
1/2 tablespoon Tamarind Juice
 (page 18)
2 cups (200 g) freshly grated
 coconut or 1 1/2 cups (120 g)
 unsweetened desiccated coconut
1/3 cup (50 g) roasted unsalted
 peanuts, skins discarded
1/4 teaspoon salt

Grind the shallots, garlic, sugar, shrimp paste and Tamarind Juice to a smooth paste in a mortar or blender. Add the grated coconut and mix well.

Dry-fry the mixture in a wok or skillet over very low heat for 10 to 15 minutes until golden brown and flaky. Add the peanuts and salt, and mix until well blended. Remove from the heat and set aside to cool. Serve in small bowls or sprinkle over rice or side dishes. *Serundeng* keeps for 2 weeks in an airtight container.

Tomato Sambal

2 tablespoons oil
6–8 shallots, peeled and sliced
5 cloves garlic, peeled and sliced
4-5 red finger-length chilies,
 deseeded and sliced
2 medium-sized tomatoes, cut in
 wedges
1 teaspoon dried shrimp paste
 (*trasi*), dry-roasted (page 13)
1 teaspoon lime juice
Salt to taste

Heat the oil in a heavy saucepan or wok. Add the shallots and garlic and stir-fry for 5 minutes over low heat. Add the chilies and stir-fry for another 5 minutes, then add the tomatoes and dried shrimp paste and simmer for another 10 minutes.

Add the lime juice. Put all the ingredients in a food processor and process coarsely. Season to taste with salt. Cool before using. This sambal can be frozen.

Basic Spice Paste

4 shallots, peeled and chopped
5 cloves garlic, peeled and chopped
2 in (5 cm) galangal, peeled and
 thinly sliced
1 teaspoon coriander seeds
1 in (2 cm) fresh turmeric root,
 peeled and sliced
3 red finger-length chilies, deseeded
 and chopped
1 in (2 cm) fresh *kencur root*,
 peeled and chopped

Bird's-eye Chili Sambal

12 bird's-eye chilies
2 tablespoons oil
1 teaspoons dried shrimp paste
 (*trasi*)
Pinch of salt

Clean and discard the stems of the chilies. Heat the oil in a wok or saucepan until smoking. Crumble the dried shrimp paste and combine with the salt.

Add the chilies, dried shrimp paste and salt to the oil, stir over high heat for 1 minute and then remove from the heat and allow to cool. Store the chilies and cooking oil in an airtight container. Keeps up to 1 week in a refrigerator.

Sambal Kecap

Sweet Soy Dip

3–4 shallots, peeled and sliced
1 red finger-length chili, deseeded
  and sliced
2 tablespoons sweet Indonesian soy
  sauce (*kecap manis*)

Combine all the ingredients, mix well and serve in a small bowl.

Crispy Fried Shallots

10–15 red Asian shallots
1 cup (250 ml) oil

Peel and thinly sliced the shallots, then pat dry with paper towels.

Heat the oil in a wok over medium low heat and stir-fry the sliced shallot until golden brown and crispy, 3 to 5 minutes. Do not allow them to burn or they will taste bitter. Drain well using a wire mesh sieve and allow to cool completely, then store in an airtight container. Reserve the **Garlic Oil** for frying or seasoning other dishes.

Chicken Stock

1 lb (500 g) chicken bones
1/2 cup (125 ml) Basic Spice Paste
  (page 72)
1 stalk lemongrass, tender inner part
  of bottom third only, lightly bruised
3 kaffir lime leaves
2 *salam* leaves (optional)
1 teaspoon black peppercorns,
  coarsely crushed
1 teaspoon salt

Rinse the bones until the water is clear. Put them in a large saucepan with cold water to cover and bring to a boil. Drain the water, wash the bones under running water. Return the bones to the pan, cover with fresh water and boil. Reduce the heat and remove any scum with a ladle.

Add all the seasoning ingredients and simmer the stock gently, uncovered for 3 to 3 1/2 hours, removing any scum. Strain the stock, cool and store in small containers in the freezer.

Crispy Peanut Wafers

1 1/2 cups (220 g) raw peanuts
1 cup (120 g) rice flour
3/4 cup (100 g) all-purpose flour
1 cup (250 ml) thick coconut milk
Oil, for deep-frying

Spice Paste
2 macadamia nuts or candlenuts,
  roughly chopped
1/2 in (1 cm) fresh turmeric root,
  peeled and sliced, or 1/2 teaspoon
  ground turmeric
2 cloves garlic, peeled
1 teaspoon coriander seeds
2 kaffir lime leaves (optional)
1/2 teaspoon salt

Dry-roast the peanuts in a wok or skillet over low heat for about 5 minutes. Remove from the heat and set aside to cool, then rub the peanuts together to remove the skins.

To make the Spice Paste, grind all the ingredients to a smooth paste in a mortar or blender, adding a little coconut milk if necessary to keep the mixture turning. Combine the ground paste and flours in a mixing bowl, add the coconut milk and stir well to obtain a smooth batter, then add the peanuts and mix well.

Heat the oil in a wok over medium heat until hot. Ladle 2 tablespoons of the batter at a time into the hot oil and deep-fry until crispy and golden brown, 3 to 5 minutes. Remove from the wok and drain the wafer on paper towels. Continue to deep-fry the wafers until all the batter is used up. Allow the wafers to cool thoroughly before storing them in an airtight container.

Palm Sugar Syrup

1 cup (200 g) shaved palm sugar or
  dark brown sugar
1 cup (250 ml) water

Bring the palm sugar and water to a boil over high heat in a saucepan. Reduce the heat to low, simmer uncovered for about 10 minutes, stirring from time to time, until the sugar is dissolved and the mixture turns syrupy. Remove from the heat and set aside to cool.

Mixed Vegetable Pickles

Acar Segar

1 small cucumber, peeled, deseeded
  and cut into matchsticks
1 small carrot, peeled and cut into
  matchsticks
8 shallots, peeled and quartered
3/4 cup (180 ml) water
3 tablespoons white vinegar
1 tablespoon sugar
1 teaspoon salt

Place the sliced vegetables in a bowl. In another bowl, combine the water, vinegar, sugar and salt, then add to the vegetables and mix well. Set aside to cure for 2 or 3 days in the refrigerator before serving. This pickle keeps for 2 weeks in the refrigerator.

Pickles with Basil

1 small cucumber, peeled and sliced
1/2 cup (25 g) bean sprouts, seed
  coats and tails discarded,
  blanched
2 shallots, peeled and thinly sliced
1 red finger-length chili, deseeded
  and sliced
1–2 bird's-eye chilies, deseeded and
  sliced
2 sprigs Asian basil, minced
3 tablespoons coarsely ground
  almonds, cashews or
  macadamia nuts
1/4 teaspoon dried shrimp paste
  (*trasi*), dry-roasted (page 13)
2 tablespoons lime or lemon juice
1/4 teaspoon sugar
1/4 teaspoon salt
1–2 tablespoons warm water

Place the sliced cucumber and bean sprouts in a bowl, then spread the sliced shallot, chilies and basil on top.

Combine the remaining ingredients in another bowl and mix well to make a thick sauce. Drizzle the sauce over the vegetables, mix well and set aside to cure for 2 to 3 hours. If storing the pickles, keep the vegetables and sauce separate. This pickle keeps for a week in the refrigerator.

Cucumber Pickles

1 medium cucumber, peeled, halved
  lengthwise, deseeded and sliced
1 tablespoon white vinegar
2 1/2 tablespoons sugar
1 teaspoon salt
2 1/2 tablespoons hot water

Place the sliced cucumber in a bowl. Combine the vinegar, sugar, salt and hot water in another bowl, then add to the cucumber and toss well. Set aside to cure for 1 hour before serving. This pickle keeps for a week in a jar in the refrigerator.

Sambal Kacang

Peanut Sauce for Satay

1 cup (150 g) roasted unsalted
  peanuts, skins discarded
3 cloves garlic, peeled
1 in (2 1/2 cm) fresh *kencur* root,
  peeled and sliced
2–3 bird's-eye chilies, deseeded
1 kaffir lime leaf
3 tablespoons sweet Indonesian soy
  sauce (*kecap manis*)
1/2 teaspoon salt
1 1/2 cups (375 ml) water
1 teaspoon lime or lemon juice
1 tablespoon Crispy Fried Shallots
  (see recipe on this page)

Grind the peanuts, garlic, *kencur* and chilies coarsely in a mortar or blender.

Combine the ground ingredients with all the other ingredients (except the lime or lemon juice and Crispy Fried Shallots) in a saucepan, mix well and simmer over medium heat for 15 to 20 minutes, stirring constantly to prevent the sauce from burning. Add more water as needed to keep the sauce a thick consistency. Remove from the heat, add the lime or lemon juice and mix well. Sprinkle the Crispy Fried Shallots over it just before serving.

Boiled Pepper Shrimp (upper left) and Fresh Tuna and Green Mango Salad (lower right)

In Indonesia these dishes would be used as side dishes to accompany rice. You can increase the quantities slightly and serve as part of a shared main meal with rice.

Fresh Tuna and Green Mango Salad

If fresh tuna is not available, use canned tuna as a substitute, although the flavor is not the same.

1–2 unripe mangoes, peeled and pitted, flesh sliced into matchsticks
1 teaspoon salt
1 lb (500 g) fresh tuna steaks, grilled and deboned, flesh flaked
2–3 shallots, peeled and sliced
1 teaspoon ground white pepper
3 tablespoons thick coconut milk

Place the mango shreds in a colander. Sprinkle the salt over them and mix well. Set aside to drain for 10 minutes, then squeeze the mango to remove as much liquid as possible.

Place the mango in a large salad bowl. Add the flaked tuna, shallots, pepper and coconut milk, and toss well. Serve chilled.

Boiled Pepper Shrimp

4 cups (1 liter) water
1¹/2 lbs (750 g) large fresh shrimp
2 red finger-length chilies, deseeded
4 red Asian shallots, peeled
2 tablespoons Tamarind Juice (page 18) or lime juice
Sprigs of fresh parsley or coriander leaves (cilantro)
Bottled sweet chili sauce

Bring the water to a boil in a large saucepan and add the shrimp. Immediately reduce the heat and simmer until the shrimp turn pink, 2 to 3 minutes. Quickly drain and plunge the shrimp into a basin of iced water for 30 seconds to stop the cooking. Drain, peel and devein the shrimp. Transfer to a serving platter and set aside.

Grind the chilies, shallots and Tamarind Juice or lime juice to a smooth paste in a mortar or blender, adding a little lime or lemon juice for a more sour taste if desired. Set aside.

Add the ground paste to the shrimp and toss gently until well coated. Garnish with parsley or coriander leaves, and serve with a small bowl of sweet chili sauce on the side.

Seasoned Fish Grilled in Banana Leaves

This recipe calls for steamed bundles of flaky, seasoned fish to be grilled directly over hot charcoal, giving an inimitable flavor.

1 lb (500 g) white fish fillets, skinned and cut into chunks
4 to 5 shallots, peeled
3 cloves garlic, peeled
2 green onions (scallions), sliced
1 teaspoon ground white pepper
1/2 cup (85 ml) thick coconut milk
1 tablespoon lime or lemon juice
1/2 teaspoon salt
2 eggs
Banana leaves or aluminum foil, cut into 8-in (20-cm) square pieces

Place the fish chunks in a blender or food processor and pulse for a few seconds, then add all the other ingredients, except the banana leaves, and grind to a thick paste. Set aside.

Scald the banana leaves by pouring boiling water over them in a basin, so they become flexible. Drain and place them on a clean work surface. Spoon 3 heaped tablespoons of the fish mixture onto each piece of banana leaf (or use aluminum foil), roll firmly and secure the ends with toothpicks. Repeat until all the fish mixture is used up.

Grill each parcel directly over hot charcoal or under a preheated broiler for 10 to 15 minutes, turning from time to time until the banana leaf wrapper is charred. Serve hot.

Balinese Satay
Sate Lilit

1 lb (500 g) ground chicken or duck
2 cups (200 g) freshly grated coconut
3 kaffir lime leaves, thinly sliced
2 tablespoons shaved palm sugar or dark brown sugar
1 teaspoon salt
24 stalks lemongrass or bamboo skewers, soaked in water
2 portions Sambal Kecap (page 73)

Spice Paste
2 macadamia nuts or candlenuts, roughly chopped
1/2 in (1 cm) fresh galangal, peeled and sliced
1/2 in (1 cm) fresh *kencur* root, peeled and sliced
1/2 in (1 cm) fresh turmeric root, peeled and sliced, or 1 teaspoon ground turmeric
2 red finger-length chilies, deseeded
4–6 shallots, peeled
2 cloves garlic, peeled
1/4 teaspoon ground cloves

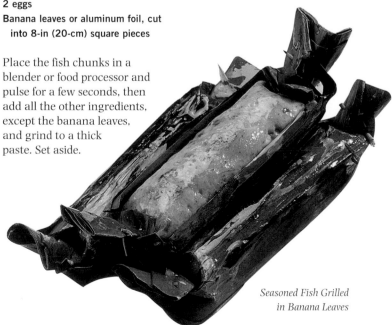

Seasoned Fish Grilled in Banana Leaves

2 teaspoons coriander seeds
$1/2$ teaspoon freshly ground black
  pepper or black peppercorns
Pinch of ground nutmeg
1 teaspoon dried shrimp paste
  (*trasi*), dry-roasted (page 13)
1 tablespoon oil

Make the Spice Paste by grinding all the ingredients, except the oil, to a smooth paste in a mortar or blender, adding a little oil if necessary to keep the mixture turning. Heat the oil in a wok over medium heat and stir-fry the ground paste for 3 to 5 minutes, then remove from the heat and set aside to cool.

When cooled, mix the Spice Paste with the ground chicken or duck and all the other ingredients, except the skewers, until well blended. Set aside to marinate for 2 hours in the refrigerator.

If using bamboo skewers, soak them in water for 4 hours before using. Mold about 2 heaped tablespoons of the meat mixture onto each lemongrass or bamboo skewer with your hands and press it together firmly to form a kebab. Repeat until all the meat mixture is used up.

Grill the skewers over hot charcoal or under a preheated broiler for 2 to 3 minutes on each side, basting with the marinade, until cooked. Turn the skewers frequently to prevent the meat from burning. Arrange the satay on a serving platter and serve hot with the Sambal Kecap dipping sauce.

Fragrant Beef Satay

Fragrant Beef Satay

$1^{1}/2$ lbs (750 g) top round beef, cubed
30 Bamboo skewers, soaked in water
  for 4 hours before using
2 portions Sambal Kacang (page 73)

Spice Paste
4 macadamia nuts or candlenuts,
  roughly chopped
2 in (5 cm) fresh galangal, peeled
  and sliced
1 in ($2^{1}/2$ cm) fresh ginger, peeled
  and sliced
2–3 red finger-length chilies, deseeded
4–5 shallots, peeled
3 cloves garlic, peeled
$1/2$ teaspoon black pepper
1 teaspoon ground coriander
3 tablespoons shaved palm sugar or
  dark brown sugar
1 teaspoon salt
2 tablespoons oil
1 *salam* leaf

Make the Spice Paste by grinding all the ingredients, except the oil and *salam* leaf, to a smooth paste in a mortar or blender, adding a little oil if necessary to keep the mixture turning. Heat the oil in a wok over medium heat and stir-fry the ground paste with the *salam* leaf for 3 to 5 minutes until fragrant. Remove from the heat and set aside to cool.

When cooled, place the Spice Paste and beef in a large bowl and mix well. Set aside in the refrigerator to marinate overnight.

Soak the bamboo skewers in water for 4 hours before using so

they do not burn when grilling the meat. Thread the marinated beef onto the skewers and grill over hot charcoal or under a preheated broiler for 2 to 3 minutes on each side, basting with the marinade, until cooked. Turn the skewers frequently to prevent the beef from burning, it should be browned on the outside and cooked on the inside.

Arrange the beef satay on a serving platter and serve with a bowl of Sambal Kecap or Sambal Kacang on the side.

Lamb Satay

Lamb Satay

$1^{1}/2$ lbs (750 g) boneless lamb
24 bamboo skewers, soaked in water
  for 4 hours before using
Lime wedges, to serve
1 portion Sambal Kecap (page 73)
1 portion Sambal Kacang (page 73)

Marinade
$1/2$ cup (125 ml) sweet Indonesian
  soy sauce (*kecap manis*)
$1/2$ teaspoon ground coriander
$1/4$ teaspoon ground white pepper
1 tablespoon lime or lemon juice

Cut the lamb or goat meat into bite-sized cubes. Combine the Marinade ingredients in a bowl and mix well. Pour two-third of the Marinade to the meat cubes, mix until well coated and allow to marinate for at least 2 hours. Reserve the remaining Marinade.

Thread the marinated meat cubes onto the bamboo skewers and grill over hot charcoal or under a preheated broiler for 5 to 7 minutes, turning and basting frequently with the reserved Marinade, until the meat is well cooked and browned on all sides. Arrange the satays on a serving platter and serve with the lime wedges and bowls of Sambal Kecap and Sambal Kacang on the side.

Classic Gado Gado
Tofu and Vegetable Salad with Peanut Dressing

1 cup (50 g) bean sprouts, seed coats and tails discarded
2 cups (180 g) spinach, rinsed, tough stems discarded
1 carrot, sliced
1 cup (100 g) green beans, cut into short lengths
1/4 head cabbage, leaves separated and sliced
2 cakes (about 7 oz/200 g each) deep-fried tofu, sliced
2 hard-boiled eggs, cut into wedges
2 tablespoons Crispy Fried Shallots (page 73)
Krupuk shrimp crackers (page 14)

Dressing
1 cup (150 g) roasted unsalted peanuts
2 cloves garlic, peeled
2–3 bird's-eye chilies or red finger-length chilies, deseeded
1 in (2 1/2 cm) fresh *kencur* root, peeled and sliced
1 kaffir lime leaf
3 tablespoons sweet Indonesian soy sauce (*kecap manis*)
1/2 teaspoon salt
2 cups (500 ml) water
1 teaspoon lime or lemon juice

To make the Dressing, coarsely grind the peanuts, garlic, chilies and *kencur* in a mortar or blender, adding a little water if necessary to keep the mixture turning. Place the ground mixture in a saucepan with all the other Dressing ingredients, except the lime or lemon juice, and simmer uncovered over very low heat for about 1 hour, stirring frequently to prevent the sauce from sticking to the pot and burning. Remove from the heat and set aside. Add the lime or lemon juice, mix well and sprinkle 1 tablespoon of the Crispy Fried Shallots over the sauce just before serving.

Bring a saucepan of water to a boil over medium heat, and briefly blanch the vegetables (about 30 seconds for bean sprouts, 1 minute for spinach, 1 to 2 minutes for carrot, and 2 to 3 minutes for green beans and cabbage). Remove from the heat and drain.

Arrange all the vegetables on a serving platter and top with the tofu and egg wedges. Garnish with the remaining Crispy Fried Shallots and drizzle the Dressing on top. Serve with the deep-fried *krupuk* on the side.

Roast Chicken Salad with Chilies and Lime

1 whole chicken, weighing about 2 1/2 lbs (1 1/4 kgs)
1/2 cup (125 ml) Basic Spice Paste (page 72)
1/2 cup (125 ml) Tomato Sambal (page 72)
3 tablespoons lime juice

Preheat oven to 350°F (180°C). Rub the chicken outside and in with the Spice Paste. Place on wire rack in oven and roast until done. When cool, remove and discard the skin. Remove the meat from bones and shred by hand into fine strips. Combine the chicken strips with the remaining ingredients. Mix well and season to taste. Serve with steamed rice.

Green Bean Salad with Steamed Chicken

No big celebration would be held without serving this ritual dish. Only the eldest and most experienced men are allowed to mix the many ingredients.

1 lb (500 g) green beans, trimmed, blanched and sliced
1/2 cup (50 g) grated coconut, roasted
3 cloves garlic, peeled, sliced and fried
2–4 bird's-eye chilies, finely sliced
1 teaspoon Bird's-eye Chili Sambal (page 72)
1 tablespoon Basic Spice Paste (page 72)
Crispy Fried Shallots (page 73)
1 teaspoon lime juice
1 teaspoon salt
1/2 teaspoon black peppercorns, crushed

Steamed Chicken
8 oz (250 g) ground chicken
2 tablespoons Basic Spice Paste (page 72)
12-in (30-cm) square of banana leaf

Combine the beans, coconut, garlic, shallots, all the chilies, and Spice Paste in a large bowl and mix well.

To prepare the Steamed Chicken, combine the ground chicken with 2 tablespoons of the Basic Spice Paste and mix well. Place the ground chicken lengthwise in the center of the banana leaf or aluminum foil and roll up very tightly. Place the roll on another sheet of aluminum foil and roll up again very tightly. Twist the ends in opposite directions to tighten the roll. Steam the roll for 20 minutes. Remove the aluminum foil and banana leaf, break up the meat with a fork to its original ground form.

Combine the ground chicken with the bean mixture, season to taste with salt, pepper, and lime juice. Garnish with Crispy Fried Shallots.

Rujak
Fruit and Vegetable Salad with Sweet Tamarind Dressing

This popular snack, an intriguing mixture of sweet, sour and spicy flavors, is prepared at countless warungs throughout Indonesia. The list of raw fruits and vegetables that can be included depends on what is available and what you feel like eating.

1/2 small pineapple, peeled, eyes and fibrous core discarded, sliced
1 unripe mango, peeled and pitted, flesh sliced
1 small cucumber, peeled, deseeded and sliced
1 green apple, rinsed and sliced
1 starfruit, sliced
1/2 small papaya, peeled, halved, deseeded and sliced

Sambal Rujak
1/2 cup (100 g) shaved palm sugar or dark brown sugar
1/2 cup (125 ml) water
1/4 cup (60 ml) Tamarind Juice (page 18)
1/2 teaspoon dried shrimp paste (*trasi*), dry-roasted (page 13)
3–4 bird's-eye chilies, left whole
1/2 teaspoon salt
1/2 cup (125 ml) water

To make the Sambal Rujak, boil the sugar and water in a saucepan, then reduce the heat to low and simmer until the syrup is thickened, about 10 minutes. Add all the other ingredients, sitr well, increase the heat to medium and bring the mixture to a boil. Reduce the heat to low again and simmer for about 5 minutes, then remove from the heat and set aside to cool. Strain the Sambal before serving.

Place all the cut fruits and vegetables in a large salad bowl,

Classic Gado Gado (Tofu and Vegetable Salad with Peanut Dressing, right) and Crispy Peanut Wafers (left, recipe on page 73)

Festive Turmeric Rice (Nasi Kuning)

drizzle the Sambal Rujak over them and toss to coat well. Serve immediately.

Festive Turmeric Rice
Nasi Kuning

Rice colored with turmeric and shaped into a cone is a common sight during festive occasions in Bali and Java. The conical shape echoes that of the mythical Hindu mountain, Meru, while yellow is the color of royalty and one of the four sacred colors for Hindus.

2 in (5 cm) fresh turmeric root, sliced
1/4 cup (60 ml) water
1 1/2 cups (300 g) uncooked rice, washed and drained
1 1/2 cups (375 ml) thin coconut milk
1/2 cup (125 ml) Chicken Stock, (page 73)
1 *salam* or pandanus leaf
1 stalk lemongrass, tender inner part of bottom third only, bruised
1 in (2 1/2 cm) fresh galangal, sliced
1 teaspoon salt

Grind the turmeric and water in a mortar until fine. Strain to extract all the juice. Discard the solids. If using ground turmeric, dissolve the powder in 2 tablespoons of water.

Combine the rice, turmeric juice, coconut milk, Chicken Stock, *salam* or pandanus leaf, lemongrass, galangal and salt in

a pot and bring to a boil over high heat. Reduce the heat to medium and simmer covered until the liquid is absorbed, 10 to 15 minutes, then reduce the heat to low and cook for 5 to 10 more minutes, until the rice is dry and fluffy. Remove from the heat and mix well. Alternatively, cook the rice and ingredients in a rice cooker.

Discard the *salam* or pandanus leaf, lemongrass and galangal. Press the cooked turmeric rice into a cone shape, if desired.

Classic Nasi Goreng
Indonesian Fried Rice

One of Indonesia's most popular dishes, Nasi Goreng is prepared in countless ways and is eaten morning, noon and night. This classic version is accompanied by fried egg, fried chicken, satay and *krupuk* (deep-fried shrimp crackers) for a substantial meal. Any sort of leftover or fresh meat or shrimp may be added, but the true flavor of Indonesia comes from the use of pungent chilies and *trasi* (dried shrimp paste).

5 cups (500 g) cold cooked rice or leftover rice
3 tablespoons oil
4 eggs
4–5 shallots, peeled and sliced
1–2 red finger-length chilies, deseeded and minced
2 cloves garlic, peeled and sliced

2 teaspoons dried shrimp paste (*trasi*), dry-roasted (page 13)
5 oz (150 g) fresh shrimp, peeled and deveined
1 cup (200 g) leftover cooked or fresh chicken, lamb or beef, diced
2 cups (250 g) thinly sliced cabbage
1 teaspoon salt
1 tablespoon sweet Indonesian soy sauce (*kecap manis*)
Sliced cucumber and sliced tomato

Accompaniments
1 portion Javanese Fried Chicken (page 84)
1/2 portion Fragrant Beef Satay (page 75)
Crispy Fried Shallots (page 73)
1 portion Sambal Kecap (page 73)
Krupuk shrimp crackers (page 14)
1/2 portion Mixed Vegetable Pickles (page 73)

Prepare the Javanese Fried Chicken, Beef Satay, Crispy Fried Shallots, Sambal Kecap and Mixed Vegetable Pickles by following the respective recipes.

Flake the cold rice with a fork or your fingers to separate the grains. Set aside.

Lightly grease a non-stick skillet with a little oil and fry the eggs sunny side up. Remove from the heat and set aside.

Heat the remaining oil in a wok over medium heat and stir-fry the shallots, garlic, minced chili and dried shrimp paste until fragrant, 1 to 2 minutes. Add the shrimp and chicken and stir-fry until almost cooked, about 2 minutes, then add the cabbage and continue to stir-fry for 2 more minutes until the meat and vegetables are cooked. (If using cooked meat, add to the wok with the cabbage and stir-fry until the cabbage is slightly wilted, about 2 minutes.) Increase the heat to high, add the rice, salt and sweet Indonesian soy sauce, and stir-fry briskly until all the ingredients are mixed well and heated through, about 2 minutes. Remove from the heat.

Transfer the fried rice to a serving platter, top with the fried eggs and arrange the fried chicken and satays on the side. Garnish with cucumber and tomato slices (if using) and serve with the Accompaniments on the side.

Classic Nasi Goreng (Indonesian Fried Rice)

Beef Ribs Soup (Konro Makasar)

Beef Ribs Soup

Konro Makasar

2 lbs (1 kg) beef spareribs
3 cups (300 g) freshly grated
  coconut, or 2 cups (150 g)
  unsweetened desiccated coconut
16 cups (4 liters) water
3 stalks lemongrass, tender inner
  part of bottom third only, bruised
1 in (2¹/2 cm) fresh galangal, sliced
3 kaffir lime leaves
1 teaspoon ground white pepper
1 teaspoon salt
Crispy Fried Shallots (page 73)

Spice Paste
3–4 shallots, peeled
3 macadamia nuts or candlenuts,
  roughly chopped
2 cloves garlic, peeled

Separate the beef ribs and cut
into lengths. Set aside.

Dry-fry the grated coconut in
a skillet over low heat, stirring
constantly until it turns golden
brown, about 10 minutes for
fresh coconut and 5 to 7 minutes for desiccated coconut. Remove from the heat and allow to
cool. While still warm, grind the
coconut in a mortar or blender
until fine. Set aside.

Prepare the Spice Paste by
grinding all the ingredients to a
smooth paste in a mortar or

blender, adding a little water if
necessary to keep the mixture
turning. Set aside.

Bring the beef and water to
a boil in a large pot and simmer
uncovered over medium heat
until the beef is tender, 30 to 40
minutes. Add the ground coconut,
Spice Paste and all the remaining
ingredients (except the Crispy
Fried Shallots), mix well and
continue to simmer for 15 more
minutes, until the beef is very
tender, but not falling off the
bones. Remove from the heat
and serve garnished with the
Crispy Fried Shallots.

Beef Soup with Chilies and Tamarind

This soup from Timor in eastern Indonesia has a wonderful sweet-sour edge to it.

8 cups (2 liters) water
2 lbs (1 kg) stewing beef
3 tablespoons oil
4–5 shallots, peeled
2 cloves garlic, peeled
1 teaspoon dried shrimp paste
  (*trasi*), dry-roasted (page 13)
2 tablespoons shaved palm sugar or
  dark brown sugar
1 teaspoon sweet Indonesian soy
  sauce (*kecap manis*)

2 tablespoons Tamarind Juice
  (page 18)
1 teaspoon salt
1–2 red finger-length chilies,
  deseeded and sliced into strips
2 green onions (scallions), cut into
  short lengths

Bring the water to a boil in a
large pot. Add the beef, reduce
the heat to low and simmer
until the meat is half cooked,
about 15 minutes. Turn off the
heat. Remove the beef from the
stock and drain. Strain and
reserve the stock.

When cool enough to handle,
cut the beef into cubes. Heat 2
tablespoons of the oil over medium heat in a skillet and pan-fry
the beef until cooked, 2 to 3
minutes. Remove from the heat
and set aside.

Grind the shallots, garlic,
dried shrimp paste and sugar to
a smooth paste in a mortar or
blender, adding a little water if
necessary to keep the mixture
turning. Set aside.

Heat the remaining oil in a
wok over medium heat and stir-
fry the ground paste until fragrant, 3 to 5 minutes. Add the
beef cubes and sweet Indonesian
soy sauce, and stir-fry for 2 minutes, then pour in the reserved
beef stock and Tamarind Juice,
and season with the salt. Bring
the soup to a boil, then simmer
uncovered until the beef is tender, 10 to 15 minutes. Adjust the
taste with more salt or Tamarind
Juice as desired, stir in the sliced
chilies and green onions, and
remove from the heat. Serve hot.

Fish Stew with Turmeric and Lemongrass

This dish is typically cooked
with fish heads in Indonesia,
as shown in the photo, but is
equally delicious with whole
fish or fillets.

1¹/2 lbs (750 g) snapper, tuna or
  sea bream fillets
1 tablespoon oil
4 cups (1 liter) water
1 teaspoon salt
3 stalks lemongrass, tender inner
  part of bottom third only, bruised
5 kaffir lime leaves
1–2 red finger-length chilies, sliced
2 green onions (scallions), cut into
  lengths
Crispy Fried Shallots (page 73)

Spice Paste
1¹/2 in (4 cm) fresh turmeric,
  peeled and sliced, or 1¹/2 teaspoons ground turmeric
2 in (5 cm) ginger, sliced
2–3 red finger-length chilies,
  deseeded
4–6 shallots, peeled
3 cloves garlic, peeled

If using whole fish, scale, gut
and clean the fish, then make
several shallow diagonal slits on
each side.

Make the Spice Paste by
grinding all the ingredients to a
smooth paste in a mortar or
blender, adding a little water if
necessary to keep the mixture
turning.

*Fish Stew with Turmeric and
Lemongrass*

Heat the oil in a wok over high heat and stir-fry the Spice Paste for 1 to 2 minutes until fragrant. Add the water, salt, lemongrass and kaffir lime leaves, and bring to a boil. Add the fish, reduce the heat to medium and return to a boil, then simmer uncovered until the fish is cooked, 7 to 10 minutes. Adjust the taste with more salt or water as desired and remove from the heat.

Transfer to a serving platter and serve hot with steamed rice, garnished with sliced chili, green onions and Crispy Fried Shallots.

Peel the papaya, cut in half lengthwise and remove the seeds. Slice the papaya lengthwise into 4 or 6 slices, then slice crosswise in slices about 1/4 in (1/2 cm) thick. Heat the stock, add the Spice Paste and bring to a boil. Simmer for 2 minutes, then add the *salam* leaves, lemongrass, and papaya and simmer gently until the papaya is tender. If the stock reduces too much, add more. Season to taste with pepper and salt and garnish with Crispy Fried Shallots.

Clear Chicken Soup

Clear Chicken Soup

4 cups (1 liter) Chicken Stock
  (page 73)
1/2 cup (125 ml) Basic Spice Paste
  (page 72)
1 teaspoon crushed black peppercorns
1 *salam* leaf (optional)
1 stalk lemongrass, tender inner part
  of bottom third only, bruised
14 oz (400 g) boneless chicken,
  skin removed, ground
Salt and pepper to taste
2 tablespoons Crispy Fried Shallots
  (page 73)

Bring the Chicken Stock to a boil in a stockpot or large saucepan. Wrap the Spice Paste and black peppercorns into a piece of cotton cloth and tie with a string. Add the Spice Paste bundle, the *salam* leaf, and lemongrass to the the soup and simmer for 10 minutes.

Add the ground chicken and simmer for 15 minutes. Remove the Spice Paste bundle from the soup and discard. Season to taste with salt and pepper. Garnish with Crispy Fried Shallots.

Green Papaya Soup

You can try making this soup with any summer squash or Chinese winter melon instead.

1 unripe papaya weighing roughly
  1 1/2 lbs (750 g)
4 cups (1 liter) Chicken Stock
  (page 73)
1 cup (250 ml) Basic Spice Paste
  (page 72)
2 *salam* leaves or bay leaves
1 stalk lemongrass, tender inner part
  of bottom third only, bruised
1/4 teaspoon ground white pepper
1 teaspoon salt
Crispy Fried Shallots (page 73)

Spinach and Tempeh in Coconut Milk

A Sumatran dish using protein-rich tempeh stewed with vegetables in a rich coconut gravy.

2 cups (500 ml) thick coconut milk
2 cloves
3 cakes tempeh (1 1/2 lbs/750 g),
  cubed
8 oz (250 g) spinach
1/2 teaspoon salt
1 green onion (scallion), sliced
1 red finger-length chilies, deseeded
  and diced

Spice Paste
1 teaspoon white peppercorns
1 1/2 in (4 cm) fresh turmeric root,
  peeled and sliced, or 1 1/2 teaspoons ground turmeric
1 in (2 1/2 cm) fresh ginger, sliced
4 cloves garlic, peeled
1 tablespoon shaved palm sugar or
  dark brown sugar

Make the Spice Paste by grinding all the ingredients to a paste in a mortar or blender, adding a little coconut milk if necessary to keep the mixture turning.

Bring the coconut milk to a boil in a saucepan. Add the Spice Paste, cloves, tempeh and spinach and bring to a boil again. Reduce the heat to low and simmer uncovered, until the vegetables are tender and the sauce has thickened, 7 to 10 minutes. Season with salt and garnish with freshly sliced green onion and chili.

Spinach and Tempeh in Coconut Milk (bottom left) and Sweet and Spicy Fried Tempeh Strips (top right, recipe on page 81)

Spicy Padang Eggs

8 hard-boiled eggs, peeled
2 cups (500 ml) thick coconut milk
1/2 turmeric leaf, shredded
1 tablespoon Tamarind Juice
 (page 18)
1/2 teaspoon salt
Crispy Fried Shallots (page 73)

Spice Paste
1 in (2 1/2 cm) fresh galangal
 sliced
1/2 in (1 cm) fresh turmeric root,
 sliced, or 1/2 teaspoon ground
 turmeric
1 in (2 1/2 cm) fresh ginger, sliced
2 to 4 bird's-eye chilies, deseeded
4–5 shallots, peeled
3 cloves garlic, peeled

Prepare the Spice Paste by grinding all the ingredients coarsely in a mortar or blender and adding a little coconut milk if necessary to keep the mixture turning. Set aside.

Bring the coconut milk slowly to a boil in a wok or saucepan. Add the Spice Paste and turmeric leaf (if using), mix well and simmer for 2 minutes. Reduce the heat to low, add the eggs and continue to simmer uncovered until the sauce thickens, 8 to 10 minutes. Season with the Tamarind Juice and salt, simmer for 1 more minute and remove from the heat. Serve hot garnished with Crispy Fried Shallots.

Spicy Padang Eggs

Sayur Asam
Vegetables in Tamarind Broth

4 cups (1 liter) water
2 *salam* leaves or bay leaves
1 in (2 1/2 cm) fresh galangal, bruised
1 fresh or frozen corn cob, cut into
 sections
2 cups (6 oz/180 g) spinach
1 cup (100 g) green beans, cut into
 short lengths
1–2 green finger-length chilies,
 deseeded and cut into short
 lengths (optional)
1/2 cup (75 g) lightly boiled raw
 peanuts or *melinjo* nuts
1/4 cup (60 ml) Tamarind Juice
 (page 18) or 4 to 6 carambola
 (*belimbing wuluh*), sliced
1/2 cup (125 g) fresh shrimp, peeled
 and deveined (optional)
1 ripe tomato, cut into wedges
2 tablespoons sugar
1/2 teaspoon salt

Spice Paste
2–3 red finger-length chilies,
 deseeded
3–4 shallots, peeled
3 cloves garlic, peeled
1/2 teaspoon salt

Grind all the Spice Paste ingredients to a smooth paste in a mortar or blender, adding a little water if necessary to keep the mixture turning. Set aside.

Bring the water to a boil over medium heat in a large saucepan. Add the Spice Paste, *salam* leaves (if using) and galangal, mix well and bring to a boil again, then simmer uncovered for 2 minutes. Add the corn and boil for 2 more minutes, then add the vegetables, chili (if using), peanuts and Tamarind Juice or carambola.

Bring the mixture to a boil and simmer until the vegetables are tender, 3 to 5 minutes. Finally add the shrimp, tomato and sugar, and simmer for 1 to 2 minutes until the shrimp turn pink. Season with the salt and remove from the heat. Serve hot as part of a rice-based meal.

Stewed Eggplant

2–3 red finger-length chilies,
 deseeded and sliced
2–3 shallots, sliced
2 cloves garlic, sliced
2 cups (500 ml) water
3 slender eggplants (1 lb/500 g),
 halved lengthwise and sliced
2 tablespoons Tamarind Juice
 (page 18)
1 ripe tomato, cut into wedges
2 teaspoons shaved palm sugar
 or dark brown sugar
1/2 teaspoon salt

Garnishes
Crispy Fried Shallots (page 73)
2 tablespoons sliced Chinese celery
 leaves
1 green onion (scallion), sliced

In a large saucepan, bring the sliced chili, shallot, garlic and water to a boil over medium heat, then simmer uncovered for 3 to 5 minutes. Add the eggplants and Tamarind Juice, and simmer until half cooked, about 2 minutes. Add the tomato and sugar, and simmer until the tomato is soft, about 2 minutes. Season with the salt and remove from the heat.

Transfer to a serving bowl and serve hot, garnished with Crispy Fried Shallots, celery leaves and green onion.

Spinach with Coconut and Spicy Dressing

10 oz (300 g) spinach, washed and
 drained
1 kaffir lime leaf
1 clove garlic, peeled
1 teaspoon shaved palm sugar or
 dark brown sugar
1 cup (100 g) freshly grated
 coconut
2–3 bird's-eye chilies or red finger-
 length chilies, deseeded
1/2 teaspoon dried shrimp paste
 (*trasi*), dry-roasted (page 13)
1 teaspoon salt
1 teaspoon lime or lemon juice
2 tablespoons warm water

2 tablespoons roasted unsalted
 peanuts
4 limes, halved, to serve

Wash the spinach well and discard the tough stems. Cut into lengths. Blanch in boiling water for 1 to 2 minutes, then set aside on a plate.

Grind the kaffir lime leaf, garlic, palm sugar and grated coconut in a blender until fine and set aside in a bowl, then grind the chilies, dried shrimp paste, salt, lime or lemon juice and water to a smooth paste.

To serve, toss the blanched spinach with the dried shrimp paste mixture. Sprinkle the grated coconut mixture and peanuts on top and serve with lime halves on the side.

Vegetables with Spicy Coconut Sauce

7 oz (200 g) green beans, cut into
 lengths
6 oz (180 g) spinach leaves
1 cup (50 g) bean sprouts, seed
 coats and tails discarded
Crispy Fried Shallots (page 73)

Coconut Sauce
1 teaspoon ground turmeric
2–3 bird's-eye chilies, or red finger-
 length chilies, deseeded
2–3 shallots, peeled
2 cloves garlic, peeled
1 teaspoon shaved palm sugar or
 dark brown sugar
1 teaspoon dried shrimp paste
 (*trasi*), dry-roasted (page 13)
1 cup (100 g) freshly grated or
 unsweetened desiccated coconut
1 cups (250 ml) water
1 *salam* leaf or bay leaf
1/4 teaspoon salt

Make the Coconut Sauce by grinding the turmeric, chilies, shallots, garlic, palm sugar and shrimp paste to a smooth paste in a mortar or blender, adding a little water if necessary to keep the mixture turning. Place the ground paste with all the other ingredients in a saucepan and simmer uncovered over medium heat for 5 to 10 minutes until the sauce thickens. Remove from the heat and set aside to cool.

Bring a saucepan of water to boil over medium heat. Blanch the vegetables for 1 to 2 minutes. Remove from the heat, drain well and arrange on a serving platter.

Asparagus in Coconut

Drizzle the Coconut Sauce over the vegetables and serve garnished with Crispy Fried Shallots or serve the sauce on the side.

Asparagus in Coconut

The young tips of several varieties of wild ferns are enjoyed in many parts of Indonesia. They are sold in wet markets throughout Southeast Asia and have an excellent flavor. Young asparagus or spinach work equally well for this dish.

2 cups (500 ml) thin coconut milk
1 lb (500 g) young asparagus, washed
2 *salam* leaves or bay leaves
1 tablespoon Tamarind Juice (page 18)
1/2 teaspoon salt

Spice Paste
1 in (2 1/2 cm) fresh galangal sliced
1/2 in (1 cm) fresh turmeric root, sliced, or 1/2 teaspoon ground turmeric
1 in (2 1/2 cm) fresh ginger, sliced
1–2 red finger-length chilies, deseeded
2–3 shallots, peeled
2 cloves garlic, peeled

Make the Spice Paste by grinding all the ingredients to a smooth paste in a mortar or blender, adding a little coconut milk if necessary to keep the mixture turning.

Bring the Spice Paste and coconut milk to a boil in a saucepan. Reduce the heat to medium and simmer uncovered for 2 minutes. Add the fern tips or asparagus, *salam* leaves and Tamarind Juice, mix well and bring to a boil again, then simmer for about 15 minutes, stirring frequently until the vegetables are tender. Season with the salt and remove from the heat.

Transfer to a serving casserole and serve immediately with steamed rice.

Sweet and Spicy Fried Tempeh Strips

Sweetened with palm sugar and spiced with galangal, lemongrass, shrimp paste, tamarind and chilies, this dish is a Javanese favorite (see photo on page 79).

2 cakes tempeh (1 lb/500 g in total)
Oil for deep-frying
2 shallots, peeled and sliced
3 cloves garlic, peeled and sliced
1–2 red finger-length chilies, deseeded and thinly sliced
1 in (2 1/2 cm) fresh galangal, sliced
2 stalks lemongrass, tender inner part of bottom third only, bruised
3 tablespoons water
1/2 teaspoon dried shrimp paste (*trasi*), dry-roasted (page 13)
3 tablespoons shaved palm sugar or dark brown sugar
2 tablespoons Tamarind Juice (page 18)
1/2 teaspoon salt

Slice the tempeh into long, narrow strips. Heat the oil in a wok over high heat and deep-fry the tempeh strips until browned and crispy, 3 to 5 minutes. Remove from the hot oil and set aside to drain on paper towels.

Drain the oil from the wok and wipe it clean. Heat 1 tablespoon of fresh oil in the wok over medium heat and stir-fry the shallots, garlic, chilies, galangal, lemongrass and dried shrimp paste for 3 to 5 minutes until fragrant. Add the palm sugar, water and Tamarind Juice, and stir-fry until the sugar has completely dissolved and begins to caramelize. Add the deep-fried tempeh strips and stir-fry until the sauce has thickened and completely coats the tempeh, 3 to 5 minutes. Season with the salt and remove from the heat. Discard the galangal and lemongrass, and garnish with sliced chili, if desired.

Pork in Sweet Soy

This Balinese sweet pork dish, with a hint of ginger and plenty of chilies to spice it up, often appears on festive occasions.

2 tablespoons oil
3–4 shallots, peeled and sliced
5 cloves garlic, peeled and sliced
1 1/2 lbs (750 g) boneless pork shoulder or leg, cubed
3 in (8 cm) ginger, peeled and sliced lengthwise
4 tablespoons sweet Indonesian soy sauce (*kecap manis*)
2 tablespoons soy sauce

Pork in Sweet Soy

1 teaspoon black peppercorns, crushed
2 cups (500 ml) Chicken Stock (page 73)
4–5 bird's-eye chilies, left whole

Heat the oil in a wok or heavy saucepan. Add the shallots and garlic and stir-fry for 2 minutes over medium heat or until lightly colored. Add the pork and ginger and continue to stir-fry for 2 more minutes over high heat. Add both types of soy sauces and black pepper and continue stir-frying for 1 minute.

Pour in the Chicken Stock and chilies and simmer over medium heat for approximately 1 hour. When done, there should be very little sauce left and the meat should be shiny and dark brown. If the meat becomes too dry during cooking, add a little Chicken Stock.

Pork with Tomatoes

A simple recipe from Kalimantan, where pork (particularly wild boar from the jungle) is popular among the Dyaks.

1 1/2 lbs (750 g) pork, cut into bite-sized chunks
4 ripe tomatoes, cut into wedges
4–6 garlic chives (*kucai*), or green onions (scallions), cut into lengths
1 stalk lemongrass, tender inner part of bottom third only, bruised
1 cup (250 ml) water

Spice Paste
1 in (2 1/2 cm) ginger sliced
2–3 red finger-length chilies, deseeded
4 shallots, peeled

Make the Spice Paste by grinding all the ingredients to a smooth paste in a mortar or blender, adding a little water to keep the mixture turning.

Bring the Spice Paste and all the other ingredients to a boil in a wok or saucepan, then simmer over medium heat until the pork is tender, 3 to 5 minutes, adding a little sugar if the tomatoes are quite sour and a little water if the sauce dries up before the meat is cooked. Remove from the heat and serve immediately with steamed rice.

Fragrant Ginger Pork

In Northern Sulawesi, where there are many Christians and Chinese, the Muslim strictures on eating pork do not apply.

1¹/₂ lbs (700 g) boneless pork shoulder or leg
2¹/₂ in (6 cm) fresh ginger, peeled and sliced
2–3 red finger-length chilies, deseeded
3 shallots, peeled
2 tablespoons oil
5 kaffir lime leaves
2 turmeric leaves (optional)
3 stalks lemongrass, tender inner part of bottom third only, sliced
¹/₂ teaspoon salt

Cut the pork into bite-sized chunks. Set aside.

Beef Rendang (Spicy Beef in Coconut)

Grind the ginger, chilies and shallots in a mortar or blender, adding a little water to keep the mixture turning. Set aside.

Heat the oil in wok over medium heat and stir-fry the ground mixture until fragrant, 3 to 5 minutes. Add the pork and all the other ingredients and stir-fry for about 2 minutes, then reduce the heat to low, cover the wok and simmer the pork in its own juices until tender, 3 to 5 minutes. Add a little warm water if the gravy dries up before the meat is cooked. Remove from the heat and serve with steamed rice.

Dry Spiced Beef

This dish is so wonderfully flavored that it's worth making a large amount. It is also excellent as a finger food with cocktails.

2¹/₂ lbs (1¹/₄ kgs) beef top round, cut in 4 steaks of 8 oz (250 g) each
8 cloves garlic, peeled
2 teaspoons coriander seeds
1 tablespoon shaved palm sugar or dark brown sugar
1–2 red finger-length chilies, deseeded
2 tablespoons galangal, sliced
2 teaspoons dried shrimp paste (*trasi*), dry-roasted (page 13)
2 cloves, ground
1 teaspoon salt
1 teaspoon black peppercorns, ground
2 tablespoons oil
2 teaspoons lime juice

Bring 20 cups (5 liters) of lightly salted water to a boil in a stockpot. Add the beef and boil for approximately 1 hour until very tender. Remove from the stock. The meat must be so tender that its fibers separate very easily. Reserve the stock. Pound the meat with a mallet until flat and then shred by hand into fine fibers.

Place the garlic, coriander, palm sugar, red chilies, galangal, dried shrimp paste, cloves, salt, and pepper in a food processor and blend coarsely, or grind in a stone mortar. Heat the oil in a heavy saucepan and stir-fry the marinade for 2 minutes over medium heat. Add the shredded beef, mix well and stir-fry until dry. Season with lime juice. Remove from the heat and allow to cool. Serve at room temperature with steamed rice.

Beef Rendang
Spicy Beef in Coconut

This is a very popular Indonesian dish, with chunks of beef stewed in coconut and spices.

2 lbs (1 kg) top round or stewing beef, cut into bite-sized chunks
2 tablespoons oil
2 cups (500 ml) coconut cream or 3 cups (750 ml) thick coconut milk
2 *salam* leaves
3 kaffir lime leaves
1 cinnamon stick
2 tablespoons shaved palm sugar or dark brown sugar
2 teaspoons salt
Crispy Fried Shallots (page 73)

Spice Paste
1 teaspoon black peppercorns
3 in (8 cm) fresh galangal, sliced
2 stalks lemongrass, tender inner part of bottom third only, sliced
2 in (5 cm) fresh ginger, sliced
3–4 red finger-length chilies, deseeded
8–10 shallots, peeled and sliced
8–10 cloves garlic, peeled

Make the Spice Paste by grinding all the ingredients very coarsely in a mortar or blender, adding a little coconut cream if necessary to keep the mixture turning.

Heat the oil in a wok over high heat and stir-fry the Spice Paste until fragrant, 1 to 2 minutes. Add the beef chunks and

all the other ingredients, except the Crispy Fried Shallots, and bring to a boil, stirring constantly. Reduce the heat to medium and simmer uncovered for about 1 hour, then reduce the heat to low and continue simmering for 1 more hour, stirring from time to time until the meat is very tender and most of the liquid has evaporated. By this time, the oil will have separated from the milk. Continue to stir-fry the beef for about 25 minutes until it turns a dark brown color, then remove from the heat.

Transfer the beef to a serving platter, garnish with Crispy Fried Shallots and serve with steamed rice. This dish actually tastes better if left to sit for several hours, or even overnight in the refrigerator, then stir-fry it again for several minutes before serving.

Lemongrass Fish

2 lbs (1 kg) freshwater fish, either whole fish or fillets
1 teaspoon salt
1 teaspoon ground white pepper
2 cups (500 ml) water
2 stalks lemongrass, tender inner part of bottom third only, bruised
2 tablespoons Tamarind Juice (page 18)
1 green onion (scallion), sliced
¹/₂ lemon, cut into wedges

Spice Paste
6 macadamia nuts or candlenuts, roughly chopped
1 in (2¹/₂ cm) fresh galangal sliced
1 in (2¹/₂ cm) turmeric root, sliced, or 1 teaspoon ground turmeric
1 in (2¹/₂ cm) fresh ginger, sliced
2–3 red finger-length chilies, deseeded
4–5 shallots, peeled
4 cloves garlic, peeled
¹/₂ teaspoon salt

If using whole fish, scale, gut and clean the fish, then make several shallow diagonal slits on each side. Season the fish with the salt and pepper, and set aside for 15 minutes.

Grind the Spice Paste ingredients to a smooth paste in a mortar or blender, adding a little water if necessary to keep the mixture turning.

Bring the Spice Paste, water, lemongrass and Tamarind Juice to a boil in a wok or skillet.

Balinese Fried Squid

Scrub and clean the lobsters. Bring the water to a boil over medium heat in a pot, add the lobsters and boil for 10 to 15 minutes. Remove them from the heat and immediately plunge them into a basin of iced water for 1 minute to cool. Strain and reserve the stock. Drain the lobsters and remove the meat from the shells. Discard the shells.

Prepare the Spice Paste by grinding all the ingredients (except the oil, *salam* leaf and Tamarind Juice) to a smooth paste in a mortar or blender, adding a little oil if necessary to keep the mixture turning. Heat the oil over medium heat in a wok or skillet and stir-fry the Spice Paste until fragrant, 3 to 5 minutes. Add the *salam* leaf and Tamarind Juice and simmer for about 2 minutes, then remove from the heat. Set aside.

In a pot, bring the lobster stock, Spice Paste, lemongrass, lime leaves and vinegar to a boil over medium heat, then simmer uncovered for 3 to 5 minutes. Add the coconut cream, mix well and bring to a boil again, then simmer for about 5 minutes. Add the lobster meat, season with the salt and simmer for 1 minute. Remove from the heat.

Transfer to a serving bowl, garnish with Crispy Fried Shallots and serve hot with steamed rice.

Reduce the heat to medium and simmer uncovered for about 10 minutes, adding more water if the sauce evaporates too quickly. Add the fish, cover and simmer until cooked, 6 to 10 minutes, turning the fish over from time to time to cook it evenly on both sides. Remove from the heat.

Transfer the fish to a serving platter and pour the sauce over it. Garnish with sliced green onion and serve hot with lemon wedges.

Balinese Fried Squid

If squid is unavailable, replace with any firm fish fillets, such as snapper or sea bass.

1 1/2 lbs (750 g) baby squid
1 tablespoon lime juice
1/2 teaspoon ground white pepper
1/2 teaspoon salt
3 tablespoons oil
4–5 shallots, peeled and sliced
1–2 red finger-length chilies, deseeded and sliced
1/2 cup (125 ml) Basic Spice Paste (page 72)
1 cup (250 ml) Chicken Stock (page 73)
5 sprigs Lemon Basil, sliced
Crispy Fried Shallots (page 73)
Sprigs of Lemon Basil, to garnish

Remove the skin of the squid and pull out the tentacles and head. Cut off and discard the head and beaky portion, but reserve the tentacles, if desired. Clean the squid thoroughly inside and out. Marinate the squid with the lime juice, pepper and salt.

Heat the oil in a wok, add the shallots, chilies and squid and stir-fry for 2 minutes over high heat. Add the Spice Paste and continue to stir-fry for 1 more minute. Pour in the Chicken Stock, add the sliced basil and bring to a boil. Reduce the heat and simmer for 1 minute.

Season with salt to taste and garnish with Lemon Basil and Crispy Fried Shallots.

Curried Lobsters

4 fresh lobsters (6 lbs/2 1/2 kgs)
6 cups (1 1/2 liters) water
2 stalks lemongrass, tender inner part of bottom third only, bruised
2 kaffir lime leaves
1/4 teaspoon white vinegar
1 1/2 cups (375 ml) coconut cream
1 teaspoon salt
Crispy Fried Shallots (page 73)

Spice Paste
3 macadamia nuts or candlenuts, roughly chopped

2–3 red finger-length chilies
4–5 shallots, peeled
3 cloves garlic, peeled
2 in (5 cm) turmeric root, sliced, or 2 teaspoons ground turmeric
2 in (5 cm) ginger, sliced
1 1/2 teaspoons coriander seeds
1/2 teaspoon dried shrimp paste (*trasi*), dry-roasted (page 13)
2 tablespoons oil
1 *salam* leaf or bay leaf
2 tablespoons Tamarind Juice (page 18)

Curried Lobsters

Classic Grilled Chicken

Ayam Panggang

This is one of Indonesia's most traditional dishes that is served on special occasions everywhere throughout the archipelago.

1 fresh chicken (2^1/4 lbs/1 kg)
2 tablespoons oil
2–3 bird's eye chilies or finger-length chilies
3 stalks lemongrass, thick bottom third only, outer layers discarded, inner part bruised
2^1/2 cups (675 ml) thin coconut milk
2 cups (500 ml) Chicken Stock (page 73)
2 *salam* leaves (optional)
1 teaspoon salt
1 teaspoon freshly ground black pepper
Sweet Indonesian soy sauce (*kecap manis*), for glazing
1 portion Sambal Kecap (page 73)

Spice Paste
3 macadamia nuts or candlenuts, roughly chopped
^{1}/2 in (1 cm) fresh *kencur* root, peeled and sliced (optional)
1 in (2^1/2 cm) fresh galangal, peeled and sliced
1 in (2^1/2 cm) fresh turmeric, peeled and sliced, or 1 teaspoon ground turmeric
4 shallots, peeled
5 cloves garlic, peeled
2 tablespoons shaved palm sugar or dark brown sugar

Clean and cut the chicken into serving pieces and press to flatten.

Make the Spice Paste by grinding all the ingredients to a smooth paste in a mortar or blender, adding a little oil if necessary to keep the mixture turning.

Heat the oil in a wok or large saucepan over medium heat and stir-fry the ground paste, together with the chilies and 2 stalks of the lemongrass until the mixture is fragrant and changes to a golden color, 3 to 5 minutes. Add the coconut milk, Chicken Stock and remaining lemongrass, and bring to a boil, then reduce the heat to low and simmer uncovered for about 5 minutes. Add the chicken, *salam* leaves, salt and pepper, and continue to simmer for about 30 minutes, turning the chicken frequently in the pan to cook it evenly and allow the spices to penetrate the meat. Turn off the heat and allow the chicken to cool in the sauce to room temperature.

Remove the chicken pieces from the sauce and dry in an open, airy place for 30 minutes, then grill the chicken pieces over hot charcoal or under a preheated broiler for 3 to 5 minutes on each side and brush with a little sweet Indonesian soy sauce to glaze the skin. Serve the grilled chicken with steamed rice, vegetables and a bowl of Sambal Kecap on the side.

Classic Grilled Chicken (Ayam Panggang)

Chicken Simmered in Mild Coconut Gravy (Opor Ayam)

Chicken Simmered in Mild Coconut Gravy

Opor Ayam

A mild dish without chilies but redolent of coriander, lemongrass, *salam* leaves and galangal, *Opor Ayam* is a universal favorite in Indonesia.

3 cups (750 ml) thin coconut milk
1 fresh chicken (2 lbs/1 kg), cleaned and cut into serving pieces
1 stalk lemongrass, thick bottom third only, outer layers discarded, inner part bruised
2 *salam* leaves or bay leaves
^{1}/2 teaspoon salt
^{1}/2 cup (125 ml) thick coconut milk

Spice Paste
5 macadamia nuts or candlenuts, roughly chopped
1 in (2^1/2 cm) fresh galangal, peeled and sliced
3 shallots, peeled
3 cloves garlic, peeled
2 tablespoons coriander seeds or 1 tablespoon ground coriander
1 teaspoon ground white pepper
^{1}/2 tablespoon shaved palm sugar or dark brown sugar

Make the Spice Paste by grinding all the ingredients to a smooth paste in a mortar or blender, adding a little coconut milk if necessary to keep the mixture turning.

Bring the thin coconut milk and Spice Paste to a boil over high heat in a wok or large saucepan. Add the chicken pieces, lemongrass, *salam* leaves and salt, mix well and bring to a boil again. Reduce the heat to low and simmer uncovered for about 30 minutes, until the chicken is cooked and the sauce has reduced by a third. Finally add the thick coconut milk, simmer for 5 more minutes and remove from the heat.

Transfer to a serving casserole and garnish with fresh chilies if desired.

Javanese Fried Chicken

Seasoned chicken that is simmered in coconut and spices until almost cooked, then flash-fried to give it a crispy coating, make this central Javanese dish a favorite.

Oil for deep-frying
2 *salam* leaves (optional)
1 fresh chicken (2^1/4 lbs/1 kg), cleaned and cut into serving pieces
2 cups (500 ml) thin coconut milk
2 limes, cut into wedges
1 portion Sambal Trasi (page 72)

Spice Paste
1 tablespoon coriander seeds or 2 teaspoons ground coriander
^{1}/2 in (1 cm) fresh galangal, sliced
^{1}/2 in (1 cm) fresh turmeric, peeled and sliced, or ^{3}/4 teaspoon ground turmeric
^{3}/4 in (2 cm) fresh ginger, sliced
4–5 shallots, peeled
3 cloves garlic, peeled
1 tablespoon shaved palm sugar or dark brown sugar
^{1}/4 teaspoon salt

Grind the Spice Paste ingredients to a smooth paste in a mortar or blender, adding a little oil if necessary to keep the mixture turning.

Heat 2 tablespoons of the oil in a wok over medium heat and stir-fry the Spice Paste and *salam* leaves until fragrant, 3 to 5 minutes. Add the chicken pieces and stir-fry to coat them well with the spices, then stir in the coconut milk and bring the mixture to a boil. Reduce the heat to low and simmer uncovered until the chicken is almost cooked and the sauce has almost dried up, about 20 minutes. Remove from the heat and set aside to cool.

Just before serving, heat the oil in a wok until very hot and dee-fry the chicken until crisp and golden brown on all sides, about 3 minutes. Serve with lime wedges and a small bowl of Sambal Trasi on the side.

Balinese Spiced Chicken
Bebek Betutu

Duck is also delicious when cooked in this way—which is essentially the Balinese equivalent of a spicy Rendang.

1 large roasting chicken or duck (about 3¹/₂ lbs/1³/₄ kgs)
2 tablespoons oil
4 cups (1 liter) thick coconut milk
2 stalks lemongrass, tender inner part of bottom third only, bruised
2 *salam* leaves (optional)
1 teaspoon salt
1 teaspoon ground black pepper

Spice Paste
3 macadamia nuts or candlenuts, roughly chopped
1 in (2¹/₂ cm) fresh galangal, sliced
1 in (2¹/₂ cm) fresh *kencur* root, peeled and sliced (optional)
1 in (2¹/₂ cm) fresh turmeric root, peeled and sliced, or 1 teaspoon ground turmeric
2–3 red finger-length chilies, deseeded
8–10 shallots, peeled
6 cloves garlic, peeled
2 cloves
2 teaspoons coriander seeds or 1 teaspoons ground coriander
¹/₄ teaspoon black pepper
¹/₄ teaspoon freshly grated nutmeg or ground nutmeg
1 teaspoon dried shrimp paste (*trasi*), dry-roasted (page 13)

Clean and cut the chicken or duck into serving pieces, then dry with paper towels.

Make the Spice Paste by grinding all the ingredients in a mortar or blender until fine, adding a little oil if necessary to keep the mixture turning.

Heat the oil in a wok over high heat and stir-fry the Spice Paste until fragrant, about 3 minutes. Add the chicken or duck pieces and stir-fry for about 5 minutes. Add the coconut milk, lemongrass, *salam* leaves, salt and pepper, mix well and bring to a boil. Reduce the heat to medium low and simmer uncovered, turning frequently, until the chicken or duck pieces are tender and the sauce has thickened, 30 to 35 minutes. Remove from the heat. Garnish with Crispy Fried Shallots and serve with fragrant steamed rice.

Chicken with Sambal

Chicken with Sambal

This recipe comes Kalimantan, where it is usually made with free-range or kampung chickens. The sour tomatoes and lemon juice makes a delicious counterpoint to the sweet spiciness of the special sambal served.

1 fresh free-range chicken (2¹/₄ lbs/1 kg), cleaned and cut into serving pieces
1 teaspoon salt
1 tablespoon lime or lemon juice
2 cups (500 ml) water
3–4 red finger-length chilies, deseeded and sliced
8–10 shallots, peeled and sliced
4 unripe tomatoes, sliced
1 sprig Asian basil
3 kaffir lime leaves
2 green onions (scallions), sliced
¹/₂ in (1 cm) fresh ginger, sliced

Fragrant Chili Sambal
¹/₄ teaspoon freshly grated nutmeg or ground nutmeg
3–4 red finger-length chilies, deseeded
5–6 shallots, peeled
3 cloves garlic, peeled
1 teaspoon salt
2 tablespoons shaved palm sugar or dark brown sugar
1 teaspoon dried shrimp paste (*trasi*), dry-roasted (page 13)
1 stalk lemongrass, tender inner part of bottom third only, bruised
1 tablespoon oil

¹/₂ in (1 cm) fresh galangal, peeled and sliced
2 *salam* leaf
2 tablespoons Tamarind Juice (page 18)

Season the chicken pieces with the salt and lime or lemon juice, then set aside to marinate for at least 20 minutes.

Make the Fragrant Chili Sambal by grinding the first 7 ingredients to a smooth paste in a mortar or blender, adding a little oil if necessary to keep the mixture turning. Heat the oil in a wok or skillet over medium heat and stir-fry the ground paste with with *salam* leaf, lemongrass and galangal until fragrant, 3 to 5 minutes. Add the Tamarind Juice and bring the mixture to a boil, then reduce the heat to low and simmer for about 1 minute. Remove from the heat and set aside to cool. Discard the *salam* leaf, lemongrass and galangal.

Bring the water to a boil in a wok or large saucepan. Add the marinated chicken and simmer uncovered over medium heat until the chicken is just tender, 5 to 10 minutes. Add all the other ingredients, mix well and cook for 15 more minutes before removing from the heat. Serve immediately with a serving bowl of Fragrant Chili Sambal on the side or serve mixed with the Fragrant Chili Sambal.

Balinese Spiced Chicken (Bebek Betutu)

Black Rice Pudding

It's hard to find a foreign visitor to Bali who does not fall in love with the wonderful nutty flavor and melt-in-your-mouth smooth texture of Black Rice Pudding, served with swirls of delicious coconut cream.

1 cup (200 g) uncooked black
   glutinous rice (see note)
3/4 cup (150 g) uncooked white
   glutinous rice
6 cups (11/2 liters) water
2 pandanus leaves, tied into a knot,
   or 1 drop vanilla extract
1/4 cup (50 g) shaved palm sugar or
   dark brown sugar
Pinch of salt
1/2 cup (125 ml) coconut cream

Rinse both types of glutinous rice in several changes of water until the water runs clear, and soak overnight.

In a saucepan, bring the glutinous rice, water and pandanus leaves or extract to a boil over medium heat and simmer uncovered for about 40 minutes, stirring occasionally until the rice is soft and cooked, with porridge-like consistency. Discard the pandanus leaves, if using. Add the palm sugar and stir until the sugar is dissolved. Reduce the heat to low and simmer for about 5 minutes before removing from the heat.

Banana Fritters (Pisang Goreng, top) and Steamed Banana Cakes (bottom)

Combine the coconut cream and salt in a bowl and mix well.

To serve, spoon the pudding into individual serving bowls and top with the salted coconut cream.

Shaved Ice Dessert
Es Campur

Indonesia has a multitude of thirst-quenching sweet snacks that are also enjoyed as desserts.

Black Rice Pudding

Known as Es Campur (Mixed Ice), the contents of this dessert depend upon the availability of the ingredients and the preference of the individual. The ones listed here are just suggestions. Popular also in the Philippines, where it is called Halo Halo.

1 portion Palm Sugar Syrup (page
   73)
2 cups (about 250 g) diced fruit
   (papaya, avocado and pineapple)
1 young coconut, flesh removed with
   a spoon, 1 cup (250 ml) of the
   coconut juice reserved (optional,
   see note)
1/2 cup (125 ml) sweetened condensed milk, cream or evaporated
   milk
Crushed ice

Drain the jelly cubes, fermented tapioca (if using) and *kolang kaling*. Cut the coconut flesh into bite-sized pieces.

Place the diced fruits with all the other ingredients, except the crushed ice, in a mixing bowl and mix well. To serve, ladle the mixture into individual glasses and top with some crushed ice.

Look for cans or bottles of young coconut flesh in Filipino stores under the name buko.

Steamed Banana Cakes

6 small or 2 large ripe bananas
11/4 cups (150 g) rice flour
4 tablespoons mung bean flour or
   tapioca flour
2 cups (500 ml) thin coconut milk
1/4 cup (50 g) sugar
Pinch of salt
Twelve 7-in (18-cm) square pieces
   of banana leaves, for wrapping
Toothpicks, to fasten

Peel and halve each small banana or if using large bananas, slice each diagonally into six thick slices. Set aside.

Combine both types of flour and 1 1/2 cups (325 ml) of the coconut milk in a bowl into a smooth batter, free of any lumps. Set aside.

Combine the remaining coconut milk, sugar and salt in a saucepan, and heat over medium heat, mixing well until the sugar is dissolved. Bring to a boil, then pour in the batter and continue to cook, stirring continously until the mixture thickens, 5 to 10 minutes. Remove from the heat and set aside to cool.

Scald the banana leaves by pouring boiling water over them in a basin, so they become flexible. Drain and place them on a clean work surface.

To wrap the cakes, spread 2 tablespoons of the flour mixture across the center of a piece of banana leaf. Lay a slice of the banana on top and then spread another 2 tablespoons of the flour mixture over it, covering the banana. Wrap by folding one side of the banana leaf over the filling, then the other, forming a tight parcel. Tuck both ends underneath and fasten with toothpicks. Continue to wrap the remaining ingredients in this manner.

Steam the parcels in a wok on a rack over boiling water or in a steamer for about 20 minutes. Remove from the heat and allow to cool before serving.

> Mung bean flour (*tepong hoen kwe*) is sold in paper-wrapped cylinders—sometimes, the flour is colored pink or green and the paper wrapper correspondingly colored. It gives a more delicate texture to desserts than rice flour, although the latter is an acceptable substitute.

Banana Fritters
Pisang Goreng

This is a great way to use up over-ripe bananas, by mashing them up with flour, sugar and coconut cream and deep-frying them.

2 large or 6 small over-ripe bananas, peeled
1 tablespoon sugar
1/2 teaspoon salt (optional)
1 tablespoon flour
1/4 cup (60 ml) coconut cream
Oil, for deep-frying

In a mixing bowl, mash the bananas with the sugar, salt (if using), flour and coconut cream into a sticky, slightly moist batter.

Heat the oil in a wok or large saucepan until very hot. Using very moist fingers, pinch about 1 heaped tablespoon of the batter, roll it into a ball and gently lower it into the hot oil. Deep-fry for 3 to 5 minutes, turning occasionally, until crispy and golden brown on all sides. Do not overcrowd the pan with the batter or the temperature of the oil will drop. Remove from the hot oil and drain on paper towels.

Transfer to a serving platter and serve warm with ice cream or a bit of coconut cream on top.

Sweet Coconut Pancakes
Dadar

These pancakes, with a sweet coconut filling known as *unti*, are a popular snack food and are sometimes eaten for breakfast.

1 cup (150 g) flour, sifted
2 eggs
2 cups (500 ml) thick coconut milk
1/2 teaspoon salt
2 tablespoons oil

Coconut Filling (*Unti*)
1/2 cup (100 g) shaved palm sugar or dark brown sugar
1/4 cup (60 ml) water
1 cup (100 g) freshly grated coconut
1/4 teaspoon salt
1 pandanus leaf, tied into a knot

Make the Coconut Filling by bringing the sugar and water to a boil in a saucepan. Reduce the heat to low and simmer uncovered for about 10 minutes, stirring occasionally, until the sugar is dissolved and the mixture turns syrupy. Add all the other ingredients and cook, stirring constantly, for 10 to 15 minutes, until the mixture dries up. Remove from the heat, discard the pandanus leaf and set aside.

To make the pancakes, combine the flour, eggs, coconut milk and salt in a mixing bowl, and whisk into a smooth batter that has a pouring consistency. Strain to remove any lumps. Lightly grease a non-stick wok or skillet and heat over low heat. Stir the batter and ladle 1 scoop (about 3 tablespoons) onto the pan and turn the pan to obtain a thin round layer, about 7 in (18 cm) in diameter. Cook until the pancake sets and begins to brown, then flip it over and cook for a few seconds on the other side, and remove from the heat. Continue to make the pancakes until all the batter is used up.

To assemble, place a pancake on a flat surface and top with 2 tablespoons of the Coconut Filling. Fold one side of the pancake over the Filling, then fold in the sides and roll up tightly into a cylinder. Assemble the remaining pancakes in the same manner.

Sweet Coconut Pancakes (Dadar)

"Japanese cuisine today is a melting pot of culinary influences from and around the world, refined and adapted to reflect local preferences in taste and presentation."

JAPAN

From the land of endless ingenuity has come a cuisine designed for the eyes as well as the palate.

Left: Everyone enjoys a box lunch, from school children and salary men to Buddhist monks.

Right: The serene beauty of Kyoto's Golden Pavilion temple is emblematic of traditional Japanese culture.

More than any other cuisine in the world, Japanese food is a complete aesthetic experience for the eyes, the nose and the palate. The presentation of food is as important as the food itself, with great care given to detail, color, form, and balance. In Japan, cuisine is culture, and culture cuisine; food is meant to create order out of chaos, complement nature from whence it came and still be presentational. It is a cuisine developed out of austerity and a sense of restraint.

The Land and its People

Japan's position north-east on the Southeast Asian monsoonal belt means the islands generally experience a temperate oceanic climate. Surrounded by sea, the Japanese have made its bounty—seaweed, fish and shellfish—a vital part of their diet. There is a Japanese saying that a meal should always include "something from the mountain and something from the sea," hence vegetables and rice. Poultry and meat are also eaten, although they

are less important than the humble soybean, which appears as nutritionally rich bean curd (*tofu*); as *miso*, fermented soybean paste used for soups and seasoning; and as soy sauce.

Over 43 percent of the nation's 124 million people is crammed into the three major coastal metropolises of Tokyo, Osaka, and Nagoya. Fully two-thirds of the land is mountainous or forested; just over 14 percent is agricultural, and a little over four percent is used for housing.

Japan is composed of four main islands—Hokkaido, Honshu, Shikoku, and Kyushu—and several thousand smaller islands stretching 1900 miles from Hokkaido to Okinawa.

Hokkaido is a land of wide expanses, dairy farms, ranches, and meadows, reminiscent of the American Midwest, and home to the Ainu, the indigenous people of Japan, a small minority. They were once hunters and fishermen who are thought to have roamed large areas of northern Honshu.

Central Japan encompasses the Sea of Japan

Each season has its special foods. Restaurants and private homes change their serving dishes to suit the season, as in this autumnal spread.

a wide variety of vegetarian foods prepared in one of five standard cooking methods. *Shojin ryori* guidelines place emphasis on food of five colors (green, red, yellow, white, and black-purple) and six flavors (bitter, sour, sweet, hot, salty, and delicate). It was an extremely important culinary influence and the tradition lives on today. *Shojin ryori* also led to the development of *cha kaiseki*, food served before the tea ceremony, in the mid–16th century.

Japan's trade with the outside world from the 14th to 16th centuries brought many new influences. Kabocha, the green-skinned winter squash, was introduced by the Portuguese in the 16th century. The Portuguese are also credited with introducing *tempura* (batter-fried foods) as well as the popular cake *kasutera* (*castilla*). A century later, the Dutch brought corn, potatoes, and sweet potatoes. European cooking created some interest and developed into what came to be known in Japan as "the cooking of the Southern Barbarians" or *Nanban ryori*.

coastal areas, where fishing villages can still be found, and the Japan Alps region centered in Nagano Prefecture, sometimes called the Roof of Japan. Three major mountain ranges traverse Nagano, and from the Koumi train line that runs through central Nagano, it is possible to enjoy views of the Japan Alps, the still-active volcano Mount Asama, and Mount Fuji, at 12,300 feet, Japan's highest mountain and a sacred symbol of the nation.

Kyushu, the third largest of Japan's islands, is renowned for its Imari and Arita pottery, hot springs resorts and active volcanoes. Nagasaki in western Kyushu was traditionally the center of trade with China and Holland and Japan's door to the outside world. Shikoku is Japan's fourth largest island.

The Ryukyu archipelago includes the southernmost province of Okinawa, comprising 160 islands, and stretches towards Taiwan.

The Making of a Cuisine

Japan's distinctive style of cuisine began to develop during the Heian Period (794–1185). The capital was moved from Nara to Kyoto, and the thriving aristocracy indulged its interests in art, literature, poetry, fine cuisine, and elaborate games and pastimes. Elegant dining became an important part of the lifestyle and the aristocracy were not only gourmets, but gourmands who supplemented their regular two meals a day with numerous between-meal snacks. Today, *Kyo ryori*, the cuisine of Kyoto, represents the ultimate in Japanese dining and features an assortment of carefully prepared and exquisitely presented delicacies.

In 1185, the government moved to Kamakura, where the more austere samurai lifestyle and Zen Buddhism fostered a more simple cuisine. *Shojin ryori* (vegetarian Buddhist temple fare), heavily influenced by Chinese Buddhist temple cooking, features small portions of

During the Edo Period (1603–1857), Japan underwent almost three centuries of self-imposed seclusion from the outside world, which led to the development of a highly refined and distinctive Japanese culture. The Meiji Period (1868–1912) marked the return of contact and trade, and the early 20th century renewed interest in things foreign.

Japanese cuisine today is a melting pot of culinary influences from and around the world, refined and adapted to reflect local preferences in taste and presentation. The desire to adapt outside influences to local tastes has produced unique blendings of East and West, including green tea ice cream, mild apple curry and seaweed-flavored potato chips, even salmon roe spaghetti!

The Chinese influence is discernible: it was from China that Japan learned the art of making bean curd (*tofu*) and how to use chopsticks. China was also the origin of soy sauce, although today's Japanese-style soy sauce is a product of the 15th century. Tea was first introduced from China in the 9th century, but gradually faded from use only to be reintroduced by a Zen priest in the late 12th century. Rice cultivation began in Japan around 300 BC and is still the cornerstone of a Japanese meal.

The Food of the People

The drastic extremes in Japan's climate—from the very cold northern island of Hokkaido to the subtropical southern islands of Okinawa—have led to the creation of regional cuisines.

In Hokkaido, which is not conducive to rice cultivation, the people have acquired a taste for potatoes, corn, dairy products, barbecued meats, and salmon. Their version of Chinese noodles, called *Sapporo ramen*, is often served with a dab of butter. Seafood *o-nabe* (one-pot stew) featuring crab, scallops, and salmon is also a specialty of the region.

There are differences in the food preferences of the residents of the Kanto region (centered around Tokyo and Yokohama) and the Kansai region (Kyoto, Osaka and environs). In the Kansai area, fermented *miso* is almost white compared with the darker brown and red *miso* favored in the Kanto region. Eastern and Western Japan are also divided by differing tastes in *sushi*, sweets, and pickles. The Kyoto area is identified with the light, delicately flavored cuisine of the ancient court, true *haute cuisine*.

Located halfway between Tokyo and Kyoto is Nagoya, known for its flat *udon* noodles and *uiro*, a sweet rice jelly. The island's famous Sanuki *udon* noodles, fresh sardines, and mandarins are popular with pilgrims visiting the Buddhist temples on Shikoku. Kyushu is known for its tea, fruits, and seafood, and for the Chinese and Western culinary influences that developed because of Nagasaki's role as a center of trade with the outside world.

On the islands of Okinawa, dishes featuring pork are favored. Sweets made with raw sugar, pineapple, and papaya are also popular, as are several powerful local drinks: *awamori*, made from sweet potatoes, and *habu sake*, complete with a deadly *habu* snake coiled inside the bottle.

The *o-bento* or box lunch is a microcosm of Japanese cuisine, consisting of white rice and an assortment of tiny helpings of meat, fish, vegetables, egg, fruit, and a sour plum (*umeboshi*), all arranged in a small rectangular box. Since only small portions of each dish are included and a well-balanced variety of foods is necessary, preparing a proper *o-bento* can be a time-consuming ritual. As with almost all Japanese dishes, attention to detail and attractive presentation are paramount. The most famous of the commercially made *o-bento* are the *ekiben*, the box lunches available at most of the nation's train stations. These vary greatly from one area of the country to another and are considered to be an important way of promoting regional delicacies, customs, and crafts.

The Four Seasons

One of the most striking aspects of Japanese cuisine is the emphasis on seasonal cuisine. Every food has its appropriate season, which not only ensures that Japanese tastes are in harmony with nature but that the cooks use the freshest possible ingredients.

By far the most important of seasonal dining specialties is *osechi ryori*, the special foods that are served during the first week of the new year. Dozens of items are decoratively arranged in tiered lacquer boxes which are brought out again and again over the first few days of the new year. Customs vary from home to home and region to region, but the typical New Year foods usually include *kamaboko* fish sausages bearing auspicious bamboo, plum, and pine designs; *konbu* seaweed rolls tied into bows with dried gourd strips; chestnuts in a sticky sweet-potato paste; herring roe, shredded carrot and white radish in a sweet vinegared dressing; and pickled lotus root. Vegetables such as *shiitake* mushrooms, radishes, lotus root, carrots, and burdock are boiled in a soy sauce and *dashi* broth. The savory steamed egg custard *chawan-mushi* is also often eaten.

The staple accompaniment for these dishes is *o-mochi*, rice cakes that can be grilled or boiled in a soup called *o-zoni*. *Mochi-gome*, a special type of glutinous rice, is prepared and molded into a ball while still hot and placed in a large round wooden mortar where it is pounded rhythmically. The final product is rolled out flat and cut into rectangular cakes.

Cherry blossom-viewing parties are a seasonal must for the majority of Japanese to signal the coming of spring. Top restaurants may serve a cup of cherry blossom tea with several delicate blossoms floating in the clear, slightly salty beverage to signal the auspicious event. Other spring delicacies include bamboo sprouts, bonito, and rape blossoms.

Summer is the time for grilled eel, which is believed to supply the energy needed to survive the sticky, humid weather. It is also the time for octopus, abalone, and fresh fruits and vegetables, especially the summer favorite, *edamame*—fresh soybeans boiled in the pod and dusted with salt—the perfect accompaniment for beer on a hot summer's night. Another summer treat is cold noodles served with a *dashi* and soy sauce dip.

Strings of persimmons drying can be seen dangling from the eaves of many a farmhouse in the countryside in autumn. This is also the season for roasted chestnuts, *soba* noodles, and mushrooms. *Matsutake*, highly prized mushrooms savored for their distinctive fragrance, appear now and are used in soups and rice dishes. Late autumn is the time for preserving the year's vegetable harvest for winter. A large variety of pickling methods are popular in Japan, the most common using *miso*, salt, vinegar or rice bran as preservatives.

Winter brings *fugu sashimi*, strips of raw blowfish which can be a deadly delicacy if the fish is not handled properly by a licensed chef. Mandarins and *o-nabe*, warming one-pot stews, are also enjoyed. On the final day of the year, it is customary to eat *soba* to guarantee health and longevity in the new year. Few things are as quintessentially Japanese as the ritual tea ceremony which encapsulates all the refinement, discipline and mystique of Japanese culture. *Cha-noyu*, the Way of Tea, began in the 15th century, and in its early form placed much emphasis on displaying and admiring imported Chinese art objects. The Way of Tea gave rise to two of the more interesting aspects of Japanese cuisine: *cha kaiseki*, Japanese *haute cuisine* designed to be served as a light meal before a tea ceremony, and *wagashi*, traditional Japanese sweets which became an important accessory to the tea ceremony from the mid–16th century.

The Japanese Kitchen and Table

Don't be misled into thinking that because the individual portions of food that make a Japanese meal are small, you'll finish a Japanese meal hungry. With the variety of tastes, textures and flavors, you're certain to feel satisfied—physically and mentally—at the end of a meal.

A Japanese meal can be divided into a beginning, a middle and an end. The beginning includes appetizers, clear soups and raw fish (*sashimi*). The middle of the meal is made up of a number of seafood, meat, poultry and vegetable dishes prepared by either grilling, steaming, simmering, deep-frying or serving as a vinegared "salad." To ensure variety, each style of preparation would be used only once for the foods making up the middle of the meal. For example, if the fish was deep-fried, the vegetables might be simmered in seasoned stock, the meat grilled and a mixture of egg and savory tidbits steamed. Alternatively, this variety of "middle" dishes might be replaced by a hot-pot (*nabe*), a one-dish combination of vegetables, seafood, meat, bean curd, and noodles. The meal concludes with rice, *miso* soup and pickles, green tea and fresh fruit—the basis of every main meal in Japan.

Accompanying dishes are varied according to availability, season, how much time you have for preparation of the meal and so on. The Japanese do not categorize their food by the basic ingredient (for example, vegetables, beef or fish), but by the method with which it is prepared. Food is thus classified as grilled, steamed, simmered, deep-fried or vinegared.

The two extremes of Japanese cuisine are a full *kaiseki ryori*, an array of a dozen or more tiny portions of food, and the basic meal consisting of boiled rice, miso soup, and pickles. If you are new to Japanese cuisine, keep the menu simple. You might like to prepare an appetizer and a couple of other dishes using fish, meat, poultry or vegetables around the basic rice, soup, and pickles. You might even limit the meal to one simple appetizer and a one-pot dish such as *sukiyaki*, followed by the rice, soup, and pickles. It is better to serve three carefully cooked, beautifully presented dishes than six less-than-perfect ones.

This beautifully presented meal shows the imaginative use of ceramics, lacquer-ware, porcelain and basketware that is typically Japanese.

In private homes and many restaurants, all the dishes making up the meal are presented at the same time. At a formal meal, the appetizers arrive first, followed by the "middle" dishes, each served in the order dictated by their method of preparation.

The presentation of Japanese food is an art that encourages the cook's imagination and creativity. Even the choice of tableware is influenced by the season and the type of food being served. Generally speaking, foods which are round, such as pieces of rolled meat or slices of lotus root, are presented on rectangular or square plates, while square-shaped foods are likely to be served on round plates for contrast. Such imagination is shown in Japan, however, that plates and bowls are not just square, rectangular or round; they might be hexagonal, semicircular, fan-shaped or resemble a leaf or shell. And, it has been said in Japan that "a person cannot go out naked in public, neither can food." In most cases, garnishes are edible.

The secret to preparing Japanese cuisine at home is an understanding of the basic ingredients and of how a meal is composed; the culinary methods used are actually very simple. But the most important requirement of all is simply a love of good food, prepared and presented with a sense of harmony.

The formal tea ceremony, with its bitter powdered green tea, led to the creation of delicate *wagashi* sweets during the 16th century.

SUGGESTED MENUS

A family meal (1)

With Japanese meals many small dishes are served, and often there is no "main" attraction—they all are! But you do not necessarily have to follow this practice.

For a family meal, you may like to serve the following:
• Thick Sushi Rolls (page 99);
• Grilled Tofu Topped with Sweet Miso (page 96) and a small side dish of Green Bean Salad with Tart Sesame Dressing (page 96) with rice;
• Jellied Plums (page 107) are a simple dessert to make but look dramatic.

A family meal (2)

Another great menu for a family dinner.
• Begin with individual bowls of Chawan Mushi (page 101);
• Miso Soup with Mushrooms (page 105) and Sake Shrimp (page 101);
• Green Tea Ice Cream is always a favorite with which to finish (page 107).

A dinner party

For a dinner party that will delight your guests, you can't go wrong with dishes such as:
• Grilled Eggplant and Shrimp with Miso Sauce (page 103), served with small side dishes of Spinach with Sesame (page 95) and Fish Tempura with Clear Dashi Broth (page 97);
• Sukiyaki (page 106) or Shabu-Shabu (page 105) that diners can cook as they eat;
• Green Tea Ice Cream (page 107) .

A melting pot menu

If you prefer a mix-and-match menu, put together a meal that features the following:
• Grilled Miso Fish (page 104) from Japan;
• Mild Chicken Curry (page 61) with Tandoori Naan (page 57) from India and a dish of Spinach with Dried Shrimp (page 134) from Malaysia/Singapore;
• Round off the meal with some homely but delicious Pineapple Tartlets (page 187) from Vietnam, served with sliced fresh fruit.

THE ESSENTIAL FLAVORS OF JAPANESE COOKING

Dried bonito and **konbu** seaweed are essential for making the clear *dashi* that is used in much of Japanese cooking. Flavorful **miso**, with **tofu** and **wakame** or **nori** seaweed, makes a quick and easy soup. Popular flavorings are **ginger**, **sake,** and **soy sauce**. **Mirin** and **rice vinegar** are added to rice for *sushi*. **Sesame paste** is used in dipping sauces.

Basic Dashi Stock

1 strip dried kelp (*konbu*), (4 in/10 cm long), wiped with a damp cloth
4 cups (1 liter) water
4 cups (50 g) dried bonito flakes

Soak the dried kelp in a saucepan of water for 1 hour. Simmer over medium heat. Just before the water comes to a boil, remove and discard the kelp. Sprinkle the bonito flakes into the water and remove the saucepan from the heat immediately. As soon as the flakes sink, strain the stock and discard the flakes.

Cold Soba Dashi Broth

1 cup (250 ml) Basic Dashi Stock (recipe above)
2 tablespoons soy sauce
1/4 cup (60 ml) *mirin*

Place all the ingredients in a saucepan, bring just to a boil over medium heat and remove from the heat immediately. Serve with cold soba noodles. Keeps refrigerated for up to 4 days.

Tempura Batter

1 egg yolk
1 cup (250 ml) ice water
1 cup (150 g) cornstarch, sifted

Put the egg yolks in a bowl and mix in the water gradually. Add the cornstarch all at once and stir briefly (preferably with a pair of chopsticks). Tempura batter should be thin and lumpy. It is best made just before cooking, however the batter can be refrigerated until required.

Sweet Vinegar

1 cup (250 ml) water
1/2 cup (125 ml) rice vinegar
1/3 cup (60 g) sugar
1 teaspoon salt

Bring the water and vinegar to a boil in a saucepan, then add the remaining ingredients and stir to dissolve the sugar and salt. Remove from the heat and set aside to cool. Use for dipping and pickling vegetables. Keeps refrigerated for up to 10 days.

Sushi Rice

1 cup (200 g) uncooked Japanese rice (yields 2 cups cooked rice)
1 1/4 cups (310 ml) water
1 strip dried kelp (*konbu*), (4 in/10 cm long), wiped with a damp cloth and quartered

Dressing
2 tablespoons rice vinegar
1 tablespoon sake
2 teaspoons sugar
1 teaspoon salt

Rinse the rice gently and drain. Cook the rice, water and kelp in a saucepan and bring almost to a boil over high heat. Reduce the heat, discard the kelp, and simmer, covered, for 15 minutes until the rice is cooked. Turn the heat off, remove the lid and cover the pan with a towel to absorb condensation. Set aside for 20 minutes. Stir the Dressing ingredients in a non-reactive bowl to dissolve the sugar. Put the cooked rice in a wide wooden tub or large bowl. Add the Dressing and stir gently in a circular motion with a wooden spoon. Ideally, the rice mixture should be fanned to keep cool it. Cover the rice with a damp cloth until ready to use. Do not refrigerate. Keep at room temperature and use within 4 hours.

Tempura Dipping Sauce

1 cup (250 ml) Basic Dashi Stock (recipe on this page)
1 1/2 tablespoons soy sauce
3 tablespoons *mirin*

Bring all the ingredients to a boil in a saucepan. Remove from the heat and cover to keep warm.

Teriyaki Sauce

1 cup (250 ml) soy sauce
1 cup (250 ml) sake
1 1/2 cups (375 ml) *mirin*
5–6 tablespoons sugar

Combine all the ingredients in a pan and bring to a boil, stirring to dissolve the sugar. Once the sugar is dissolved, remove from the heat and pour the sauce into a bowl.

Pickled Ginger

Gari

8 oz (250 g) young ginger, peeled and thinly sliced diagonally
1/2 cup (85 ml) rice vinegar
2 tablespoons *mirin*
2 tablespoons sake
5 teaspoons sugar

Rinse the ginger slices thoroughly and blanch in boiling water and set aside to drain. Add the rest of the ingredients into a saucepan and bring to a boil, stirring to dissolve the sugar. Set aside to cool. Place the ginger in a sterilized jar and pour the vinegar mixture over it. Cover and keep for 3–4 days before using. The ginger keeps well refrigerated for 1 month—it may develop a pale pink color as it ages. Serve with sushi and other Japanese dishes.

Ponzu Dipping Sauce

1 strip dried kelp (*konbu*), (about 2 in/5 cm long), wiped with a damp cloth
1/3 cup (85 ml) *yuzu* orange, or lemon or lime juice
1/3 cup (85 ml) soy sauce
2 tablespoons *mirin*
1 1/2 tablespoons *tamari* or dark soy sauce
2 tablespoons Basic Dashi Stock (recipe on this page)
2 tablespoons hot water

Heat the dried kelp over a gas flame or under a broiler (grill) until crisp and fragrant, then put in a bowl or jar with all the other ingredients. Cover and refrigerate for 3 days, then strain. Can be stored for up to a year.

Sesame Dipping Sauce

5 tablespoons white sesame seeds
1 tablespoon miso
2 tablespoons *mirin*
1 tablespoon *tamari* or dark soy sauce
1 tablespoon soy sauce
1 tablespoon lime or lemon juice
1/2 tablespoon sugar
1/2 teaspoon grated young ginger
1/4 teaspoon ground red pepper
1/4 cup (85 ml) water

Dry-roast the white sesame seeds in a skillet until light golden

brown. Do not burn the seeds or it will taste bitter. Place the warm toasted seeds and all the other ingredients in a blender. This sauce is best prepared a day ahead for the flavors to blend. Keeps refrigerated for 2 to 3 days.

Sashimi Soy Dip

Tosa Shoyu

3 tablespoons sake
1/2 cup (125 ml) soy sauce
2 tablespoons *tamari* soy sauce or *mirin*
1 strip dried kelp (*konbu*), (about 2 in/5 cm long), wiped with a damp cloth
1/2 cup (5 g) dried bonito flakes

Place all the ingredients in a small saucepan and simmer on medium-low heat for 5 minutes. Allow to cool, then strain and discard solids. The sauce can be stored for up to a year if kept refrigerated in a jar. Use as a dipping sauce for sashimi.

Chicken Yakitori Glaze

1/2 cup (125 ml) chicken stock
1/3 cup (85 ml) sake
1/2 cup (125 ml) *mirin*
1/2 cup (125 ml) soy sauce
2 tablespoons sugar

Place all the ingredients in a small saucepan and bring to a boil. Reduce the heat and simmer for 20 minutes, or until the sauce is reduced to half the original volume. The sauce keeps refrigerated for up to 1 month. Use this sauce for brushing when grilling chicken yakitori.

Sukiyaki Sauce

6 tablespoons soy sauce
5 tablespoons *mirin*
5 tablespoons sake
5–6 tablespoons sugar
1 1/2 cups (375 ml) chicken stock or 1 1/2 cups (375 ml) Basic Dashi Stock (recipe on this page)

Combine all the ingredients in a pan and bring to a boil, stirring to dissolve the sugar. Once the sugar is dissolved, remove from the heat and pour the sauce into a bowl.

Spinach with Sesame

Spinach with Sesame

This simple but tasty appetizer is served at room temperature.

10 oz (300 g) spinach, washed and
 left whole, thick stems removed
4 cups (1 liter) water
1 tablespoon salt
3 tablespoons sesame seeds
1 tablespoon sugar
2 tablespoons Basic Dashi Stock
 (page 94)
Nori strips, to wrap
Thin *nori* strips, to garnish

Bring the water and salt to a boil. Lightly blanch the spinach leaves until they are soft but not soggy. Drain in a colander and cool under running water. Drain again, pressing on the spinach with your hands or the back of a wooden spoon to remove excess water. Lay the spinach on a bamboo rolling mat and roll up tightly to squeeze out any remaining moisture and shape into a roll.

Dry-roast the sesame seeds in a skillet until light golden brown, stirring constantly. Take care not to burn the seeds as this would make them taste bitter. Grind, using a mortar and pestle or a spice grinder, to a coarse, grainy paste. Add the sugar and *dashi* stock to smoothen the mixture into a creamy paste.

Just before serving, slice the rolled spinach into short sections. Wrap the *nori* strip around each section like a belt, top with a little sesame sauce and sprinkle with the shredded *nori*.

Mixed Chicken and Vegetable Yakitori

These grilled chicken and vegetables skewers are very popular in Japan and abroad.

10 oz (300 g) boneless chicken
 thighs, cubed
2 leeks, cut into lengths
4 oz (125 g) chicken livers, halved
8 fresh shiitake mushrooms, stems
 discarded and caps halved
12 small Japanese green peppers or
 2 large bell peppers, deseeded and
 cut into strips
6 stalks asparagus, cut into lengths
36 bamboo skewers, soaked in water
 for 1 hour before grilling
Oil, to baste
1 portion Chicken Yakitori Glaze
 (page 94)

Chicken Meatballs
10 oz (300 g) ground chicken
2 teaspoons sugar
2 teaspoons soy sauce
1 teaspoon fresh ginger juice
1 egg, lightly beaten
2 teaspoons bread crumbs
2 teaspoons cornstarch
4 cups (1 liter) Basic Dashi Stock
 (page 94)
3 tablespoons sake

Condiments
Seven-spice chili powder (*shichimi*)
Sansho pepper powder
1 lemon, cut into wedges

Prepare the Chicken Meatballs by combining the ground chicken with the sugar, soy sauce, ginger juice, egg, bread crumbs and

cornstarch, mixing well. Scoop 1 tablespoon of the chicken mixture and shape into small meatballs, 3/4 in (2 cm) in diameter. Bring the dashi stock and sake to almost a boil. Gently drop the chicken meatballs into the simmering stock, a few at a time, and simmer until the meatballs change color. Thread the meatballs onto the skewers. Reserve the stock.

Alternate the pieces of chicken thigh and leek onto skewers and set aside. Thread the chicken livers onto skewers and set aside. Thread all the vegetables onto skewers and brush lightly with oil and set aside.

Heat a charcoal barbecue or grill and cook the skewers. When the food is half-cooked, brush with the Chicken Yakitori Glaze and return to the grill briefly. Baste the food a couple more times during cooking, but take care not to overcook. Sear the vegetables quickly on the grill until done.

Strain the dashi stock and serve together with the yakitori. Serve with the range of Condiments.

Grilled Eggplant with Ginger and Bonito Flakes

1 lb (500 g) slender Japanese
 eggplants
4 tablespoons Basic Dashi Stock
 (page 94) or 1/4 teaspoon dashi
 stock granules dissolved in 4 tablespoons hot water
1 tablespoon soy sauce
1 in (21/2 cm) young ginger, grated
1/2 cup (5 g) dried bonito flakes

Prick the skin of the eggplants in a few places with a toothpick to prevent them from bursting during cooking. Grill the eggplants under a very hot broiler or grill, turning frequently until the skins are slightly blackened and the flesh is soft.

Remove from the grill, plunge into a basin of cold water, drain and peel off the skins. Cut the eggplant into strips lengthwise or crosswise into sections.

Combine the *dashi* stock and soy sauce in a bowl. Arrange the eggplants on individual serving plates and drizzle with a bit of the sauce mixture. Top with grated ginger and sprinkle with bonito flakes.

Rice with Vegetables and Mushrooms

Mountain vegetables, sold as Wild Sansai Plants—usually a mixture of bracken, fern tips, nameko mushrooms and other mountain greens—are packed in water and sold in Japanese markets. They have a wonderful "woodsy" flavor and interesting texture that transforms plain rice into a treat. Any mixture of fresh mushrooms, works well in this recipe.

11/2 cups (300 g) uncooked
 Japanese rice
21/2 cups (625 ml) water
1 tablespoon sake
1 tablespoon soy sauce
1 packet mountain vegetables
7 oz (200 g) mixed fresh mushrooms
3 pieces fried tofu slices (*aburage*)
Kinome leaves or chopped parsley

Rice Seasoning
1 teaspoon salt
1 teaspoon sake
1 teaspoon soy sauce
1 teaspoon mirin

Rinse and wash the rice gently. Place the rice and 21/2 cups (625 ml) water in a deep saucepan and set aside to soak for 20 minutes.

Rinse, drain the mountain vegetables and place in a small bowl. Add the sake, soy sauce and mushrooms, mix well and set aside for 5 minutes.

Add the Rice Seasoning to the saucepan of soaking rice, together with the seasoned vegetables and stir. Cover the saucepan and bring to a boil over high heat for about 5 minutes, or until the water is almost fully absorbed, then stir. Reduce the heat and simmer gently, covered, for 15 minutes until the rice is cooked. Remove from the heat, place a towel over the rice (to absorb moisture) and cover with the lid. Set aside for 20 minutes.

Pour boiling water over the tofu slices to remove excess oil. Drain and pat dry with paper towels. Cut in half lengthwise, and then cut into short, narrow strips. Stir the fried tofu slices into the rice, garnish and serve hot.

Mountain vegetables are available in packets of 5–61/2 oz (150–200 g). Substitute 1 lb (500 g) of mixed fresh mushrooms, if desired.

Grilled Tofu Topped with Sweet Miso

Small blocks of tofu topped with three different types of miso make a colorful and unusual appetizer.

2 cakes firm tofu (about 1 lb/500 g)

Miso Toppings
6 tablespoons white miso
3 tablespoons sake
3 tablespoons *mirin*
1 tablespoon sugar
1/2 teaspoon very finely grated *yuzu* orange or lemon peel
1/3 cup (10 g) *kinome* or watercress

Red Dengaku Miso
3 tablespoons red miso
1 1/2 tablespoons sake
1 1/2 tablespoons *mirin*
1/2–1 tablespoon sugar
1 tablespoon water

Wrap the tofu in a clean cloth to remove excess moisture. Place it between two cutting boards for 20 minutes. Cut the tofu into half horizontally and then into quarters to obtain rectangular strips.

Make the light yellow and green Miso Toppings by combining the miso, sake, *mirin* and sugar in a saucepan and bring almost to a boil. Reduce the heat and simmer for 5 minutes, stirring to dissolve the sugar. Divide the mixture into two bowls. Add the grated citrus peel to one bowl, stir and set aside.

To make the green topping. Grind the greens using a mortar and pestle or finely mince.

Squeeze to obtain a small quantity of green juice. Add this to the other bowl of the miso mixture. Stir and set aside.

For the red topping, put the ingredients for the Red Dengaku Miso in a small saucepan. Bring almost to a boil. Reduce the heat and simmer for 5 minutes, stirring to dissolve the sugar. Remove from the heat. Set aside.

Grill the pieces of tofu under a broiler for 1 minute until lightly browned on both sides. Spread each piece of the tofu with one of the three toppings and return to the grill briefly until brown on the top. If you like, carefully insert a skewer into each tofu rectangle as shown. Serve hot.

Green Bean Salad with Tart Sesame Dressing

10 oz (300 g) green beans
Finely shredded *nori*

Tart Sesame Dressing
4 tablespoons ground sesame paste
1/2 tablespoon soy sauce
1/2 teaspoon salt
1 tablespoon sugar
1 tablespoon rice vinegar or lemon juice
2 tablespoons Basic Dashi Stock (page 94)

Blanch the beans in a saucepan of lightly salted water for about 2 to 3 minutes until just tender. Drain and cool under cold running water, then slice into lengths.

Mix the Tart Sesame Dressing ingredients in a bowl. Divide the

beans into four serving bowls, top each with a spoonful of the Dressing and garnish with the shredded *nori*.

Substitute ground sesame paste with tahini or peanut butter. If using tahini, increase the amount of sugar and lemon juice by 1/2 tablespoon. If using peanut butter, use 1/2 tablespoon sugar and 1 1/2 tablespoons lemon juice.

Cold Dashi Custard Tofu
Tamago Dofu

This chilled custard makes a refreshing summer appetizer, and looks as lovely as it tastes when garnished with sprigs of shiso flowers or leaves. If these are not available, use decorative sprigs or petals of any edible flowers. Flowering basil is one such good substitute.

3 eggs, lightly beaten
3/4 cup (175 ml) Basic Dashi Stock (page 94)
1–1 1/2 tablespoons soy sauce
1 teaspoon *mirin*
4 medium cooked shrimp (optional)
2/3 cup (150 ml) Cold Soba Dashi Broth (page 94)
Grated *yuzu* orange, lime or lemon peel, to garnish
Shiso flowers or thinly sliced *shiso* leaves, to garnish

Combine the eggs dashi stock, soy sauce and mirin in a bowl

and stir the mixture gently. Pour it into a small, square or rectangular, heat-proof bowl or dish measuring about 4 in (10 cm) on each side. Steam over medium heat for about 25 minutes until it sets. Set aside to cool, cover and chill until needed.

Slice the custard into four, and place each piece in a small glass or china bowl. Place a shrimp, if using, on top of each piece of custard and spoon the Cold Soba Dashi Broth over it. Garnish with the grated citrus peel and *shiso* flowers or leaves. Serve chilled.

Seared Tataki Beef

1 lb (500 g) beef sirloin, cut into 4
1 teaspoon salt
1 medium onion
Ohba or *shiso* leaves or sprigs of watercress, to garnish
7 oz (200 g) daikon radish (about 3 in/8 cm), peeled and thinly sliced
Thinly sliced green onions (scallions), to garnish
4 tablespoons finely grated daikon radish mixed with 1/4 teaspoon ground red pepper, to serve
Ponzu Dipping Sauce (page 94)

Heat a skillet until very hot. Sprinkle the beef with salt and sear it for a few seconds on each side, just until the color changes. Remove and cut into very thin slices.

Peel the onion, cut in half

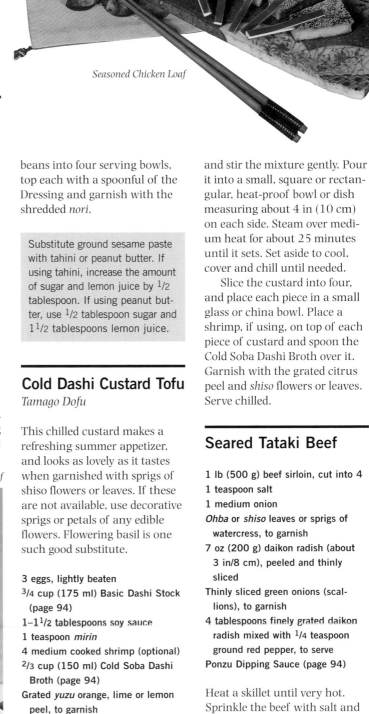
Seasoned Chicken Loaf

Seared Tataki Beef

lengthwise, then into very thin slices across. Break up the slices with your fingers and put in ice water to chill. Rinse, drain and dry the onion slices.

To serve, lay the beef slices in a circle on a large platter. Arrange the greens in the center, topped with the sliced daikon and onions. Garnish with green onions and place small mounds of the grated daikon on the side. Serve with a small bowl of the Ponzu Dipping Sauce.

Seasoned Chicken Loaf

Tiny poppy seeds scattered over the top of this seasoned chicken loaf are supposedly reminiscent of sand on a beach. In this dish, also known as "Wind in the Pines," sesame seeds can be used in place of poppy seeds if these are not available.

14 oz (400 g) boneless chicken
2 eggs, lightly beaten
2 teaspoons minced young ginger
2 tablespoons red miso
2 teaspoons sake
2 teaspoons soy sauce
2 tablespoons sugar
2 teaspoons cornstarch
1 tablespoon fine white poppy seeds or sesame seeds
Bamboo sticks or ice-cream sticks

Grind the chicken in a food processor to make a paste. Add all the other ingredients except the poppy or sesame seeds and process until well mixed.

Line the base and the sides of an 8-in (20-cm) square baking pan with baking paper or oiled foil. Put in the chicken mixture, spreading evenly, then sprinkle with the poppy seeds. Preheat the oven to 350°F (180°C). Set the baking pan with the chicken into a larger heat-proof tray half-filled with water and bake for about 30 minutes, until the center is firm.

Remove the pan from the oven and pull up the sides of the baking paper or foil to lift the loaf out of the pan. Cut the loaf into rectangles or fan shapes and skewer onto the sticks. Serve at room temperature.

Fish Tempura with Clear Dashi Broth

4 oz (125 g) fresh whitebait, cleaned, washed and patted dry
2 tablespoons cornstarch
Oil, for deep-frying
7 oz (200 g) daikon radish (about 3 in/8 cm), peeled and grated
4 cups (1 liter) Basic Dashi Stock (page 94)
2 teaspoons soy sauce
2 teaspoons sake
1/4 teaspoon salt, or more to taste
Mitsuba leaves or blanched chrysanthemum greens or spinach

Tempura Batter
1 egg yolk
2 tablespoons ice water
2 tablespoons cornstarch, sifted

Mix the Tempura Batter ingredients together in a bowl. Heat the oil in a wok. Shake the whitebait and cornstarch together in a plastic bag. Remove the coated whitebait and then dip into the Batter. Fry in hot oil until crisp and light golden. Drain on paper towels and set aside in a warm place.

Place the grated daikon in a muslin cloth, gently squeeze and discard the juice. Bring the *dashi* stock, soy sauce and sake almost to a boil in a saucepan and add the grated daikon. Turn off the heat, and season the soup with salt to taste.

Stir and ladle the soup into four soup bowls and add the fried fish just before serving. Topped with the sprigs of *mitsuba* or the blanched chrysanthemum greens or spinach.

Fish Tempura with Clear Dashi Broth

Hot Soba Noodle Soup with Tempura

Hot Soba Noodle Soup with Tempura

7 oz (200 g) soba noodles or buckwheat pasta
12 cups (3 liters) water
1 teaspoon salt
Finely sliced green onions (scallions)
Seven-spice chili powder (*shichimi*)

Hot Soba Dashi Broth
4 cups (1 liter) Basic Dashi Stock (page 94)
3 tablespoons soy sauce
1 tablespoon *mirin*

Tempura Batter
1 egg yolk
1 cup (250 ml) ice water
1 cup (150 g) cornstarch

Tempura
8 fresh medium shrimp
Cornstarch, for dusting
4 fresh shiitake mushrooms, stems discarded, caps left whole
4 *shiso* leaves
Oil, for deep-frying

In an uncovered saucepan, boil the noodles in plenty of lightly salted water for 4 to 5 minutes, drain and chill in cold water, then drain again. Set aside.

To make the Hot Soba Dashi Broth, place all the ingredients into a saucepan, bring to a boil and immediately remove from the heat. Set aside in a warm place.

Make the Tempura Batter by mixing the egg yolk, ice water and cornstarch in a bowl and stir briskly. The Batter should be slightly lumpy.

To prepare the Tempura, peel the shrimp, discard the heads and keep the tails intact. Slit the back of each shrimp and devein.

Cold Soba Noodles with Assorted Toppings

Make several small incisions crosswise along the underside of the shrimp to prevent it from curling during the frying process.

Preheat the oil in a wok or saucepan until very hot. Dust each shrimp with the cornstarch, shake off any excess, then dip in the Tempura Batter and deep-fry in very hot oil for 1–2 minutes until light golden. Drain on paper towels. Dip the shiitake mushrooms and *shiso* leaves in the Batter and deep-fry. Drain on paper towels.

Divide the soba noodles into four bowls and ladle the broth over the noodles. Top with 2 shrimp, mushroom and *shiso* leaf in each bowl, and garnish with the green onions and a sprinkling of seven-spice chili powder.

Cold Soba Noodles with Assorted Toppings

Soba noodles made from buckwheat flour are eaten both cold and hot in Japan. These chilled noodles are wonderful in summertime, and the toppings can be varied according to the ingredients on hand.

1 packet dried soba noodles or buckwheat pasta (about 7 oz/200 g)

2 cups (500 ml) Cold Soba Dashi Broth (page 94)

Simmered Shiitake Mushrooms
12 dried black Chinese mushrooms, rinsed and soaked in 3/4 cup (185 ml) water for 10 minutes to soften, stems discarded and soaking liquid reserved, or 20 fresh shiitake mushrooms, stems discarded, soaked in 1/2 cup (125 ml) water
1 1/2 teaspoons sugar
1 1/2 teaspoons soy sauce

Tempura Fritters
1/2 burdock root peeled and grated
1 small carrot, peeled and grated
1 onion, very thinly sliced
1 tablespoon minced *mitsuba* or parsley leaves
Oil, for deep-frying
1 egg yolk
4 tablespoons ice water
4 tablespoons cornstarch

Toppings
4 teaspoons wasabi paste
4 tablespoons finely shredded *nori*
2 eggs, lightly beaten, fried as a thin omelet, then very thinly sliced
8 *shiso* leaves, very thinly sliced
2 green onions (scallions), white part only, finely sliced into shreds
1 1/4 oz (40 g) salmon or tuna, poached and flaked or 3/4 oz (20 g) salted salmon flakes (*shio zake*)
2 tablespoons *konbu tsukudani* (kelp simmered in soy sauce, *mirin* and sugar)

Boil the noodles in plenty of lightly salted water for 4 to 5 minutes, uncovered, drain and chill in cold water. Drain again and refrigerate. Simmer the Cold Soba Dashi Broth over medium-high heat for 10 minutes and set aside.

To cook the Simmered Shiitake Mushrooms, combine all the ingredients in a saucepan and bring to a boil. Reduce the heat and simmer for 10 minutes and set aside to cool. Drain and slice the mushroom caps very finely.

Prepare the tempura batter by mixing the egg yolk, ice water and cornstarch in a bowl and stir briskly. The batter should be slightly lumpy. Heat the oil in a frying pan until very hot. Combine and mix the tempura vegetables in a bowl. Take a small handful of the vegetables and dip it in the batter, remove with a slotted spoon. Gently slide the vegetables into the hot oil and deep-fry until light golden brown. Drain on paper towels and set aside.

When serving, arrange small portions (enough for two mouthfuls) of the noodles in small bowls. Pour a little broth over the noodles and add the preferred combination of Toppings. Repeat, varying the combination of Toppings.

Thick Sushi Rolls

Thick Sushi Rolls

3 cups (600 g) cooked Sushi Rice (page 94)
1 Japanese cucumber, quartered
6–8 fresh medium shrimp, cooked, peeled and halved lengthwise
4 sheets toasted *nori*, each about 8 x 7 in (20 x 18 cm)
4 heaped tablespoons Shrimp Flakes (page 99) or salted salmon flakes (*shio zake*)
1 portion Simmered Shiitake Mushrooms (page 98)
Pickled Ginger (page 94)
Sashimi Soy Dip (page 94)

Japanese Omelet
3 eggs
4 tablespoons Basic Dashi Stock (page 94)
2 tablespoons *mirin*
1 1/2 teaspoons sugar
1/4 teaspoon salt
Oil, for greasing

Make 1 1/2 portions of Sushi Rice. Cover and set aside.

Combine all the Japanese Omelet ingredients in a bowl, stir gently until the sugar has dissolved. Heat a small omelet pan over medium heat. Brush lightly with oil. Lower the heat. Slowly pour enough egg mixture to make a thin omelet into the pan. Swirl the pan for the mixture to spread evenly. Break up any bubbles that may form.

When the egg is about to set, fold two sides of the omelet toward the center, overlapping each other. Remove and set onto a dry plate. Cook a second omelet. When the egg is set at the bottom and still moist on top, place the first omelet in the center of the pan and fold the two sides over. Remove and set aside on the dry plate again. Repeat with the remaining egg mixture until all is used up. Set the omelet onto a kitchen towel, roll and squeeze gently to remove moisture. Unroll and flatten the omelet. Slice lengthwise into long rectangular strips.

Place a *nori* sheet on a bamboo mat and spread a quarter portion of the Sushi Rice on the *nori*, leaving $^1/_2$ in (1 cm) of the *nori* exposed along the top. Sprinkle 1 tablespoon of the Shrimp Flakes along the center of the rice. Lay a quarter of the seasoned mushrooms over it. Place a quarter of the omelet strips, cucumber and shrimp along the center of the rice.

First, roll the mat once over the ingredients, pressing the ingredients in to keep the roll firm. Lift the mat and complete the roll, pressing the mat firmly all around. Unroll the mat, and use your finger to ensure that the roll is sealed. Roll the sushi rice again, using fingers to press the roll into a circle. Remove and slice each roll in half, and cut each half into four pieces. Repeat with the remaining fillings to make another three rolls. Serve with the Pickled Ginger and Sashimi Soy Dip on the side.

Thin Sushi Rolls

Three different fillings are used in this recipe for *nori*-wrapped rolls of vinegared rice—tuna, cucumber and pickled daikon—the last is available in plastic packets in Japanese stores. Other fillings may also be used —for example carrot, crabstick and omelet strips.

2 cups (400 g) cooked Sushi Rice (page 94)
2 teaspoons wasabi paste
3 sheets toasted *nori*, each about 8 x 7 in (20 x 18 cm), halved
Pickled Ginger (page 94)
Sashimi Soy Dip (page 94)

Thin Sushi Rolls and Sushi Rice with Assorted Toppings

Fillings
1 Japanese cucumber
5 oz (150 g) pickled daikon radish
7 oz (200 g) fresh tuna

While the rice is cooking, deseed the cucumbers and cut into quarters lengthwise. Slice the pickled daikon into long, thin strips. Cut the tuna into long strips. Set the Fillings aside.

Place a halved *nori* sheet on a bamboo rolling mat with the shiny side down. Spread $^1/_3$ cup (70 g) of the cooked Sushi Rice evenly on the *nori* sheet, leaving a border of about $^1/_2$ in (1 cm) exposed along the top edge. Dab a little wasabi along the center of the rice. Place 2 strips of the cucumber across the center of the wasabi.

To roll, hold the edge of the mat nearest to you with one hand, press the cucumber with the other hand to hold it in place, and roll the mat over the rice. Lift the top of the mat and complete the roll, squeezing gently along the length of the roll. Unroll the mat, and press to seal. Roll the sushi in the mat again. Slice the roll in half, and cut both rolls twice to give six uniform pieces. Repeat with the remaining cucumber, daikon radish and tuna fillings. Serve with the Pickled Ginger and Sashimi Soy Dip on the side.

Sushi Rice with Assorted Toppings

Sushi rice, topped with seafood and eggs, is served in a bowl. Vegetables or cooked meat can be added for variety. This is eaten as a one-bowl meal, or served in a large bowl to be shared.

2–3 cups (400–600 g) cooked Sushi Rice (page 94)
1 tablespoon dried whitebait or silverfish, dry-fried for about 5–10 minutes in a pan until crisp (optional)
3 eggs, lightly beaten and fried as an omelet, then very thinly sliced
8 fresh medium shrimp, cooked, peeled, deveined, sliced butterfly style
3 oz (90 g) fresh tuna, cut into strips
1 piece (2 oz/60 g) squid, blanched lightly and cut into strips
1 strip (3 oz/90 g) barbequed eel
Nori, thinly shredded, to garnish
Pickled Ginger (page 94)
Sashimi Soy Dip (page 94)
Wasabi paste

Shrimp Flakes
5 oz (150 g) fresh small shrimp, peeled and deveined
1 egg yolk
2–3 teaspoons sugar
$^1/_2$ teaspoon salt

Prepare the Shrimp Flakes by simmering the shrimp in a

saucepan with a little salted water until the shrimp change color. Drain, cool and blend in a food processor. Place the ground shrimp into a bowl and add the egg yolk, sugar and salt and mix well. Place the mixture in a pan and dry-fry over very low heat, stirring constantly, for about 10 minutes or until almost dry and flaky. Transfer to a dry plate and set aside. This can be kept refrigerated for a week.

Mix the Sushi Rice with the dried whitebait (if using) in a wide wooden bowl. With the back of a spoon, pack the rice into four lacquer bowls or boxes and level the surface.

Scatter the sliced omelet over the rice and top with the shrimp, tuna, squid and eel. Garnish with the shredded *nori* and Shrimp Flakes, and serve with Pickled Ginger, Sashimi Soy Dip and wasabi paste on the side.

Silverfish are tiny fish sold cured or dried in packets, and barbequed eel is available either canned or in vacuum packs. Other non-traditional ingredients such as barbequed pork or beef, smoked oysters or salmon may also be used. Substitute Shrimp Flakes with prepared salted salmon flakes (*shio zake*).

Assorted Sashimi

Beef Sushi
Gyu-Nigiri

Well-marbled beef is normally used for this dish, which is the Japanese equivalent of Italian carpaccio. If you prefer, the beef may be quickly seared on the outside before slicing, and may also be marinated beforehand with Teriyaki Sauce (page 94) and barbequed.

1 cup (150 g) cooked Sushi Rice (page 94)
5 oz (150 g) prime marbled beef sirloin, very thinly sliced
1 teaspoon crushed garlic
Shiso flowers or alternative garnish
Benitade or alfalfa sprouts
4 tablespoons pickled young ginger slices, to serve
Ponzu Dipping Sauce or Sashimi Soy Dip (page 94), for dipping

Cut the beef into thin slices about $2^{1}/2$ in (6 cm) long by $^{3}/4$ in (2 cm) wide by $^{1}/4$ in (3 cm) thick. Hold a beef slice in one hand and, using a small spoon, spread a little of the crushed garlic on it. Moisten your other hand and pinch a heaped tablespoonful of the Sushi Rice and form a smal cylinder in the palm of your hand. Lay the rice onto the seasoned side of the beef and press lightly, for the beef to adhere to the rice.

Arrange on a platter and garnish with the *shiso* flowers, *benitade* or alfalfa sprouts. Serve with the pickled ginger and Ponzu Dipping Sauce.

Assorted Sashimi

A wide variety of seafood is enjoyed raw as sashimi in Japan, each one sliced in different ways depending upon the texture of the particular ingredient. Sashimi is served with a variety of garnishes, condiments and dipping sauces. You may decide to serve just one or two types of fish, or a range of seafood, but whatever you choose, be absolutely certain that it is fresh.

8 fresh medium shrimp
4 oz (125 g) freshly shucked scallops
$^{1}/2$ teaspoon oil
5 oz (150 g) fresh tuna fillet
5 oz (150 g) fresh salmon fillet
5 oz (150 g) fresh mackerel or snapper fillet
8 oz (250 g) daikon radish (about 4 in/10 cm), grated into long thin shreds
4 *shiso* leaves
4 teaspoons wasabi paste
Sashimi Soy Dip (page 94), to serve

Peel and clean the shrimp, but leave the head and tail on for a more authentic appearance.

Clean and dry the scallops. Heat the oil in a pan until moderately hot and sear the scallops for 30 seconds on each side. Remove from the heat and set aside.

Slice the tuna and salmon fillets on the diagonal into strips about $^{1}/2$ in (1 cm) wide and $1^{1}/2$ in (3 cm) long. The mackerel or snapper can either be sliced paper-thin or cut into decorative shapes.

Arrange the shrimp, scallops and cut fish on a serving platter. Garnish with the daikon, *shiso* leaves and wasabi paste, and serve with small bowls of Sashimi Soy Dip.

Fresh Shellfish Sashimi

Cockles, also known as ark shell, can reach a diameter of 5 in (12 cm) in Japan. The best quality cockles are harvested in spring, and only the freshest ones are eaten raw. Expert sashimi chefs have a beautiful way of slicing fresh shellfish and a unique method of tenderizing

the meat in preparation for a delightfully mouth-watering sashimi treat—by flinging the meat onto the cutting board several times!

8–12 fresh cherrystone clams or scallops, in the shell
7 oz (200 g) daikon radish (about 3 in/ 8 cm), cut into shreds
Ohba or *shiso* leaves, to garnish
Shiso flowers or alternative garnish
Benitade or alfalfa sprouts
Wasabi paste, to serve
Sashimi Soy Dip (page 94)

Open the shellfish by inserting a knife along the back of the shells and cutting the muscles. Remove the meat, discarding the hard parts and entrails. Slit the cockles or clams down the center, without cutting through, and open to form a butterfly shape. Cut several shallow slits on the outside of the cockle meat. Cut in half and tenderize if needed.

Arrange the shellfish on the shredded daikon or on the leaves, and garnish with the *shiso* flowers and *benitade*. Serve with the wasabi paste and dip.

Fresh Shellfish Sashimi

Seared Tuna with Tangy Dressing

Seared Tuna with Tangy Dressing

Tataki means "to pound" and refers to the method in which seasoned meat is lightly beaten with a knife to enhance its flavor. Lightly seared fish is marinated with tangy seasonings in this refreshing dish—a perfect starter for hot summer months.

Oil, to grease pan
12 oz (375 g) fresh tuna fillet
3 green onions (scallions), thinly sliced into shreds
1 in (2¹/2 cm) young ginger, finely shredded
1–2 cloves garlic, minced
¹/2 lemon, thinly sliced
¹/2 cup (85 ml) Ponzu Dipping Sauce (page 94)
4 oz (125 g) daikon radish (about 2 in/5 cm), sliced into thin strips
Chrysanthemum flowers, to garnish
1 heaped tablespoon grated daikon radish mixed with ¹/4 teaspoon seven-spice chili powder (shichimi) or ground red pepper

Heat a lightly greased frying pan. Sear the fish until the outside of the flesh just turns white. Using a pair of chopsticks, turn and sear the other side, then immediately chill in the refrigerator or freeze to stop the fish from cooking further.

Once the fish has cooled, wipe away any moisture and marinate the whole fillet in half of the green onions, ginger, garlic, lemon and half of the Ponzu Dipping Sauce. Pat the fish with the side of a knife to help the sauce penetrate. Chill in the refrigerator for a minimum of 10 minutes. Cut the marinated fish into small slices.

Arrange the fish and lemon slices on a bed of daikon strips. Sprinkle the remaining sliced green onions, ginger, garlic and the edible flowers over the fish. Serve chilled or at room temperature with the remaining Ponzu Dipping Sauce in a small bowl and seasoned grated daikon on the side.

Chawan Mushi
Steamed Egg Custard Cups

This traditional silky smooth egg custard dish may be served as an appetizer or main course. Blanched vegetables such as asparagus, carrots and spinach may be substituted for the chicken and shrimp. In Japan, chawan-mushi is prepared and served in tall, dainty teacups and eaten with a bamboo spoon.

3 oz (90 g) chicken breast, thinly sliced
5 teaspoons soy sauce
2 large or 3 medium eggs
1¹/3 cups (350 ml) Basic Dashi Stock (page 94) or ²/3 teaspoon dashi stock granules dissolved in 1¹/3 cups (350 ml) hot water
1 teaspoon mirin
8 gingko nuts, peeled, blanched and skins removed (optional)
4 fresh shiitake mushrooms, stems discarded, caps left whole
4 fresh medium shrimp, peeled and deveined, heads and tails intact
4 mitsuba or watercress stems, cut into sections
Grated yuzu orange or lemon peel

Marinate the sliced chicken in 2 teaspoons of soy sauce for about 10 minutes. Drain and set aside.

To prepare the custard, break the eggs in a large bowl and stir gently with chopsticks or a fork. Do not beat or allow bubbles to form in the eggs. Combine the dashi stock with the remaining soy sauce in a saucepan and place over medium heat. Heat until almost to a boil, then quickly remove from the heat. Add the mirin and stir.

Pour the dashi mixture, while still hot, in a slow, steady stream into the eggs, stirring gently to blend. Strain the egg and dashi mixture through a fine sieve.

Evenly divide and place the chicken, followed by gingko nuts, mushroom caps, shrimp and mitsuba or watercress into four small but heat-proof cups or bowls. Slowly pour an equal amount of egg and dashi mixture down the side of the cups. Seal each cup with foil, a heat-proof plate or a lid.

Heat water in a large steamer, and place the custard cups on the rack. Steam over medium-high heat for 1 minute, then reduce the heat to low and steam for another 15 minutes. Insert a knife or fork into the custard; it is cooked when the knife or fork comes out clean. Remove from the steamer and garnish with the grated yuzu orange or lemon peel. Serve immediately.

Sake Shrimp

12–16 fresh large shrimp
1 cup (250 ml) Basic Dashi Stock (page 94)
²/3 cup (150 ml) sake
1 teaspoon sugar
3 teaspoons soy sauce
1 in (2¹/2 cm) young ginger, bruised
16 snow peas or 2 cups sliced spinach or Chinese cabbage

Trim the whiskers and legs of each shrimp. Using a small knife, make a small incision along the mid-section in the back of the shrimp and devein by gently pulling out the intestinal tract.

Blanch the vegetables in lightly salted water for 2 minutes. Drain and portion into individual serving platters. Set aside.

Place the shrimp in a pan with the dashi stock, sake, sugar, soy sauce and ginger. Cook over high heat for 3 to 4 minutes, or until the shrimp turns pink. Remove the shrimp from the heat. Serve the warm broth on the side if desired. Peel the shrimp, keeping the heads and tails intact. Serve immediately on the bed of greens.

Sake Shrimp

Fried Pork Cutlets

Tonkatsu

These deliciously fried cutlets (*tonkatsu*) make a satisfying lunch served with a bowl of rice, a dollop of hot prepared mustard, some thinly sliced cabbage and a splash of *tonkatsu* sauce. Bottled *tonkatsu* sauce is widely available in well-stocked supermarkets. Alternatively, make your own using 1 part Worcestershire or steak sauce and 5 parts tomato ketchup.

4 cups (600 g) cooked rice
4 sprigs *mitsuba* or parsley
Prepared Japanese mustard paste
Tonkatsu sauce, to serve

Pork Cutlets
1 lb (500 g) pork loin
Salt and pepper, to taste
2 tablespoons cornstarch
1 egg, lightly beaten
1/2 cup (30 g) bread crumbs

Oil, for deep-frying

Sauce
3 medium onions, thinly sliced
2 teaspoons oil
1 cup (250 ml) Basic Dashi Stock
  (page 94)
4 tablespoons *mirin*
4 tablespoons soy sauce
4 teaspoons sugar
2 eggs, lightly beaten (optional)

First cut the pork loin into four steaks. Make small incisions along the fatty edges to prevent the steaks from curling during frying. Season the meat lightly with salt and pepper, dust with cornstarch on both sides, dip in

Fried Pork Cutlets (Tonkatsu)

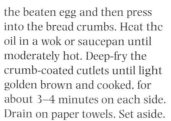

the beaten egg and then press into the bread crumbs. Heat the oil in a wok or saucepan until moderately hot. Deep-fry the crumb-coated cutlets until light golden brown and cooked, for about 3–4 minutes on each side. Drain on paper towels. Set aside.

To prepare the Sauce, heat the oil in a skillet and fry the onions for 2 minutes. Remove the onions and set aside. Add the *dashi* stock, *mirin*, soy sauce and sugar in a pan. Stir and simmer on high heat for 5 minutes. Add the onions, stir and remove the skillet from the heat. Add the beaten eggs, if using and stir gently. Set aside.

Scoop the rice into four large bowls and pour the Sauce and onions over it. Place a cutlet into each bowl, garnish with the *mitsuba* or parsley. Serve hot.

Pork with Ginger

1 lb (500 g) pork loin
1 large onion, thinly sliced
1 tablespoon oil
7 oz (200 g) cabbage cut into squares
1 cup (200 g) Japanese green peppers or bell peppers, deseeded and cut into squares

Seasoning
4 teaspoons juice of grated young ginger
3 tablespoons sake
2–3 tablespoons soy sauce
1 teaspoon dark soy sauce or *tamari* soy sauce
2–3 teaspoons sugar

Mix the Seasoning ingredients together in a bowl and set aside.

Slice the pork into very thin pieces. To thinly slice the pork, wrap it in plastic and place it in the freezer for 20 minutes or until it is half-frozen. Remove the plastic and slice the pork across the grain with a very sharp knife into very thin sheets.

Heat 1/2 tablespoon oil in a frying pan or wok. Stir-fry the onions over high heat for 1 minute, then add the cabbage and green peppers and stir-fry for another 2 minutes. Remove and set aside.

Vegetables Simmered in Dashi and Sake

In the same pan, heat the remaining oil. Add the pork and stir-fry over very high heat for 5 minutes, or until it is cooked. Add the Seasoning and stir, then add the vegetables, mix well and serve hot with steamed rice and soup, if desired.

Vegetables Simmered in Dashi and Sake

An array of vegetables simmered in dashi and rice wine creates this hearty stew which is surprisingly light and, at the same time, healthy and delicious. Any combination of vegetables may be used, depending on availability and personal preference. The amount of stock called for in this recipe is sufficient for about 1 1/2 lbs (750 g) of vegetables.

1 1/2 lbs (750 g) combination of four or five types of root vegetables, such as daikon radish, burdock root, lotus root, potatoes and pre-cooked bamboo shoots
4 fresh shiitake mushrooms, stems discarded, caps halved
12 snow peas or sugar snap peas
5 oz (150 g) boneless chicken, cut into bite-sized strips (optional)

2 teaspoons oil
3 cups (750 ml) Basic Dashi Stock
  (page 94)
1/3 cup (85 ml) soy sauce
1/2 cup (125 ml) sake
2–3 tablespoons sugar

Peel and cut all the root vegetables into bite-sized chunks. Bring a small saucepan of lightly salted water to a boil. Boil the different types of vegetables separately for about 5 minutes each. Repeat with the *konnyaku*.

Scald the shiitake mushrooms and the sugar snap peas. Blanch the chicken pieces in hot water for 20 seconds. Drain, chill in ice water and drain again.

Heat the oil in a frying pan, add the mushrooms, snow peas and chicken, stir briskly, remove from the heat and set aside.

Bring the *dashi* stock, soy, sake and sugar to a boil in a deep saucepan. Add the parboiled vegetables and mushrooms, and simmer gently for 15–20 minutes, or until all the vegetables are tender.

Portion the snow peas, chicken and the cooked vegetables into individual bowls. Pour the hot broth over and serve immediately.

Grilled Eggplant and Shrimp with Miso Sauce

In this dish, the rather bland flavor of eggplant is transformed by a robust miso sauce.

1 lb (500 g) slender Japanese eggplants
2 tablespoons oil
8 fresh medium shrimp, peeled and deveined (optional)
12 snow peas, to garnish (optional)

Miso Sauce
3 tablespoons red miso
1 teaspoon sake
1 teaspoon *mirin*
2 teaspoons sugar
2 tablespoons water

Combine all the Miso Sauce ingredients in a small saucepan and gently heat on low for 3 minutes, stirring constantly until the sugar has dissolved and the alcohol has evaporated, then set aside.

Blanch the snow peas for 1 minute, drain and set aside to cool.

Blanch the shrimp until just cooked and pink, or for about 1 minute, and set aside.

Cut the eggplants in half lengthwise and score, making criss-cross incisions. Place the eggplants on a baking tray and brush with the oil. Grill for 7 minutes on each side, or until tender. Alternatively, bake at 400°F (200°C) for 15 minutes until tender.

Spread the Miso Sauce on the open face of the eggplants and grill or bake for another 2 minutes. Remove from the heat and serve the eggplant pieces garnished with the snow peas and shrimp.

Instead of grilling or baking, the eggplants are usually cut into bite-sized pieces, deep-fried and drained. It is then mixed with the Miso Sauce (omit the water in this case), and serve with the snow peas and shrimp on the side.

Grilled Fish with Salt

This is perhaps the simplest and also the tastiest method of cooking whole fish. Pressing the fish liberally with salt before grilling helps keep in the moisture and gives the fish an attractive snowy coat. Grilled fish is usually served with grated daikon on the side, drizzled with soy sauce, and eaten with hot steamed rice.

4 small to medium whole fish, such as mackerel, trout, flounder, sole or pomfret
1 tablespoon coarse salt

Lemon wedge
4 oz (125 g) daikon radish (about 2 in/5 cm), grated and lightly squeezed to remove moisture

Pickled Lotus Root
1/2 cup peeled and thinly sliced lotus root
3 tablespoons Sweet Vinegar (page 94)
1 red finger-length chili, deseeded
1/4 cup (75 ml) Ponzu Dipping Sauce (page 94)

Prepare the Pickled Lotus Root in advance as it needs to marinate. Blanch the sliced lotus root in water for 30 seconds, drain and place it in the Sweet Vinegar. Heat the chili in a dry pan for a few seconds, then add it to the Sweet Vinegar. Pour in the Ponzu Dipping Sauce. Stir and refrigerate for several hours.

Clean, scale and rinse the fish thoroughly. Dry with a paper towel and make two deep incisions crosswise on each side. Put a skewer through the fish. Sprinkle both sides of the fish lightly with salt, then press a liberal amount of salt onto the tail and fins.

Cook the fish over a moderately hot charcoal fire or under a broiler, turning it with the skewer to avoid damaging the skin, until the fish is golden on both sides and cooked through. Turn the fish only once. Wrap the tail in aluminum foil halfway through to avoid it getting too charred, if necessary. Serve on a plate garnished with the lemon wedge, grated daikon and soy sauce with the Pickled Lotus Root on the side.

Seared Tuna Seaweed and Cucumber Salad

An excellent combination of lightly seared or blanched tuna (the outside cooked for a few seconds while the inside is still raw), crunchy cucumber slices and chewy wakame seaweed.

8 oz (200 g) fresh tuna
Oil, to sear
1 1/2 heaped tablespoons dried *wakame* seaweed, rinsed and soaked in water to soften
1 small Japanese cucumber
1 teaspoon salt
1 green onion (scallion), white part only, thinly sliced, to garnish

Miso Mustard Dressing
5 1/2 tablespoons white *miso*
1 1/2 teaspoons sesame paste or smooth peanut butter
2 1/2 tablespoons rice vinegar
1/2–1 tablespoon sugar
2 teaspoons soy sauce
1–2 teaspoons prepared Japanese mustard paste

In a small bowl, mix all the ingredients for the Miso Mustard Dressing and set aside.

Heat a skillet with a few drops of oil and lightly sear the tuna for a few seconds on all sides. Alternatively, boil a cup of water in a saucepan. Using a pair of chopsticks, plunge the tuna in the boiling water for 5 to 10 seconds until the flesh on the outside starts to turn pinkish white. Remove and chill in ice water for a few seconds, drain and cut into sashimi-thin slices.

Rub 1/2 teaspoon of the salt onto the cucumber skin. Then, halve the cucumber lengthwise and cut into paper-thin strips. Sprinkle with the remaining salt, mix and set aside for 5 minutes. Rinse off the salt and gently squeeze out the moisture.

Arrange the tuna, *wakame* and cucumber on a platter. Top with a little of the Dressing and garnish each serving with strips of green onion.

Grilled Fish with Salt

Chicken Wings Braised in Ginger and Soy

Chicken Wings Braised in Ginger and Soy

This dish is made using *sato-imo*, also known as taro potatoes, which have a delicious creamy texture when thoroughly cooked. As *sato-imo* are not readily available, baby potatoes—or any boiling potato or yams—may be used instead. Tasty and easy to prepare, more vegetables can be added to make a complete one-dish meal.

1 lb (500 g) chicken wings
3 tablespoons sake
2 teaspoons oil
3/4 in (2 cm) young ginger, sliced
5 green onions (scallions), cut into sections
14 oz (400 g) baby potatoes or *sato-imo* potatoes, peeled
2–3 tablespoons soy sauce
2 teaspoons dark soy sauce or *tamari* soy sauce
2–3 teaspoons sugar
12 snow peas or sugar snap peas

Marinate the chicken wings in the sake for 30 minutes. Heat the oil in a pan and stir-fry the wings until they change color. Add the ginger, green onions and enough water to just cover the chicken. Cover the pan and simmer for 5 minutes.

Add the potatoes, soy sauce and sugar, and stir. Simmer, covered, over medium heat for 20 minutes or until potatoes are soft.

Blanch the snow peas in lightly salted water and set aside.

Dish the chicken wings and potatoes into four bowls and serve warm with snow peas on the side.

Grilled Miso Fish

This is an exquisite way to prepare white fish fillets like cod, seabass or snapper. For maximum flavor, begin preparing this dish 3 days in advance.

1–1 1/2 lbs (500–750 g) cod or seabass fillets
1 1/2 cups (300 g) white miso
1/3 cup (85 ml) sake
1/2 teaspoon sugar
1/2 teaspoon ground red pepper (optional)
2 tablespoons *mirin*, for basting
4 oz (125 g) daikon radish (about 2 in/5 cm), freshly grated or 4 pieces pickled daikon, to serve
Soy sauce, to serve

Cut the fish into four serving pieces. Combine the miso, sake, sugar and ground red pepper (if using) in a bowl. Add the fish fillets and rub the marinade into the fish so that they are well coated. Cover and marinate in the refrigerator for 1–3 days.

Remove the fillets and scrape off the miso. Cut a shallow cross on the surface of each fillet and broil under low heat for about 20 minutes or until the fish is cooked. Brush the fillets with *mirin* each time you turn them over to add a shiny glaze to the fish, Serve immediately with the grated or pickled daikon and osy sauce on the side.

Steamed Fish with Noodles in Clear Broth

7 oz (200 g) red snapper or redfish
1/2 teaspoon salt
4 oz (125 g) dried fine wheat noodles (*somen*) or angel hair pasta
3 1/2 oz (100 g) *shimeji* mushrooms
1 heaped tablespoon grated daikon radish, mixed with 1/4 teaspoon ground red pepper
2 green onions (scallions), white part only, very thinly sliced

Clear Broth
1 cup (250 ml) Basic Dashi Stock (page 94)
1 tablespoon sake
1 tablespoon *mirin*
1/2 teaspoon soy sauce
Salt, to taste

To make the Clear Broth, bring all the ingredients to a boil in a saucepan over medium-high heat. Remove from the heat and set aside in a warm place.

Sprinkle the fish with salt, then slice into four pieces. Place on a heat-proof dish and steam for 5 minutes. Remove and set aside.

Cook the noodles in lightly salted boiling water, until soft. Drain and immediately rinse under cold water and drain again.

Divide the noodles into four individual serving bowls. Place a piece of fish and portion the *shimeji* mushrooms on the noodles in each bowl. Return to the steamer. Steam the fish again over rapidly boiling water for 5 minutes.

Remove the bowls from the steamer and pour in the Clear Broth. Serve with grated daikon on the side and garnish with the green onions.

Miso Soup with Mushrooms

Nameko mushrooms are attractive reddish brown mushrooms with a smooth texture that are excellent fresh, although other fresh mushrooms may be used as substitutes if fresh *nameko* are not available.

4 cups (1 liter) Basic Dashi Stock (page 94)
4 tablespoons miso
5 oz (150 g) *nameko* or other fresh mushrooms, rinsed
1 cake silken tofu, diced (8 oz/250 g)
4 teaspoons very finely sliced green onions (scallions)

Bring the *dashi* stock to a boil in a saucepan. Reduce the heat and add the miso, stirring to dissolve. Quickly add the mushrooms and tofu, and allow them to heat through, but do not let the soup boil. Remove from the heat.

Stir, then ladle the soup into four individual bowls. Sprinkle with the green onions and serve hot.

Grilled Miso Fish

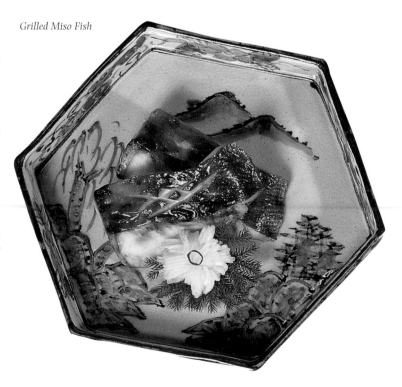

Sirloin Steak Teriyaki

Miso Soup with Clams

30 littleneck clams or other baby
    clams (about 8 oz/250 g)
2 cups (500 ml) water
2 cups (500 ml) Basic Dashi Stock
    (page 94) or 1 teaspoon dashi
    stock granules dissolved in 2 cups
    (500 ml) hot water
3 tablespoons miso
Sprigs of *mitsuba* leaves, parsley
    or watercress, to garnish
Sansho powder, to taste

Soak the clams in cool, lightly
salted water for 20 minutes,
then scrub with a brush. Bring
the water to a boil in a saucepan,
then add the clams and cook for
about 3 minutes or until the
clams open. Remove from the
heat. With a slotted spoon, portion the cooked clams into four
soup bowls.

Strain and reserve the clam
stock. Rinse the saucepan well,
pour the clam stock, then the
dashi stock into the saucepan
and bring to a boil. Lower the
heat, add the miso to the stock
and stir to dissolve. Remove
from the heat immediately. Stir,
then ladle the soup over the
clams and serve garnished with
mitsuba leaves and a sprinkling
of *sansho* powder.

Grilled Clams with Miso and Mushrooms

16 large clams
8 fresh shiitake mushrooms, stems
    discarded, caps quartered
2 tablespoons bottled Japanese
    Mayonnaise, add 1 tablespoon
    white miso, 1/2 teaspoon lemon juice
    or a pinch of grated citrus peel
1/2 tablespoon white miso
1/2 teaspoon finely grated *yuzu*
    orange or lemon peel

Steam the clams using lightly
salted water and remove from
the heat immediately when the

shells open. Drain the clams and
remove the meat, reserving the
shells. Cut each clam in half.
Put 2 clam pieces and mushrooms on each reserved shell.

Mix the Japanese Mayonnaise,
miso and *yuzu* peel together and
top each clam shell with about
1/2 teaspoon of the mixture.
Grill under low heat for 2 minutes, then serve immediately.

Sirloin Steak Teriyaki

1 lb (500 g) beef tenderloin, cut
    into bite-sized cubes
8 small Japanese green peppers,
    cut into 8 strips

Fried Vegetables
1 teaspoon oil
2 cups (100 g) bean sprouts
1 cup fresh oyster mushrooms, ends
    trimmed or fresh shiitake mush-
    rooms, stems discarded
1 tablespoon sake
1/4 teaspoon freshly ground black
    pepper
1/2 teaspoon salt

Teriyaki Steak Sauce
6 1/2 tablespoons (100 ml) soy sauce
6 1/2 tablespoons (100 ml) sake
2/3 cup (150 ml) *mirin*
2 tablespoons sugar

Make the Teriyaki Steak Sauce
by combining all the ingredients
in a saucepan and bring to a
boil over medium heat. Simmer
for about 15 minutes until the
sauce is reduced to about 1 cup.

If using Japanese green peppers, make a small slit in the side
of each. Thread the Japanese
peppers or bell pepper strips onto
skewers and grill until done.

Thread the steak on skewers
and grill until about half-
cooked. Brush with the Steak
Sauce and return to the grill for
another 30 seconds or so. Turn
the steak over and brush again.
Grill for another 30 seconds,
then give the steak a final
brushing and cook for 30 seconds on each side until nicely
glazed.

To cook the Fried Vegetables,
heat the pan over high heat, add
the oil and stir-fry the bean
sprouts and mushrooms briskly.
Season with the sake, pepper and
salt. Stir-fry for 1–2 minutes, or
until just cooked. Portion onto
individual serving plates.

Remove the skewers from the
peppers and steak and serve
immediately with the vegetables
on the side.

Shabu-shabu
Mongolian Hotpot

1 lb (500 g) well-marbled, prime
    beef sirloin
1 packet (3 1/2 oz/100 g) dried *shi-
    rataki* or bean thread noodles
10 oz (300 g) Chinese cabbage
2 leeks, white part only
1 bunch (8 oz/250 g) chrysanthemum
    leaves, washed, hard stems discarded
7 oz (200 g) *enokitake* mushrooms
1 cake (8 oz/250 g) silken tofu, cubed

Shabu-shabu (Mongolian Hotpot)

8 fresh shiitake mushrooms, stems discarded, caps cross-cut

Stock
6 cups (1 1/2 liters) water
1 strip dried kelp (*konbu*), (4 in/10 cm long), wiped with a damp cloth and halved
1 teaspoon salt

Accompaniments
Ponzu Dipping Sauce (page 94)
4 tablespoons finely grated daikon radish with 1/4 teaspoon ground red pepper
Sesame Dipping Sauce (page 94)
4 tablespoons minced green onions (scallions)

Place the Sesame and Ponzu Dipping Sauces into separate dipping bowls. Place the grated daikon and green onions into individual saucers.

Slice the beef following the instructions used for Sukiyaki (recipe on this page). Cook the noodles, if using, in boiling water until soft (see packet instructions). Drain, rinse in cold water, drain again and set aside.

Slice the cabbage thinly, keeping the leaves and stems separate. Slice the leeks on the diagonal. Slice the hard ends of the *enokitake* mushroom stems and discard. Arrange the beef, noodles, vegetables and tofu on a serving platter or basket.

To prepare the Stock, place a large metal or ceramic casserole on a hot plate or gas burner in the center of the table and add the water and kelp. When the water comes to a boil,

quickly remove the kelp with chop sticks and discard. Add the salt and stir to dissolve.

Each person may now select morsels of food and immerse it in the Stock with chopsticks until it is cooked. Skim the Stock of any foam that surfaces during cooking. Have some boiling water at hand, to add to the Stock while cooking, should it dry up too quickly. The noodles are usually cooked last, by which time the Stock would have become a rich soup. Serve with the Ponzu Dipping Sauce mixed with the grated daikon, and the Sesame Dipping Sauce mixed with the green onions.

Mixed Seafood Hotpot

5 oz (150 g) each of any of the following seafood ingredients: fresh shrimp, clams, shucked oysters, scallops and fish fillets
5 oz (150 g) chicken fillets
1 packet (3 1/2 oz/100 g) dried *shirataki* or bean thread noodles
1 small carrot, peeled and sliced
1/2 small Chinese cabbage
2 leeks, white part only, cut diagonally
12 fresh shiitake mushrooms, stems discarded, caps cross-cut 4 oz (125 g) *enokitake* mushrooms
1 cake (8 oz/250 g) soft tofu, cubed
1 bunch chrysanthemum greens
Ponzu Dipping Sauce (page 94)

Stock
7 cups (1 3/4 liters) Basic Dashi Stock (page 94)

4–5 tablespoons soy sauce
2 tablespoons *mirin*
8 oz (250 g) daikon radish, sliced

Place all the Stock ingredients in a large pan and simmer on medium heat for 15 minutes. Set aside and keep warm.

Peel and devein the shrimp, keeping the heads and tails intact. Scrub the clams clean and soak in lightly salted water for 20 minutes. Rinse the oysters thoroughly with lightly salted water. Drain in a colander and set aside. Slice the fish fillets into bite-sized pieces. Blanch the fish quickly in boiling water until it just changes color, then drain and set aside.

Slice the chicken fillets into bite-sized pieces and blanch in boiling water and leave to chill in a small bowl of ice water. Drain, rinse in cold water, drain again and set aside.

Cook the noodles in boiling water until soft (see packet instructions). Drain and set aside. Blanch the carrots and cabbage. Drain and set aside. Wash the chrysanthemum greens, discard the hard stems and cut them into lengths. Arrange all the ingredients attractively on a large platter.

Pour the Stock into a heatproof casserole and set it on a hotplate or gas burner at the center of the table. To cook, place the chicken and clams in the Stock, followed by half of the fish, shrimp, oysters, noodles and vegetables. Wait until the ingredients are cooked, before adding the remaining ingredients. Serve with Ponzu Dipping Sauce and soy sauce.

Sukiyaki
Beef Hotpot with Vegetables

One of the most popular Japanese dishes abroad, sukiyaki became known in Japan around the turn of the century, when the Japanese began eating beef (previously prohibited by Buddhist law). There are two styles of sukiyaki: the Osaka style involves preparing the Sukiyaki Sauce at the table each time a new ingredient is cooked; in the Tokyo style (followed in this recipe) the sauce is made in advance, and served with the cooked food.

1 lb (500 g) well-marbled prime beef sirloin, very thinly sliced
1 packet (3 oz/90 g) dried *shirataki* or bean thread noodles or arrowroot starch noodles
1 large onion, peeled and sliced
2 leeks, white part only, sliced diagonally
1 bunch chrysanthemum leaves, hard parts of stems discarded, washed
12 fresh shiitake mushrooms, stems discarded, caps cross-cut
4 oz (125 g) enokitake mushrooms, hard part of stems discarded
1 cake (8 oz/250 g) firm tofu, sliced into rectangles
1 gluten cake (*fu*) or grilled bean curd (*yakidofu*), sliced into rectangles
4 eggs (optional), to serve
1 portion Sukiyaki Sauce (page 94)

To thinly slice the beef, wrap it in shrinkwrap and place it in the freezer for 20 minutes or until it is half-frozen. Remove

Mixed Seafood Hotpot

Sukiyaki (Beef Hotpot with Vegetables)

Jellied Plums

A simple dessert, with large grapes or plums set in jellied plum wine *(umeshu)*. If Japanese plum wine is not available, substitute with any other fortified fruit wine, such as peach or raspberry.

8 large seedless grapes or plums
2¹/2 envelopes (25 g) unflavored Japanese gelatin powder
¹/4 cup (60 ml) water
1 small bottle Japanese plum wine (*umeshu*)
2¹/2 tablespoons (30 g) sugar
1 teaspoon cognac or brandy
8 porcelain teacups or jelly molds

Blanch the grapes or plums in hot water for about 10 seconds, drain and put in cold water to chill for a few seconds. Peel, halve and set aside.

Stir the gelatin and water in a non-reactive saucepan. Simmer over medium heat, stirring constantly, until the gelatin is dissolved and smooth. Add the plum wine and sugar, stir until the sugar is melted. Remove from the heat, add the cognac and stir.

Portion the grapes or plums into the teacups. Pour the liquid jelly into the teacups and chill until the jelly sets.

the plastic, slice and reserve some beef fat to use for greasing the pot. Slice the beef across the grain with a very sharp knife into very thin sheets.

Cook the noodles in boiling water until soft (see packet instructions). Drain, rinse in cold water, drain again and set aside.

Arrange the beef, noodles, vegetables and tofu on a large platter or basket. Crack the eggs into individual dipping bowls.

Place a large iron skillet or Dutch oven on top of a hot plate or gas burner on the table. Heat the pot and grease with a chunk of the reserved beef fat or small amount of vegetable oil. Add a small portion of the sliced beef and vegetables and tofu, pour a little of the Sukiyaki Sauce over the ingredients and simmer. When the ingredients are cooked, each person helps himself to the food from the hotpot. If desired, the food can be dipped into the lightly stirred egg before eating. Serve with steamed rice.

Green Tea Ice Cream

Finely powdered green tea gives a uniquely Japanese flavor to this delightfully rich ice cream.

2¹/4 oz (75 g) green tea powder
¹/3 cup (75 ml) cognac or brandy
5 cups (1¹/4 liters) fresh milk
1 cup (250 ml) heavy cream
1¹/3 cups (100 g) skimmed milk powder
1³/4 cups (350 g) sugar
Sweetened *azuki* beans

Place the green tea powder in a bowl, add the cognac and mix well.

Pour the fresh milk, cream, milk powder and sugar into another bowl and mix well. Transfer to a saucepan and bring to a boil over moderate heat. Remove from the heat and allow to cool to a lukewarm temperature, then add the green tea mixture and mix well.

Chill immediately in the freezer section of the refrigerator until ice crystals start to form around the edges of the container. Pour the mixture into a blender or food processor and blend for a few seconds to break up the crystals. Leave the mixture to freeze in a plastic container. For an interesting variation, serve topped with sweetened *azuki* beans.

Green Tea Ice Cream

An old Korean saying reads: "A man can live without a wife but not without *kimchi.*"

KOREA

A rugged land of mountains, forests, and jagged coastline has produced an equally robust, and delicious, cuisine.

Left: A stall operator in a Korean market prepares for a busy day.

Right: Chinese cabbage on sale at an auction market.

Many factors have contributed to the evolution of Korean cooking over the centuries, and the most important of these are the geography and climate, the importance of medicinal vegetables and herbs, and the various influences that have presented themselves throughout the history of this Land of Morning Calm.

Mountains, Forests, and Seas

The Korean peninsula juts out like a spur from the Asian mainland, just below Manchuria in north-eastern China, and eastern Siberia. To the west lies the Yellow Sea and China; to the east the East Sea and Japan. Scattered off the jagged coastline are some 3,000 islands. But apart from the encircling sea, Korea is a land of mountains. Only 20 percent of the country consists of arable land, and of this a large proportion is represented by the rice-growing Honam plain in southwest Korea.

Korea is also rich in forests with mountain parks full of juniper, bamboo, willow, red maples, and flowering fruit and nut trees such as apricot,

pear, peach, plum, cherry, persimmon, chestnut, walnut, ginkgo, and pine nut. Korea has four distinct seasons: spring and autumn are temperate, winter and summer verge on the extremes. Winter is particularly cold, with temperatures dropping to 24°F (-15°C) or less, and it often lasts from November until late March. This climate, in combination with the mountainous interior, has given Koreans an appetite for hearty, stimulating food, which helps to keep out the cold and produce energy—meat, soup, chilies, garlic, ginseng, and many medicinal vegetables, berries, and nuts. At the same time, the four seasons have guaranteed the Koreans a steady flow of seasonal produce. The lowland fields provide excellent grains and vegetables, while the uplands grow wild and cultivated mushrooms, roots, and greens.

The surrounding seas produce a host of fish, seafood, seaweed, and crustaceans. However, it is the sense of food as medicine and long-term protection that has governed the evolution of the Korean diet. Even raw fish sashimi is given extra vitality by being seasoned with red chili. Most meals are served with a gruel or a soup, as well as the ubiquitous, fortifying *kimchi* and a range of vegetarian side dishes collectively known as *namul*, which are delicately seasoned with soy, seasame, and garlic.

Medicinal Foods

Koreans often look to herbal remedies for illnesses, the result of their grounding in Chinese medical belief about the yin-yang balance of the body and the warming-cooling properties of certain foods. The most common medicinal foods used in cooking are dried persimmon, jujube (red dates), pine seeds, chestnut, ginkgo, tangerine, and ginseng. The sapodin in garlic, which Koreans often eat raw wrapped in a lettuce leaf round barbecued meat, is said to cleanse the blood and aid digestion. Chicken and pork are considered the first steps to obesity, so are largely avoided. Nuts are supposed to be good for pregnancy as well as the skin; jujube and bellflower root for coughs and colds; raw potato juice for an upset stomach; while dried pollack with bean sprouts and tofu is said to be good for hangovers.

In the past, close to the forests and mountain streams, Buddhist monks studied the scriptures; they also developed a "mountain cuisine" that has become the foundation of Korean cooking today. For example, meat, which is forbidden to the Buddhist monk, and anything that is strong smelling, such as garlic and green onion, did not feature in temple cuisine. While modern Korean Buddhism is not so rigid about garlic, this cuisine has retained its traditional dependence on roots, grasses, and herbs. Other stalwarts of the Korean table originate from the mountains, too, such as vegetable pancakes or *jeon*, which are usually filled with lentils or leeks and are sometimes fashioned in the shape of a flower.

Kimchi, Spices, and Ginseng

Even today it is virtually impossible to find a Korean house, apartment, or monastery without rows of big, black enameled *kimchi* pots on the porch or balcony, or, in the snowy months, beneath the earth. *Kimchi* can be preserved for a long time. Its hot and spicy taste stimulates the appetite, and it is nutritious, providing vitamins, lactic acid, and minerals otherwise lacking in the winter diet. The introduction of chili into the pickling process of vegetables in the 17th century, a process that dates back a thousand years or more, was an important innovation in Korean food culture. Using chilies in combination with vegetables and fish resulted in a unique method of food preservation and led to the adoption of *kimchi* as a Korean staple. Red chili and garlic are the mainstays of the basic *kimchi* formula, which calls for heads of fresh cabbage to be cut open, salted, placed in brine with lots of red chili and garlic and set to ferment. In summer, when fermentation is rapid, *kimchi* is made fresh every day. In winter, the big *kimchi* pots are packed in straw and buried in the earth to prevent freezing, then left to ferment for months. There are literally hundreds of *kimchi* types.

Wrapped kimchi (*bossam kimchi*), comprising seafood such as octopus, shrimp, and oyster; white cabbage kimchi (*baek kimchi*), mainly made in the south and containing pickled fish, and sometimes eaten with noodles in winter; stuffed cucumber kimchi (*oisobaegi*), made with cucumbers stuffed with seasonings; hot radish kimchi (*kkaktugi*), made with Korean white radishes cut into small cubes, seasoned and fermented; "bachelor" radish kimchi (*chonggak kimchi*), made with small salted white radishes and anchovies; and sliced radish and cabbage kimchi (*nabak kimchi*), with small pieces of white radish or cabbage pickled in seasoned brine, mixed with whole green or red chilies, and served chilled.

There are also many fermented pastes and sauces for dipping,

called *chang*. Every restaurant and home has its own formula for making *chang*. Based on a fermented mash of soybeans, the three most common varieties are *kan chang* (dark and liquid), *daen chang* (thick and pungent), and *gochu chang* (fiery and hot).

Ginseng (*insam*) is also a staple of the Korean diet; it is also one of Korea's most universally recognized symbols. The roots are grown in long, neat rows protected from the elements by thatched shelters. After harvesting, they are washed, peeled, and dried, then sorted according to age and quality into white ginseng types. Red ginseng, which is regarded by Koreans as the very best, is steamed before being dried in the sun, which is believed to increase its medicinal powers. Koreans consume an enormous amount of ginseng—as root, pills, capsules, candies, chewing gum, cigarettes, tonics, and beauty products. Ginseng tea (*insam-cha*) is a national drink, and is available in tea shops everywhere. Perhaps the most famous ginseng dish is ginseng chicken soup (*samgyetang*). The chicken is stuffed with ginseng, jujube, sticky rice, and garlic, then stewed. The result is a sweet, tender, flavorsome dish that is sublimely cooling on hot summer days.

Table Settings and Etiquette

Korean table settings are classified into 3-*cheop*, 5-*cheop*, 7-*cheop*, 9-*cheop*, and 12-*cheop*, according to the number of side dishes served at a meal. For an everyday Korean meal, the average family takes about four side dishes, along with rice—traditionally the center of all table arrangements—soup, and *kimchi*. The main meals include breakfast, which is the most fortifying meal of the day, a lighter lunch (called *jeomsin*, which means "to lighten the heart"), and a not-too-heavy dinner.

The basic *bansang* setting includes seven side dishes with boiled rice, soup, three seasoning sauces—such as red chili paste, *kimchi*, and hot radish *kimchi*—and two heavier soups, such as hot pollack or rib stew. These soups are considered an accompaniment to the meal and not a starter. Except for the individual bowl of rice and soup, the dishes are shared. Rice, soup, and stews are eaten with spoons, and the rather dry side dishes are eaten with metal chopsticks, but spoon and chopsticks are not used at the same time. Bowls and plates are also not raised from the table.

The Korean barbecue is well-known throughout the world and in Korea it is a popular way of cooking beef in restaurants and in street stalls. At home, families usually use a table-top grill on which to cook *bulgogi* and *galbi* ribs.

The ceremonial aspect of Korean dining has been greatly influenced by Confucianism and the royal court. There are abundant archives of royal dishes in Korea, and some of them can still be experienced in their entirety. For example, *gujeolpan* (nine-sectioned royal platter) is served in an octagonal lacquered platter with nine compartments. Delicate pancakes are placed in the center, surrounded by eight other treasures to be carefully interwoven into the pancakes. Another royal delicacy is *shinseolo*, which comes in a brass pot with a chimney.

Many families also own a special pot used in steamboat or fire-kettle meals. This unusual vessel has a central chimney surrounded by a moat which is filled with morsels of food and kept in the fridge until ready to eat. An hour or more before mealtime, coals are lit in an outside barbecue so that when the vessel is removed from the fridge and placed at the dining area, the glowing red coals can be inserted into the chimney. A hot broth is poured into the moat and is kept hot by the chimney. Diners are then able to select food items from the hot broth—this is a delicious and very social way of dining!

SUGGESTED MENUS

Family meals

Enjoy a Korean-style family meal at home with rice and:
• Classic Chinese Cabbage Kimchi (page 112);
• Tofu with Spicy Sauce (page 112);
• Rice Bowl with Beef and Vegetables (page 115)

Dinner parties

For a smart dinner party with Korean dishes, serve rice and:
• Seafood Hotpot (page 113);
• Classic Chinese Cabbage Kimchi (page 112);
• Ginseng Chicken Soup (page 113);
• Barbecued Beef (page 114).

Finger food

For fun snacks and appetizers that can be eaten with the fingers, try:
• Seafood Pancakes (page 112);
• Grilled Beef Ribs (page 114);

A melting pot menu

For an interesting tasting menu that takes in many special Asian dishes, serve your guests:
• Miso Soup with Mushrooms (page 104) from Japan;
• Barbecued Beef (page 114) from Korea with plain rice;
• Spicy Pomelo or Grapefruit Salad (page 160) from Thailand;
• Shaved Ice Dessert (page 86) from Indonesia or seasonal fresh fruits as dessert.

THE ESSENTIAL FLAVORS OF KOREAN COOKING

Ingredients common to the Koeran pantry include Korean chili in its many guises: **fresh red chili** is used in the preparation of *kimchi*, **chili flakes**, **chili powder**, and **chili threads** are all made from dried red chilies and are used as garnishing items and to add heat to a dish. **Chili paste** is available from Korean stores. Korean **medium grain rice** would be ideal but Japanese rice is an acceptable substitute (do not use long or short grain rice.) If you are not making your own ***kimchi,*** then keep a steady supply on hand for every meal.

Classic Chinese (Napa) Cabbage Kimchi

Classic Chinese (Napa) Cabbage Kimchi

Kimchi—a fermented vegetable condiment—is served with every Korean meal. This classic kimchi is made with Chinese cabbage, chives, daikon radish and leek, and is seasoned with chili, garlic and ginger. For a sour kimchi, cover and store in a cool place for 1–2 days to ferment, then keep refrigerated for up to 3 months. Kimchi can also be eaten fresh.

1 large Chinese or Napa cabbage
3/4 cup (210 g) sea salt, coarse salt or pickling salt
8 cups (2 liters) water

Kimchi Spice Mixture
4 tablespoons glutinous rice flour
1 1/2 cups (375 ml) water
3 tablespoons crushed garlic
1/2 in (2 cm) ginger, crushed
4 tablespoons fish sauce
8–10 tablespoons ground red pepper
1/2 tablespoon sugar
8 oz (250 g) daikon radish (about 4 in/10 cm), sliced into strips
1 1/2 cups (90 g) Chinese chives, sliced into lengths
1/2 leek, thinly sliced diagonally

Rinse the cabbage, remove two outer leaves and set aside. Halve the rest of the cabbage lengthwise. Rub 1/4 cup of the sea salt between all the leaves and place the cabbage in a large plastic tub or container. Add the remaining salt and the water. Place a big plate on top of the cabbage to weigh it down and keep the cabbage immersed in the brine. Soak for 4 to 6 hours or more, until the stems soften and bend without breaking.

To make the Kimchi Spice Mixture, first make a glutinous rice flour paste by heating the flour and the water in a small saucepan. Stir constantly until it thickens, about 4 minutes, then set aside to cool. Once it has

cooled, combine with the garlic, ginger, fish sauce, red pepper and sugar in a large bowl and mix well. Add the daikon, chives and leek, mix gently and set aside.

After the cabbage has finished soaking, rinse the leaves thoroughly under running water. Fill a container with water and shake the two halves of the cabbage backwards and forwards vigorously to remove the salt. Squeeze the cabbage firmly to remove excess water and set aside to drain.

Rub the Kimchi Spice Mixture all over the cabbage and in between leaves. Press the leaves together and place into a large airtight container. Top with the reserved outer leaves and cover. Leave to stand unrefrigerated overnight, then refrigerate.

> To make **fresh kimchi**, first cut the cabbage into bite-sized pieces, then sprinkle the sea salt and soak in the water for 2 hours and continue with the recipe. Never use a reactive metal to store kimchi; use porcelain, stainless steel or sturdy plastic.

Seafood Pancakes

Pancakes are very popular in Korea. As seafood is widely available in most parts of the country, pancakes made with oysters, fish or mixed seafood are often found. Plenty of green onions add extra flavor to this version.

1/3 cup (40 g) glutinous rice flour
1/3 cup (40 g) rice flour
1/3 cup (50 g) flour
1 large egg, lightly beaten
1 teaspoon salt
1/2 teaspoon ground white pepper
3/4 cup (185 ml) water
8 teaspoons oil
12–16 green onions (scallions), cut into lengths, or length of the skillet
1/2 cup (100 g) fresh oysters, rinsed and drained or 3/4 cup (150 g) mixed seafood—fish, clams, shrimp

and squid—cut into small pieces
1 red finger-length chili, deseeded and sliced into long, thin strips

Garlic Soy Dip
3 tablespoons soy sauce
1/2–1 tablespoon rice vinegar
1 teaspoon minced garlic
1/2 teaspoon sesame oil
1 teaspoon toasted sesame seeds
1/4 teaspoon ground black pepper

Mix all the Garlic Soy Dip ingredients in a bowl. Set aside.

Combine the flours, egg, salt and pepper in a mixing bowl, gradually stirring in the water to make a smooth, thin batter. Keep 4 tablespoons of the batter aside, divide the rest into 4 portions.

Heat 2 teaspoons of the oil in a skillet (diameter of 6 in/15 cm). When the oil is moderately hot, add 1 portion of the batter and spread it over the base of the skillet to make a thin pancake.

Lay the green onion sections in neat rows on the batter, then scatter the oysters and sliced chili on top. Drizzle 1 tablespoon of the reserved batter over the green onions and oysters to secure to the pancake. Cook for 2 to 3 minutes over medium heat until the pancake is golden brown underneath and the top starts to set. Turn the pancake over and cook for another minute. Repeat with the remaining portions of batter to make 4 pancakes. Serve hot with little bowls of the Garlic Soy Dip.

Tofu with Spicy Sauce

A deliciously simple way of serving tofu. A light side dish, perfect on a hot summer night.

1 lb (500 g) silken or soft tofu, chilled and cut into 4 pieces

Seafood Pancakes

1 green onion (scallion), minced
1/2 red finger-length chili, deseeded and minced

Spicy Sesame Sauce
1 tablespoon soy sauce
1 teaspoon sesame oil
1 clove garlic, finely minced
1/2 red finger-length chili, minced
1 teaspoon ground red pepper
1 teaspoon water
2 teaspoons toasted sesame seeds, crushed
2 green onions (scallions), minced

To make the Spicy Sesame Sauce, combine all the ingredients, mix well and set aside.

Place the 4 pieces of tofu into individual serving bowls, or into one large bowl if using a whole piece of tofu. Drizzle the Spicy Sesame Sauce over the tofu and garnish with the green onion and chili. Serve as an appetizer or as a side dish with steaming hot rice.

Spicy Beef Soup

1 lb (500 g) beef flank or shin beef, halved
6 cups (1 1/2 liters) water
1 portion Prepared Bracken (see recipe below) or 3 cups (150 g) chopped spinach, blanched in boiling water to soften
2 cups (100 g) bean sprouts
2 leeks, halved lengthwise and cut into lengths
2 eggs, lightly beaten

Seasoning
1 tablespoon soy sauce
1 1/2 teaspoons crushed garlic
4 teaspoons ground red pepper
1 1/2 teaspoons chili bean paste (*gochujang*)
1 teaspoon sesame oil
1/2 teaspoon sugar
1/2 teaspoon salt

Prepared Bracken
1 1/2 cups (20 g) dried bracken
Pinch of salt
1 teaspoon soy sauce
1 teaspoon garlic, finely diced
1 teaspoon oil
1/4 cup (60 ml) water
1/2 teaspoon sesame oil

To make the Prepared Bracken, first rinse the dried bracken and soak in water overnight. Alternatively, dried bracken can be rinsed and boiled in water for 30 to 40 minutes to soften. Drain and season with the salt, soy sauce, garlic and oil. Mix well. Heat a small skillet and stir-fry the seasoned bracken for 2 minutes. Add the water and stir-fry on medium heat until dry, about 3 minutes. Remove the bracken from the heat. Drizzle the sesame oil and mix well.

Combine all the ingredients for the Seasoning and set aside.

Place the beef and water in a pot and bring to a boil. Cover, then reduce the heat and simmer for about 1 1/2 hours until the beef is tender. Remove the beef from the pot, to cool and thinly sliced.

Bring the beef broth to a boil, then cover and simmer over low heat.

If using spinach instead of bracken, mix the softened spinach with 1/2 teaspoon soy sauce and 1 teaspoon peeled and crushed garlic, mix well and set aside.

Combine the Seasoning with the bracken and shredded beef. Add the beef, bracken, bean sprouts and leeks to the simmering broth and allow to heat through, about 5 minutes. Just before serving, pour the beaten eggs slowly into the soup, stirring gently at the same time. Remove from the heat immediately and serve with bowls of steaming hot rice.

Classic Kimchi Stew with Beef and Tofu

The liberal amount of ground red pepper in this satisfying soup is excellent for clearing the nasal passages, and is regarded by many as a remedy for the symptoms of the common cold in Korea. Eaten with steamed rice, it's a meal on its own. The stew is usually served in a cast iron, clay or stoneware pot which can be placed over direct heat.

2 teaspoons oil
8 oz (250 g) beef sirloin, thinly sliced or boneless pork ribs, sliced
1/2 large onion, thinly sliced
1–2 teaspoons minced garlic
2 cups (350 g) sliced kimchi and 3/4 cup (185 ml) kimchi juice
3 1/2 cups (875 ml) beef stock
8 oz (250 g) firm tofu, thickly sliced
2–4 teaspoons ground red pepper
1 tablespoon soy sauce
1–2 teaspoons sugar
1 leek, sliced diagonally
2 green onions (scallions), sectioned
1 red finger-length chili, sliced

Heat the oil in a pot and stir-fry the beef until it changes color. Add the onion, garlic, kimchi and stir-fry for 2 to 3 minutes. Add the beef stock and bring to a boil, then reduce the heat and simmer for another minute.

Add the kimchi juice, tofu, red pepper, soy sauce, sugar and leek. Return the soup to a boil and cook for 2 minutes, then sprinkle the green onions and sliced chili. Serve hot.

Seafood Hotpot

2 lbs (1 kg) fresh crabs/crab claws
20 clams, soaked in lightly salted water for 20 minutes, and scrubbed with a brush
2 tablespoons soybean paste (*deonjang*)
1 tablespoon chili bean paste (*gochujang*)
7 cups (1 3/4 liters) water
7 oz (200 g) daikon radish (about 3 in/8 cm), halved lengthwise and quartered
1 tablespoon soy sauce
2 slices ginger, minced
1 tablespoon ground red pepper
1 tablespoon minced garlic
1 1/2 teaspoons salt
1–2 red or green finger-length chilies, deseeded and sliced
1 small leek, white part only, thinly sliced
2 bunches chrysanthemum greens (*tung ho*) or Chinese celery leaves, sliced

Clean and quarter the crabs. Crack open the crab claws to allow the flavors to penetrate.

Mix the soybean and chili bean paste with 1 cup (250 ml) water, then mash and strain into a large pot. Add the remaining water to the pot and simmer over medium high heat for 5 minutes.

Add the daikon, crab, soy

Ginseng Chicken Soup

sauce and ginger to the boiling stock, and simmer for 7–10 minutes on medium high heat.

Add the red pepper, garlic, salt and clams, stir and simmer for 3 more minutes, until the clams are opened.

Add the chilies, leek and chrysanthemum greens or Chinese celery leaves, and leave to cook for another minute. Remove from the heat and serve with rice and pan-fried sweet green chili or other fried foods.

> Substitute fresh crabs with pre-cooked crab claws or jumbo shrimp. If using, add this into the pot during the last 3 minutes of cooking.

Ginseng Chicken Soup

2 spring chickens (about 1 lb/500 g each), or 1 large chicken (3 lbs/ 1 1/2 kgs)
2 pieces finger-thick fresh ginseng roots, washed or 3 tablespoons dried ginseng shavings or 4 tablespoons dried ginseng roots and tails
1 teaspoon salt
1/4 teaspoon ground white pepper
2 dried red dates
2 thin slices ginger
8 cloves garlic, peeled and left whole
1 leek, green part only, or green onions (scallions) sliced diagonally, to garnish

Stuffing
1/2 cup (100 g) uncooked glutinous rice, soaked in boiling water for 30 minutes, then drained
4 dried red dates

4 chestnuts (optional)
1/2 teaspoon salt

Salt and Pepper Dip
1 tablespoon salt
1 teaspoon ground black pepper

Combine the ingredients for the Stuffing and mix well. Divide into two portions and set aside.

Combine the Salt and Pepper Dip ingredients. Set aside.

Rinse the chickens inside and out, then pat dry with paper towels. Stuff the chickens with the Stuffing, but do not pack the mixture too tightly as it will swell during cooking. Close the cavity of the chicken by threading a skewer in and out of the flap.

Place the chickens in a pot large enough to hold them, then add enough water to cover. Add the ginseng, salt, pepper, dried red dates, ginger and garlic, and bring to a boil. Cover, then reduce the heat and simmer gently. Turn the chicken and continue to cook until the chicken is very tender and the flesh is almost falling off the bone; about another 40 to 50 minutes for 2 spring chickens or 1 hour for a large chicken.

To serve, remove the chicken from the pot and cut into halves or quarters. Return the chicken to the soup and serve in bowls. If preferred, serve the soup in small bowls and the chicken on a separate platter and garnish with the leek. Serve with the Salt and Pepper Dip, and bowls of kimchi on the side.

Barbecued Beef

Beef Bulgogi

Traditional *bulgogi* is made by cooking very thin strips of marinated beef over a charcoal fire using a special domed griddle with holes. These days, it is more likely to be cooked on a tabletop gas grill or in a cast iron skillet in the kitchen. If possible, barbecue the beef over wood or charcoal to get that good old-fashioned flavor. Thanks to the excellent marinade, the meat will still taste good when cooked in a skillet or frying pan.

1 1/2 lbs (750 g) sirloin or rib eye beef, thinly sliced
1 onion, sliced
1 leek, diagonally sliced into very thin strips
8 fresh shiitake mushrooms, stems discarded and caps sliced (optional)
Toasted sesame seeds, to garnish

Bulgogi Marinade
1 1/2–2 tablespoons minced garlic,
4–5 tablespoons soy sauce
2 tablespoons soft brown sugar
2 tablespoons corn or sugar syrup
1/2 teaspoon ground black pepper
2 tablespoons rice wine or sake
1 tablespoon sesame oil
1 large nashi pear, grated
2 green onions (scallions), finely sliced
1/2 cup (125 ml) beef stock

Mix all the Bulgogi Marinade ingredients together and combine with the beef in a large bowl. Cover and marinate for 2 hours.

Heat a large skillet or frying pan, add the beef, onion, leek and mushrooms, and stir-fry over high heat for about 4 minutes, or until the beef is cooked.

Garnish with the sesame seeds. Serve with the chili bean paste (*gochujang*), lettuce leaves, sesame leaves, sliced raw garlic and sliced green chili on the side.

Barbecued Beef (Beef Bulgogi)

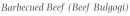

Arrange these ingredients and the meat on a leaf, then wrap and dip the parcel in a spicy sauce before eating.

Wrap the beef in plastic wrap and chill in the freezer for 30 minutes. Remove the plastic wrap and slice the beef very thinly, and then into strips. Alternatively, heat a barbecue or grill and cook the beef over high heat.

Grilled Beef Ribs

2 lbs (1 kg) beef short ribs, cut into 1 1/2-in (4–cm) lengths

Marinade
2 tablespoons garlic, peeled and crushed
1 teaspoon grated ginger
1/4 cup (60 ml) soy sauce
1 tablespoon honey
4 tablespoons soft brown sugar
1/2 teaspoon ground black pepper
2 tablespoons rice wine or sake
1 1/2 tablespoons sesame oil
1 large nashi pear, grated
2 green onions (scallions), minced

If using frozen ribs, the bones may be dark red in color. If so soak the ribs in cold water for 20 minutes. Drain and squeeze gently to remove excess water.

Combine all the Marinade ingredients together, except the green onions. Add the Marinade to the beef ribs and mix well. Then add the green onions and toss lightly. Cover and marinate for at least 4 hours.

Heat a grill or broiler and grill the ribs for 3 to 4 minutes on each side, or until browned and cooked through. Serve with lettuce, perilla leaves, raw garlic and chili bean paste on the side.

Transparent Noodles with Beef and Vegetables (Japchae)

Seasoned Korean Vegetables

Side dishes of blanched vegetables, delicately seasoned and prepared with minimum oil, are almost invariably served as part of a main Korean meal. All kinds of vegetables like spinach greens, mushroom, eggplant, daikon radish, cucumber and fresh bean sprouts can all be prepared in this fashion.

10 oz (300 g) spinach, washed and drained
8 oz (250 g) bamboo shoots, slivered
1 tablespoon sesame oil
2 teaspoons toasted sesame seeds, crushed
1 teaspoon salt
20 fresh shiitake mushrooms (about 5 oz/150 g), stems discarded and caps sliced
1/3 cup (80 ml) water
1 1/2 tablespoons soy sauce
2 tablespoons rice wine or sake
1 teaspoon sugar
Toasted sesame seeds, to garnish

Cover the bottom of a large saucepan or pot with water and bring to a boil. Blanch the spinach. Drain and roughly chop the spinach and squeeze out any excess liquid. Combine the spinach with 1 teaspoon of the sesame oil, 1 teaspoon of the crushed sesame seeds and a 1/2 teaspoon of the salt. Arrange the spinach neatly on a serving dish. Repeat with the bamboo shoots and arrange them neatly beside the spinach.

Place the mushrooms in a small saucepan and add the water, the remaining sesame oil, soy sauce, rice wine and sugar. Bring to a boil, cover, and simmer for 5 minutes, or until the mushrooms are cooked.

Arrange the mushrooms beside the other vegetables on the serving dish . Sprinkle the toasted sesame seeds and serve warm or at room temperature.

If fresh shiitake mushrooms are not available, substitute 15 dried black Chinese mushrooms. Soak for 30 minutes before use.

Transparent Noodles with Beef and Vegetables

Japchae

A delicious and simple recipe, this popular party dish is also ideal for lunch or as a light meal.

10 oz (300 g) rib eye or other beef fillet, cut into thin strips
3 tablespoons vegetable oil
1 large egg, lightly beaten

Marinade
1 tablespoon soy sauce
1 tablespoon sugar
2 teaspoons sesame oil
3 cloves garlic, peeled and crushed
5 green onions (scallions), cut into lengths

Noodles
1 packet (10 oz/300 g) dried sweet potato starch noodles or thick Chinese glass noodles
1 tablespoon soy sauce
1–2 tablespoons sugar
1 tablespoon sesame oil
1 teaspoon salt
1/4 teaspoon ground white pepper

Vegetables
1 onion, thinly sliced
4 dried black Chinese mushrooms, rinsed, soaked in hot water for 30 minutes to soften, stems discarded and caps thinly sliced

1/2 cup (15 g) small dried wood ear
  mushrooms, rinsed, soaked in hot
  water for 10 minutes to soften,
  then cut into thin strips
1 carrot, cut in sections, then into
  thin strips
1 medium zucchini, cut in sections,
  then into thin strips
1 bell pepper, cut into thin strips
1 tablespoon soy sauce
1/2 teaspoon salt
1/2 cup (125 ml) water

Combine the beef and the Marinade, mix well and set aside for 30 minutes.

Bring a pot of water to a boil and cook the noodles for 8 minutes (see packet instructions). Drain well, season with the soy sauce, sugar, sesame oil, salt and pepper, and set aside.

Heat 1/2 tablespoon of the oil in a skillet and add the egg. Swirl the egg to make a very thin omelet. Slice the cooked egg into long, thin strips.

Heat 1 tablespoon of the oil in the same skillet over high heat and stir-fry the beef until cooked, 2 to 3 minutes, then set aside.

To prepare the Vegetables, heat the remaining oil in a wok over medium heat. Add the onion and stir-fry until transparent. Add the mushrooms and stir-fry for 2 minutes. Then increase the heat slightly and add the carrot, zucchini and bell pepper. Stir-fry for another 2 minutes. Add the soy sauce, salt and water. Stir-fry until the Vegetables are tender and the liquid has evaporated.

Toss the Noodles, Vegetables and beef together. Garnish with the fried egg and serve.

Rice Bowl with Beef and Vegetables
Bibimbap

Bibimbap is a healthy and hearty everyday dish of steamed rice, vegetables and meat. It is a meal on its own. Add a dollop of *gochujang*, mix it all up, and enjoy!

4 cups (800 g) freshly cooked short-grain rice, kept hot
Chili bean paste (*gochujang*)

Seasoned Vegetables
1 zucchini, sectioned and cut into thin strips
1 carrot cut into thin strips
10 oz (300 g) spinach leaves, sliced
2 cups (100 g) soybean or mung bean sprouts, tails discarded
1 teaspoon crushed garlic
1 teaspoon sesame oil
1 teaspoon salt
1 portion Prepared Bracken (page 113) (optional)

Beef
8 oz (250 g) ground beef or very thinly sliced sirloin beef
2 teaspoons soy sauce
1 teaspoon garlic
1 teaspoon sesame oil
1 teaspoon sugar
1/2 teaspoon ground black pepper

Simple Daikon Salad
8 oz (250 g) daikon radish halved, sliced into thin strips
3/4–1 tablespoon ground red pepper
1 teaspoon minced garlic
3/4 teaspoon salt
1 teaspoon brown sugar
1 teaspoon toasted sesame seeds
1/4 teaspoon sesame oil (optional)

Rice Bowl with Beef and Vegetables (Bibimbap)

Prepare the Seasoned Vegetables by bringing a pot of water to a boil and blanching the zucchini. Drain, then toss the zucchini in 1/4 teaspoon garlic, 1/4 teaspoon sesame oil and 1/4 teaspoon salt. Repeat with the carrot, spinach and soybean sprouts separately.

To make the Daikon Salad, combine the daikon and ground pepper, and mix well. Toss the daikon gently with the remaining ingredients and set aside.

Combine the ingredients for the Beef and mix well. Heat a nonstick skillet over high heat and dry-fry the ground beef for 2 to 3 minutes until the color changes. Remove from the heat.

Scoop the cooked rice into 4 bowls and top with a portion of the vegetables, Prepared Bracken, seasoned beef and daikon, and serve with chili bean paste.

Fried Kimchi Rice

This is a handy way of using leftover cooked rice, which can be kept refrigerated in a covered container (in fact, rice kept overnight is best for all fried rice dishes, as the rice is completely dry). In this recipe, the rice is stir-fried with shredded beef, spicy kimchi, onion, green onions and garlic, and seasoned with soy sauce and sesame oil for a quick and tasty dish. Ideal for a light lunch or supper.

7 oz (200 g) ground beef or beef sirloin, cut into thin strips
1 1/2 tablespoons soy sauce
2 cloves garlic, peeled and crushed
1 tablespoon oil
1/2 teaspoon sugar
1 small onion, diced
1 cup (250 g) firmly packed, sliced kimchi
3 cups (600 g) cold cooked rice, preferably short-grain rice
1 small bell pepper, diced (optional)
3 green onions (scallions), thinly sliced
1 green finger-length chili, sliced
1 tablespoon sesame oil
Black sesame seeds, to garnish

Season the beef in a bowl with the soy sauce and garlic, mix well and set aside for 5 minutes.

Heat 1/2 tablespoon of the oil in a wok over high heat and stir-fry the beef with the sugar, onion and kimchi until the onion softens, about 1 to 2 minutes. Remove and set aside.

Reduce the heat to medium, add the remaining oil to the wok and heat until the oil is very hot. Add the rice and stir-fry for 30 seconds, then add the beef, bell pepper, green onions and chili. Stir-fry until heated through, then transfer to a serving bowl and drizzle the sesame oil. Garnish with the black sesame seeds and serve.

Grilled Korean Beef Steak

This recipe for grilled beef couldn't be easier. Start with thinly sliced good quality beef steak, grill it on a tabletop grill, and serve with sesame oil, salt and pepper, and a tangy Mustard and Lemon Sauce. The succulent, tender meat confirms the old saying that simple things in life are often the best.

1 teaspoon oil
4–8 cloves garlic, peeled and thinly sliced (optional)
1 lb (500 g) high quality beef sirloin, wrapped in plastic wrap, chilled in the freezer for 30 minutes, then thinly sliced
4 cloves raw garlic, to serve

Sesame Sauce
1/2 tablespoon sesame oil
1/2 tablespoon salt
1/4 teaspoon freshly ground black pepper

Mustard and Lemon Sauce
2 teaspoons prepared Japanese or Chinese mustard
1 tablespoon brown sugar
1 teaspoon vinegar
4 teaspoons water
2 1/2 tablespoons lemon juice

Combine the Sesame Sauce ingredients and set aside.

Combine the Mustard and Lemon Sauce ingredients and set aside.

Heat the oil in a nonstick skillet and stir-fry the sliced for 30 seconds. Remove from the heat and set aside.

Place the beef slices in a hot nonstick skillet or on a tabletop grill, and quickly sear it on 1 side. Turn the meat over and quickly sear on the other side. Serve the grilled meat with the Sesame Sauce, Mustard and Lemon Sauce, and both roasted and raw garlic.

“Malaysians and Singaporeans of all ethnic backgrounds view eating as a communal activity—as a quick visit to any food court will show you.”

MALAYSIA & SINGAPORE

Cultural exchanges between the Chinese, the Indians, and the Malays have made the peninsula a true culinary melting pot.

Left: Malay food can now be found on many a smart restaurant's menu but the flavors remain true to the *kampung* (village).

Right: Rice is the staple food in both countries and comes in many varieties.

It is not possible to live cheek by jowl with people of another ethnic community without picking up ideas on food. Over the centuries, the Malay peninsula saw sailing ships arriving from the west from Arabia, India and, much later on, from Europe. From the east came Chinese junks, Siamese vessels, and the inter-island sailing craft of the Buginese and Javanese people of the Indonesian archipelago. This has resulted in a melting pot culture, where the delicacy of Chinese cooking, the exuberance of Indian spices and the fragrance of Malay herbs co-exist.

The original people of the peninsula—known collectively as *orang asli*—consist of about twenty different tribes belonging to two distinct linguistic groups. Later arrivals to the area, who spread south from Yunnan in southern China and began settling in Malaysia around 4000 years ago, are the ancestors of today's dominant ethnic group, the Malays.

The ethnic and social structures of the Muslim Malaccan sultanate were to change irrevocably from the 16th century. Since then it has witnessed the settlement of the Portuguese, the Dutch and, in the 19th century, the British. With the British came large numbers of Chinese and Indian workers, which changed the face of the country forever.

In 1963, the Federation of Malaysia was formed, consisting of the states of the peninsula; Singapore, the island at the tip of the peninsula, and the former British colonies of Sabah and Sarawak. Singapore broke away in 1965, and has since come into its own as an important entrepôt. Today Singapore is one of Asia's most dynamic and modern cities.

The Land and its People

Their location near the equator means that Malaysia and Singapore are humid and steamy all year-round. Tropical rains frequently bring fresh-

During the Feast of the Hungry Ghosts, offerings of food and incense are made to the spirits.

ness during the afternoons, and in contrast with the usually hot days, nights are balmy and the early mornings fresh and cool.

The postcard-pretty tropical landscape—rice paddies, beaches fringed by groves of coconut palms—exists along the coasts, and much of the lush alluvial plains of the peninsula's west coast is planted with palm oil and rubber. Orchards proliferate here and luscious tropical fruits such as the highly prized durian, furry rambutan, mangosteen, starfruit, and *langsat* can be found. To the far north of the peninsula, the climate is often dry and the landscape of endless paddy fields relieved by abrupt limestone hills.

The temperate climate on the main mountain range that runs north-south along the peninsula, the Banjaran Titiwangsa, makes getaways such as Cameron Highlands perfect not only for holiday makers but for the tea plantations and market gardens that provide much of the fresh produce for the peninsula's markets.

The generally muddy coastal waters of the Malacca Straits on the west coast are ideal for crabs and shellfish. The small *kampungs* (villages) along the east coast are ideal fishing grounds and make their livelihood from the South China Sea.

Over on the Borneo peninsula, Sabah has a mountain range that culminates in Southeast Asia's tallest peak, Mount Kinabalu (13,455 feet). Much of the terrain of Sarawak is low-lying.

Singapore is for the most part low-lying, and urban development has accelerated swamp reclamation and deforestation. Dense equatorial rain forests and a few low hills which once shaped the landscape have given way to a dense cover of high-rise office blocks, shopping complexes, condominiums, and public housing. Singapore has

grown almost none of its food for decades; much of its scarce land is devoted to industry and housing its population.

Located as they are in the middle of the world, and with produce coming in from all over, few foods are ever out of season in Singapore and Malaysia.

The Making of a Cuisine

Perhaps the contemporary food of Malaysia and Singapore is best represented by the open-air eating stalls. Here, you might start dinner with some *popiah* (spring roll), move on to a fish-head curry and spicy *kangkung* with rice, and take home a packet of *hokkien mee* for supper. Almost any self-respecting Malaysian or Singaporean cook can whip up a tasty Malay-style chicken or fish curry, *roti canai* or *murtabak*, or a very fine Chinese stir-fry.

When Chinese merchants sailed their junks across the South China Sea, they set in train a process that was to have a profound influence on the region. A few of these Chinese traders stayed on in the Malay peninsula, often marrying local women and forming the beginnings of Nonya or Straits-Chinese culture. The British encouraged Chinese migration to supply labor for the tin mines. Thousands of Chinese workers poured in to Singapore and the Malay peninsula. Others headed straight for the gold mines and coal fields of Sarawak to try their luck, or moved to British North Borneo (now Sabah) to work on the land.

The Chinese brought with them the cooking styles of their homeland, mostly the southern provinces of Guangdong and

Fukien, and introduced to the indigenous people of the Malay peninsula and northern Borneo a range of ingredients now used by every ethnic group in Malaysia and Singapore today: noodles, bean sprouts, tofu, and soy sauce. In turn, the Chinese developed a penchant for spices and chilies.

Like their Chinese counterparts, Indian traders have been recorded in the region for more than a thousand years, but it was in the 19th century that they came to Malaya in large numbers as contract laborers.

Malay cuisine is the link between Indonesia to the west and south, and Thailand to the north. Although the results are rather different, there is overlap, especially with the food of nearby Sumatra and, in the northern states of Malaysia, with Thailand. Although Malay food is not as prominent in Singapore as Chinese, familiar favorites such as the *korma*, *rendang*, chicken curry, and various *sambals* are very much part of a mainstream diet.

While the Malays, Chinese and Indians continue to create their traditional foods, cross-cultural borrowing in the kitchen has led to a number of uniquely "Malaysian" and "Singaporean" dishes, such as *mee goreng* and *rojak*.

The Food of the People

Despite regional differences, Malay food can be described as spicy and flavorful, although this does not necessarily mean chili-hot. But you can rest assured that even if the main dishes are not hot, there'll be a chili-based *sambal* on hand.

Over the centuries, traditional Southeast Asian spices have been joined by Indian, Middle Eastern, and Chinese spices, so the partnership of coriander and cumin (the basis of many Malay "curries") is enhanced by pepper, cardamom, star anise, and fenugreek.

The Malaysian northern states of Kedah, Perlis, and Kelantan, all of which border Thailand and Trengganu, show distinct Thai influences. (So, too, does Penang.) Fiery hot chilies, so much a part of Thai food, are popular in the northern states. In addition to Malaysian herbs such as lemongrass, pandan leaf, the fragrant leaf of the kaffir lime, and the pungent polygonum or *daun kesum*, *daun kemangia*, a basil popular in Thailand, leaves of a number of rhizomes such as turmeric and zedoary (known locally as *cekur*), and the wonderfully fragrant wild ginger bud are used. Tamarind, sour carambola, and limes give food a tangy and fragrant sourness.

Food without seasoning is unthinkable—even a piece of fish is rubbed with ground turmeric and salt before cooking. Many of the seasonings that enhance Malay food are not dried spices but rhizomes such as fresh turmeric and *lengkuas* (galangal), and other "wet" ingredients such as chilies, onions, and garlic. Fresh seasonings and dried spices are pounded to a fine paste and cooked gently in oil before liquid—either creamy coconut milk or a sour broth—is added, together with the vegetables, meat or fish.

Produce from the sea is an important part of the Malay diet. Tiny dried anchovies (*ikan bilis*) and dried shrimp are popular flavorings, and dried shrimp paste (*belachan*) is used to give an inimitable finish to many dishes.

The *kenduri* or feast is one time when Malay cuisine comes into its own. All the women of the family or village take out their giant cooking pots and work through the night, scraping and squeezing coconuts for milk, pounding shallots, garlic, chilies, and spices, cutting and chopping, simmering and stirring, until they have created an impressive array of fish curries, *gulai* (curries) of vegetables bathed in coconut milk and seasoned perhaps with fresh shrimp; coconut-rich *rendang* of beef or chicken, tingling hot shrimp *sambals*, and a colorful array of desserts. With their innate courtesy and hospitality, the Malays consider it an honor to be able to invite any fortunate passer-by to join in the *kenduri*.

Nonya—the Food of Love

The so-called Straits-born Chinese, descendants of early settlers in Penang and Malacca, combine elements of both Chinese and Malay culture, quite unlike the mass of Chinese migrants who arrived around the turn of this century and up until the 1930s. These pioneering Chinese traders took Malay wives, although as time went on, children of these early mixed marriages generally married pure Chinese or the children of other Straits Chinese. The women, known as *Nonyas*, and the men, *Babas*, generally spoke a mixture of Malay and Chinese, dressed in modified Malay style, and combined the best of both cuisines in the kitchen.

A selection of pickles to be served with the main meal.

Nonya cakes are renowned for their richness and variety. Most are based on Malay recipes, using freshly grated tapioca root, sweet potato, agar-agar, glutinous rice, palm sugar, and coconut milk

The Kitchen and Table

Whatever the ethnic community in Malaysia and Singapore, eating is a communal activity, whether at home or in a restaurant. The assortment of dishes appear all at once, diners get individual servings of rice and then help themselves to the dishes using a serving spoon. One exception to this is the Chinese banquet, a formal eight or ten-course dinner, where the dishes appear sequentially.

"Don't use your fingers" is not an admonishment you will hear often in Malaysia and Singapore. Indians, Malays, and Straits Chinese will tell you that curry and rice taste best when you can literally feel the food with your fingers. Eating with your hand has its own etiquette too. Only the right hand is used, and just the tips of the fingers; the palm is kept perfectly clean. Washing the hands before eating is not only polite but more hygienic. In the finer Indian and Malay restaurants, a waiter will bring a bowl of warm water before and after a meal. In the more pedestrian curry shops or "banana leaf" restaurants, there will be a row of wash basins and soap for customers to clean up. Even with clean hands, diners should touch only the food on their plate, never that in the communal dishes, and the left hand is used to hold the serving spoon to keep it clean.

Chinese food is more likely to be eaten with chopsticks, although at some Chinese food stalls and in many Chinese homes, forks, spoons, and plates are used. However, at a ten-course Chinese meal, chopsticks are *de rigueur*. Sucking or licking the tips of the chopsticks is impolite and contact between mouth and the tips is kept to a minimum. Spoons are set out for larger mouthfuls. Often before and always at the end of the meal, hot towels are handed round for cleaning the face and hands.

Although Chinese tea is the traditional drink with Chinese food, there is nothing quite like beer to take the heat off your tongue and to cool you down when you eat spicy food on a steamy evening.

Most urban kitchens in Malaysia and Singapore these days are a curious blend of old and new: the microwave next to the mortar and pestle; the food processor next to a well-seasoned wok.

Above: A spread of Nonya food, which is often time consuming to prepare but well worth the effort. *Below right:* The owner of a hawker stall in Singapore entices customers with his fresh produce.

Typical Chinese ingredients (such as tofu, soy sauce, preserved soybeans, black shrimp paste, sesame seeds, dried mushrooms, and dried lily buds) were blended with Malay herbs, spices, and fragrant roots. Being non-Muslim, the Straits Chinese cooked pork dishes in the Malay style, and added distinctive local ingredients (coconut milk, spices, and sour tamarind juice) to basic Chinese recipes.

Distinct differences evolved between the cuisine of the Penang Nonyas and that of Malacca. In Penang, which is geographically much closer to Thailand, the Nonyas developed a passion for sour food (using lots of lime and tamarind juice), fiery hot chilies, fragrant herbs, and pungent black shrimp paste. Malacca Nonyas prepare food that is generally rich in coconut milk and Malay spices (such as coriander and cumin), and usually use more sugar than their northern counterparts.

Many fruits and vegetables were prepared in imaginative ways by the Nonyas. Unripe jackfruit, the heart of the banana bud, sweet potato leaves, and tiny sour carambola were all transformed in the kitchen, added to and blended with aromatics such as the kaffir lime leaf, polygonum or *laksa* leaf, zedoary, fresh turmeric leaves, and pandan.

One of the most popular Nonya dishes among Malaysians of any background is *laksa*, a rice-noodle soup that marries Malay seasonings with Chinese noodles.

SUGGESTED MENUS

A family meal

For a family dinner, serve the following with rice:
• Nonya Chicken Curry (page 131), a little bit of Shrimp Sambal (page 133) and Spicy Curried Pumpkin (page 134);
• Sago with Honeydew and Coconut Cream (page 135) is a popular sweet treat with both the young and old.

Snacks

Chicken Curry Puffs (page 123) are great as a mid-morning or afternoon snack. The Pancakes with Sweet Coconut Filling (page 135) and Coconut Mango Pudding (page 135) would normally be eaten in-between meals as fillers in Malaysia and Singapore.

A light lunch

The recipes in this chapter are particularly well suited to smorgasbords. For a light lunch:
• Fresh Spring Rolls (page 122) make a delighful start;
• Shrimp Noodle Soup (page 126) or Indian Mee Goreng (page 127);
• finish with some sliced fresh fruit.
Other great lunch dishes include Claypot Rice (page 130) or Classic Hainanese Chicken Rice (page 129).

A dinner party

For a formal dinner, impress your guests with these dishes:
• Chicken Satay with Satay Peanut Sauce (page 124) and Spicy Chicken Soup with Noodles (page 124)
• Hot and Sour Malay Fish Curry (page 134) or the Singapore Chili Crab (page 133), which is a sure-fire hit;
• Chilled Almond Jelly with Lychees (page 135) is a good way to round off the meal.

A melting pot menu

You could start your Asia-wide menu with
• Laksa Noodle Soup with Spicy Coconut Broth (page 127);
• Fried Pork Cutlets (page 102) from Japan are an interesting blend of East and West, serve with Vietnamese Water Spinach with Yellow Bean Sauce (page 181);
• finish with the wonderful Shaved Ice Dessert from Indonesia (page 86).

THE ESSENTIAL FLAVORS OF MALAYSIAN AND SINGAPOREAN COOKING

The aromatic curry pastes need **chilies**, **garlic**, **ginger**, **limes**, **lemongrass**, and **shallots**, but these ingredients are also used by themselves. **Coconut milk** and **palm sugar** are frequently added to soften the heat of curries and, in desserts, the fragrant **pandanus leaf** is used. **Rice** and **soy sauce** are must-haves.

Chicken Stock

3 lbs (1 chicken kgs) chicken bones
  or ¹/2 chicken
2 in (5 cm) ginger, sliced
3 green onions or shallots
1 celery stalk, leaves attached,
  roughly chopped
1 teaspoon peppercorns
10 cups (2 liters) water

Combine all the ingredients in a large stock pot and bring to a boil over high heat. Reduce the heat and simmer for 1 hour. Discard the solids and strain the stock through the sieve. The stock can be frozen for up to 3 months.

Sambal Belachan
Shrimp Paste Chili Dip

12 red finger-length chilies, deseeded
  and sliced
2 tablespoons dried shrimp paste
  (*belachan*), dry-roasted (page 13)
²/3 cup (165 ml) water
¹/4 cup (60 ml) lime juice

Blend the chilies and dried shrimp paste with the water until coarse. Season with the lime juice. Keeps for 3 weeks in the refrigerator. Serve with rice, noodles and as a dip.

Basic Chili Sauce Dip

4 red finger-length chilies, deseeded
  and sliced
3 tablespoons water
2 tablespoons white vinegar
1 tablespoon sugar
¹/2 teaspoon salt

Blend the chilies and water in a mortar or blender. Add the

Basic Chili Sauce Dip

Fresh Spring Rolls (Popiah)

blended mixture and the rest of the ingredients to a pan and bring to a boil. Then remove from the heat and set aside to cool. Serve with fried rice, noodles, fritters and deep-fried foods. Keeps refrigerated for up to 3 months.

Crispy Fried Shallots or Garlic and Garlic Oil

30 shallots or 30 cloves garlic,
  peeled and thinly sliced
¹/2 cup (125 ml) oil

Heat the oil in a wok and gently stir-fry the sliced shallots or garlic over medium heat until light golden brown and crips, about 5 to 7 minutes. Do not allow them to burn or they will taste bitter. Drain, cool completely and store in an airtight container.
  Reserve the **Shallot** or **Garlic Oil** for frying or seasoning other dishes.

Popiah Wrappers

¹/2 cup (75 g) rice flour
1¹/2 tablespoons plain flour
¹/4 teaspoon salt
2 eggs
¹/2 teaspoon oil
1 cup (250 ml) water

Sift the flours and salt together

into a bowl. In another bowl, mix the eggs, oil and water. Add the flour mixture a little at time, mixing well to obtain a smooth batter. Set the batter aside in the refrigerator for at least 1 hour.
  Grease a nonstick pan with oil. Ladle 2 tablespoons of the batter onto the pan and swirl it quickly to make a very thin pancake. Cook over medium heat until the batter sets, about 2 minutes. Place the cooked wrapper on a plate. Repeat until all the batter is used up.

Dried Cucumber Acar

2 cucumbers, halved lengthwise,
  seeds removed
1 large carrot, peeled

Dressing
³/4 cup (150 ml) distilled white
  vinegar
3 tablespoons sugar
¹/2 teaspoon salt
Pinch of ground turmeric
2 shallots, sliced
¹/2 in (1 cm) ginger, finely sliced
1 clove garlic, peeled and shredded
2 tablespoons raisins

Cut the carrot and cucumbers into matchstick pieces 1 ¹/2 in (3 cm) long. Dry them in the sun for 2 hours. Combine the vinegar, sugar, salt, and turmeric and bring to a boil. Remove from the heat and cool. Add the

shallots, ginger, garlic, and raisins and mix with the cucumbers and carrot. Store in the refrigerator up to 1 month.

Chili Ginger Sauce

4 red finger-length chilies, sliced
1¹/4 in (3 cm) ginger, sliced
3 cloves garlic
5 tablespoons water
1¹/2 tablespoons sugar
1¹/2 tablespoons lime juice
1 teaspoon salt
¹/2 teaspoon sesame oil

Grind the chilies, ginger, garlic with water in a mortar or blender. Season with the sugar, lime juice, salt and sesame oil. Keeps in the refrigerator for 1 week. Serve with chicken rice.

Fresh Spring Rolls
Popiah

This Nonya version of a popular Chinese snack uses fresh ready-to-eat wrappers and is substantial enough for an entire meal. Popiah wrappes are similar to fresh Filipino wrappes, lumpia. They are available in the refrigerator or freezer sections in Asian supermarkets. You can choose to make your own by following the recipe on page 122.

4 tablespoons oil

3 eggs, lightly beaten

20 large fresh popiah wrappers (page 122)

20 long lettuce leaves

Sweet black sauce (*tim cheong*)

10 cloves garlic, ground to a paste

6 red finger-length chilies, deseeded and sliced, then ground to a paste

1 cup (50 g) bean sprouts, blanched and drained well

1/3 cup (60 g) coarsely ground roasted peanuts

3 tablespoons Crispy Fried Shallots (page 122)

Filling

8 shallots, halved

8 cloves garlic, halved

2 tablespoons fermented soybean paste (*tau cheo*)

1 *bangkuang* (jicama) (about 1 lb/ 500 g), peeled and sliced

1 cake deep-fried tofu (8 oz/250 g), thinly sliced or 1 cake firm tofu (8 oz/250 g), deep-fried and sliced

1 teaspoon dark soy sauce

1 1/2 tablespoons sugar

1/2 teaspoon salt

4 oz (125 g) small fresh shrimp, peeled and deveined

1/4 small cabbage, thinly sliced

1 cup (100 g) green beans, thinly sliced

Grease an omelet pan with 1/2 teaspoon of the oil and fry the eggs to make 3 very thin omelets. Slice the omelets into shreds and set aside.

To make the Filling, grind the shallots and garlic, and mix with the fermented soybean paste. Heat the rest of the oil in a pan over medium heat and stir-fry the paste mixture until fragrant, about 3 minutes. Spoon 1 tablespoon of the fried paste into a small bowl and set aside. Add the *bangkuang* to the remaining fried paste in the pan and cook for 5 minutes until soft. Then add the tofu and cook over low heat for 15 to 20 minutes. Season with the soy sauce, sugar and salt. Remove from the heat and set aside.

Place 1 teaspoon of the reserved paste in a wok with the shrimp. Stir-fry for 3 minutes until the shrimp are cooked and place in a small bowl. Repeat with the cabbage and beans, and place the cooked ingredients in another 2 bowls.

To serve, place the prepared ingredients on a table. Lay a popiah wrapper on a plate and place a lettuce leaf on it. Spread a little sweet black sauce, garlic

Chicken Curry Puffs

paste and chili paste on the leaf. Add a portion of the *bangkuang*, shrimp, cabbage, beans, bean sprouts, peanuts and Crispy Fried Shallots. Fold in the sides of the popiah wrapper, roll and serve immediately.

Chicken Curry Puffs

A perennial favorite originally created by Indian cooks and enjoyed by every Malaysian.

Filling

5 tablespoons oil

1 medium onion, diced

1 tablespoon grated ginger

3 1/2 teaspoons meat curry powder

1/2 teaspoon ground red pepper

1/2 teaspoon ground turmeric

2 large potatoes (1 lb/500 g total), peeled, boiled and diced

2 teaspoons sugar

1/2 teaspoon ground black pepper

1 teaspoon salt

2 cups chicken meat (14 oz/400 g) or 2 large chicken breasts, cooked and diced

1/4 cup (60 ml) water

Pastry

3 1/3 cups (500 g) flour

2/3 cup (150 g) butter or margarine

3/4 cup + 4 teaspoons (200 ml) water

1/2 teaspoon salt

Heat the oil in a skillet over medium heat and gently stir-fry the onion and ginger until the onion turns light golden brown. Add the curry powder, ground red pepper and turmeric, and stir-fry for 3 minutes or until fragrant. Add the potatoes, sugar, pepper and salt, and stir-fry for another 10 minutes. Then, add the chicken and

water, and cook for 7 minutes, or until the mixture is almost dry. Remove from the heat and set aside to cool.

Knead the Pastry ingredients into a smooth dough. Cover with a damp cloth and set aside to rest in a warm place for 30 minutes to 1 hour.

Divide the dough into 2 portions. Roll each half on a lightly floured surface to 1/8 in (3 mm) thick. Use a curry puff cutter or a cookie cutter, to cut the dough into circles 4 in (10 cm) in diameter. Spoon 1 tablespoon of the Filling onto the center of each circle. Fold the dough over to form a crescent and crimp and roll the edges to form a simple wave pattern, sealing the package well. Repeat until all the Filling and Pastry are used up.

Deep-fry each puff in hot oil until light golden brown on both sides. Alternately, bake at 350°F (180°C) for 30 minutes until light golden brown. Serve hot or at room temperature.

Pork Ribs Wrapped in Pandanus Leaves

> Not all types of margarine are suitable to make the Pastry because of their high moisture content. The Malaysian brand, Planta, is recommended while Crisco is a suitable substitute.

Pork Ribs Wrapped in Pandanus Leaves

The elusive fragrance of pandanus leaves permeates a number of rice, meat and chicken dishes of Malay or Nonya origin, while pandanus essence extracted from the leaves is often used in cakes and desserts. If pandanus leaves are not available, substitute parchment paper.

3 shallots, peeled

5 cloves garlic, peeled

3 tablespoons Worcestershire sauce (purchased)

2 tablespoons sweet plum sauce or honey

1 1/2 tablespoons steak sauce (purchased)

1 tablespoon hoisin sauce

1/2–1 teaspoon five spice powder

4 tablespoons oil

1 teaspoon sesame oil

1 1/2 lbs (750 g) meaty pork ribs or chicken thighs, cut into serving pieces

24 pandanus leaves, rinsed and dried

Oil for deep-frying

Grind the shallots and garlic in a mortar and mix with all the other ingredients, except the meat, pandanus leaves and oil for deep-frying. Rub this mixture into the meat and set aside to marinate for 2 hours.

Chicken Satay with Satay Peanut Sauce.

adding a little oil if necessary to keep the blades turning.

Heat the oil in a saucepan over medium heat and stir-fry the Spice Paste for 3 to 5 minutes until fragrant. Add the peanuts, tamarind juice and water, and season with the salt and sugar. Reduce the heat to low and cook for 3 more minutes, stirring constantly. Remove from the heat. Transfer to a bowl and serve warm or at room temperature.

You may substitute 1/2 cup (6 tablespoons) crunchy peanut butter for the crushed peanuts. Add the peanut butter to the sauce and mix thoroughly, then remove from the heat. Satay Sauce can be made in large quantities and kept in the the refrigerator for 2–3 weeks or frozen for 3 months.

Spicy Chicken Soup with Noodles
Soto Ayam

As the ancestors of many Malay Singaporeans originally came from Java, it's not surprising that this Javanese noodle soup is found at most Singapore food centers. It's ideal as a light luncheon dish or even as a starter.

1 fresh chicken (1 1/2 kg/3 lbs)
8 cups (2 liters) water
1 teaspoon salt
1 teaspoon pepper
2 oz (50 g) dried glass noodles, soaked in hot water to soften, then drained
6 slices of Lontong (compressed rice), cubed, or 2 cups (400 g) cold cooked rice (optional)

Wrap each piece of pork rib or chicken thigh in a pandanus leaf, tying it in a simple knot so the meat is enclosed as in photo on page 123.

Deep-fry the meat parcels in very hot oil for 3 to 5 minutes until cooked. Serve hot, still in the pandanus leaf, allowing each diner to unwrap his or her own portions.

Chicken Satay

The tantalising aroma of seasoned mutton, beef or chicken cooking over a charcoal fire, anointed from time to time with oil spread with a "brush" of fragrant lemongrass, is irresistible. It's no wonder this Malay dish is an all-time favorite.

1/2 teaspoon ground red pepper
2 tablespoons sugar
1/2 teaspoon salt
1 teaspoon ground turmeric
4 chicken legs and thighs, deboned and cut into 3/4-in (2-cm) cubes
12 skewers soaked in water for 1 hour
1 stalk lemongrass, tender inner part of bottom third only, for brushing
Oil for brushing
Satay Peanut Sauce (see recipe on this page), for dipping
Cucumber, sliced, to serve

Onion, sliced, to serve
Ketupat, quartered, to serve (optional, see note)

Spice Paste
1 tablespoon coriander seeds
2 stalks lemongrass, tender inner part of bottom third only, sliced
5 shallots, peeled and halved
2 cloves garlic, peeled and halved
2 tablespoons oil

Grind the Spice Paste ingredients in a mortar or blender, adding the oil to keep the blades turning. Mix the paste with the ground red pepper, sugar, salt and ground turmeric, and marinate the chicken cubes for at least 12 hours.

Thread 4 to 5 pieces of the marinated chicken onto each skewer until all the chicken pieces are used up. Grill the chicken over a hot charcoal fire, constantly brushing with a stalk of lemongrass dipped in the oil. Turn the skewers frequently to prevent the meat from burning. The chicken should be slightly charred on the outside and just cooked on the inside. Alternatively, grill the chicken under an oven broiler for 10 minutes on each side.

Serve with a bowl of Satay Sauce and sliced cucumber, raw onion and Ketupat or boiled rice on the side.

Ketupat are compressed rice cakes. They are packed in beautifully woven cases of coconut leaves or daun palas (see photo) and boiled in water. The rice takes the shape of the case and is usually served quartered. These traditional festive cakes dress every table during many celebrations in Malaysia. Ketupat are sold in many Malay food stores.

Satay Peanut Sauce

4 tablespoons oil
1/2 cup (75 g) roasted peanuts, skins discarded and coarsely ground
1/2 tablespoon tamarind pulp, soaked in 2 tablespoons water, mashed and then strained to obtain juice
1/2 cup (125 ml) water
1/4 teaspoon salt
1 tablespoon sugar

Spice Paste
1 tablespoon coriander seeds
1/2 teaspoon cumin seeds
2 stalks lemongrass, tender inner part of bottom third only, sliced
3/4 in (1 1/2 cm) galangal root, sliced
4 dried chilies, soaked in warm water
3 cloves garlic, peeled and halved
2 shallots, peeled and halved

Grind the Spice Paste ingredients in a mortar or blender,

Spicy Chicken Soup with Noodles (Soto Ayam)

6 quail eggs, peeled and halved, or
  2 hard-boiled eggs, peeled and
  quartered
1¹/2 cups (75 g) bean sprouts,
  rinsed
5 tablespoons coarsely chopped
  Chinese celery or parsley leaves
Crispy Fried Shallots (page 122),
  to garnish
Sambal Belachan (page 122), to
  serve
3 small limes (limau kasturi) or
  regular, halved, to serve

Spice Paste
8 macadamia or candlenuts, roughly
  chopped
2¹/2 in (6 cm) fresh turmeric root,
  peeled and sliced, or 2 teaspoons
  ground turmeric
2 in (5 cm) fresh ginger, peeled and
  sliced
24 shallots, peeled
10 cloves garlic, peeled
3 tablespoons oil
3 stalks lemongrass, tender inner
  part of bottom third only, bruised
2 in (5 cm) fresh galangal root,
  peeled and sliced
8 kaffir lime leaves
2 tablespoons ground coriander

Place the chicken and water in a
pot and simmer over low heat
for 30 minutes. While the chick-
en is simmering, make the Spice
Paste. Grind the macadamia or
candlenuts, turmeric, ginger,
shallots and garlic in a blender
until fine, adding a little oil if
necessary to keep the blades

turning. Heat the oil in a wok
and stir-fry the ground paste
with the remaining Spice Paste
ingredients for 4 to 5 minutes
until fragrant.

Add the cooked Spice Paste
to the pot with the chicken and
continue to simmer for 20 more
minutes until the chicken is
cooked. Season with salt and
pepper, and remove from the
heat. Remove the chicken from
the stock, and cool. Debone the
chicken and shred the meat into
long strips. Strain the stock well,
and return to the pot to keep
warm.

Portion the noodles, Lontong
or cooked rice, chicken strips,
hard-boiled eggs, bean sprouts
and celery leaves into 6 serving
bowls. Fill each bowl with the
warm stock and garnish with the
Crispy Fried Shallots. Serve hot
with a bowl of Sambal Belachan
and lime halves on the side.

Superior Wonton Soup

Superior Wonton Soup

Juicy, stuffed dumplings or wonton in soup are found in Chinese
restaurants throughout the world.
This version is made with an
excellent stock—made from *ikan
bilis*, dried scallops and chicken.

1 cup (100 g) snow peas or 1¹/2
  cups (100 g) bok choy, blanched
  for a few seconds and sliced
6 dried black Chinese mushrooms,
  soaked, boiled and caps thinly
  sliced
Pepper to taste (optional)
Green finger-length chili, sliced
Soy sauce
Chili Ginger Sauce (page 122)

Basic Stock
10 oz (300 g) chicken bones or
  chicken meat
3 dried scallops
¹/2 cup (90 g) dried *ikan bilis*
5 stalks celery ribs, cut into lengths
3 cloves garlic, peeled and bruised
1 medium carrot, cut into chunks
¹/2 in (1 cm) ginger, bruised
¹/2 teaspoon white peppercorns
10 cups (2¹/2 liters) water

Wonton Wrappers
1³/4 cups (270 g) flour
¹/2 cup (125 ml) water
1 egg

Filling
7 oz (200 g) medium fresh shrimp,
  peeled and deveined

5 oz (150 g) ground chicken or pork
8 water chestnuts, peeled and diced
1¹/2 oz (50 g) dried black fungus, or
  4 dried black Chinese mushrooms,
  soaked in water for 15 minutes to
  soften
1 egg, beaten
2 teaspoons rice wine or sake
2 teaspoons soy sauce
1 teaspoon oyster sauce
1 teaspoon grated ginger juice
¹/2 teaspoon sesame oil
1 teaspoon cornstarch
1 teaspoon sugar
¹/2 teaspoon salt
¹/2 teaspoon ground white pepper

Place the Basic Stock ingredients in a stockpot and bring to a
boil. Skim the surface, lower the
heat and simmer, covered, for 1
hour. Strain the stock well and
discard the solids. Reserve 6
cups (1¹/2 liters) of the stock.

Make the Wonton Wrappers
by kneading the flour, water and
egg for 10 minutes into a
smooth dough. Set the dough
aside to rest for 15 minutes.
Pinch about 1 tablespoon of the
dough and roll it into a small
ball. Place the dough ball on a
work surface and flatten it with
your palm. Roll the dough out
into a 3¹/2 in (9 cm) circle and
set aside on a dry plate. Repeat
with the rest of the dough to
make at least 15 wrappers in all.

To make the Filling, chop the
shrimp, chicken, water chestnuts and black fungus or mushrooms together with a cleaver
until fine. Add all the other
ingredients and mix well.

Place a wrapper on a lightly
floured surface and scoop 1 teaspoon of the Filling onto the
center of a wrapper and dab a
little water on the wrapper all
around the Filling. Fold the
wrapper up like a pouch and
press the edges to seal it. Repeat
until all the Filling is used up to
make 15 wonton pouches.

Bring the reserved stock back
to a boil, add the wonton and
simmer for 3 to 5 minutes or
until they rise to the top. Add
the snow peas, mushrooms and
pepper. Remove from the heat
and serve immediately with
small bowls of sliced green
chilies in soy sauce and Chili
Ginger Sauce on the side.

Wonton wrappers are available
ready-made in the refrigerator
sections of most supermarkets.
If using frozen wrappers, allow
them to thaw to room temperature before using. If you are
unable to find dried scallops
(which are very expensive),
substitute 1 lb (500 g) of pork
bones to make the stock.

Shrimp Salad with Sweet and Sour Dressing

Contrasting flavors and textures bring excitement to this combination of vegetables, shrimp, herbs and crunchy *krupuk* shrimp crackers. It makes a delicious starter to any meal.

1 head soft-leaf lettuce, torn into shreds (optional)
1 small carrot, cut into matchsticks
4 oz (125 g) daikon radish, cut into matchsticks
1 cucumber, halved lengthwise, deseeded and thinly sliced
1 starfruit or green apple, halved lengthwise and thinly sliced
2 ripe tomatoes, cut into wedges
8 oz (250 g) fresh shrimp, poached for 1 minute, then peeled and deveined
Coriander leaves (cilantro), to garnish
Crispy Fried Shallots (page 122)
Krupuk (deep-fried shrimp crackers), to garnish (optional)
Fried peanuts, skins removed and coarsely ground, to garnish (optional)

Sweet Sour Dressing
7–10 red finger-length chilies, deseeded and sliced
3–4 cloves garlic, peeled and bruised
$^1/_2$ cup (125 ml) Chinese plum sauce or $^1/_2$ cup (125 ml) tamarind juice (from 2 heaped tablespoons tamarind pulp mashed with $^1/_4$ cup (60 ml) water and strained) mixed with 1 tablespoon sugar
$^1/_2$ cup (125 ml) Palm Sugar Syrup
$^1/_2$ cup (125 ml) lime juice
1 tablespoon soy sauce
$^1/_2$ tablespoon sesame oil

To make the Sweet Sour Dressing, grind the chilies and garlic in a mortar or blender, adding a little of the plum sauce or tamarind juice to keep the blades turning. When finely ground, add all of the other Dressing ingredients and grind again. Set aside in a small bowl.

Prepare the rest of the ingredients and portion them onto 6 serving plates. Pour a little of the Dressing over each serving and top with the fresh coriander leaves, crispy shallots, *krupuk* and a generous helping of peanuts. Or serve the prepared ingredients with the dressing on the side.

Shrimp Noodle Soup
Hae Mee

The flavor of this simple noodle dish depends on the richly flavored stock made from both fresh and dried shrimp, and pork or chicken. This soup is traditionally served with delicious, crunchy pork cracklings: some may omit these for health reasons but they make all the difference to the flavor of the dish.

8 cups (2 liters) water
8 oz (250 g) large fresh shrimp, shelled and deveined, heads and shells reserved for the Stock
$1^1/_2$ oz (50 g) fatback (pork fat) or salt pork, cubed
1 lb (500 g) fresh yellow wheat noodles (Hokkien *mee*)
1 cup (50 g) bean sprouts, rinsed, or a few leafy greens
1 green onion (scallion), thinly sliced
Ground white pepper

Shrimp Noodle Soup (Hae Mee)

Stock
1 tablespoon oil
4 oz (100 g) small fresh shrimp
3 tablespoons dried shrimp
1 dried chili, whole
5 shallots, diced
5 cloves garlic, minced
10 whole white peppercorns, ground and dry-fried until fragrant
8 oz (250 g) pork or chicken bones
1 tablespoon sugar
$^1/_4$ teaspoon salt

Bring the water to a boil in a pot, add the shelled shrimp and boil for 2 minutes. Drain the shrimp and set aside, reserving the shrimp broth to make the Stock.

To make the Stock, heat the oil in a pot over medium to low heat and stir-fry the reserved shrimp heads and shells with the small fresh shrimp, dried shrimp and dried chili for 5 minutes. Crush the ingredients in the pot firmly with the back of a wooden spoon against the side of the pan, then add all the other Stock ingredients, except the sugar and salt, and add the reserved shrimp broth. Simmer gently over low heat, uncovered, for 20 minutes until the liquid is reduced to three-quarters of the original amount.

Heat the sugar in a small skillet with 1 tablespoon of water and cook, stirring constantly, over medium heat until it caramelizes, about 1 minute. Add this caramel syrup to the Stock and mix well. Remove from the heat and strain the Stock, pressing the solids firmly with the back of a spoon to extract all the liquid, then season with the salt. Keep the Stock hot if using immediately.

While the Stock is cooking, fry the fatback (pork fat), if using, in a wok over medium heat until the oil runs out and the pork is crisp and golden, 3 to 5 minutes. Drain and set aside. Alternatively, bake the fatback (pork fat) in a preheated oven at 350°F (180°C) for 5 to 10 minutes.

Scald the noodles in boiling water for 1 minute to heat through, then divide them into 4 serving bowls. Top each serving with bean sprouts or leafy greens, ladle the hot Stock over and add some shrimp into each bowl. Sprinkle the fried pork, green onion and add a liberal dash of white pepper. Serve immediately with sliced red chili in a bowl of soy sauce or with the sambal of your choice.

Penang Laksa
Penang-style Noodle Soup with Tamarind Broth

There are two definite groups in Malaysia: those who prefer Laksa Lemak, noodles in coconut gravy, and those who prefer the sour, fragrant Penang version with a pronounced fishy flavor.

3 medium fresh mackerel or small tuna (about $1^1/_4$ lbs/650 g total), cleaned and left whole
8 cups (2 liters) water
4 tablespoons tamarind pulp, soaked in 1 cup (250 ml) water, mashed and then strained for juice
2 wild ginger buds (*bunga kantan*), sliced
3 sprigs laksa leaves (*daun kesum*), washed and sliced
2 tablespoons sugar
1 lb (500 g) fresh round rice noodles (*laksa noodles*) or 8 oz (250 g) dried rice noodles

Spice Paste
2 stalks lemongrass, tender inner part of bottom third only, sliced
1 in ($2^1/_2$ cm) turmeric root, sliced, or 2 teaspoons ground turmeric
5 dried red chilies, soaked in warm water and cut into lengths
7 red finger-length chilies, sliced
10 shallots, peeled and halved
1 teaspoon dried shrimp paste (*belachan*)

Garnishes
1 small cucumber, peeled, deseeded and thinly sliced
6 sprigs laksa leaves (*daun kesum*), sliced
Few sprigs mint, torn
1 large red onion, sliced
3 red finger-length chilies, sliced
$^1/_2$ fresh small pineapple, peeled and sliced into small pieces
4–6 hard-boiled quail eggs, halved or 3 hard-boiled chicken eggs, peeled and quartered (optional)
1 heaped teaspoon black shrimp paste (*hay koh*), diluted in 2 tablespoons warm water

Simmer the cleaned fish in the water for 5 minutes until cooked. Remove the fish and set aside to cool. Strain the fish stock carefully and pour into a large pan with the tamarind juice, ginger buds, laksa leaves and sugar. When cool enough to handle, debone the fish and coarsely flake the flesh with a fork.

*Laksa Noodle Soup
with Spicy Coconut Broth*

Grind the Spice Paste ingredients to a paste in a mortar or blender, adding a little oil if necessary to keep the blades turning. Add the Spice Paste to the pan with the fish stock. Add half of the flaked fish and simmer for 20 to 30 minutes.

Blanch the noodles in boiling water and drain. If using dried noodles, boil them for about 7 minutes and drain or see packet instructions for preparation. Divide the noodles into 6 serving bowls and ladle the fish stock to almost fill each bowl. Garnish each bowl with the rest of the flaked fish and a helping of various Garnishes. Serve with a bowl of the diluted black shrimp paste (*hay koh*) on the side.

Laksa Noodle Soup with Spicy Coconut Broth

This Nonya version of Laksa from Malacca is light and soupy. It is infused with wild ginger buds to give a distinctly delicate fragrance.

5 tablespoons oil
9 sprigs laksa leaves (*daun kesum*), sliced
3 wild ginger bud (*bunga kantan*), thinly sliced
5 cups (1¹/4 llters) water
1¹/2 cups (375 ml) thick coconut milk
1–2 teaspoons sugar
2 teaspoons salt
1 lb (500 g) fresh yellow wheat noodles (*mee*) or 8 oz (250 g) dried noodles, blanched and drained
1 chicken breast, poached in ¹/2 cup (125 ml) water and thinly sliced
8 oz (250 g)) medium fresh shrimp, peeled and deveined and poached

1¹/2 cups (75 g) bean sprouts, blanched

Spice Paste
5 macadamia or candlenuts, roughly chopped
1 stalk lemongrass, tender inner part of bottom third only, sliced
³/4 in (2 cm) galangal root, sliced
¹/4 in (¹/2 cm) turmeric root, sliced or ¹/2 teaspoon ground turmeric
10 red finger-length chilies, deseeded and sliced
10 shallots, peeled and halved
3 cloves garlic, peeled and halved
1 teaspoon dried shrimp paste (*belachan*)

Garnishes
1 small cucumber, thinly sliced
3 eggs, beaten and fried into thin omelets, then thinly sliced
2 red finger-length chilies, sliced
2 green onions (scallions), sliced
6 tablespoons Sambal Belachan (see page 122)
6 small limes (*limau kasturi*), halved

Grind the Spice Paste ingredients in a mortar or blender, adding a little of oil if necessary to keep the blades turning.

Heat the remaining oil in a saucepan over medium heat and stir-fry the Spice Paste for 5 to 7 minutes. Add 6 sprigs of the laksa leaves, 2 wild ginger buds and water, and bring to a boil. Then add the thick coconut milk and season with sugar and salt. Reduce the heat and simmer very gently, uncovered for 10 to 15 minutes until the oil separates from the milk.

Blanch the fresh noodles in boiling water for a few seconds to heat through. If using dried noodles, boil them for about 7

minutes and drain or see packet instructions for preparation.

Divide the noodles, chicken, shrimp and bean sprouts into 6 individual serving bowls and top each with the remaining laksa leaves and ginger bud slices. Pour the coconut gravy over the noodles and garnish with cucumber, eggs, chilies and green onions. Serve with a small bowl of the Sambal Belachan and lime halves on the side.

The coconut gravy can be prepared in advance and the garnish readied, although not sliced to ensure maximum fragrance and freshness. If fresh noodles are not available, use dried rice vermicelli (*meehoon*) or any dried Chinese wheat noodles.

Indian Mee Goreng
Indian Fried Noodles

Although noodles were brought to Singapore by the Chinese, all the other ethnic groups have enthusiastically adopted and adapted them to suit their tastes. This spicy dish—which you cannot find in India—is well-balanced by the sweetness of fresh tomatoes and tomato sauce.

4 tablespoons oil
1 cake firm or pressed tofu (8 oz/250 g total), cubed
6–8 dried chilies, soaked in warm water to soften, then ground to a paste, or 3–5 tablespoons ground red pepper
5 cloves garlic, minced
1 teaspoon dried shrimp paste (*belachan*)
5 oz (150 g) boneless chicken or lamb, thinly sliced
5 oz (150 g) fresh shrimp, peeled and deveined
14 oz (400 g) fresh yellow wheat noodles (Hokkien *mee*)
2 cups (200 g) *choy sum*, washed and sliced

2 tablespoons soy sauce
3 tablespoons tomato ketchup
¹/2 teaspoon salt
¹/2 cup (125 ml) Chicken Stock (page 122)
2 eggs, beaten
1 onion, diced
1 tomato, diced, or 2 tablespoons tomato purée
1 red finger-length chili, sliced
1 green finger-length chili, sliced
2 cups (100 g) bean sprouts, seed coats and tails discarded
¹/2 teaspoon ground white pepper

Garnishes
Coriander leaves (cilantro) or Chinese celery, coarsely chopped
Green onions (scallions), sliced (optional)
Crispy Fried Shallots (page 122), (optional)
Small limes (*limau kasturi*), halved

Heat 2 tablespoons of the oil in a large wok and stir-fry the tofu cubes over medium heat until golden brown, about 7 minutes. Remove from the oil and set aside to drain on paper towels.

In the same wok, add the rest of the oil and stir-fry 3 to 5 tablespoons of the chili paste or the ground red pepper with the garlic and dried shrimp paste for 3 minutes until fragrant. Add the sliced chicken or lamb and stir-fry until it turns opaque, about 3 minutes. Then add the shrimp and stir-fry until the shrimp are cooked, another 2 minutes.

Add the noodles and *choy sum*, mix well, and cook for 1 minute. Then add the soy sauce, tomato ketchup, salt and Chicken Stock.

Indian Fried Noodles (Mee Goreng)

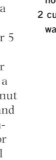

*Fried Kway Teow
(Char Kway Teow)*

Cook for 3 minutes until the liquid is absorbed by the noodles and the mixture is dry.

Push the noodles to one side of the wok with the spatula. Add the eggs and scramble. Then stir the noodles and the eggs together until the eggs are cooked. (Add a little more chicken stock for a moister Mee Goreng.)

Add the onion, tomato, fresh chilies and bean sprouts, and stir-fry for 3 minutes. Then add the fried tofu and mix well until heated through. Season with the ground pepper. Garnish with coriander leaves, green onions, Crispy Fried Shallots and serve fresh limes on the side.

If preferred, substitute spinach or cabbage for the *chye sim.*

Fried Kway Teow

Char Kway Teow

Fresh flat rice noodles (*kway teow*) stir-fried with seafood and chili paste is practically Singapore's national dish.

4 tablespoons oil
5 cloves garlic, minced
3¹/2 oz (100 g) red snapper fillet, sliced (optional)
8 oz (250 g) medium fresh shrimp, shelled and deveined
7 oz (200 g) squid, cleaned and sliced
1–2 tablespoons chili paste
2 sweet dried Chinese sausages (*lap cheong*), blanched and thinly sliced
1 lb (500 g) fresh flat rice noodles (*kway teow*) or 8 oz (250 g) dried rice sticks, blanched in hot water and drained
1 cup (100 g) *choy sum*, washed and cut into lengths

1 tablespoon soy sauce
1–2 tablespoons dark soy sauce
1/2 teaspoon sugar (optional)
3 eggs, lightly beaten
3/4 cup (40 g) bean sprouts
1 red finger-length chili, thinly sliced
1/2 teaspoon salt
1/2 teaspoon ground white pepper

Heat 2 tablespoons of the oil in a wok over high heat and stir-fry the garlic until light brown, about 1 minute. Add the seafood, chili paste and Chinese sausages, and stir-fry for another 2 minutes.

Add the noodles and *choy sum,* and stir. Then season with the soy sauces and sugar, and stir to mix well.

Push the noodles to the side of the wok, reduce the heat to medium, add the rest of the oil and the beaten eggs. Scramble the eggs, then stir-fry with the rest of the ingredients in the wok to mix well, about 1 minute.

Add the bean sprouts and chili, and stir-fry for another 1 to 2 minutes. Season with salt and pepper, and serve immediately.

Yen's Crispy Brown Noodles with Gravy

This version of a Cantonese-style dish—deep-fried coils of crisp, light brown noodles bathed in a delicate and delicious sauce—is named after the chef who created it.

5 oz (150 g) dried wheat noodles (*yee mien*)
3 cups (300 g) mustard greens or spinach, hard ends trimmed
Oil for deep-frying
3 cloves garlic, minced

5 oz (150 g) medium fresh shrimp, peeled and deveined
5 oz (150 g) chicken or pork, thinly sliced
2 cups (500 ml) water
1 tablespoon oyster sauce
1 tablespoon soy sauce
1 teaspoon dark soy sauce
1/2 teaspoon sesame oil
1/2 teaspoon ground white pepper
1 tablespoon cornstarch mixed with 3 tablespoons water
2 eggs, lightly beaten
Thinly sliced red finger-length chilies
Soy sauce

Place the dried noodles in a colander, sprinkle a few drops of cold water and set aside to soften for 10 minutes. Cut the vegetables into 1¹/2-in (4-cm) lengths.

Heat the oil in a wok over medium heat and deep-fry the noodles a handful at a time, turning them over until crispy and golden, about 1 minute. Drain the cooked noodles and set aside on a platter. Repeat with the remaining noodles.

Reserve 1 tablespoon of the oil in the wok and drain off the rest. Wipe the wok clean, return the reserved oil to the wok and stir-fry the garlic for a few seconds until golden brown. Add the shrimp and chicken or pork and stir-fry until cooked, about 2 to 3 minutes. Add the water, oyster sauce, soy sauces and sesame oil. Season with the pepper and bring to a boil. Then add the vegetable and simmer for a minute until the vegetable is wilted.

Add the cornstarch mixture and cook, stirring continuously, until the sauce thickens and clears, about 2 minutes. Then add the beaten eggs and cook until they set. Ladle into individual bowls and serve with the crunchy noodles. Alternatively, place the crunchy noodles in a bowl and ladle the cooked mixture over it. Serve hot, with a small bowl of sliced chili and soy sauce on the side.

Dried yee mien noodles are light beige in color. They should have a firm and crunchy texture after cooking. The distinctive flavor of this noodle makes this simply named dish worth trying. Packets of dried yee mien noodles are available in Chinese provision shops.

Rice Noodles in Spicy Tamarind Gravy

Mee Siam

This Nonya specialty—noodles in a spicy sweet and sour broth—is a popular snack at food stalls throughout Singapore.

30 dried chilies, cut into lengths, deseeded and soaked in water to soften
3 tablespoons oil
8 oz (250 g) dried rice vermicelli (beehoon), soaked in hot water to soften
2 cups (100 g) bean sprouts, rinsed, seed coats and tails removed
4 cakes deep-fried tofu or aburage (about 7 oz/200 g total), diced, or 2 cakes pressed tofu (10 oz/300 g), diced and pan-fried until golden brown
8 oz (250 g) medium fresh shrimp, boiled for 1 to 2 minutes in 3 cups (750 ml) water, drained, shelled and deveined, shrimp stock reserved
8 quail eggs, halved, or 2 hard-boiled eggs, shelled and cut into wedges
2 green onions (scallions) or garlic chives (*koo chye*), cut into lengths
Sambal Belachan (page 122)
4 small limes (limau kasturi), halved

*Rice Noodles in Spicy
Tamarind Gravy (Mee Siam)*

Sauce

8–10 shallots, peeled

5 tablespoons dried shrimp, soaked in water to soften

10 macadamia or candlenuts, roughly chopped

6 cloves garlic, peeled

1 teaspoon *belachan* (dried shrimp paste)

5 tablespoons oil

1/2 cup (75 g) unsalted peanuts, roasted and coarsely crushed

3 tablespoons black bean paste (*tau cheo*), mashed

6 tablespoons sugar

6 tablespoons tamarind pulp mashed with 1 cup (250 ml) warm water, squeezed and strained for juice

1 stalk lemongrass, tender inner part of bottom third only, bruised

1/2 tablespoon dark soy sauce

1 teaspoon salt

1 teaspoon pepper

Grind the dried chilies to a paste in a blender, transfer to a small bowl and set aside.

Prepare the Sauce by grinding the dried shrimp, macadamia or candlenuts, shallots, garlic and *belachan* in a blender, adding a little oil if necessary to keep the blades turning. Heat the oil in a wok over medium heat and and gently stir-fry the ground paste for 5 minutes. Add the peanuts, black bean paste and sugar, and stir-fry for another minute. Add the reserved shrimp stock, tamarind juice, lemongrass and soy sauce, and bring to a boil. Reduce the heat and simmer gently, uncovered, for 5 minutes. Season with salt and pepper. Remove from the heat and keep warm.

Heat the oil in a wok and stir-fry 3 tablespoons of the reserved chili paste for 1 minute. Then add the noodles and continue to stir-fry just long enough to coat with the paste so they take on a red color, about 1 minute.

To serve, divide the noodles into 4 individual bowls. Top the noodles with bean sprouts, fried tofu, shrimp and eggs. Ladle the hot Sauce over and garnish with green onions or chives. Serve with a small bowl of Sambal Belachan and lime halves on the side.

Classic Hokkien Mee

Braised Noodles with Seafood Hokkien Style

As the majority of Singapore's Chinese population is Hokkien, this is an all-time favorite noodle dish. A combination of fresh yellow wheat noodles (Hokkien mee) and rice vermicelli are stir-fried with a mixture of seafood, vegetables and pork. The whole lot is then bathed in rich stock and seasoned to perfection. Robust rather than refined, it makes an excellent lunch or late-night snack.

8 oz (250 g) medium fresh shrimp, shelled and deveined, shells and heads reserved to make stock

1 small squid or fish fillet, cleaned and sliced

31/2 oz (100 g) pork fillet or belly pork, very thinly sliced

2 cups (500 ml) water

1/3 cup (90 ml) oil

4 cloves garlic, minced

8 oz (250 g) fresh yellow wheat noodles (Hokkien mee)

5 oz (150 g) dried rice vermicelli (beehoon), soaked in hot water to soften, then cut into short lengths

5 stalks *choy sum* or *bok choy* leaves, rinsed and sliced

1 cup (50 g) bean sprouts

2 tablespoons soy sauce

1/2 teaspoon ground white pepper

1 egg, lightly beaten

Fresh coriander leaves (cilantro), chopped, or finely shredded carrot, to garnish (optional)

Sambal Belachan (page 122)

Small limes (limau kasturi), halved, to serve

Make a stock by placing the shrimp, reserved shrimp shells and heads, squid or fish, pork and water in a pot and bringing it to a boil for 2 to 3 minutes. Strain and reserve the stock. Set the seafood and meat aside. Discard the shrimp shells and heads.

Heat the oil in a wok over medium heat, add the garlic and stir-fry for a 1 minute until light brown. Add the shrimp, squid and pork, and stir-fry briskly for a few seconds. Then add 11/2 cups (375 ml) of the stock and simmer for another minute.

Increase the heat to high, add both types of noodles, *choy sum*, bean sprouts, soy sauce and pepper. Stir-fry briskly until all ingredients are mixed, about 2 to 3 minutes. Then add the egg and cook for about a minute until the egg is cooked. Garnish with fresh coriander leaves or shredded carrot, if using. Serve with a small bowl of Sambal Belachan and lime halves on the side.

Classic Hainanese Chicken Rice

Classic Hainanese Chicken Rice

The classic Singapore dish made with fresh chicken to achieve a perfect combination of flavors and textures, accompanied by fluffy rice cooked in chicken stock, soup and 3 types of sauces.

8 cups (2 liters) Chicken Stock (page 122)

1 large fresh chicken (about 11/2 kg/3 lbs), cleaned and patted dry

1 teaspoon soy sauce

1/4 teaspoon sesame oil

1 green onion (scallion), thinly sliced, to garnish

1 sliced tomato, to garnish

1 sliced cucumber, to garnish

Sprigs of coriander leaves (cilantro), to garnish

Chicken Rice

1 tablespoon oil or chicken fat

1 clove garlic, unpeeled

1 slice of fresh ginger, peeled and bruised

2 cups (400 g) uncooked long-grain rice, rinsed and drained

2 pandanus leaves, tied in a knot (optional)

Sauces

1 portion Chili Ginger Sauce (page 122)

5 cm (2 in) fresh ginger ground with 1 tablespoon water

2 tablespoons dark soy sauce

Bring the Chicken Stock to a rolling boil in a pot and add the chicken. Turn off the heat, cover and let the chicken steep for 15 minutes. Remove the chicken from the stock, plunge into iced water to cool for 1 minute then drain. Bring the stock back to a boil, return the chicken to the pot and repeat the steeping process 3 more times. Remove the chicken and set aside to cool. Keep the stock warm to cook the Chicken Rice. When cool enough to handle, cut the chicken into serving pieces. Drizzle the soy sauce and sesame oil over and garnish with coriander leaves.

To cook the Chicken Rice, heat the oil in a pan over medium to high heat and brown the garlic and ginger, about 1 minute. Add the rice and stir-fry until fragrant, about 2 minutes. Add the pandanus leaves, if using, and 4 cups (1 liter) of the reserved stock, and bring it to a boil. Reduce the heat and simmer, covered, for 15 to 20 minutes until the rice is cooked. Alternatively, cook the seasoned rice in a rice cooker.

Place each of the Sauces in separate serving dishes. Pour the remaining chicken stock into small individual bowls and garnish with freshly sliced green onion. Serve the chicken with the hot Chicken Rice, Sauces, sliced tomato and cucumber, and small bowls of the Chicken Stock on the side.

Claypot Rice

A simple Cantonese one-pot dish, in which rice is cooked with succulent chunks of chicken, Chinese sausage, Chinese mushrooms and seasonings. The Chinese believe that a claypot is essential to ensure the correct flavor and fragrance of this dish, though any other type of covered earthenware container could be used.

1 lb (500 g) boneless chicken meat, cut into bite-sized chunks
6 dried black Chinese mushrooms, soaked to soften, stems discarded, caps quartered
1 tablespoon oil
2 cups (400 g) uncooked long-grain rice, washed and drained
1¹/2 cups (375 ml) Chicken Stock (page 122)
1 sweet dried Chinese sausage (*lap cheong*), sliced
1¹/2 in (4 cm) ginger, thinly sliced
1 green onion (scallion), sliced

Marinade
1 tablespoon oil
3 tablespoons oyster sauce
1 tablespoon rice wine or sake
1 tablespoon soy sauce
1 teaspoon dark soy sauce
1 teaspoon sugar
¹/2 teaspoon sesame oil
¹/2 teaspoon ground white pepper
¹/2 tablespoon cornstarch

Combine the Marinade ingredients in a small bowl and pour

Claypot Rice

over the chicken and mushrooms, and mix to coat them well. Set the chicken and mushrooms aside to marinate for at least 2 to 4 hours.

Heat the oil in a large seasoned claypot over high heat and stir-fry the drained rice for 2 minutes in the oil until lightly browned. Add the chicken stock, bring to a boil, then reduce the heat and simmer, covered, over low heat for 15 minutes.

Spread the marinated chicken and mushrooms, sausage and ginger on top of the rice. Cover again and cook for another 10 minutes. Remove from the heat, garnish with freshly sliced green onion and serve.

> Claypots are the Chinese version of a casserole dish. While claypots are cooked on the stovetop, casseroles are usually bound for the oven. The design of the claypot ensures that food stays piping hot even if the meal is delayed. To season a new claypot, immerse it completely in water for 24 hours, or see package instructions.

Special Fried Rice

This version of fried rice from a Nonya kitchen gets its distinctive flavor from the tiny dried salted fish used by Chinese cooks. Smaller than the usual Malay *ikan bilis*, they are sometimes called silverfish.

3 tablespoons oil
¹/2 cup (80 g) very small dried salted fish or bits of salted fish
3 cloves garlic, minced
1 chicken breast (4 oz/125 g), diced
5 oz (150 g) medium fresh shrimp, peeled and deveined
3 eggs, beaten
4 cups (800 g) cold cooked rice or leftover rice
1 tablespoon soy sauce
¹/2 teaspoon salt
¹/2 teaspoon pepper
¹/4 teaspoon sesame oil (optional)
1 cup (75 g) bean sprouts
2 green onions (scallions), thinly sliced

Heat the oil in a wok and stir-fry the dried salted fish until brown and crispy. Remove from the oil and drain. In the same wok, gently stir-fry the garlic for a few seconds, then add the chicken

and shrimp, and stir-fry for 3 to 4 minutes. Increase the heat and add the eggs, stirring until the eggs are cooked.

Add the rice and stir-fry over high heat until the rice is heated through. Then add the rest of the ingredients and stir-fry for another 3 minutes. Add the crispy silverfish or salted fish and stir to mix well. Serve immediately.

> Leftover rice kept overnight is preferred for any fried rice dish, as it is drier and firmer, and will result in a better textured fried rice dish.

Chicken Devil Curry

This Eurasian dish may be too spicy for some. The large amount of chilies makes the name "Devil's Curry" appropriate, which is based on the Indian Vindaloo Curry with its blending of spices and vinegar. A Malaysian touch is given with fresh lemongrass and galangal. To help reduce the heat, swirl a little plain yogurt into the curry or serve a small bowl of cold yogurt on the side.

4 tablespoons oil
5 cloves garlic, sliced
2 onions, quartered
2 in (5 cm) ginger, thinly shredded
2 red finger-length chilies, halved lengthwise
1 chicken (2 lbs/1 kg), cut into serving pieces
1 lb (500 g) potatoes, peeled and halved
1¹/2 teaspoons salt
1 teaspoon dark soy sauce
2–4 tablespoons sugar
¹/2 cup (125 ml) white vinegar
2–3 cups (500–750 ml) water

Spice Paste
1 teaspoon brown mustard seeds, soaked in water for 5 minutes
2 stalks lemongrass, tender inner part of bottom third only, sliced
1 in (2¹/2 cm) galangal root, sliced
1¹/4 in (3 cm) turmeric root
15 dried chilies, cut into lengths, soaked to soften and deseeded
30 shallots, peeled and halved

Grind the Spice Paste ingredients, adding a little oil if necessary to keep the blades turning.

Heat 2 tablespoons of the oil in a wok and stir-fry the garlic, onions, ginger and chilies for 2

Nonya Chicken Curry (Ayam Limau Purut, left) and Vegetables in Coconut Milk (Nonya Sayur Lemak, recipe on page 134)

minutes. Drain the fried mixture and set aside.

Stir-fry the ground Spice Paste with the remaining 2 tablespoons oil in the wok over medium to high heat for 5 to 7 minutes. Add the chicken, potatoes, salt and soy sauce, and cook for 10 minutes. Then add the sugar, vinegar and water. Add a little more vinegar for a more sour curry if preferred. Reduce the heat and simmer, uncovered, for 20 minutes until the chicken is cooked.

Add the reserved fried mixture and mix well. Transfer the curry to a platter and serve hot with freshly cooked rice.

Nonya Chicken Curry
Ayam Limau Purut

4 tablespoons oil
1 chicken (about 2 lbs/1 kg), cut into serving pieces
1 slice *asam gelugur* (optional)
1/2 cup (125 ml) water
1 cup (250 ml) thick coconut milk
4 kaffir lime leaves
1 1/2 teaspoons salt
1–2 tablespoons fresh lime juice

Spice Paste
1 1/4 in (3 cm) galangal root, sliced
1 stalk lemongrass, tender inner part of bottom third only, sliced
8–10 red finger-length chilies, sliced
2 medium onions, quartered
3 cloves garlic, peeled and halved
1 teaspoon ground turmeric

Grind all the Spice Paste ingredients in a mortar or blender, adding a little oil if necessary to keep the blades turning.

Heat the oil in a wok and stir-fry the Spice Paste over medium heat for 7 minutes, until fragrant. Add the chicken, *asam* and water, and simmer for 10 minutes.

Add the coconut milk and lime leaves, and simmer, uncovered, for 10 minutes until the chicken is tender. Season with salt and fresh lime juice.

Indian Mutton Curry
Kambing Korma

2 lbs (1 kg) mutton or lamb, cubed
9 cups (2 1/4 liters) water
2 in (5 cm) fresh ginger, sliced
10 green finger-length chilies, deseeded
10 shallots, peeled
10 cloves garlic, peeled
3 tablespoons oil
4 large onions, peeled and sliced
6 cardamom pods, bruised
20 raw cashew nuts, ground
5 star anise pods
4 cinnamon sticks
6 tablespoons meat curry powder
1 sprig curry leaves
3 potatoes, peeled and cubed
1 cup (250 ml) plain yogurt
1 1/2 teaspoons salt
1 tablespoon ground white pepper
2 tablespoons tamarind pulp mashed with 4 tablespoons warm water, squeezed and strained for juice
4–6 green finger-length chilies, halved lengthwise and deseeded
6 small tomatoes, quartered

Cover the mutton with 8 cups (2 liters) water in a pot. Grind the ginger, chilies, shallots and garlic in a mortar or blender, adding 1 cup (250 ml) of water to keep the blades turning. Add the ground mixture to the pot and bring to a boil. Reduce the heat and simmer, uncovered, until the meat is tender, about 1 1/2 hours for mutton and 1 hour for lamb.

Heat the oil in a skillet and stir-fry the onions for 3 minutes. Add the cardamom pods, candlenuts or cashew nuts, star anise, cinnamon, curry powder and curry leaves and stir-fry for 5 minutes until fragrant. Remove from the heat and add the fried mixture to the pot with the mutton.

Add the potatoes, yogurt, salt, pepper and tamarind juice, and continue to simmer until the meat is soft and cooked through, about 20 to 30 minutes. Add the green chilies and tomatoes if using and stir. Serve immediately with freshly cooked white rice.

Indian Mutton Soup
Sup Kambing

Also known as Sup Tulang or Bone Soup, this dish is one of the more popular hawker dishes in Singapore. It makes a great late-night meal or luncheon served with lots of crusty French bread to soak up the soup.

2 in (5 cm) fresh ginger, sliced
6 cloves garlic, peeled
2 lbs (1 kg) meaty mutton or lamb ribs
1 onion, sliced or 5 shallots, sliced
1 heaped tablespoon ground coriander
1 teaspoon ground fennel
1 teaspoon ground cumin
1/2 teaspoon ground turmeric
1 1/2 teaspoons salt
1 teaspoon ground black pepper
8–12 cups (2–3 liters) water
1/2 tablespoon oil
2 leeks, white part only, sliced (optional)
5 cardamom pods, bruised
3 star anise pods
1 cinnamon stick
1 tomato, cut into wedges
Crispy Fried Shallots, to garnish (page 122)
Chinese celery or coriander leaves (cilantro), chopped, to garnish

Grind the ginger and garlic together in a mortar to a paste. Place the paste in a pot with the mutton or lamb ribs, onion, coriander, fennel, cumin and ground turmerics. Season with the salt and pepper. Add 12 cups (3 liters) of water if using mutton,

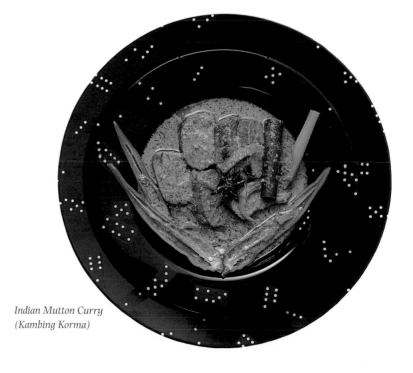

Indian Mutton Curry (Kambing Korma)

but only 8 cups (2 liters) if using lamb, which will cook more quickly. Simmer over medium heat, uncovered, until the meat is soft, about 1 1/2 hours for mutton and 1 hour for lamb.

Heat the oil in a skillet over medium heat and stir-fry the leeks, cardamom, star anise and cinnamon until the leeks are tender, about 5 minutes.

Add the fried mixture to the mutton soup and simmer for another 2 minutes. Then add the tomato and stir to mix well. Serve garnished with Crispy Fried Shallots and Chinese celery leaves, and crusty French bread on the side.

Fragrant Beef Rendang

No festive occasion is complete without this rich Sumatran dish where beef is cooked to melt-in-the-mouth tenderness in a fragrant coconut gravy. This rendang actually tastes better the next day!

1 cup (100 g) grated fresh coconut
4 tablespoons oil
1 stalk lemongrass, tender inner part of bottom third only, bruised
1/2 cinnamon stick (1 1/4 in/3 cm)
2 cloves
4 star anise pods
2 cardamom pods
1 lb (500 g) topside or stewing beef, cubed
1 cup (250 ml) thick coconut milk
1 slice *asam gelugur* or 2 teaspoons dried tamarind pulp soaked in 1/2 cup (125 ml) water, mashed and strained for juice

2 kaffir lime leaves, very thinly sliced
1 turmeric leaf, very thinly sliced
1 1/2 teaspoons sugar
1 tablespoon soy sauce

Spice Paste
2 stalks lemongrass, tender inner part of bottom third only, sliced
3/4 in (2 cm) galangal root, sliced
3/4 in (2 cm) ginger, sliced
10 dried chilies, cut into lengths and soaked in warm water
2 shallots, peeled and halved
2 cloves garlic, peeled and halved

Dry-fry the grated coconut in a wok or skillet, stirring constantly over low heat for 10 minutes until brown. Grind the coconut in a mortar while it is still hot and crispy. If a little oil oozes out, mix it into the coconut. Set aside.

Grind the Spice Paste ingredients in a mortar or blender, adding a little oil if necessary to keep the blades turning.

Heat the oil over medium heat in a saucepan, add the Spice Paste, lemongrass cinnamon, cloves, star anise and cardamom pods, and stir-fry for 5 to 7 minutes until fragrant.

Add the beef, coconut milk and *asam* or tamarind juice and stir. Reduce the heat and simmer, uncovered, stirring frequently until the meat is almost cooked, about 45 minutes.

Add the lime and turmeric leaves, and the ground coconut, and season with the sugar and soy sauce. Simmer until the meat is very tender and the gravy has dried up, about 1 to 1 1/2 hours. Serve with rice.

Fragrant Beef Rendang

Spicy Oxtail Stew

Oxtail has long been a popular Singapore dish, prepared almost as an English-style stew by Hainanese cooks. This is a simple, delicious recipe, richly flavored with the silky texture of oxtail enhanced by Malay or Indonesian spices.

2 lbs (1 kg) oxtail, fat trimmed off and cut into serving pieces
8–10 cups (2–2 1/2 liters) water
1/2 teaspoon salt or more to taste
1/2 teaspoon pepper
Crispy Fried Shallots (page 122)

Marinade
1 in (2 1/2 cm) turmeric root, peeled and sliced, or 1 teaspoon ground turmeric
1 1/2 in (4 cm) galangal root, sliced
10–12 red finger-length chilies, deseeded and sliced
5–10 bird's-eye chilies (*chili padi*), deseeded and sliced
10 shallots, peeled
8 cloves garlic, peeled
2 stalks lemongrass, tender inner part of bottom third only, sliced
1/2 cup (125 ml) water
1/2 cup (150 g) tamarind pulp, mashed with 1 1/2 cups (375 ml) warm water, squeezed and strained for juice
5 kaffir lime leaves, very thinly sliced
3 tablespoons tomato paste or 5 tablespoons tomato ketchup
1 tablespoon sugar (if using tomato ketchup, omit this)

To make the Marinade, grind the turmeric, galangal, chilies, shallots, garlic and lemongrass in a mortar or blender until smooth, adding a little water if necessary to keep the blades turning. Combine the ground mixture with the rest of the Marinade ingredients. Rub the Marinade into the oxtail and set aside to marinate for at least 2 hours or overnight.

Bring the water to a boil in a pot. Add the marinated oxtail, reduce the heat and simmer, covered, over low heat for 30 minutes. Then simmer, uncovered, for another 30 minutes until the oxtail is tender and the broth is reduced by half. Stir periodically to prevent the meat from burning and add more water if the broth evaporates too quickly.

Season with the salt and pepper and garnish with Crispy Fried Shallots (if using). Serve hot with freshly steamed rice.

Black Pepper Crab

This is a truly original Malaysian dish—begin with fresh crabs and seasonings, spice it up with black pepper and curry leaves, enrich with butter and finally, toss in some chili padi for a knock–out result.

2 tablespoons dried shrimp
1 1/2–2 kg (3–4 lbs) fresh crabs
1/4 cup (60 ml) oil
2 tablespoons butter
2 shallots, minced
7 cloves garlic, minced
1 tablespoon fermented soybean paste (*tau cheo*), mashed
3 1/2 tablespoons black peppercorns, cracked or coarsely ground
1/2 cup (20 g) curry leaves
10 red or green bird's-eye chilies (*chili padi*), whole
3 tablespoons sugar
2 tablespoons dark soy sauce
1 tablespoon oyster sauce
1/4 cup (60 ml) water

Rinse and drain the dried shrimp. Then dry roast them in a skillet for 2 to 3 minutes. Allow to cool, then grind coarsely in a mortar or blender.

To prepare the crabs, lift the triangular-shaped "apron" on the underside of the crab. Insert your thumb between the body and topshell at the rear of the crab and pull the topshell off. Discard the grey gills on either side of the body and any spongy grey matter. Clean the crab thoroughly, then rinse and drain. Quarter the crabs and crack the claws so the spices can penetrate.

Heat the oil in a wok and stir-fry the crabs over high heat for 5 minutes. Cover the wok and let the crabs cook for another 5 minutes. Remove from the heat and set the crabs aside on a rack to allow the oil to drain.

In the same wok, melt the butter in the remaining oil over medium heat. Stir-fry the shallots, garlic, fermented soybean paste, dried shrimp, black peppercorns, curry leaves and chilies until fragrant, about 3 to 5 minutes. Add the crabs and the remaining ingredients. Cook for 5 to 10 minutes until the crabs are pink and cooked through.

Singapore Chili Crab

Another Singapore original—a spicy and sweet tomato sauce, enhancing the delicious taste of fresh crabs. Sold in hawker centers and seafood restaurants in the country, and not to be missed when visiting the island state.

3 fresh crabs (5 lbs/2¹/₂ kg total)
Oil for deep-frying
1 cup (250 ml) Chicken Stock
  (page 122)
1 egg, lightly beaten
1 tablespoon cornstarch dissolved in
  3 tablespoons water
¹/₂ teaspoon salt
1 teaspoon white pepper
1 green onion (scallion), thinly sliced

Sauce
4 tablespoons oil
8 cloves garlic, minced
1 large onion, diced
2 in (5 cm) young ginger, sliced
2 teaspoons fermented soybean
  paste (*tau cheo*)
3–5 red finger-length chilies,
  deseeded and sliced
2 tomatoes, diced
4 tablespoons sweet bottled chili sauce
4 tablespoons bottled tomato ketchup
1 teaspoon sesame oil
1 tablespoon soy sauce
1 tablespoon sugar
1 teaspoon ground red pepper
¹/₂ teaspoon ground white pepper

Clean and quarter the crabs, cracking the pincers to allow the flavors to penetrate. Pat dry, then deep-fry the crabs in 2 batches in hot oil in a wok for 3 minutes until the shells turn bright red. Remove from the heat and set aside to drain.

To make the Sauce, drain the oil in the wok and pour 4 tablespoons of fresh oil into it. Stir-fry the garlic, onion, ginger, black bean paste and chilies over high heat until fragrant, about 1 to 2 minutes. Add the tomatoes, chili sauce, tomato ketchup, sesame oil, soy sauce and sugar, and mix well. Then reduce the heat and simmer for 1 minute. Add the ground red pepper, if using, and season with the pepper.

Return the crabs to the wok and toss to coat with the Sauce. Add the chicken stock and cook over high heat for 3 minutes. Add the egg and cornstarch, and stir until the Sauce thickens, about 1 minute. Season with the salt and pepper. Garnish with the green onion and serve.

Singapore Chili Crab

Butter Shrimp

A relatively recent Malaysian creation, this dish combines traditional Malay, Chinese, Indian and Western ingredients, highlighting the fresh seafood available all year from the waters surrounding Malaysia.

1¹/₄ lbs (650 g) large fresh shrimp
Oil for deep-frying
2–3 tablespoons butter
15 bird's-eye chilies (*chili padi*),
  bruised or left whole
10–15 curry leaves
3 cloves garlic, minced
¹/₂ teaspoon salt
1 cup (100 g) fresh grated coconut,
  dry-fried until golden brown

1 teaspoon rice wine or sake
1 tablespoon sugar
¹/₂ teaspoon soy sauce

Slice the shrimp lengthwise, through the shells, and gently devein them. Then trim the feelers and the legs. Pat the shrimp dry with paper towels and deep-fry them in hot oil until golden brown, about 3 minutes. Remove from the oil and set aside to drain.

Melt the butter in a saucepan and stir-fry the chilies, curry leaves, garlic with the salt for 2 minutes. Add the shrimp, grated coconut, wine, sugar and soy sauce, and stir-fry briskly over high heat for 1 to 2 minutes. Serve immediately.

Shrimp Sambal
Sambal Udang

¹/₄ cup (60 ml) oil
2 tablespoons shaved palm sugar or
  dark brown sugar
1¹/₂ teaspoons salt
3 tablespoons thick coconut milk
4 tablespoons lime juice
1 lb (500 g) fresh medium shrimp,
  peeled and deveined

Spice Paste
1 macadamia or candlenut, chopped
5 dried chilies, cut into lengths and
  soaked in warm water, then drained
2–5 red finger-length chilies, sliced
  and deseeded
¹/₂ in (1 cm) ginger, sliced
1 red onion, sliced
5 cloves garlic, peeled and halved
2 tablespoons water

Grind the Spice Paste ingredients to a paste in a mortar or blender, adding a little oil if necessary to keep the blades turning.

Heat the oil in a wok and stir-fry the Spice Paste over medium to high heat for 5 to 7 minutes until fragrant. Add the palm sugar, salt and coconut milk, and bring to a boil. Add the lime juice and shrimp, and cook over high heat for 3 minutes until the shrimp are cooked. Serve with rice.

Teochew Steamed Fish

1 whole pomfret or other white fish,
  about 1¹/₂–2 lbs (750 g–1 kg), or
  4–6 fish fillets (about 2 lbs/1 kg)
¹/₄ cup (50 g) pickled mustard cabbage (*kiam chye*), soaked, drained
  and thinly sliced
1 medium tomato, cut into wedges
2 in (5 cm) ginger, thinly sliced
1 red finger-length chili, deseeded
  and thinly sliced lengthwise
3 or 4 sour plums
1 green onion (scallion), cut into
  lengths
2 dried black Chinese mushrooms,
  soaked in water to soften, stems
  discarded, caps sliced
¹/₄ cup (50 g) pork, thinly sliced

Seasonings
1 tablespoon soy sauce
¹/₄ cup (60 ml) Chicken Stock
  (page 122)
1 teaspoon Garlic Oil (page 122)
1 teaspoon rice wine or sake
¹/₂ teaspoon sugar
¹/₄ teaspoon sesame oil

*Shrimp Sambal
(Sambal Udang)*

Clean the fish and pat it dry thoroughly. Mix the Seasonings in a large bowl until the sugar is completely dissolved. Add all the other ingredients to the bowl and mix well.

Place the fish on a plate or tray that fits inside a steamer or wok that can be covered. Spread the Seasoning mixture over the fish. Cover the steamer or wok and steam the fish over rapidly boiling water for 10 to 15 minutes until the fish is cooked. Do not overcook or the texture of the fish will be spoiled.

> Preserved mustard cabbage (*kiam chye*) is slightly sour and extremely salty. This heavily salted pickled cabbage needs to be soaked in fresh water for at least 15 minutes to remove some of the saltiness. **Salted plums** are lightly pickled in brine and sold in jars. They are sour and the seeds need to be removed before using. The Japanese version is called *umeboshi*.

Hot and Sour Malay Fish Curry

Ikan Asam Pedas

1/3 cup (85 ml) oil
1/2 in (1 cm) galangal root, bruised
3–4 pieces *asam gelugur* or 11/2 heaped tablespoons tamarind pulp soaked in 4 tablespoons water, mashed and strained to obtain juice
21/2 cups (625 ml) water
6 thick fish fillets (11/2 lbs/750 g)
4 sprigs laksa leaves (*daun kesum*), minced
3 tablespoons thick coconut milk
2 teaspoons sugar
1 teaspoon salt
Dried Cucumber Achar (page 122)

Spice Paste
2 macadamia or candlenuts, chopped
15 dried chilies, cut into lengths and soaked in warm water
10 shallots, peeled and halved
4 cloves garlic, peeled and halved
1/2 teaspoon ground turmeric
1 cup (250 ml) water

Grind the Spice Paste ingredients to a paste in a mortar or blender, adding a little oil if necessary to keep the blades turning.

Heat the oil in a pot over medium heat and stir-fry the Spice Paste and galangal for 5

Spinach with Dried Shrimp (Kangkung Belachan)

minutes until fragrant. Add the *asam gelugur* or tamarind juice and 1/2 cup (125 ml) water, and cook for 5 minutes.

Add the rest of the water and bring to a boil. Then add the fish, laksa leaves, coconut milk and season with the sugar and salt. Simmer, uncovered, for another 5 minutes until the oil separates from the coconut milk. Serve with freshly cooked white rice and a small bowl of Dried Cucumber Achar on the side.

Spinach with Dried Shrimp

Kangkung Belachan

A popular method of cooking this excellent leafy green vegetable using both Malay and Chinese seasonings.

11/2 lbs (750 g) *kangkung* (water spinach or regular spinach), trimmed, wilted leaves discarded
2–3 tablespoons oil
3 tablespoons dried shrimp, soaked in water to soften, then coarsely ground in a mortar or blender
2–4 teaspoons sugar
1 teaspoon sesame oil
1 tablespoon soy sauce
1 red finger-length chili, thinly sliced
1/2 teaspoon salt
1/2 teaspoon pepper

Spice Paste
1 in (21/2 cm) ginger, sliced
5–8 red finger-length chilies, deseeded and sliced
6 shallots, peeled
6 cloves garlic, peeled
2 teaspoons dried shrimp paste (*belachan*)

Use only the tender tips and leaves of the *kangkung*, and discard the tough stems. Wash the leaves and stems thoroughly in several changes of water to remove any grit.

Grind the Spice Paste ingredients in a mortar or blender, adding a little oil if necessary to keep the blades turning.

Heat the oil in a wok and stir-fry the ground dried shrimp and the Spice Paste over medium heat for 5 to 7 minutes until fragrant. Add the sugar, sesame oil, soy sauce and sliced chili, and stir to mix well. Increase the heat to high, add the *kangkung* and stir-fry briskly until the vegetable is slightly wilted, about 3 minutes. Season with the salt and pepper. Best served hot.

Vegetables in Coconut

Nonya Sayur Lemak

A Nonya adaptation of the popular Malay-style vegetable dish simmered in a lightly spiced coconut milk.

1 carrot
1 slender Asian eggplant
1/4 small *bangkuang* (jicama), peeled
3 long beans or 12 green beans
1/4 small cabbage
1 cake firm tofu (8 oz/250 g), drained
Oil for shallow-frying (about 3 tablespoons)
11/2 (375 ml) cups water
11/2 cups (375 ml) thick coconut milk
1 teaspoon salt

Spice Paste
3 macadamia or candlenuts, roughly chopped

1 teaspoon dried shrimp, soaked for 5 minutes in warm water and drained
2 red finger-length chilies, sliced
5 shallots, peeled and halved
1/2 teaspoon ground turmeric
1/2 teaspoon dried shrimp paste (*belachan*)

Grind the Spice Paste ingredients in a mortar or blender, adding a little oil if necessary to keep the blades turning.

Cut the carrot and eggplant into long strips. Slice the *bangkuang*, long beans or green beans into strips of the same length. Then slice the cabbage into bite sized chunks.

Pan-fry the tofu in the oil in a large wok over medium heat until golden brown, about 3 minutes on each side. Remove from the oil. Set aside to drain on paper towels. Let it cool, then cut the tofu into 8 pieces.

In the same wok, stir-fry the Spice Paste over medium heat for 5 minutes until fragrant. Add the water and coconut milk, and slowly bring to a boil. Stir in prepared vegetables and then bring to a boil. Reduce the heat, add the tofu and simmer, uncovered, for 5 minutes until the vegetables are just cooked. Serve hot.

Spicy Curried Pumpkin

Gourds are very popular among Malaysians of southern Indian origin, especially the sweet-tasting pumpkin that complements a mild mixture of curry spices used in this dish.

2 tablespoons oil
1 tablespoon brown mustard seeds
2 sprigs curry leaves
1 medium onion, diced
2 teaspoons chicken curry powder
1 teaspoon ground red pepper
1/2 teaspoon ground turmeric
1/2 small pumpkin (about 1 lb/500 g), peeled and cut into chunks
11/2 cups (375 ml) water
1 teaspoon salt

Heat the oil in a wok over high heat and stir-fry the mustard seeds and curry leaves for 2 minutes until the seeds pop. Add the onion and stir-fry gently for 3 minutes until the onion is light golden brown.

Add the curry, chili and ground turmeric, and stir-fry for 30 seconds. Then add the pumpkin chunks and stir to coat them well with the spices. Slowly add the water, stirring constantly, and season with the salt. Simmer, uncovered, over medium heat until the pumpkin is tender and dry, about 15 to 20 minutes. Best served hot.

Pancakes with Sweet Coconut Filling

Kueh Dadar

A Nonya version of the Malay Kueh Dadar is often served with a coconut sauce as a teatime treat or snack, but also makes a wonderful dessert.

Batter
1 cup (150 g) flour
1/4 teaspoon salt
1 egg, lightly beaten
1/3 cup (85 ml) fresh milk
1/2 teaspoon pandanus or vanilla extract
1 cup (250 ml) water
2 teaspoons melted butter or oil

Sweet Coconut Filling
3 cups (300 g) fresh grated coconut
1 1/2 cups (375 ml) water
3 pandanus leaves (optional)
1/4 teaspoon salt
3/4 cup (150 g) shaved palm sugar or dark brown sugar

Coconut Sauce
1/2 cup (125 ml) thick coconut milk
1/2 cup (125 ml) cup water
3 pandanus leaves or 1/4 teaspoon pandanus extract
1 teaspoon sugar
1 teaspoon cornstarch
1/4 teaspoon salt

First make the Batter by sifting the flour and salt together into a bowl. Add the egg, milk, pandanus extract and water, and stir until the batter is smooth. Add the butter or oil and mix well. Cover and allow the Batter to stand for 20 to 30 minutes.

Place all the Sweet Coconut Filling ingredients in a saucepan and simmer over low heat, stirring occasionally, for about 30 minutes, until thick and almost dry. Be careful not to burn the sugar. Remove from the heat, transfer to a small bowl and set aside to cool. Then discard the pandanus leaves, if using.

Combine the Coconut Sauce ingredients in a saucepan and stir continuously over low heat

for 15 minutes until the sauce thickens. Discard the pandanus leaves, if using and strain to remove any lumps. Set aside in a warm place.

To cook the pancakes, grease a non-stick griddle with a little butter and spoon 3 tablespoons of the Batter onto it to make a pancake about 6–8 in (15–20 cm) in diameter. Cook over low heat until the pancake sets and browns, about 2 minutes. Flip the pancake over and cook for a few seconds. Remove from the heat and set aside on a plate. Repeat until all the Batter is used up.

To serve, place 2 tablespoons of the filling on one side of each pancake, fold the sides in and roll up. Repeat until all the filling and pancakes are used. Serve warm with a little Coconut Sauce drizzled on top.

> The unused Batter tends to thicken as you cook the pancakes. Thin it down with a tablespoon or two of water as you go along.

Chilled Almond Jelly with Longans

A classic Chinese restaurant dish that is very easy to make and can be prepared well in advance. What a great way to end a Chinese dinner!

3 cups (750 ml) water
2 tablespoons agar-agar powder
1 cup (250 ml) fresh milk
1/2 cup (125 g) sugar
2 teaspoons almond essence
One (20-oz/600-g) can longans or lychees, with canning syrup, chilled
Ice cubes (optional)

Pour the water into a deep saucepan and sprinkle the agar agar powder over it. Stir gently and slowly bring to a boil over medium heat. Then reduce the heat and simmer gently over low heat for 5 minutes. Add the milk and sugar, and continue to stir until the sugar is completely dissolved. Then add the almond essence and gently simmer for another minute. Pour the mixture into a square or rectangular dish and leave to set, then refrigerate until required.

Just before serving, pour the chilled longans or lychees and

their canning syrup into a large bowl. Cut the almond jelly into squares and add to the bowl. Add a few ice cubes, if desired, and serve immediately.

Coconut Mango Pudding

Delicate and light, garnish these simple puddings with fresh mango and other fruits to create an elegant dessert.

4 cups (1 liter) water
1/2 cup (125 g) sugar
2 tablespoons gelatin powder
1 cup (250 ml) thick coconut milk
1/2 cup (125 ml) fresh milk
2 eggs, beaten
1 large mango (about 1 lb/500 g), peeled, pitted and puréed
1 large mango (about 1 lb/500 g), peeled, pitted and diced
1 large mango (about 450 g), peeled, pitted and sliced to garnish
Strawberries, kiwi or other fruits

Combine the water, sugar and gelatin powder in a saucepan and stir constantly over low heat until completely dissolved, about 7 to 10 minutes.

Remove from the heat, add the coconut milk or cream, fresh milk, eggs and mango purée, and mix well. Then add the diced mango and mix again.

Pour the mixture into small molds and refrigerate until set. Garnish with the sliced mango, strawberries and kiwis or other fruits (if using) and serve.

Sago with Honeydew and Coconut Cream

7 tablespoons dried sago pearls
9 cups (2 1/2 liters) water
1/2 cup (100 g) sugar
1 ripe honeydew melon
1 1/2 cups (375 ml) coconut cream

Rinse the sago pearls, place in a pot and bring to a boil with 8 cups (2 liters) water, stirring constantly for 15 minutes. Remove the pot from the heat, cover and set aside for 5 minutes. Drain the sago pearls, discarding the water. Rinse the sago under cold running water, drain again and set aside.

Boil the sugar and 1/2 cup (125 ml) water to make a golden syrup. Remove from the heat and set aside to cool.

Peel the honeydew, halve, deseed, and discard the soft center. Blend half the melon flesh in a juicer or process in a blender with 1/2 cup (125 ml) water. Cube the other half of the melon flesh or shape into small balls with a melon baller. Mix the cooked sago pearls, coconut cream, honeydew juice and cubes, and drizzle a little sugar syrup over to taste. Serve well chilled.

Coconut Mango Pudding

"In this land of over 7000 islands, regional diversity cannot only be seen but tasted."

THE PHILIPPINES

Compared to her neighbors' fiery fare, Philippine cuisine is more reserved: a gentle cuisine accented by strong-flavored condiments.

Left: Bananas, gourds and tomatoes are not only for eating. Local produce is used to decorate the houses in Lucban during the fiesta of San Isidro Labrador.

Right: Emerald green rice terraces are part of the spectacular scenery in the cordillera of Northern Philippines.

The land and the waters gave the Filipinos their food. Over 7000 islands are surrounded by seas, threaded by rivers and brooks, edged by swamps, and dotted with lakes, canals, ponds, and lagoons, providing a multitude of fish and aquatic life that make up the basic food of Filipinos. This variegated land of mountains and plains, shores and forests, fields and hills is inhabited by land, water, and air creatures that generously transform into regional dishes.

Culinary Adaptation

Foreign influences made a deep impact on native island culture. Chinese traders had been coming to the islands since the 11th century and many stayed on. Their foodways also stayed. Perhaps they cooked the noodles of home; certainly they used local condiments; surely they taught their Filipino wives their dishes, and thus Filipino-Chinese food came to be. The names identify them: *pansit* (Hokkien for something quickly cooked) are noodles; *lumpia* are vegetables rolled in edible wrappers; *siopao* are steamed, filled buns; *siomai* are dumplings. All, of course, came to be indigenized—Filipinized by the ingredients and by local tastes. Today, for example, *pansit Malabon* has oysters and squid, since Malabon is a fishing center; and *pansit Marilao* is sprinkled with rice crisps, because the town is within the Luzon rice bowl. When restaurants were established in the 19th century, Chinese food became a staple of the *pansiterias*, with the food given Spanish names for the ease of the clientele: thus *comida China* (Chinese food) includes *arroz caldo* (rice and chicken gruel); and *morisqueta tostada* (fried rice).

In the 16th century, the Spanish colonizers imported Christianity, and the culture related to colonization lasted three centuries. The food influences the Spaniards brought with them were from both Spain and Mexico, as it was through the vice-royalty of Mexico that the Philippines were governed. This meant the production of food for an elite, non-food-producing class, and a food for which many ingredients were not locally available.

Fil-Hispanic food had new flavors and ingredients—olive oil, paprika, saffron, ham, cheese, cured sausages—and new names. *Paella*, the dish cooked in the fields by Spanish workers, came to be a festive dish combining pork, chicken, seafood, ham, sausages, and vegetables, a luxurious mix of the local and the foreign. *Relleno*, the process of stuffing festive capons and turkeys for Christmas, was applied to chickens, and even to *bangus*, the silvery milkfish. Christmas, a new feast for Filipinos that coincided with the rice harvest, came to feature not only the myriad native rice cakes, but also *ensaymadas* (*brioche*-like cakes buttered, sugared and cheese-sprinkled) to dip in hot thick chocolate, and the apples, oranges, chestnuts, and walnuts of European Christmases. Even the Mexican corn *tamal* turned Filipino, becoming rice-based *tamales* wrapped in banana leaves.

After the Revolution of 1889, the Battle of Manila Bay, and the pact of exchange between the US and Spain, the Philippines became an American colony. The Americans introduced to Philippine cuisine the ways of convenience: pressure-cooking, freezing, pre-cooking; sandwiches, and salads; hamburgers, fried chicken, and steaks.

National and Regional Dishes

Several dishes comprise the "national" cuisine: *bistek* (beef and onion rings braised in soy sauce); *lumpia* (spring rolls); and the popular *adobo*—chicken and pork stewed in vinegar and soy sauce, garlic, peppercorns, and bay leaf. Every province boasts of having the best version of *adobo*. Manila's is soupy with soy sauce and garlic. Cavite cooks mash pork liver into the sauce. Batangas adds the orange hue of annatto; Laguna likes hers yellowish and piquant with turmeric. Zamboanga's *adobo* is thick with coconut cream.

Three other items represent mainstream tastes and might be called "national" dishes. *Sinigang*, the lightly boiled, slightly sour soup, has a broth as tart as the heart (or taste buds) desires. An array of souring agents—unripe guavas; tamarind leaves and flowers; belimbi; tomatoes—help make a home-cooked *sinigang* of seafood or meat and vegetables as varied as the 7107 islands. There is the stew known as *dinuguan*—basically pig blood and innards simmered with vinegar and hot peppers. Most regions do the *dinuguan* stew in their own versions. Finally there's *lechon*, the whole roast pig or piglet, star of many fiesta occasions. *Lechon* is slowly roasted over live coals, basted regularly—and made crisp and luscious. The tasty sauce is concocted from the pig's liver, simmered with vinegar, sugar, and herbs.

The Philippine archipelago has conjured a people with a stubborn sense of regional identity. The scattered island geography sustains multiple cultures—and many distinctly different cuisines, all alive and well. Regionalism can be sensed—rather, tasted—on Philippine islanders' taste buds. While Filipino food comprises essentially a simple, tropical cuisine, diverse styles have evolved among seven major regions of the 7107 islands.

The northwest coast of Luzon is the Ilocos region, a strip of land between the mountains and the sea, where five provinces share the same language, food, and tough challenges of nature. Ilocanos eat meat sparingly, preferring vegetables and rice as the bulk of their diet. *Pinakbet* is a popular vegetable medley identified with the Ilocanos, a combination of tomatoes, eggplant, and bitter melon, lima beans, okra, and squash—all bound together with *bagoong*, a salty sauce made from fermented fish or shrimp.

Two cuisines in the rice-and-sugar lands of Central Luzon— Pampanga and Bulacan—claim superiority over the other. Many exotic dishes are attributed to land-locked Pampanga: fried catfish with *buro*, a fermented rice sauce; fermented crabs; frogs or milkfish in a sour soup; fried mole crickets, and cured pork slices called *tosino*. From here comes *bringhe* (a fiesta rice made with coconut milk);

ensaymada, a buttery bun; *leche flan*, a crème brûlée made with water buffalo milk; and a great array of sticky rice cakes. In Bulacan cooking, river fish are boiled with citrus or in palm wine, then flamed. Eels are simmered in coconut cream; saltwater fish, in vinegar and ginger. Mudfish are fermented or packed in banana stalks and buried in live coals; crabs sautéed with guava; shellfish flavored in a gingery broth. Bulakeños specialize in meat dishes: a chicken "sits" in a claypot lined with salt and is slowly roasted. Typically, Bulakan cooks claim the best *relleno* and *galantina* (stuffed chicken rolls); *estofado* (pork leg) and *asado* (pot roast); as well as *kare-kare* (oxtail stewed in peanut sauce).

The Bicol Region—six provinces along the southeastern peninsula of Luzon—is synonymous with *gata* or coconut cream. Chili and *gata* come together deliciously, especially in the famous Bicol dish called *pinangat*. Little bundles of *gabi* (taro) leaves are filled with shredded taro leaves and bits of tasty meat; the bundles are simmered in *gata*, and laced with a fistful of chilies.

The Visayas are the big island group in the center of the archipelago, where several cuisines reflect the influence of the Chinese community and the taste of the seas. Iloilo City is famous for its delicious noodle soups. *Pancit molo* is a hearty soup designed around shrimp-and-chicken-and-pork dumplings. From Iloilo also, the delectable *lumpiang ubod*: heart of palm in soft crêpes. Bacolod and Iloilo share credit for *binakol*, a chicken soup based not on chicken stock but on *buko*, the sweet water of the young coconut.

In Mindanao, the frontier land of the far south, everyday cuisine is more Malay in influence and distinctly exotic in taste. Spices are used liberally: turmeric, ginger, garlic, chilies, and roasted coconut. Seafood eaten raw, broiled, or fried; or put in soups with lemongrass, ginger, and green papayas; or coconut cream and turmeric. Chicken is served in curry; or combined with taro in a stinging soup. Glutinous rice is often mixed with shrimp, spices, or coconut milk; or cooked with turmeric and pimento. Finally is Zamboanga, a Catholic town with a distinct Spanish accent. *Cocido*, the traditional Sunday platter, is prepared like its Iberian prototype, with sausage, salted pork, pork ribs, sweet potatoes, corn, and cooking bananas.

The Filipino Table

Whether at home or out in a restaurant, Filipinos love to eat communal-style, all together in an informal social gathering called a *salu-salo*. The components of a typical Filipino meal—fresh fish or other seafood; chicken, pork or beef; vegetables; hearty soups mixed with coconut and noodles—are arrayed around a large container of steamed white rice. Eating is done frequently. On an ordinary day, there are generally five small but tasty meals to munch through— breakfast; morning *merienda* (10 am snack); lunch; afternoon *merienda* (4 pm snack), and dinner. Filipinos eat rice from morning until night, supported by rice cakes, nuts, and sugary snacks in between. Plus there's happy hour and the traditional *pulutan* or finger-foods, the sometimes exotic "appetite-ticklers" that accompany the pre-dinner beer.

What's most unique to the Filipino eating tradition is the *saw-sawan*—the mixing and matching of cooked foods with salty, sour or savory dipping sauces, called *sawsawan*. These myriad table sauces in tiny plates turn the bland white rice and the simply roasted seafood and meats into a meal that's sour, salty, sweet-salty or even bitter-sour—as one chooses. The most common condiments are: *patis* (fish sauce), *toyo* (dark soy sauce), *suka* (native vinegar), and *bagoong* (fermented shrimp paste). These conspire tastily with garlic, ginger, red chilies, peppercorns, onions, tomatoes, *wansoy* (cilantro), belimbi (a sour fruit), and *kalamansi* (the small, sweet native lime).

SUGGESTED MENUS

Family meals

For an easy family meal at home, serve rice and:
• Chicken Rice Soup with Ginger (page 141);
• Beef and Vegetable Tamarind Stew (page 142);
• Chicken Vermicelli (page 141);
• Halo Halo (page 143).

Dinner parties

For a fun Filipino party, serve rice with:
• Shanghai-style Eggrolls (page 140);
• Seafood Paella (page 141);
• Chicken Adobo (page 142);
• Stuffed Crab (page 142).

Finger food

Pulutan, or finger food to accompany alcoholic drinks, are very popular, so crack open a beer and nibble on:
• Shrimp and Tofu Fritters (page 140)
• Shanghai-style Eggrolls (page 140)

Sweet snacks are often eaten throughout the day:
• Rice Patties with Sweet Grated Coconut (page 143)

A melting pot menu

For a sampling of various Asian flavors, serve:
• Beef Soup with Chilies and Tamarind (page 78) from Indonesia;
• Chicken Adobo (page 142) from the Philippines and Shrimp Sambal (page 133) from Malaysia with plain rice or with *Chapati* Indian Unleavened Flatbreads (page 56);
• Indian Kulfi Ice Cream (page 65) for dessert.

THE ESSENTIAL FLAVORS OF FILIPINO COOKING

Flavorings essential to Filipino cooking include *bagoong* (salty, fermented fish paste), *patis* (fish sauce), *toyo* (soy sauce), and *suka* (native vinegar; substitute with white vinegar). Other common ingredients include fresh **red chilies** and small **bird's-eye chilies**, **coconut milk**, **kamias** (belimbi; substitute with citrus juice or tamarind), fresh **cilantro** (coriander leaves), *kalamansi* limes, Spanish *chorizo* **sausage**, and **tamarind** pulp (and sometimes leaves if available). *Lumpia* (spring roll) wrappers are a must too and are readily avialable.

Garlic Soy Vinegar Dip

3 cloves garlic, crushed
1/4 cup (60 ml) soy sauce
1/3 cup (90 ml) Filipino vinegar (*suka*) or apple cider vinegar
1/4 teaspoon salt
1/4 teaspoon ground pepper
Pinch of ground red pepper, chili powder or dried chili flakes

Mix all the ingredients and serve in dipping bowls with grilled meats. Keeps in the refrigerator for 6 weeks.

Shrimp and Tofu Fritters

This crunchy appetizer is great as an afternoon snack between meals (*merienda*), or as a cocktail snack in the evening with drinks (*pulutan*).

12 fresh medium shrimp (about 8 oz/250 g), heads and legs discarded, shells left on
2 cups (100 g) bean sprouts, rinsed, shells and tails discarded
1/2 small cake (3 1/2 oz/100 g) pressed tofu, drained and diced
4 oz (125 g) ground chicken
2 tablespoons fermented baby shrimp (*bagoong alamang*)
Oil for deep-frying
1 portion Garlic Soy Vinegar Dip (recipe above), to serve

Batter
2 eggs, beaten
1 teaspoon baking powder
1/4 cup (30 g) cornstarch
3/4 cup (100 g) plain flour
1/2 cup (125 ml) water
1/2 teaspoon freshly ground black pepper

Make the Batter by whisking the eggs, baking powder, cornstarch, flour and water together in a bowl to form a smooth, thin batter. Season with the black pepper.

Heat the oil in a wok or saucepan. Add the shrimp, bean sprouts, tofu, chicken and fermented shrimp to the Batter and mix well. Ladle about 3 tablespoons of the mixture into the hot oil, ensuring that each portion contains 1 shrimp and bits of all the other ingredients. Fry for 3 minutes until the fritters are golden brown, then remove with a slotted spoon and drain on paper towels. Repeat until all the mixture is used up. Serve the fritters with small bowls of Garlic Soy Vinegar Dip on the side.

Shanghai-style Eggrolls

8 oz (250 g) ground pork
8 oz (250 g) fresh shrimp, peeled and ground
3/4 cup (175 g) water chestnuts or jicama (*singkamas*), diced
1 medium carrot, peeled and cut into short strips
3 cloves garlic, minced
1 green onion (scallion), thinly sliced
1 teaspoon soy sauce
1/2 teaspoon salt
1 teaspoon ground black pepper
15 eggroll wrappers (see note)
Oil for deep-frying

Sweet and Sour Sauce
1 cup (250 ml) water
3 tablespoons tomato ketchup
3 tablespoons sugar
1/4 teaspoon salt
1/4 teaspoon hot sauce (Tabasco)
2 teaspoons cornstarch dissolved in 4 teaspoons water

Prepare the Sweet and Sour Sauce by combining all the ingredients in a saucepan. Bring to a boil and simmer for 5 minutes or until the sauce thickens.

Mix the pork, shrimp, water chestnuts, carrot, garlic, green onion and soy sauce in a bowl. Season with the salt and pepper.

Place 1 heaped tablespoon of the filling on each eggroll wrapper. Roll the wrapper up tightly and seal the ends with a few drops of water. Repeat until all the filling is used up.

Heat the oil in a wok. Deep-fry the prepared eggrolls in the hot oil until light golden brown. Remove with a slotted spoon and drain on paper towels. Serve with a bowl of Sweet and Sour Sauce on the side.

Eggroll wrappers are sold in various sizes. This recipe calls for 5 in (12 1/2 cm) square wrappers. They are sold in packets of 25 or 50 wrappers in the refrigerator or freezer section of supermarkets. If using larger wrappers, double the amount of filling used in each eggroll.

Ground Beef Stew
Picadillo

A popular Spanish-influenced dish that is so quick and easy to prepare. It may be served as a soup or stew depending on the amount of liquid added. Absolutely delicious with rice!

1 1/2 tablespoons oil
5 cloves garlic, minced
10 shallots or 1 onion, diced
4 small tomatoes, diced
12 oz (350 g) ground beef
1 tablespoon fish sauce (*patis*)
1/2 teaspoon freshly ground black pepper
2 potatoes, peeled and cubed
4 cups (1 liter) water
Parsley or coriander leaves (cilantro), coarsely chopped, to garnish

Heat the oil in a saucepan and stir-fry the garlic until golden brown. Add the shallots or onion and stir-fry for 2 minutes. Then add the tomatoes and cook until they soften.

Add the ground beef and season with the fish sauce and pepper. Stir-fry for 5 minutes to brown the meat. Add the potatoes and water, and bring to a boil. Reduce the heat and simmer, uncovered, over low heat until the beef and potatoes are cooked, about 20 minutes (add more water if needed or if you prefer a more soupy dish).

Ladle the stew into a large serving bowl and garnish with fresh parsley or coriander leaves. Serve hot with white rice.

Cuban-style Rice

A hearty rice dish with a strong Caribbean influence—featuring ground meat and vegetables in a delicious sauce served with fried plantains and eggs.

3 tablespoons oil
2 cloves garlic, minced
4 shallots, diced
1 small tomato, diced
8 oz (250 g) ground beef
8 oz (250 g) ground pork
2 tablespoons soy sauce
1/2 tablespoon Worcestershire sauce
1/4 cup (40 g) raisins
1/2 teaspoon salt
1/4 teaspoon ground black pepper
1/2 cup (75 g) fresh or frozen peas
3 tablespoons olive oil or peanut oil
5 oz (150 g) small plantains or unripe bananas, peeled, sliced lengthwise
4 eggs
4 cups (400 g) freshly cooked rice, kept warm

Heat the oil in a saucepan and stir-fry the garlic until golden brown. Add the shallots and stir-fry until translucent. Add the tomato and cook until it softens. Add the beef, pork, soy and Worcestershire sauces, and cook over medium heat for 15 minutes or until the meat is browned.

Add the raisins, salt and pepper, and stir constantly. Add the peas and braise for 5 more minutes. Remove from the heat.

Ground Beef Stew (Picadillo)

Seafood Paella

In a skillet, heat the olive oil and fry the plantain slices until they are soft and caramelized on both sides, 5–7 minutes. Then fry the eggs sunny-side up.

Arrange the cooked rice, meat, fried plantains and eggs on a large serving platter. Serve hot.

Chicken Rice Soup with Ginger

4 tablespoons oil
4 tablespoons minced garlic
1 large onion, diced
2 in (5 cm) ginger, thinly sliced
3/4 cup (150 g) uncooked rice, washed and drained
7 cups (1 3/4 liters) water
1 lb (500 g) boneless chicken, cut into bite-sized pieces
1 1/2 teaspoons fish sauce (patis)
Ground black or white pepper
Green onion (scallion), thinly sliced
Pinch of saffron
Kalamansi limes or regular limes

Heat 2 tablespoons of the oil in a pot and stir-fry half of the garlic until golden brown. Add the onion and ginger and stir-fry until the onion is translucent.

Add the rice and stir-fry for 5 minutes until lightly browned. Add the water and cover the pot. Increase the heat and bring the mixture to a boil, stirring occasionally. Then reduce the heat, add the chicken and simmer for another 30 minutes or until the rice and chicken are cooked.

While the rice is cooking, heat the remaining oil in a skillet and stir-fry the rest of the garlic until crisp and golden brown. Drain on paper towels and set aside.

When the rice and chicken are cooked, add the fish sauce or salt, stir and continue to simmer over low heat for another 2 minutes. Serve in individual soup bowls seasoned with black or white pepper. Garnish with the green onion, fried garlic and saffron, and serve with lime halves on the side.

Seafood Paella

A Filipino adaptation of the famous Valencian dish that makes a satisfying one-pot meal for 4–6 people. Your guests will not believe how simple it is to prepare!

10 fresh shrimp (7 oz/200 g), shelled and deveined, tails intact
Salt and pepper, to taste
2 fresh crabs (3 lbs/1 1/2 kg)
5 cups (1 1/4 liters) water
2 medium squid (about 10 oz/ 300 g), cleaned and cut into rings
1/2 cup (125 ml) olive oil
8 oz (250 g) pork tenderloin, cut into bite-sized pieces
1/2 teaspoon paprika or ground red pepper
2 tablespoons minced garlic
1/2 medium onion, diced
One 3-in (8-cm) chorizo de Bilbao or pepperoni sausage, thinly sliced
2 cups (400 g) uncooked long-grain rice
4 tablespoons canned tomato purée
1 bay leaf
1 bell pepper, deseeded and cut into chunks
Generous pinch of saffron mixed with 1 teaspoon water
1/2 cup (60 g) fresh or frozen green peas
2 hard-boiled eggs, quartered or sliced

Season the shrimp lightly with the salt and pepper, and set aside.

Boil the crabs in the water for 20 minutes or until cooked. When cooked, remove the crabs, quarter them, crack the shells and claws, and set aside. Reserve the water.

Blanch the squid in the reserved crab water until cooked, about 3 minutes. Remove the squid and set aside in a bowl of cold water. Strain and reserve 3 3/4 cups (925 ml) of the crab-squid broth.

Preheat the oven to 350°F (180°C). Heat the olive oil in a large skillet or casserole dish. Add the pork, paprika, garlic, onion and *chorizo* slices, and stir-fry for a few minutes. Then add the rice and stir-fry until lightly browned. Add the tomato purée, reserved broth and bay leaf, and stir for a few minutes. Add the bell pepper and saffron, and bring to a boil.

Remove from the heat and bake in the preheated oven, uncovered, for 30 minutes. Arrange the seasoned shrimp, crab, squid and peas on the rice, and bake for another 5 minutes. Remove from the oven and decorate with the hard-boiled eggs. Transfer to the dining table and serve immediately.

Chicken Vermicelli

Noodles signify long life and Filipinos consume an abundance of them. This is a popular Chinese-influenced dish in which glass noodles made from mung beans are the main ingredient.

4 tablespoons oil
8 cloves garlic, minced
1 large onion, diced
1 chicken breast, boiled and sliced
10 dried black Chinese mushrooms, soaked in warm water to soften, drained and thinly sliced
3 cups (750 ml) Chicken Stock (page 122)
1/2 small carrot, cut into matchsticks
1/2 leek, cut into matchsticks
1 bunch Chinese celery leaves or Italian parsley, thinly sliced
6 oz (175 g) dried cellophane (glass) noodles (*sotanghon*), soaked in water for 10 minutes to soften and then cut into lengths
1 1/2 tablespoons fish sauce (*patis*)
Ground black pepper, to taste
Green onion (scallion), thinly sliced
Kalamansi limes or regular limes

Heat the oil in a wok and stir-fry the garlic until golden, then stir-fry the onion until translucent. Add the chicken and mushrooms, and stir-fry for 2 minutes. Add the stock and bring to a boil. Add the carrot, leek and celery leaves, and cook for 3 minutes.

Add the dried noodles and cook for 3 minutes, seasoning with the fish sauce and pepper.

Chicken Vermicelli

Remove from the heat and transfer the food to a serving platter. Garnish with freshly sliced green onion and serve hot with limes on the side.

Stuffed Crabs

Rellenong is a culinary technique inherited from Spain. This dish highlights the delicacy and richness of the shellfish.

3–4 lbs (1¹/2–2 kgs) fresh crabs
2 onions, finely minced
8 garlic cloves, finely minced
1 lb (500 g) ground pork
4 eggs
Salt and ground black pepper
Oil for frying

Steam the crabs. Remove the shells and flake the meat. Do not remove the claws and legs.

In a mixing bowl, combine the crabmeat, onion, garlic, pork, 1 egg, salt and pepper. Return the mixture to the shells.

Beat the other eggs and dip the crab shells into the beaten egg. Fry in small amount of oil until golden brown.

Chicken Simmered in Tomatoes and Pimentos

2 tablespoons olive oil
1 chicken (2 lbs/1 kg), cut into serving pieces
2 cloves garlic, peeled and crushed
1 large onion, diced
1 lb (500 g) ripe tomatoes, diced or one 14-oz (400-g) can whole peeled tomatoes, diced

2 bay leaves
1 teaspoon salt or to taste
¹/2–1 tablespoon ground black pepper
1¹/2 cups (375 ml) water
2 large potatoes, peeled and cubed
1 cup (125 g) pimentos, drained or 1 red bell pepper, deseeded and diced

Heat the oil in a large saucepan and lightly brown the chicken. Remove the chicken and set aside. Add the garlic and stir-fry until golden brown, then stir-fry the onion until translucent. Return the chicken to the saucepan, add the tomatoes, bay leaves, salt, pepper and water, and simmer over low heat for 20 minutes.

Add the potatoes and simmer for 15 minutes, then add the pimentos and simmer for another 5 minutes. Remove from the heat and serve immediately.

Chicken Adobo

Adobo, meaning cooked in vinegar and garlic, is the national dish of the Philippines. This *adobo* is enriched with coconut milk and turmeric.

1 chicken (2 lbs/1 kg), cut into serving pieces
1 tablespoon oil
1 cup (250 ml) thick coconut milk
2–4 finger-length green chilies (*siling mahaba*), whole
¹/2 tablespoon fish sauce (*patis*)

Marinade
1 tablespoon grated turmeric root or 1¹/2 teaspoons ground turmeric
10 cloves garlic, minced

¹/4 cup (60 ml) Filipino vinegar (*suka*) or apple cider vinegar
¹/2 teaspoon salt
¹/4 teaspoon ground black pepper

Combine the Marinade ingredients in a large bowl, add the chicken and mix well. Marinate the chicken overnight in the refrigerator. Drain the chicken and reserve the Marinade.

Heat the oil in a saucepan and stir-fry the marinated chicken until lightly browned, about 5 minutes.

Add the reserved Marinade and coconut milk or cream, and simmer, uncovered, over low heat until the sauce thickens and the oil separates from the milk, about 30 minutes. Add the chilies and season with the fish sauce. Mix well and serve immediately.

Beef and Vegetable Tamarind Stew

Beef Sinigang

Sinigang, the quintessential Filipino dish, consists of meat or seafood prepared in a delicious spicy stew with vegetables and a fragrant tamarind gravy.

4 cups (1 liter) water
1 lb (500 g) beef ribs or stewing beef, cut into pieces
4 small tomatoes, sliced or one 10-oz (300-g) can peeled tomatoes
4 finger-length green chilies (*siling mahaba*), whole
1 small onion, sliced
2 heaped tablespoons tamarind pulp mixed with 1 cup (250 ml) warm water, mashed and strained to obtain juice
3 potatoes (14 oz/400 g), peeled and cut into chunks
7 oz (200 g) green beans, cut into lengths
1 lb (500 g) water spinach, washed and trimmed, leaves and stalks separated, stalks cut into lengths or 8 oz (250 g) spinach leaves, washed
1 tablespoon fish sauce (*patis*)
Ground black pepper, to taste

Bring the water to a boil in a saucepan. Add the beef, tomatoes, chilies, onion and tamarind juice, and simmer for 20 minutes.

Add the potato chunks and simmer for another 25 minutes. When the potatoes are tender, add the green beans and spinach

stalks and cook for 3 minutes. Season with the fish sauce or salt and a pinch of pepper.

Add the spinach leaves and cook for another 3 minutes until the leaves are wilted. Serve hot with freshly steamed rice.

Rich Beef Stew

Caldereta

Caldereta, another dish tracing its roots to Spain, is a rich stew made of beef stir-fried in olive oil and simmered in tomato sauce. Originally, goat meat was used for this dish, but pork or chicken may be substituted.

¹/4 cup (60 ml) olive oil
6 cloves garlic, minced
2 medium onions, diced
1¹/2 cups (125 g) diced fresh tomatoes or one 14-oz (400-g) can peeled tomatoes
1 bell pepper, deseeded and sliced
1 lb (500 g) beef sirloin, cubed
4 oz (125 g) beef liver, cubed
2–3 cups (500–750 ml) beef stock or 1 teaspoon beef stock granules mixed with 2–3 cups (500–750 ml) hot water
1 tablespoon tomato paste
1 teaspoon ground black pepper
¹/2 cup (50 g) green olives
1–2 dill pickles, cubed
3–4 finger-length chilies (*siling mahaba*), sliced
¹/2 cup (125 ml) whipping cream
¹/2 cup (1¹/2 oz/50 g) grated Parmesan cheese
1 red bell pepper or pimento, cut into strips, to garnish (optional)

Heat the oil in a saucepan and stir-fry the garlic until golden brown, then stir-fry the onions until translucent. Add the tomatoes and bell pepper, and cook until they soften. Add the beef and liver, and stir-fry for a few minutes. When the liver is cooked, remove it from the saucepan and set aside in a small bowl.

Add the beef stock and tomato paste, and simmer over low heat until the beef is tender, about 45 minutes. Season with the pepper.

Add the olives, dill pickles and chilies. Mash the liver with a fork and return to the saucepan.

Cook until the sauce thickens, about 5 to 7 minutes, then add the cream and cheese, and mix well. Remove from the heat, transfer to a platter and garnish with the bell pepper or pimento strips.

Chicken Adobo (left) and Chicken Simmered in Tomatoes and Pimentoes (right)

Filipino-style Beef Steak (Bistek, left) and Rich Beef Stew (Caldereta, right)

Filipino-style Beef Steak
Bistek

1¹/2 lbs (750 g) beef sirloin or skirt steak, cut into thin fillets
2 tablespoons kalamansi lime juice or lemon juice
2 tablespoons soy sauce
2 teaspoons ground black pepper
3 tablespoons oil
1 medium onion, sliced into rings
Salt to taste

Marinate the beef slices in the kalamansi lime juice, soy sauce and pepper overnight in the refrigerator.

Heat the oil in a skillet and pan-fry the beef until medium-rare, about 30 seconds on each side. Remove from the heat.

In the remaining oil, stir-fry the onion until it is browned. Season the beef with a sprinkling of salt and drizzle a little of the pan juice over the steak. Garnish with the onion slices and serve.

Rice Patties with Sweet Grated Coconut

2 cups (250 g) glutinous rice flour
1 cup (250 ml) water
3 cups (450 g) freshly grated coconut mixed with 2 cups (400 g) sugar
Toasted sesame seeds

In a mixing bowl, knead the rice flour and water to make a smooth dough that holds together and separate cleanly from the pan. With floured hands, pinch off about 1¹/2 tablespoons of the dough and shape into a small patty, about 2 in (5 cm) in diameter and about ¹/2 in (1 cm) thick. Set aside on a dry plate. Repeat with the rest of the dough to make about 30 patties in all.

Place the sweetened coconut into a bowl. Drop the patties into a saucepan of boiling water. When they float to the top, scoop them out with a slotted spoon, drain and place into the bowl with the coconut. Garnish with sesame seeds, if using, and serve hot or at room temperature.

Halo Halo
Exotic Fruit Mix

Known as the "Queen of Desserts"—this is the Philippine's most beloved treat. It features exotic fruits and sweets that Filipinos enjoy. This indulgent recipe from Gene Gonzalez at Cafe Ysabel in Manila calls for everything all at once, but you can easily substitute or reduce the number of ingredients to simplify the preparation.

Topping
¹/2 cup (125 ml) pandanus syrup (see note) or maple syrup
1¹/2 cups (375 ml) evaporated milk or fresh cream
4 tablespoons *pinipig* or rice crispies
4 scoops French vanilla ice cream

Base
4 teaspoons sweet red azuki beans
4 teaspoons sweet yellow mung beans
4 tablespoons banana or boiled plantain, mashed
4 tablespoons boiled and mashed purple yam (*ube*)
4 tablespoons coconut sport (*macapuno*)

4 tablespoons coconut gelatin (*nata de coco*)
4 tablespoons palm nuts (*kaong*)
4 tablespoons sweet creamed corn
Shaved ice

Crème Caramel
¹/2 cup (100 g) brown sugar
¹/2 cup (60 ml) water

Make the Crème Caramel by boiling the brown sugar and water in a saucepan, stirring continuously over medium heat until the sugar is melted and turns golden brown. Pour the syrup into flan molds or custard cups and set aside for a minute to allow the Caramel to harden.

Fill the bottom halves of four serving bowls with the Base ingredients. Cover with shaved ice to reach the top of the bowls.

Drizzle the pandanus syrup or maple syrup and milk or cream over each bowl. Top with a tablespoon each of the Crème Caramel and *pinipig*, and a scoop of the ice cream. Serve immediately.

To make pandanus syrup, blend 4 pandanus leaves in a food processor with ¹/4 cup (60 ml) water, then add 3 tablespoons sugar and heat in a saucepan until it thickens. Strain to remove the bits of pandanus leaves.

Halo Halo (Exotic Fruit Mix)

"Sri Lankan cuisine is a cuisine expressed in spices—cinnamon, cloves, nutmeg, coriander, mace, pepper, cardamom, red chilies, mustard seeds, cumin, fenugreek, and turmeric are all used to flavor curries, while some add flavor to desserts and cakes."

SRI LANKA

Coursing through the cuisine of Sri Lanka is a great observance to details and tradition. It truly is like tasting history.

Left: Stilt fishermen wedge wooden poles into rock crevices to use as a perch while fishing.

Right: (Clockwise from top left) cinnamon, cloves, nutmeg, coriander, mace, pepper, cardamom, dried red chilies, mustard seeds, cumin, fenugreek, fennel, and turmeric.

Sri Lanka, the fabled island of sapphires, rubies, and other precious stones, is home to one of Asia's least known cuisines. Rarely found in restaurants outside the island itself, Sri Lankan fare is often mistaken for yet another Indian regional cuisine. To the culinary explorer, however, Sri Lankan food is as intriguing and unique as the many other customs of this island paradise.

Multiethnic Influences

Sri Lanka, formerly known as Ceylon, is located off India's southeast coast. The rugged terrain of the central highlands—characterized by high mountains and plateaus, steep river gorges, and swathes of tea plantations—dominates much of the island. This falls away to sandy lowlands, rice paddies, and long stretches of palm-fringed beaches. Sri Lankan cuisine, which is based upon rice with vegetable, fish, or meat curries, and a variety of side dishes and condiments, reflects the geographical and ethnic differences of the land.

The multiethnic mix of people living on this small island comprises Sinhalese, Tamils, Moors (Muslims), Burghers and Eurasians, Malays, and Veddhas. Over the centuries, the cooking of the Sinhalese has evolved into two slightly different styles: coastal or "low country" Sinhalese, and Kandy or "upcountry" Sinhalese. Regardless of where they live, the staple food for Sinhalese (and indeed, for all Sri Lankans) is rice. This is usually accompanied by a range of spiced vegetables, fish, poultry, meat, or game dishes.

In coastal Sinhalese cuisine, fish, and other seafood feature far more widely than poultry or meat, and coconut milk is the preferred base for curries. One Sinhalese specialty from the coast is *ambulthiyal*, or sour claypot fish. At its best in the Southern town of Ambalangoda, *ambulthiyal* is a dish of *balaya* (bonito) which uses *goraka* (gamboge) as both a flavoring and a preservative. Crab curries and numerous shrimp dishes are also popular. An ingredient known as Maldive fish is widely used as a seasoning throughout Sri Lanka, but especially in coastal regions. It is made from a type of bonito (also known as skipjack) which is boiled, smoked, and sun-dried until it is rock hard.

Kandy, the heart of upcountry Sri Lanka, remained an independent Sinhalese kingdom until the British finally took over in 1815, thus it largely escaped the social and culinary influences of the Portuguese and Dutch. Many Kandian curries are made with unusual ingredients such as young jackfruit, jackfruit seeds, cashews, breadfruit, and green papaya, while various edible flowers such as turmeric, hibiscus, and sesbania may end up in an omelet or curry. Game, including deer and wild birds, was also an upcountry favorite.

The first Tamils are believed to have arrived at about the same time as the Indo-Ayrans, around 2,000 years ago. Successive waves of Tamils from southern India established themselves in Sri Lanka, mostly in the north, on the Jaffna peninsula. Popular Tamil dishes found in Sri Lanka include *rasam*, a spicy sour soup that is an aid to digestion; *kool*, a thick seafood soup originating from Jaffna fisherfolk; *vadai*, or deep-fried savories made with black gram flour; and many types of vegetable *pachadi*, where cooked vegetables are tossed with curd or yogurt, and freshly grated coconut. *Thosai*, slightly sour pancakes made with black gram and rice flours, constitute another delicious Tamil contribution to the culinary scene.

Malays, who were brought by the Dutch, have intermarried with the Muslim community and brought with them several dishes which have since become part of the Sri Lankan kitchen. *Sathe* is the Sri Lankan equivalent of satay, or cubes of meat threaded on skewers and served with a peanut and chili sauce. Other Malay dishes include *gula melaka* (sago pudding with jaggery), *nasi kuning* (turmeric rice), *barbuth* (honeycomb tripe curry), *seenakku* and *parsong* (two types of rice flour cakes.)

Colonial Tastes

The wave of Western expansionism, which began at the end of the fifteenth century, was also to have a significant impact on Sri Lanka. Colonialism affected not only the agriculture, social structure, and religions of the country, but also the cuisine. The first Portuguese ships chanced upon Sri Lanka in the early sixteenth century and set about trading in cinnamon and other spices. There followed four hundred years of Western presence in the form of Portuguese, Dutch, and finally the British before Sri Lanka regained her independence in 1948. The Portuguese introduced a number of plants they had discovered in the Americas, the most important being chili, as well as corn, tomatoes, and guavas. It is hard to imagine Sri Lankan cuisine without chili, but prior to the introduction of this taste-tingling plant, all Asians had to rely on pepper for heat. The Portuguese impact on the cuisine of Sri Lanka has lasted until today, but almost exclusively in the area of rich cakes: *bolo de coco* (a coconut cake), *foguete* (deep-fried pastry tubes with a sweet filling), and *bolo folhadao* (a layered cake). The Dutch left a number of cakes to become part of the culinary legacy of Sri Lanka, and particularly of the Burgher community, including *breudher*, a rich cake made with yeast. Dutch meatballs, or *frikadel*, appear as part of a cross-cultural dish served on special occasions in many Sri Lankan homes. *Lampries* (a corruption of the Dutch *lomprijst*) combines these meatballs with a typically Sinhalese curry made with four types of meat and a tangy *sambol*, all wrapped up in a piece of banana leaf and steamed. Another Dutch recipe is *smore*, or sliced braised beef.

Spice and Other Things Nice

Spices, so important to the Sri Lankan kitchen, actually helped shape the history of the island. The Portuguese arrived at the beginning of the sixteenth century, and it was Sri Lanka's famous cinnamon which became the prime source of revenue for the Europeans. Sri Lanka's cinnamon trees, which grew wild on the southern and western coasts of the island, were said to produce the finest cinnamon in the world. Cinnamon was still the most important source of revenue by the time the Dutch seized control of the island. They introduced penalties to protect it, making it a capital offence to damage a plant, and to sell or to export the quills or their oil. The Dutch did eventually succeed in cultivating cinnamon, but still relied largely on the wild supply. By the nineteenth century, however, the supremacy of cinnamon was challenged by the cheaper cassia bark grown elsewhere in Asia. Cardamom, indigenous to both Sri Lanka and southern India, was another valuable spice which flourished in the wetter regions of the country. All of Sri Lanka's spices are used to flavor savory dishes such as curries; some also add their fragrance and flavor to desserts and cakes. Spices such as cinnamon therefore command a very important position in Sri Lankan culture, not only as culinary flavorings but also by virtue of their having played such a major role in the country's history.

The Sri Lankan Table

Breakfast in Sri Lanka is often a batter of rice flour cooked in special hemispherical pans to make *appa* or hoppers. These are small, bowl-shaped pancakes with a soft, bready center and crisp brown edges that goes well with treacle and buffalo-milk yogurt. Crack an egg into the middle of a hopper before turning the pan results in an egg hopper; these go best with thick, highly spiced *sambol*. Another rice-batter dish, called the "string hopper," is quite different. These are tangled little circles of steamed noodles usually served with a *hodhi* or thin curry sauce.

Sri Lankans lunch between noon and two, often with a plate of "short eats." These divide equally between crisply baked filo-dough biscuits and *frikadels* or deep-fried rolls or balls. The interiors are filled with meat, fish, or vegetables. Short eats are joined by *vadai*, or deep-fried donuts of lentils, spices, and flour. Another common snack is *roti*, a square or triangular wrap of dough stuffed with fresh chilies, onions, vegetables, and cooked egg, meat, or fish, which is fried on a searing sheet-metal griddle over a propane burner. Many prefer a rice-and-curry lunch packet. Inside a banana leaf or thin plastic wrap is a cup or two of boiled rice, a piece of curried chicken, fish, or beef for non-vegetarians, or simply some curried vegetables.

A proper rice-and-curry dinner involves three or more accompaniments, at least two of them vegetables. When choosing which curries to serve with the rice, Sri Lankan cooks ensure that there is a variety of textures as well as flavors, with at least one fairly liquid, or soupy, curry to help moisten the rice, and usually a relatively dry curry with a thick gravy. One of the curries will most likely be a spiced lentil dish, and there is sure to be at least one pungent side dish or condiment known as a *sambol*. These *sambol*, also know as "rice pullers," are guaranteed to whet the appetite with their basic ingredient—anything from onion to bitter gourd, dried shrimp to salted lime—heightened by the flavors of chili, onion, salt, and Maldive fish. One of the most popular *sambol*, *pol sambol*, is made with freshly grated coconut.

There are few native desserts but many *rasokavili* or sweets. *Kaum* is a battercake made of flour and treacle deep-fried in coconut oil. *Aluvas* are thin, flat, diamond-shaped halvas, or wedges of rice flour, treacle, and sugar cane. Coconut milk laboriously boiled down with jaggery and cashew nuts yields *kalu dodol*. *Kiribath*, a festive dish of rice cooked in milk, is the first solid food fed to babies. *Kiri peni* or "curd and honey" is buffalo-milk yogurt and treacle.

SUGGESTED MENUS

Family meals

For a simple family meal, serve plain basmati rice and Coconut Sambol (page 148) with:
• Eggplant Pickles (page150);
• Tamarind Claypot Fish (page 148) or Fish Lemon Stew (page 149)
• Spicy Lamb Curry (page 151);
• Fresh fruits for dessert.

Dinner parties

For a dinner party with a Sri Lankan seafood theme, serve plain basmati rice and Bird's-eye Chili Sambol (page 148) with:
• Butter Rice (page 148);
• Eggplant Pickles (page 150);
• Crab curry (150);
• Fish Lemon Stew (page 149);
• Fresh fruits for dessert.

One pot meals

These make an ideal lunch or dinner, served with plain rice.
• Spicy Lamb Curry (page 151) accompanied by Eggplant Pickles (page 150)
• Beef Smore (page 151) with plain rice

A melting pot menu

For a fun pan-Asian menu, serve:
• Eggplant Pickles (page 150) from Sri Lanka as a starter;
• Green Chicken Curry with Basil and Eggplant (page 163) from Thailand with plain rice;
• Creamy Shrimp Curry (page 62) from India;
• Grilled Eggplant Salad (page 28) from Burma;
• Sweet Rice Pudding (page 65) from India for dessert.

THE ESSENTIAL FLAVORS OF SRI LANKAN COOKING

Ingredients common to the Sri Lankan pantry include dried spices such as **cardamom**, **cinnamon**, **cloves**, **coriander**, **cumin**, **fennel**, **fennugreek**, **mustard seeds**, and **turmeric**. A good supply of **basmati rice** is a must. Fresh or dried **curry leaves**, fresh **cilantro**, **coconut milk**, and **tamarind** are also easy to come by and will prove indespensible. **Fresh green chilies** are used in curries and *sambols*, **dried red chilies**, **chili flakes**, and **chili powder** are common too. If **Maldive fish** is unavailable, substitute with small dried shrimps.

Sri Lanka, famous for its pristine beaches and stunning landscapes, also boasts one of the most intriguing cuisines in Asia. The fruits of land and sea are plentiful, and sitting down to a Sri Lankan meal is a truly fantastic epicurean adventure.

Roasted Curry Powder

This is used as an ingredient in curries or can be sprinkled on vegetables before serving.

1/2 teaspoon fennel seeds
1/2 teaspoon cumin seeds
1/2 teaspoon fenugreek seeds
1 1/2 teaspoons ground cinnamon
6 cardamom pods
1/2 cup (100 g) coriander seeds
6 cloves

Dry-roast all the ingredients in a skillet over low heat, stirring constantly, until the spices become a deep golden color. Grind them to a fine powder in an electric blender. Store in an air-tight container.

Coconut Gravy

1 tablespoon fenugreek seeds
2 cups (500 ml) chicken stock
1 large red onion, finely chopped
2 sprigs curry leaves
2 pieces pandanus leaf
3 cloves garlic, finely chopped
1 small cinnamon stick
4 cardamom pods, crushed
2 green finger-length chilies, deseeded and finely sliced
1 teaspoon ground turmeric
2 teaspoons dried shrimp or fish, ground to a powder in a blender
2 cups (500 ml) coconut milk
Salt and lemon juice to taste

Wash the fenugreek seeds and soak them in the chicken stock in a saucepan for 30 minutes. Add all the remaining ingredients except the coconut milk, salt, and lemon juice. Bring to a boil and simmer on very low heat until the onions are tender.

Add the coconut milk and heat the entire mix to boiling point, then reduce the heat and simmer for about 5 minutes. Remove from heat and cool slightly. Add the lemon juice and salt to taste

Coconut Sambol

1 teaspoon chopped dried chili
1 tablespoon finely chopped onion
1 teaspoon pepper
1 teaspoon dried shrimp or fish, ground to a powder in a blender
2 cups (200 g) grated fresh coconut or 1 1/2 cups (120 g) unsweetened desiccated coconut, moistened
3 tablespoons lime juice
Salt to taste

Grind together the chili, onion, pepper, and Maldive fish. Add the grated coconut and season with lime juice. Mix well by hand to ensure all the coconut is coated. Best served freshly made.

Bird's-eye Chili Sambol

1/2 cup (100 g) bird's-eye chilies
1/2 onion, sliced
1 teaspoon pepper
3 tablespoons lime juice
Salt to taste

Combine the chilies and onions and grind finely in a blender. Add the pepper, lime juice, and salt. Best when served freshly made. Store in a covered container in a cool place and use as desired.

Butter Rice

1/4 cup (50 g) butter or ghee
1/2 onion, finely chopped
2 curry leaves
2 cardamom pods, crushed
2 cloves
1/2 small cinnamon stick
2 1/2 cups (500 g) uncooked Basmati or other long-grained rice, washed
3 cups (750 ml) Chicken Stock (page 73)
1/2 teaspoon salt
1 small potato, peeled and sliced into matchsticks, then deep-fried
1 tablespoon roasted cashew nuts
1 teaspoon sultanas

Heat the butter and fry half the onion until golden. Add the curry leaves, spices and rice. Fry over medium heat for 5 minutes, stirring continuously, then add the stock, and salt. Bring to a boil, reduce the heat, cover, and simmer for 30 minutes.

Meanwhile, in a separate skillet, fry the remaining onion and set aside to be used as garnish.

Butter Rice

When the rice is cooked, remove the spices, place the rice on a platter and garnish with fried potato matchsticks, roasted cashews, sultanas, and reserved fried onions.

Tamarind Claypot Fish

The southwestern coastal town of Ambalangoda first made this dish famous. The tamarind both imparts its characteristic sharp taste and also acts as a preservative. Even in Sri Lanka's heat and humidity, an *ambulthiyal* can keep for up to a week. Serve with plain rice.

1 tablespoon tamarind pulp soaked in 4 tablespoons water
1 lb (500 g) tuna or other firm fish
Juice of 1 lime
2 teaspoons ground red pepper
1 teaspoon ground pepper
Salt to taste
1/2 cup (125 ml) water
6 cloves
1 slice of ginger
5 cloves of garlic
1 sprig curry leaves

Soak the tamarind pulp in 4 tablespoons water, stir and strain, discarding any solids.

Cut the fish into eight pieces, wash them well with the lime juice and arrange the pieces in a single layer in a pan.

Tamarind Claypot Fish

Blend the tamarind water, ground red pepper, pepper, salt, and a little water to a paste. Mix this paste with the fish in the pan, coating each piece thoroughly. Add the cloves, ginger, garlic, curry leaves, and the water, and bring to a boil. Simmer until all the gravy has reduced and the fish pieces are quite dry, about 15 minutes.

Add the ground red pepper, tumeric, and curry powder, the diced tomato, and salt. Cook, stirring frequently, until the tomato is fully mashed, about 10 minutes.

Add the shrimp and simmer until cooked, about 3 minutes. Finally, add the thick coconut milk and bring to a boil again. Remove from heat and serve.

Fish Lemon Stew

Shrimp in Coconut Curry Gravy

2 tablespoons oil
3/4 cup (100 g) minced onion
6–7 cloves garlic, chopped
1 tablespoon minced ginger
1 sprig curry leaves
1 cinnamon stick
1–2 green finger-length chilies
1 teaspoon ground red pepper
1 teaspoon ground turmeric
4 teaspoons Roasted Curry Powder
1 large tomato, diced
Salt to taste
1 lb (500 g) medium shrimp, peeled and deveined, with tails intact
1 1/2 cups (375 ml) thick coconut milk

Heat the oil in a pan and fry the onion, garlic, ginger, curry leaves, cinnamon and green chilies until the onion is golden brown.

Stir-fried Spicy Shrimp

1 lb (500 g) medium shrimps, peeled and deveined, with tails intact
Salt to taste
2 teaspoons coarsely pounded red chilies
1 teaspoon turmeric powder
1 teaspoon lime juice
1–2 teaspoons oil
1 cup (200 g) sliced onions
5 cloves garlic, sliced
2 green finger-length chilies, sliced
1 small cinnamon stick
1 teaspoon crushed peppercorns
1 small tomato, cut in wedges
1 sprig curry leaves

Rub the shrimp with the salt, red chilies, turmeric, and lime juice and allow to marinate for 20 minutes. Heat the oil in a wok and quickly stir-fry the shrimp at high heat until half done, about 2 minutes. Remove from the pan and set aside.

In the same pan, fry the onions, garlic, green chilies, cinnamon, pepper, tomato wedges, and curry leaves until crispy, about 3 minutes. Mix in the shrimp and cook them while tossing to coat the shrimp completely, for 3 minutes or until done.

Fish Lemon Stew

Seer, or Spanish mackerel, is Sri Lanka's tastiest fish. Besides pan-frying, there are many other ways to bring out its flavors, as in this delicate stew recipe.

1 lb (500 g) Spanish mackerel fillets (substitute with kingfish or cod)
Salt and pepper to taste
1 teaspoon ground white pepper
3 tablespoons vegetable oil
2 red onion, 1 diced and 1 sliced into rings
2 sprigs curry leaves
4 cloves garlic, finely chopped
2 green finger-length chilies, finely sliced
4 cardamom pods, crushed
1/2 teaspoon fenugreek seeds
1 stalk lemongrass, tender inner part of bottom third only, finely sliced
2 teaspoons ground coriander
1 teaspoon ground cumin
1/2 teaspoon ground turmeric
1 cup (250 ml) coconut milk
Juice of 1 lemon

Season the fish fillets with salt and pepper. Heat the oil until hot in a large stir-fry pan and sear the fillets to firm the flesh, then set aside.

Reheat the oil and add the diced onion (not the onion rings), curry leaves, garlic, green chilies, cardamom pods, fenugreek and lemongrass. Stir-fry over medium heat until fragrant.

Shrimp in Coconut Curry Gravy (left) and Stir-fried Spicy Shrimp (right)

Add the coriander, cumin, and turmeric, and stir-fry until the oils are released and their aroma is strong. Add the coconut milk and bring to a boil. Lower the heat and add the onion rings and the fish fillets. Simmer until the onion rings and fish fillets are tender, about 15 minutes. Remove from heat. Cool slightly and add the lemon juice to taste.

Crab Curry

Sri Lankan crab is famous throughout the region. Fresh crabs, so plentiful in the seas here, are simmered to perfection in a spiced coconut curry gravy.

4 lbs (2 kgs) fresh crabs
1 red onion, sliced
2 green finger-length chilies, chopped
3 1/2 tablespoons Roasted Curry Powder (page 148)
2 teaspoons ground turmeric
1/2 teaspoon ground red pepper
1 teaspoon ground fenugreek
2 teaspoons tamarind pulp soaked in 2 tablespoons water, stirred and strained to obtain juice
1 sprig curry leaves
2 cups (500 ml) water
4 cups (1 liter) thick coconut milk
1/2 teaspoon ground mustard
Juice of 1 lime
Salt and pepper to taste

Beef Smore

Clean the crabs, divide each into 4 portions, and place in a large pan. Add all the other ingredients except coconut milk, mustard powder, lime juice, and salt.

Bring to a boil then add the coconut milk, return the mixture to simmering point, and simmer gently for 20 minutes. Add the lime juice, mustard powder, and salt, and stir for a few minutes until the flavors are married.

Remove from the heat and serve hot.

Beef Smore

A dish of Dutch origin. In Sri Lanka, beef smore is a real treat—a whole beef filet or loin which is slowly simmered in a spicy coconut milk gravy and then sliced and served in its own gravy. Eat with rice or breads of your choice.

1 lb (500 g) beef sirloin
2 tablespoons white vinegar
Salt and pepper to taste
2 tablespoons ghee or vegetable oil for stir-frying
2 sprigs curry leaves
1 stalk lemongrass, tender inner part of bottom third only, finely sliced
1 onion, sliced
1/2 teaspoon ground red pepper
1–2 green finger-length chilies, deseeded and finely sliced
1 cup (250 ml) coconut milk

Pierce the beef all over with a fork or skewer and marinate in vinegar, salt and pepper for 2 to 4 hours.

Heat the ghee or oil until very hot and sear the beef until lightly browned on all sides. This seals the meat and helps to retain the juices. Remove the meat from the pan and set aside.

Crab Curry

To the same pan add the curry leaves, lemongrass, onions, and green chilies. Fry until half cooked, about 3 minutes. Add the ground red pepper and mix well. Return the beef to the pan and add the coconut milk. Stir well and simmer until the coconut milk reduces into a thick gravy and the meat is done to your liking, about 25–35 minutes.

Remove from the heat, slice the meat to the desired thickness and pour the gravy over the slices.

Pork Curry

2 tablespoons oil
1 onion, chopped
5 cloves garlic, chopped
1 in (3 cm) ginger, chopped
1 stalk lemongrass, tender inner part of bottom third only, chopped
1 lb (500 g) boneless pork, cubed
2 teaspoons tamarind pulp soaked in 2 tablespoons water, stirred and strained to obtain juice
1 3/4 cups (400 ml) water
2 sprigs curry leaves
4 teaspoons Roasted Curry Powder (page 148)
1 teaspoon crushed black pepper
2–3 cloves
1/2 small cinnamon stick

Heat the oil in a pan and stir-fry the onion, garlic, ginger, and lemongrass until the onion is golden brown.

Add all the remaining ingredients and bring to a boil. Reduce the heat and simmer uncovered until the gravy is thick and the pork tender, about 25 minutes.

Spicy Lamb Curry

2 tablespoons oil
1 onion, chopped
5 cloves garlic, chopped
1 in (3 cm) ginger, chopped
2 green finger-length chilies, chopped
1 stalk lemongrass, tender inner part of bottom third only
1/2 small cinnamon stick
2–3 cardamom pods, crushed
1 lb (500 g) boneless lamb, cubed
6 teaspoons Roasted Curry Powder (page 148)
1 teaspoon ground red pepper
2 teaspoons ground turmeric
1 teaspoon ground black pepper
2 large tomatoes, diced

3/4 cup (200 ml) thick coconut milk
Salt to taste

Stir-fry the onion, garlic, ginger, green chilies, lemongrass, cinnamon, and cardamoms in oil until the onion is golden brown.

Add the lamb and stir well to coat, then add the curry, chili, and tumeric powders, the pepper, and the tomatoes. Cook over medium heat until the meat becomes tender, about 40 minutes. Add the thick coconut milk, bring to a boil and simmer a few minutes longer, adjust the seasoning, and serve.

Eggplant Pickles

2 tablespoons oil
1 lb (500 g) eggplant (aubergine), thinly sliced
1 small onion, sliced into thin rings
1 teaspoon ground mustard
1 teaspoon sugar
1/2 teaspoon ground turmeric
3 tablespoons vinegar
2–3 green finger-length chilies, halved lengthwise
2 tablespoons dried shrimp or fish, ground to a powder in a blender
Salt and pepper to taste

Heat the oil and fry the eggplant until golden brown. Remove and set aside to cool.

In the same pan, add the onion and stir-fry until soft. Add the remaining ingredients and the fried eggplant. Cook for 10 to 15 minutes. Serve at room temperature as an accompaniment to other dishes.

Green Mango Curry

This classical Sinhalese dish can be traced back to the fifth century, when it was served at the court of King Kasyapa of Sigiriya.

1 tablespoon oil
1 onion, chopped
6 cloves garlic, chopped
1/2 in (1 cm) ginger, chopped
2 sprigs curry leaves
2 red finger-length chilies, sliced
4 teaspoons Roasted Curry Powder (page 148)
1/2 small cinnamon stick

1 teaspoon salt
1 lb (500 g) green mangoes, peeled and pitted, flesh cut into long, thick strips
1/3 cup (100 ml) thin coconut milk
2 teaspoons ground mustard
3 tablespoons vinegar
3/4 cup (200 ml) thick coconut milk
1 tablespoon sugar

Heat the oil in a pan and stir-fry the onion, garlic, ginger, curry leaves, and red chilies until the onion is soft.

Add the curry powder, cinnamon, salt, mango, and thin coconut milk. Bring to a boil and simmer until the mango is just tender, about 10 minutes.

Meanwhile, mix the mustard with a little vinegar to form a paste. Stir the mustard paste into the thick coconut milk and, when the mango is tender, add the mustard and thick coconut milk, and the sugar, to the curry.

Bring to a boil, reduce the heat, and simmer for about 5 minutes. Adjust the seasoning. The gravy should be thick enough to thoroughly coat the mango.

Spicy Lamb Curry (above) and Pork Curry (below)

"The secrets of classic Thai cooking have been likened to culinary treasures."

THAILAND

From the Kingdom of Sukhothai comes a cuisine that balances the sweet and the sour with the hot and the salty.

Left: Floating markets, where everything you might need is piled onto a boat and paddled along rivers and canals.

Right: A woman winnowing wheat.

The Thais have a saying, *gan gin gan yu*—as you eat, so you are, which perfectly encapsulates their approach to food. Whether Thai cuisine comes about because of the fresh ingredients used, or the meticulous act of preparation, or the seasoning or garnishing is immaterial; Thai food has an elegance and refinement that is all its own. The only country in Southeast Asia to remain independent during the era of colonization, Thailand's blends of hot and sweet, sour and salty are different from the dishes of its neighbors, even though they may use some of the same ingredients: chili, garlic, lemongrass, fish sauce, palm sugar, and lime.

It is easy to see an analogy between the various aspects of Thai culture, including its cuisine. One of the most notable characteristics of Thai decorative art, for instance, is its passion for intricate detail, particularly apparent in complex mosaics of colored glass and porcelain that adorn so many

religious buildings. From afar, these suggest a solid, seamless pattern; only on closer inspection are the separate components revealed, and the skillful way they have been put together. So, too, in Thai cuisine, a wide variety of elements has been brought together and artfully composed into something that is intrinsically quite special.

The Land and its People

A stone tablet credited to King Ramkhamhaeng of Sukhothai, the first independent Thai kingdom founded in the early 13th century, bears the couplet: "In the water there are fish, in the fields there is rice." This testifies to a natural abundance that was to sustain a series of capital cities along the length of the fertile Chao Phraya River valley and, more specifically, to the two mainstays of the Thai diet then and now. Rice culture came with the earliest settlers, long before the Thais themselves arrived on the scene, and led to a vast complex of paddy fields watered by an intricate system of canals, rivers and reservoirs. Fish were plentiful, not only in the waterways, but also in the seas.

Other ingredients were gradually added over the centuries from a wide variety of cultures: from China and India, from Persia (modern-day Iran) and Portugal. Even such a seemingly essential element as the pungent chili was, in fact, from South America. However these ingredients came, though, they were subtly modified and refined into a cuisine that is today distinctively Thai.

Like its cuisine, Thailand encompasses a wide range of topography that covers some 198,500 square miles over some 73 provinces (*changwat*). To the north is a complex system of forested mountain ranges divided by the fertile Ping, Yom, Wang, and Nan river valleys. The northeast consists of a sparsely vegetated, semi-arid plateau that stretches to the Mekong River. The flat central plains, watered by the Chao Phraya River, form one of the richest rice-growing regions on earth. The colorful checkerboard of paddy fields, orchards and vegetable gardens that makes up these plains sustains the greater part of the country's agricultural and industrial growth. The mountainous southern isthmus, extending down to the border with Malaysia, is bordered on one side by the Gulf of Thailand and on the other by the Indian Ocean.

The Thais are an agricultural people. Even today, despite the growth of urban areas, the great majority of the population can be found in villages; most villagers still derive their living from agriculture. The tropical climate allows year-round cultivation of rice, fruits and vegetables. There are three distinguishable seasons: wet (June to October), cool (November to February), and hot (March to May).

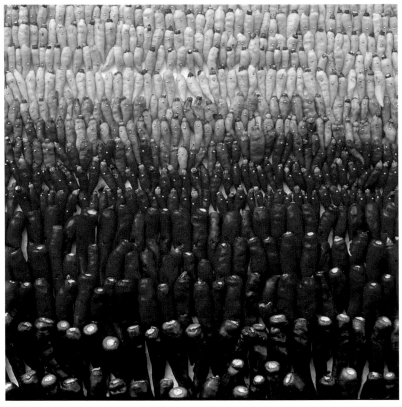
Chilies pinned out in the sun to dry.

Evidence of settlers dates back to the Paleolithic age some 500,000 years ago. The most extensive prehistoric remains come from the northeast, where a remarkable culture flourished from around 4000 BC. to just after the start of the Christian era. Indian traders later established ports along the southern peninsula, bringing not only Buddhism but numerous cultural and culinary influences. Mon settlers arrived around the same time in the Chao Phraya valley and founded the Dvaravati kingdom, to be replaced eventually by the Khmers.

Between the 7th and 11th centuries, the ethnic Thais, originating as a minority group from the northern parts of Burma and southern China, gradually migrated southward in search of greater independence and fertile land. By the 13th century, the Thais had established themselves in such numbers that they were eventually able to overthrow their Khmer overlords and establish a kingdom of their own.

This kingdom was called Sukhothai (Sanskrit for "Dawn of Happiness"), and though its power lasted less than two centuries, its influence proved far more enduring. Under King Ramkhamhaeng, the Thai alphabet was devised, works of Buddhist art were created and a truly indigenous Thai culture emerged.

Ayuthia, the next capital, began in 1350 as a small city-state on the Chao Phraya River and over the next 400 years became one of the most cosmopolitan cities in Southeast Asia. In this period, first contact was made with Europe and an active trade established with other Asian countries. Ayuthia fell to an invading Burmese army in 1767. King Rama I founded the present Chakri Dynasty in 1782 and moved the capital across the Chao Phraya to what is now Bangkok.

Bangkok prospered and the Chinese immigrants and Western traders who were drawn in large numbers to it brought diversity to the new city. By the end of 19th century, Bangkok was on its way to becoming a modern, Western-style city—at least in appearance.

The Making of a Cuisine

Little is known about the cooking of Sukhothai, but rice and fish were no doubt major ingredients. Fruits were plentiful, as were mushrooms that grew wild in the forests and a variety of vegetables. One item not present, however, was the chili, which was either brought directly by the Portuguese, who opened relations in 1511, or came via Malacca or India. Simon de la Loubere, who came with a French diplomatic mission in 1687, was struck by the fact that the people ate sparingly. Good salt was rare, and despite its abundance, fresh fish was seldom eaten. Jesuit missionary Nicolas Gervaise noted that *kapee*, the popular fermented shrimp paste, "has such a pungent smell that it nauseates anyone not accustomed to it," and gives perhaps the first general recipe for a typical Thai condiment based on it: "salt, pepper, ginger, cinnamon, cloves, garlic, white onions, nutmeg, and several strongly flavored herbs . . . mixed in considerable quantities with this shrimp paste."

The complex seasonings that we now regard as typical of Thai cuisine, including chilies, were certainly well established by the Rattanakosin, or Bangkok, period. Sir John Bowring regarded the essential sauce *nam prik* as "one of the most appetite-exciting condiments."

Alongside the development of this individual cuisine was a more refined one that prevailed in royal and aristocratic households, "Palace cooking," which focused on subtlety and visual appeal.

The Food of the People

Thai food today may be plain or fancy: a dish can be prepared in a few minutes over a charcoal brazier or require hours of chopping, grinding and carving. It may vary considerably from region to region. Always, though, it remains a singular creation, not quite like any of the influences that have shaped it over the centuries.

In the mountainous north, where borders are shared with Burma and Laos, the cuisine is as distinctive as the handicrafts for which the region is noted. Here, the earliest Thais settled on their migration southward from China, forming first a group of small city-states and then a loose federation known as Lanna, with Chiang Mai as the principal city.

The north has retained much of its native culture: its language, crafts, customs, and food. Instead of the soft-boiled rice of the central region, northerners prefer a steamed glutinous variety, rolled into small balls and dipped into liquid dishes. Curries of the region tend to be thinner, without the coconut milk widely used in central and southern cooking. There is also a distinctive local version of *nam prik ong*, a basic dipping sauce served with raw vegetables and crispy pork skin, as well as a pork sausage called *naem*, eaten plain with rice or mixed into various dishes. When it is in season, the favorite local fruit is the succulent longan, which grows in almost every compound.

The influence of neighboring Burma and Laos is apparent in many northern dishes. The former for the popular khao soi, a curry broth with egg noodles and chicken, pork or beef, and *gaeng hang lay*, a pork curry seasoned with ginger, tamarind, and turmeric; the latter for *nam prik noom*, a sauce with a strong chili-lime flavor, and *ook gai*, a red chicken curry with lemongrass.

Northeastern Thailand was long regarded as remote from the cosmopolitan world of Bangkok—not so much because of geography as a perceptible social prejudice on the part of city dwellers. Isan, as Thais call the northeast, was the poorest of the country's four main regions; its infertile soil and devastating droughts frequently drove farmers to the capital in search of work. The people of Isan have a definite skill for transforming food in ways that show both imagination and ingenuity. Barbecued chicken (*gai yang*) is grilled with lashings of peppery sauce and garlic, while catfish is the base of a delectable curry and *laab* dip is made with raw meat and ground roasted rice. Some of the region's delicacies are unique: grubworms, grasshoppers, ant eggs, snail curry, and fermented fish of exceptional pungency. Increasingly, the less challenging dishes typical of the region have won widespread admiration, and some diners are known to look upon a properly prepared *som tam* (spicy green papaya salad) or *laab* (even spicier minced pork or chicken) as being the true marks of a superior Thai cook. Perhaps because chilies add such character to the most mundane dish, northeasterners tend to use them with greater abandon than Thais of other areas.

Much northeastern cooking reflects the influence of Laos just across the Mekong River—not surprising, since many residents are ethnically Lao. Dill (*pak chee Lao* or "Laotian coriander") is widely used as a garnish, and glutinous rice is preferred. Also of Lao origin and popular on festive occasions is *khanom buang*, a crispy crêpe stuffed with dried shrimp, bean sprouts and other ingredients.

Southern Thailand, by contrast, is nurtured by rain that falls for eight months of the year. Cultivated areas tend to be vast rubber and coconut plantations rather than the rice fields and fruit orchards of the central plains. Coconuts growing plentifully everywhere provide milk for thickening soups and curries, oil for frying and grated flesh as a condiment for many dishes. Thousands of boats fish the surrounding waters from villages along the coastlines on the Gulf of Thailand and the Indian Ocean, bringing back seafood for local consumption and profitable export.

The south is home to most of Thailand's two million Muslims, its largest religious minority. In other southern places like Songkhla and the island of Phuket, the Chinese predominate. Southern food reflects the cross-pollination. Seafood may be prepared simply, grilled or steamed; or baked in a claypot with thin noodles and garlic; or included as the main component of *tom yam*, the ubiquitous Thai soup laced with lemongrass and chilies. In general, southerners like their food chili-hot, and are fond of the bitter taste of a flat, native bean called *sataw*, which other Thais tend to find less appealing. Small, juicy pineapples are a popular end to a meal.

Contributions from other cultures include *gaeng mussaman*, an Indian-style curry of chicken or beef perfumed with cardamom, cloves and cinnamon; Malay fish curries; and Indonesian satay.

The central plains is the Thai heartland. Here, you'll find the best jasmine rice, pearly white and fragrant, and mangoes, durians, mangosteens, rambutans, guavas, papayas and pomelos, even grapes. Vegetables such as cabbage, mushrooms, water convolvulus (water spinach), cucumber, tomatoes, and pumpkins, as well as more recent introductions like asparagus and baby corn, are grown in vast quantities.

Food in the villages amid the fields tends to be plain: rice with stir-fried vegetables, fish from a nearby canal or river, perhaps some minced chicken with garlic, chilies, and basil and a salad of salted eggs, chilies, and green onion (scallion) with a squeeze of lime.

In Bangkok, everything is available, even the most exotic regional delicacies, if you know where to look. The city streets are punctuated with the many fast foods based on Chinese noodles, prepared at a moment's notice at any sidewalk café or by vendors who push their carts along residential streets. Tasty, nourishing, occasionally even distinguished, these quick meals epitomize the busy life of Bangkok and also the Thai capacity for making something special out of simple ingredients. Such is its popularity that Thai street food has evolved into a distinctive culinary category all its own, generally characterized by speed of preparation and easy portability of equipment.

Palace Cooking

Dr Malcolm Smith, who served as physician to some members of the Thai royal family in the early years of this century, describes the innermost part of Bangkok's mile-square Grand Palace known as the "Inside," where the women of the court lived, thus: "A town complete in itself, a congested network of houses and narrow streets, with gardens, lawns, artificial lakes, and shops. It had its own government, its own institutions, its own laws and law-courts. It was a town of women, controlled by women."

At its peak, during the reign of King Rama V (Chulalongkorn), the "Inside" had a population estimated at nearly 3000, a select few of them bearing the exalted rank of Queen but the great majority ladies-in-waiting and lower attendants. The inner palace can be viewed as a kind of ultra-exclusive finishing school where the most refined aristocratic skills were perfected and passed on.

The royal women learned how to prepare various foods that were not merely more subtle in flavor than their outside versions, but highly memorable in visual appeal. The most visible of palace skills was the art of fruit and vegetable carving, garnishes and delicacies that sometimes required as long to prepare as the dishes that they adorned.

The hallmarks of so-called "palace food"—which was, in fact, to be found in most aristocratic homes as well—were painstaking hours of preparation and a highly refined style of presentation. *Foi thong*, for instance, is a blend of egg yolks and sugar transformed into a nest of silky golden threads, while *look choop* are tiny imitation fruits shaped by hand from a mixture of sweet bean paste and coconut milk, tinted to exactly match their real-life models.

When royal polygamy ended under King Rama VI, the ladies of the "Inside" and their numerous attendants gradually left their protected existence. Fortunately, palace cooking did not vanish with the hidden world but survived through the descendants of the royal women. In recent years, it has been discovered by a wider public through several restaurants that take pride in their re-creations of this unique cuisine.

The Thai Kitchen and Table

The hospitality and generosity of the shared Thai table is easily achieved in the home. In this section you will find recipes for popular Thai salads, curries, soups, steamed, deep-fried and stir-fried dishes, grilled dishes, desserts, relishes, and accompaniments. When cooking, try to use only the freshest ingredients. Taste as you go along, and aim to balance the flavors and textures within the dish and between the compilation of dishes to be served.

Kantoke, a meal taken while seated at a low round table, is a traditional way of dining in the north of Thailand.

Rice is the mainstay of Thai meals, mostly steamed long-grain jasmine rice, a nod to the traditions and ritual of its cultivation. All other dishes—salads, curries, soups—are called *gap kao*, to be served with rice; they are mere condiments. There is no set progression of dishes; all main course dishes are served at once. When cooking for a gathering of four, rather than increase the quantity of a single dish, do as the Thais do and increase the variety of dishes: perhaps a soup, a curry, a salad, a steamed dish, and a selection of relishes. Diners are free to help themselves, in any order they want, mixing dishes at will and seasoning them with a wide variety of condiments to achieve the desired taste.

The ideal Thai meal is a harmonious blend of the spicy, sweet, hot, wet, mild, crisp, sour, and soft, and is meant to be satisfying to the eye, nose, and palate. Complex dishes are accompanied by simpler ones: the richness of this dish may be cut by the piquancy of that, the saltiness of this recipe is a perfect foil for another. As a result the palate is not overwhelmed; there is give and take. The Thais call this harmonious layering of flavor upon flavor *rot chart*—the heart and soul of true Thai cuisine.

Many Thai desserts are based on glutinous rice, coconut milk, palm sugar, pandan leaf, and agar-agar, but the most common dessert is one or more of the abundant fresh fruits, usually brought out after the other dishes have been removed. On special occasions, more elaborate desserts such as *foi thong* (golden threads) or banana-leaf cups of *takaw*, a confection of tapioca starch, sugar and coconut that comes in a wide variety of forms, may be served.

Snacks are so popular in Thailand they deserve special mention. They may consist of nothing more than freshly sliced fruit sprinkled with salt, sugar, dried chilies or a combination of these seasonings. Or they may be a selection of traditional sweets. Some vendors offer noodle creations. To produce the universally popular *kwayteow*, a bowl of freshly cooked rice noodles is given a few ladles of meat stock, topped with cooked pork or chicken, and sprinkled with sugar, crushed peanuts, and dried chili flakes. For *pad thai*, noodles are quickly stir-fried with garlic, green onions (scallions), salted dried shrimp, and a variety of spices. Whether eaten in a restaurant, on a city sidewalk, on the open verandah of a farm house, even in the middle of a rice field at harvest time, a Thai meal is nearly always a social affair.

SUGGESTED MENUS

Family meals

For a simple family meal, try serving steamed jasmine rice with:
• Tom Yam Goong (page 161);
• Dry Beef Curry (page166) and Chinese Broccoli with Crispy Pork or Bacon (page162);
• finish with Bananas in Sweet Coconut Milk (page 169);

or

• Green Papaya Salad (page 160);
• Red Chicken Curry with Bamboo Shoots (page 164) served with rice;
• fresh fruit like jackfruit, mango, or rambutan.

A dinner party

For a stylish dinner party, serve:
• Steamed Seafood Parcels with Coconut (page 158)
• Spicy Pomelo or Grapefruit Salad (page 160), the Fried Fish with Chili Shrimp Paste Sauce (page 167) and Roast Duck Curry (page 164);
• Red Ruby Chestnuts in Sweet Coconut Cream (page 169) as a palate cleanser.

Finger food

The appetizers in this section make particularly good finger food—try the following at your next party or picnic:
• Minced Pork and Shrimp Dumplings (page 159);
• Chicken Wrapped in Pandanus Leaves (page 164);
• Steamed Seafood Parcels with Coconut (page 158).

A melting pot menu

For a refined but simple Asian tasting menu:
• Grilled Shrimp on a Sugar Cane Skewer (page 178) from Vietnam as a starter;
• Indonesian Pork in Sweet Soy (page 81) with Stir-fried Vegetables (page 43) from China combine well for a main course that is not too heavy;
• Candied Apples (page 47), also from China, are a delicious dessert with which to finish.

THE ESSENTIAL FLAVORS OF THAI COOKING

Thai cuisine uses the redolent **fish sauce** in almost everything besides desserts. The curries are built on subtle blends of **cilantro**, **lemongrass**, **galangal**, **chilies**, and **kaffir lime leaf** and **rind**. Other typically Thai flavors include **Thai sweet basil** (*horapa*), **ginger**, **shrimp paste,** and **tamarind**. **Coconut milk** and **palm sugar** are added to curries and sweets. Staples you will need include **jasmine** and **glutinous rice**.

Thai Chicken Stock

5–6 1/2 lbs (2 1/2–3 1/4 kgs) chicken bones or 1/2 whole chicken
6 quarts (5 1/2 liters) water
1 1/2 cups (250 g) chopped onion
3/4 cup (125 g) chopped celery
1 tablespoon coriander seeds
1 teaspoon black peppercorns

Wash the bones in cold water then put in a stockpot and cover with cold water. Bring rapidly to a boil, then drain and discard water. Cover the bones with 5 1/2 liters of water and add all the other ingredients. Simmer for 3 hours, removing the scum as it accumulates. Strain through a muslin cloth. The stock can be put in 1-liter containers and frozen for up to 3 months. Home made chicken stock greatly improves the flavor of all recipes where stock is specified. Yields 8 cups (2 liters) of stock.

Shrimp Chili Paste

1/2 cup (125 ml) oil
8 shallots, sliced
6 cloves garlic, sliced
1 cup (120 g) dried shrimp
1/2 cup (10 g) dried chilies, cut roughly
1 tablespoon palm sugar
3 tablespoons fish sauce
2 1/2 tablespoons Tamarind Juice (page 18)

Heat the oil in a wok and fry the shallots and garlic until golden brown; remove from the oil and set aside. Add the dried shrimp and chilies and fry until golden brown; remove from the oil and set aside. In a food processor or blender, process the shallots, garlic, shrimp, chilies and sugar with a little oil from the wok to keep the blades turning. Add the fish sauce, Tamarind Juice and salt and blend to obtain about 1 3/4 cups (435 ml) of paste.

Red Curry Paste

1 tablespoon coriander seeds
1 teaspoon cumin seed
5 dried red chilies, slit lengthwise, deseeded and soaked in hot water for 15 minutes
3 tablespoons sliced shallots
8 cloves garlic, smashed

2–3 thin slices galangal
2 tablespoons sliced lemongrass (tender inner part of bottom third only)
2 teaspoons grated kaffir lime rind
1 tablespoon chopped coriander root
10 black peppercorns
1 teaspoon dried shrimp paste (*kapee*), dry-roasted (page 13)

Dry-fry the coriander and cumin seeds in a frying pan over low heat for about 5 minutes, then grind to a powder in a blender or mortar and pestle. Add the remaining ingredients, except the dried shrimp paste, and grind well. Add the dried shrimp paste and grind again to obtain about 3/4 cup (180 ml) of fine-textured curry paste.

Mussaman Curry Paste

3 tablespoons sliced shallots
1 tablespoon chopped garlic
1 teaspoon sliced galangal
1 tablespoon sliced lemongrass (tender inner part of bottom third only)
2 cloves
1 tablespoon coriander seeds
1 teaspoon cumin seeds
5 black peppercorns
3 dried chilies, sliced open, deseeded and soaked in water for 15 minutes
1 teaspoon salt
1 teaspoon dried shrimp paste (*kapee*), dry-roasted (page 13)

Dry-fry the shallots, garlic, galangal, lemongrass, cloves,

Steamed Seafood Parcels with Coconut

coriander and cumin seeds in a wok over low heat for about 5 minutes, then grind to a powder in a mortar and pestle or blender. Add the rest of the ingredients, except the shrimp paste, and grind to mix well. Combine the ground mixture and shrimp paste and grind again to obtain 1/2 cup (125 ml) of fine-textured curry paste.

Green Curry Paste

1 tablespoon coriander seeds
1 teaspoon cumin seeds
5–10 green bird's-eye chilies
3 tablespoons sliced shallots
3 cloves garlic, sliced
1 teaspoon sliced galangal
1 tablespoon sliced lemongrass (tender inner part of bottom third only)
1/2 teaspoon grated kaffir lime rind
1 teaspoon chopped coriander root
5 black peppercorns
1 teaspoon salt
1 teaspoon dried shrimp paste (*kapee*), dry-roasted (page 13)

Dry-fry the coriander and cumin seeds in a wok over low heat for about 5 minutes, then grind to a powder. Add the rest of the ingredients, except the dried shrimp paste, and grind to mix well. Add the dried shrimp paste to the spice mixture and grind to obtain 1/2 cup (125 ml) of fine-textured curry paste.

Thai people love good food, and the emphasis on quality applies to both palace cuisine and street food. An array of sweetmeats and treats is available—Thais seem to find it more satisfactory to eat a little of this and a little of that—along the *klongs* and sidewalks, and outside offices and shopping centers. The ready-to-eat delicacies may include barbecued or grilled food on or off skewers, salads, noodle soups, wrapped in dough or edible leaves, or be a sweet. Here are a few dishes that would work well as finger food.

Steamed Seafood Parcels with Coconut

These seafood parcels are steamed in small cups made of banana leaf. You may use aluminum foil or small cupcake tins. You can also make one large cake about 1 in (3 cm) thick, in an 8 x 8 in (20 x 20 cm) heatproof cake or brownie dish, and then slice it into squares for serving.

3/4 cup (180 ml) coconut cream
1 teaspoon rice flour
4 oz (100 g) boneless white fish fillets, cut into thin slices
4 oz (100 g) fresh shrimp, peeled and deveined, cut into small pieces
4 oz (100 g) squid, cleaned and cut into tiny pieces
2 eggs, beaten
2 tablespoons fish sauce
1 1/4 cups (300 ml) coconut milk
1/2 cup (20 g) finely chopped Thai basil leaves (*horapa*)
2 tablespoons very thinly sliced kaffir lime leaves
Coriander leaves (cilantro), to garnish
1 red finger-length chili, thinly sliced
Banana leaf cups 2 in (5 cm) square

Spice Paste
10–15 dried chilies, slit open lengthwise, deseeded and soaked in water
3 cloves garlic
4 slices galangal
2 teaspoons chopped coriander (cilantro) root
1 teaspoon grated kaffir lime rind
5 black peppercorns
1/2 teaspoon salt
1 teaspoon dried shrimp paste (*kapee*), dry-roasted (page 13)

Mix the coconut cream with the rice flour and bring to a boil, stirring until thick. Remove from the heat and cool for topping.

Grind the Spice Paste ingredients in a blender or a mortar and pestle. Mix the Spice Paste with the fish, shrimp, squid, egg and fish sauce. Then add the coconut milk, a little at a time. Add half the basil and kaffir lime leaves and mix in.

Place one of the remaining basil leaves in the bottom of each cup or at the bottom of a heatproof baking dish, fill with the seafood mixture, cover and steam for 15 minutes.

Remove the cups from the steamer, and top each one with a little of the boiled coconut cream, coriander leaves, kaffir lime leaf and sliced chili.

Return to the steamer an cook for 1 more minute.

Minced Pork and Shrimp Dumplings

The color of these delicate dumplings is obtained by soaking a blue flower (*anchun*), although commercial food coloring can be substituted.

Filling
1/2 cup (80 g) roasted unsalted peanuts, chopped
1/2 teaspoon salt
2 tablespoons sugar
4 oz (100 g) ground pork

5 oz (150 g) ground shrimp
1/2 cup (125 g) chopped preserved salted radish
2 tablespoons oil

Dumplings
1/4 cup (30 g) tapioca flour
About 2 tablespoons dried *anchun* flowers or 1/2 teaspoon blue food coloring
2 cups (250 g) rice flour
1/4 cup (60 ml) coconut milk
2 tablespoons oil
1/4 cup (60 ml) water
1/2 cup (125 ml) coconut cream
Banana leaf or aluminum foil

Stir-fry all the Filling ingredients together in the oil until cooked and let cool.

Make the Dumplings by mixing all the ingredients together. Cook over low heat, stirring constantly, until the mixture turns into an elastic dough. Cover with plastic wrap while making the individual Dumplings to prevent the dough from drying out.

Pinch off a small ball of dough and flatten into a circle about 2 1/2 in (6 cm) in diameter. Place a teaspoonful of the Filling in the center of the dough and pinch the edges together to enclose. Use special tongs or pinch to give the Dumplings a flower shape. Place on an oiled banana leaf or aluminum foil and put about 1 teaspoon of coconut cream over

the top of each Dumpling to prevent it from drying out.

Steam the dumplings for 8 minutes until cooked. Serve warm on a bed of crisp-fried golden garlic and top with coconut cream.

Crispy Shrimp Cakes

Street vendors in coastal towns, especially around Songkhla, Surat Thani and Phuket, offer a highly seasoned version of this snack made with fish.

1 1/4 lbs (650 g) fresh shrimp, shelled and deveined
1/3 cup (50 g) ground pork or chopped ham or bacon
1 teaspoon salt
1/2 teaspoon sugar
1 cup (60 g) bread crumbs
2 kaffir lime leaves, very thinly sliced
4 cups (1 liter) oil for deep-frying

Sweet and Spicy Pickled Vegetables
1 cup (250 ml) distilled white vinegar
1/2 cup (100 g) sugar
3–5 bird's-eye chilies
3–5 shallots, sliced
2 tablespoons sliced cauliflower
2 tablespoons finely sliced baby corn or cabbage
2 tablespoons sliced baby cucumber
1 tablespoon grated ginger

To prepare the Sweet and Spicy Pickled Vegetables, bring the

vinegar and sugar to a boil, then set aside to cool. Add the remaining ingredients, mix and set aside.

Finely chop the shrimp and pork or oil together or process in a blender until they form a rough paste. Add the salt, sugar, kaffir lime leaves, and half the bread crumbs, then shape into flat, round patties. Coat the outside of the patties with the remaining bread crumbs.

Place the oil in a pan or wok and heat. Deep-fry the patties in the oil until golden brown and fragrant.

Serve hot with the Sweet and Spicy Pickled Vegetables.

Fried Shrimp with Sweet and Sour Sauce

1 lb (500 g) fresh shrimp
1 egg, lightly beaten
1 1/2 cups (100 g) fine bread crumbs
Oil, for deep frying

Sweet and Sour Sauce
1/2 in (1 cm) fresh ginger, peeled
2–3 whole shallots, peeled
4 tablespoons white vinegar
3 tablespoons sugar
1/2 teaspoon salt
2 tablespoons tomato ketchup
1–2 tablespoons hot sauce (Sriracha or Tabasco)

Peel the shrimp, discarding the heads but leaving the tail sections intact. Devein and flatten into a butterfly shape by pressing gently with the hand.

To prepare the Sweet and Sour Sauce, grill the ginger and shallots under the broiler, turning until brown on all sides, about 8 minutes. Place the ginger, shallots, vinegar, sugar, salt and ketchup in a pan and bring to a boil. Reduce to medium heat and simmer until all the sugar has dissolved. Remove the ginger and shallots from the pan. Bring to a boil again, then add the hot sauce. Simmer until just thickened, then remove from the heat. Set aside to cool.

Heat the oil in a medium saucepan. Dip the shrimp in the egg and bread crumbs. Deep-fry until golden brown and serve with the Sweet and Sour Sauce.

Fried Shrimp with Sweet and Sour Sauce

Most Thai salads are hot and sour. You can vary the combination of greens and spices, it is important to balance the flavors of the dressing.

Thai soups are usually light, accentuated with fresh aromatics, and have the four main flavors—hot, sour, sweet, and salty. They are drunk throughout a meal, but make a perfectly acceptable first course to a dinner party with an Asian theme.

Spicy Pomelo or Grapefruit Salad

Large round pomelos, the Asian equivalent of grapefruit, are generally bitter-sweet, and are eaten as a fruit as well as mixed with sour, spicy ingredients and shrimp or chicken to make a salad. This salad goes well with rice and other cooked dishes.

1 pomelo or 2 large grapefruits
2 tablespoons lime juice
1 tablespoon fish sauce
1 tablespoon sugar
5 oz (150 g) boiled or grilled shrimp, shells removed
2 cups (200 g) cooked chicken breast, shredded
2 tablespoons grated fresh or dried unsweetened coconut
1/2–1 tablespoon dried shrimp, soaked in warm water for 5 minutes and drained, lightly pounded or processed
1 dried chili, deseeded and chopped
1/4 cup (60 ml) coconut cream

Spicy Pomelo or Grapefruit Salad

Peel the pomelo and shred the flesh, removing the seeds. (If using grapefruit, peel and section, removing all the skins.)

Place the lime juice, fish sauce and sugar in a bowl and stir well to dissolve the sugar. Then add the shrimp, chicken and grated coconut. Mix well.

Add the pomelo or grapefruit and grated coconut. Toss lightly.

Serve sprinkled with chopped dried shrimp and chili, and drizzled with a little coconut cream, if using.

> If you are using grapefruit, it may be necessary to add extra sugar.

Green Papaya Salad

This healthy mixture of raw vegetables captures the essential flavors of Thailand: chili hot, redolent with garlic and fish sauce, and sour with lime juice. The unripe papaya, contrasts in texture with crunchy raw beans and peanuts. If unripe papaya is not available, very thinly sliced cabbage may be substituted.

2–5 bird's-eye chilies
2 tablespoons unsalted roasted peanuts or cashew nuts
1 tablespoon dried shrimp, soaked in warm water for 5 minutes and drained
5 cloves garlic
10 oz (300 g) unripe green papaya, peeled and shredded using a sharp knife or vegetable grater

1/2 cup (50 g) long beans or green beans, cut into pieces
6 ripe cherry tomatoes, quartered, or 1 large tomato, in wedges
3 tablespoons lime juice
1 tablespoon chopped palm sugar or dark brown sugar
1 tablespoon fish sauce
2 cups raw vegetables (cabbage, water spinach, broccoli, asparagus)
3 sprigs Thai basil (*horapa*)

Take the chilies, peanuts, dried shrimp and garlic and pound roughly in a mortar and pestle or process very briefly in a blender. The mixture should be coarse, not smooth.

Combine the mixture in a bowl with the shredded papaya, beans and tomato. Mix well and add the lime juice, palm sugar and fish sauce.

Serve accompanied by other raw vegetables (cabbage, water spinach, broccoli or asparagus) and sprigs of Thai basil.

> Prepare the salad immediately before serving, otherwise the papaya will lose its firm texture.

Grilled Beef Salad
Yum Nua

This salad is an ideal way to use up any leftover roast or grilled beef. Lamb may also be substituted for a delightful variation on this classic dish. Lettuce is often added to this dish although in Thailand it is often served mainly with cucumber, Chinese celery and herbs (mint and coriander leaves).

1 lb (450 g) beef sirloin or leftover roast or steak
1 tablespoon uncooked long grain or jasmine rice
1/2 cup (75 g) sliced cucumber
1/2 cup (20 g) sliced Chinese celery
1 large tomato or 6 cherry tomatoes, sliced
5–7 shallots, thinly sliced
1/2 cup (20 g) mint and coriander leaves (cilantro) to garnish
Small head of lettuce (optional), washed and torn

Dressing
2 tablespoons lime juice
1 tablespoon fish sauce
3 teaspoons sugar
1/2 teaspoon crushed dried chilies or ground red pepper

If using uncooked beef fillet, sear, chargrill or roast the beef to taste, then slice thinly and set aside.

Dry roast the rice grains in a wok or pan over medium heat until lightly browned. Remove from the pan and grind the roasted rice lightly in a mortar and pestle or blender. Set aside.

Mix all the Dressing ingredients in a large mixing bowl. Add the sliced beef, cucumber, Chinese celery, tomato wedges and shallots to the bowl and toss to coat. Add the lettuce (if using) and toss again.

Transfer to a serving dish and serve garnished with the roasted rice, mint and coriander leaves (cilantro).

Mixed Vegetable Soup

This is less a soup in the Western sense than vegetables, with a little pork, chicken, and shrimp, simmered in seasoned stock.

5 cups mixed vegetables, such as summer squash or zucchini (courgette), pumpkin, straw mushrooms, baby corn, green beans, cut into bite-sized pieces
5 oz (150 g) lean pork, thinly sliced
5 oz (150 g) chicken, thinly sliced
5 oz (150 g) fresh shrimp, peeled but with tails left intact
4 cups (1 liter) Thai Chicken Stock (page 158)
2 tablespoons fish sauce
1 cup (40 g) lemon basil leaves (*manglak*)

Seasoning
10 black peppercorns
1/2 tablespoon dried shrimp paste (*kapee*), dry-roasted (page 13)
10 shallots
1/4 cup (30 g) dried shrimp

Place all the Seasoning ingredients in a mortar or blender and pound or blend until fine. Add to the Chicken Stock and bring to a boil, stirring to prevent sticking. Add the vegetables, pork, chicken and shrimp and simmer until just cooked. Season to taste with fish sauce or salt, then remove from heat. Add the basil leaves and serve.

Creamy Chicken Soup with Coconut Milk

A delightful soup, rich with coconut milk and fragrant with the elusive flavor of galangal. Reduce the amount of chilies if you don't want the soup to be too spicy.

4 cups (1 liter) Thai Chicken Stock (page 158)
2 stalks lemongrass, tender inner part of bottom third only, smashed with the back of a cleaver
2 in (5 cm) galangal root, peeled and sliced thinly
3 kaffir lime leaves, torn into small pieces
12 oz (375 g) boneless chicken, cut into small pieces
12 fresh or canned straw mushrooms or small button mushrooms, sliced in half
1 teaspoon salt
4 tablespoons lime juice
3 tablespoons fish sauce
1/2 teaspoon sugar
3 cups (750 ml) thin coconut milk
2–3 red bird's-eye chilies, bruised

Place the Chicken Stock in a pot and add the lemongrass, galangal and kaffir lime leaves. Bring to a boil over medium heat. Add the chicken, mushrooms, salt, lime juice, fish sauce and sugar. Reduce the heat to low and cook slowly, uncovered, for 10 minutes or until the chicken changes color, then add the coconut milk and chilies. Bring almost to a boil, stirring constantly for 2–3 minutes, then remove from the heat and serve.

Sour Seafood Soup with Vegetables

Tamarind Juice adds a special touch to this relatively mild soup, which is full of vegetables, shrimp, and chopped fish.

3 cups (750 ml) water
8 oz (250 g) fresh white fish fillets
4 oz (100 g) fresh shrimp
12 fresh or canned straw mushrooms or small button mushrooms, sliced in half
1/2 cup (125 g) sliced daikon radish
1/2 cup (125 g) sliced green papaya
1/2 cup (50 g) sliced green beans
1/2 cup (60 g) cauliflower, broken into florets
3/4 cup (50 g) sliced Chinese cabbage
4 tablespoons Tamarind Juice (page 18)
2 tablespoons lime juice
1 tablespoon chopped palm sugar or dark brown sugar
1 teaspoon salt

Spice Paste
3 dried chilies, deseeded and soaked until soft
2 teaspoons chopped garlic
2 teaspoons chopped shallots
1 teaspoon chopped krachai

Bring the water to a boil in a large pot.

Sour Seafood Soup with Vegetables

Place the fish fillets and shrimp in the boiling water and simmer for about 8 minutes until cooked. Remove the seafood with a slotted spoon. Let it cool. Chop up the fish. Reserve the stock. Set the seafood aside.

Grind the Spice Paste ingredients in a blender or mortar and pestle, then place the Spice Paste in a pan with the reserved stock, fish and vegetables. Bring to a boil and simmer until just cooked, about 10 minutes. Add the Tamarind Juice, lime juice, sugar and salt.

Serve hot, topped with the shrimp.

Tom Yam Goong
Shrimp Soup with Lemongrass

One of the best known Thai dishes abroad, this flavorful but spicy soup is hot, sour and fragrant, an ideal accompaniment to other Thai dishes and rice. The kaffir lime leaves, galangal and lemon grass are what give this soup its tangy flavor, but are not meant to be eaten, so tell your guests to avoid them while eating the broth, shrimp and mushrooms.

4 cups (1 liter) Thai Chicken Stock (page 158)
3 kaffir lime leaves
2 in (5 cm) galangal root, sliced
3–4 coriander roots, washed
3 stalks lemongrass, tender inner part of bottom third only, smashed with back of a cleaver
6–8 fresh medium shrimp, shells intact
1 cup (100 g) fresh or canned straw mushrooms or small button mushrooms, sliced in half
5–10 bird's-eye chilies, smashed
3 tablespoons lime juice
1/2 tablespoon fish sauce
3 sprigs fresh coriander leaves (cilantro)

Creamy Chicken Soup with Coconut Milk

Bring the stock to a boil and add the kaffir lime leaves, galangal, coriander roots and lemongrass. Simmer for 15 minutes.

Add the shrimp, mushrooms and chilies, and simmer for 3 minutes. Add the lime juice and fish sauce (which is very salty) to taste. The soup should be spicy-sour and a little salty. Serve garnished with fresh coriander leaves (cilantro).

Do not overcook the shrimp or they will become tough. Any variety of seafood may be substituted for or added to the shrimp—including sliced fish, crab or squid.

Glass Noodle Soup

5 oz (150 g) ground pork or chicken
1/2 teaspoon soy sauce
4 cups (1 liter) Thai Chicken Stock
  (page 158)
1/4 teaspoon ground white pepper
3 white peppercorns, crushed
5 cloves garlic, crushed
1 1/2 oz (50 g) dried glass noodles
  (bean thread or cellophane noodles), soaked in warm water for
  about 5 minutes to soften
1 teaspoon fish sauce
6 dried black Chinese mushrooms,
  soaked in hot water to soften,
  stems discarded, caps sliced
1/4 teaspoon sugar
1 green onion (scallion), cut into pieces
2 tablespoons chopped coriander
  leaves (cilantro)

Mix the meat, soy sauce and ground white pepper together well, and form into small, roughly shaped meatballs.

Stir-fried Asparagus with Shrimp

Heat the Chicken Stock in a pot, add the crushed peppercorns and garlic, and bring to a boil. Place the meatballs in the boiling stock and then add the noodles, fish sauce, mushrooms and sugar. Simmer until the meatballs are cooked. Add the green onions and coriander leaves and remove from the heat immediately. Serve accompanied by rice.

Stir-fried Asparagus with Shrimp

2 tablespoons oil
3 cloves garlic, peeled and minced
10 oz (300 g) young asparagus, cut
  into bite-sized lengths
5 oz (150 g) shrimp, peeled and
  deveined, tails intact
1 teaspoon soy sauce
2 teaspoons oyster sauce
1 teaspoon fish sauce
1/4 teaspoon sugar
1/2 cup Thai Chicken Stock (page 158)
1 teaspoon cornstarch mixed in
  2 tablespoons water
1/4 teaspoon ground white pepper

Heat a wok until very hot then add the oil. When the oil is hot, add the garlic and stir-fry until fragrant, about 1 minute. Add the asparagus and shrimp and stir-fry until the asparagus is just tender and shrimp turn pink, 3–4 minutes.

Add the soy sauce, oyster sauce, fish sauce and sugar. Stir-fry then add the Thai Chicken Stock and cornstarch mixture and simmer for 1 minute.

Transfer to a plate, sprinkle with pepper and serve hot.

In Thailand main courses are usually served with rice. The dishes are served at once, and stay on the table throughout the meal. The recipes here serve four as part of a shared meal.

Chinese Broccoli with Crispy Pork or Bacon

Vegetables are frequently cooked with a little meat, poultry or seafood to add flavor and a contrasting texture.

10 oz (300 g) Chinese broccoli
  (*kailan*) or broccoli stems
3 tablespoons oil
1 tablespoon minced garlic
4 tablespoons oyster sauce
1/4 teaspoon salt
1/4 teaspoon ground white pepper
1 teaspoon sugar
1/2 cup (125 ml) Thai Chicken Stock
  (page 158) or water
5 oz (150 g) crispy roasted pork or
  bacon, sliced into bite-sized pieces

Discard the leaves and tough bottom part of the broccoli stems. Peel the skin off the tender stems and discard. Cut the stems into lengths.

Heat the oil in a wok. When it is very hot, fry the garlic until fragrant, about 1 minute, then add the broccoli and stir-fry for 5–6 minutes. Add all the seasonings and Chicken Stock. Add the crispy pork and stir-fry to heat through. Do not overcook. Serve immediately.

Stir-fried Mixed Vegetables

8 oz (250 g) Chinese broccoli
3–4 cabbage leaves, sliced
1/2 cup (100 g) sliced carrots
1/2 cup (100 g) cauliflower florets
1/2 cup (50 g) snow peas
1/2 cup (40 g) baby sweet corn
2 tablespoons oil
3 tablespoons minced garlic
5 fresh shiitake or black Chinese
  mushrooms, stems removed and
  sliced
1/2 cup (125 ml) Thai Chicken Stock
  (page 158) or water
3 tablespoons oyster sauce
1/2 tablespoon soy sauce
1/2 teaspoon dark soy sauce
1 tablespoon fish sauce
Dash of rice wine, sherry or sake
1/2 teaspoon ground white pepper
1/2 teaspoon sugar

Heat a wok until lightly smoking and add the oil. When hot, add the garlic and stir well for 1 minute, or until fragrant. Add the mushrooms and stir-fry for 1 minute.

Add the vegetables and Chicken Stock or water to the wok and stir-fry for about 8–10 minutes until just cooked; the vegetables should still be slightly crisp. Add the oyster, soy and fish sauces and wine, then sprinkle with pepper and sugar. Mix well and cook for 1 minute.

Serve accompanied with rice.

Southern Rice Salad

This is a popular way of using left-over rice and makes an ideal light lunch. The seasonings can be varied according to taste and availability; not all ingredients used in this recipe are shown in the photograph on this page

2 cups (200 g) cooked rice
1 cup (100 g) grated coconut,
  browned in an oven or dry-roased
  in a pan for 5–8 minutes
1 small pomelo or grapefruit, peeled
  and sectioned
1 small green mango, grated
1/2 cup (60 g) dried shrimp, soaked
  and lightly pounded or processed
1/2 cup (25 g) bean sprouts
1/2 cup (20 g) finely sliced lemongrass (tender inner part of bottom
  third only)

Southern Rice Salad

1/4 cup (25 g) sliced green beans
1 egg, beaten, cooked into an omelet
and thinly sliced
2 dried red chilies, deseeded and finely sliced or pounded
1 tablespoon very finely sliced kaffir lime leaves
1/2 cup (25 g) chopped coriander leaves (cilantro) or Thai basil leaves (*horapa*)
4 oz (100 g) cooked shrimp
1 green onion (scallion), minced
Lime wedges

Sauce
1/2 cup (125 ml) water
2 tablespoons chopped preserved salted fish or anchovies in brine
1 tablespoon chopped palm sugar or dark brown sugar
2 kaffir lime leaves, thinly sliced
1 tablespoon very finely sliced lemongrass (tender inner part of bottom third only)

Put all the Sauce ingredients in a pan, bring to a boil and simmer for 5 minutes. Remove from the heat, strain and set aside.

Place the rice in small bowls, each holding about half a cup. Press down then invert onto a large serving platter. Arrange the rest of the raw ingredients around the edge of rice in separate piles.

To eat, spoon some rice onto individual plates and take a little of each ingredient to mix with the rice according to taste. Spoon the sauce over the top.

Shrimp Fried Rice

3 tablespoons oil
4 cloves garlic, minced
1 slice bacon, thinly sliced
8 oz (250 g) fresh shrimp, peeled and deveined
3 eggs, beaten
4 cups (400 g) cooked rice, cooled
2 tablespoons fish sauce
1 tablespoon soy sauce
1/2 tablespoon sugar
1/4 teaspoon white pepper
1/2 cup (75 g) sliced onion
1 green onion (scallion), chopped
2 tablespoons chopped coriander leaves (cilantro)

Accompaniments
Sliced cucumbers
Sliced tomatoes
Chopped green onions (scallions)
Sliced chillies
Fish sauce

Heat a large wok or skillet until smoking and add the oil. Add the garlic and stir-fry for 1 minute or until fragrant. Add the bacon and shrimp and stir-fry for 1 minute or until the shrimp turn pink.

Add the eggs and scramble until cooked. Add the rice, fish and soy sauces, sugar and white pepper. Continue to stir-fry until the rice is hot, reducing the temperature if necessary. Add the onion and green onions.

Garnish with coriander leaves and serve with Accompaniments.

Pad Thai

Fried Rice Stick Noodles with Shrimp

Dried rice-flour noodles are used for this dish, one of the dozens of noodle creations found in Thailand. The pickled Chinese radish is available in cans, usually packed in China.

5 tablespoons oil
1 cake pressed bean curd, diced
5 cloves garlic, minced
5 shallots, minced
1 tablespoon dried shrimp, soaked for 5 minutes in water, drained, lightly pounded or processed
1 tablespoon chopped pickled Chinese radish
10 oz (300 g) dried rice-stick noodles, soaked in warm water to soften, drained well
1 teaspoon dried chili flakes or ground red pepper

3 eggs
2 cups (100 g) bean sprouts
1/4 cup (10 g) garlic chives or spring onions, sliced into lengths
2 tablespoons crushed peanuts
5 oz (150g) fresh shrimp, peeled and deveined, and grilled

Sauce
3 tablespoons shaved palm sugar
3 tablespoons fish sauce
3 tablespoons tamarind pulp soaked in 1/2 cup water, then strained to remove seeds and fibers

Place all the Sauce ingredients in a small saucepan and bring to a boil. Reduce heat and simmer for 3–5 minutes. Remove from heat and set aside.

Heat 3 tablespoons oil in a large pan and stir-fry bean curd till lightly brown, about 5 minutes. Drain and set aside.

Stir-fry garlic and shallots over high heat for 2 minutes. Add dried shrimps and pickled radish and fry for another 3 minutes. Add noodles and bean curd and stir-fry to mix, then add Sauce and dried chili flakes. Continue to stir-fry over medium heat.

Push noodles to one side. Add 2 tablespoons oil, break the eggs into the pan and scramble till cooked, then mix eggs and noodles together.

Add half the bean sprouts and garlic chives or spring onions. Mix together thoroughly and remove from heat.

Serve garnished with the remaining bean sprouts and chives, crushed peanuts and grilled shrimp, if using.

This dish can be prepared in advance by cooking it until the chicken is tender. Add the basil and chilies when reheating the dish just before serving.

Green Chicken Curry with Basil and Eggplant

A fragrant, creamy curry which is always popular. Remove the skin from the chicken if you wish to reduce the fat.

1/2 cup (125 ml) coconut cream
3 tablespoons Green Curry Paste (page 158)
12 oz (375 g) boneless chicken breast, thinly sliced
1 1/2 cups (375 ml) thin coconut milk
2 kaffir lime leaves
1 1/2 tablespoons fish sauce
1 teaspoon sugar
5 oz (150 g) eggplant, cut into bite-sized pieces
1/4 cup (10 g) Thai basil leaves (*horapa*)
2–3 red finger-length chilies, deseeded and cut in strips

Place the coconut cream in a saucepan and heat over low to medium heat until it begins to have an oily sheen. Add the Green Curry Paste and stir well.

Pad Thai (Fried Rice Stick Noodles with Shrimp)

Chicken Wrapped in Pandanus Leaves

Add the chicken and cook until it changes color. Add the coconut milk, kaffir lime leaves, fish sauce and sugar. Bring to a boil, then add the eggplant. Simmer over low heat until the chicken is cooked, about 15 minutes, then add the basil and chilies. Remove from the heat and serve.

Chicken Wrapped in Pandanus Leaves

Fragrant screwpine or pandanus palm leaves add their subtle fragrance to this deep-fried chicken dish, which is the Thai version of the popular Chinese Chee Pow Gai (Paper-wrapped Chicken).

1 lb (500 g) boneless chicken meat
16 pandanus leaves
Oil for deep-frying

Marinade
2 tablespoons soy sauce
1 tablespoon oyster sauce
1 teaspoon sugar
2 teaspoons sesame oil
2 cloves garlic and 3 coriander
    roots, pounded together to a paste

Sauce
1 teaspoon white sesame seeds
1 cup (250 ml) distilled white vinegar
1/2 cup (100 g) sugar
2 tablespoons dark soy sauce
1 teaspoon fish sauce

Cut the chicken meat into bite-sized chunks. Mix the Marinade ingredients well into the chicken. Set aside in the refrigerator to marinate for 3 hours.

To prepare the Sauce, dry-fry the sesame seeds in a skillet for 2 minutes or until lightly browned. Set aside. Mix the remaining Sauce ingredients together in a bowl, then add the sesame seeds and set aside.

Wrap two or three pieces of the chicken in each pandanus leaf to form a knot (see photo). Alternatively, wrap each pandanus leaf around the chicken to form a bundle and secure with a toothpick.

Heat the oil in a wok or small frying pan. Deep-fry the chicken until fragrant, about 5 minutes. Serve with the Sauce and steamed rice.

> If pandanus leaves are not available, add a few drops of pandan essence to the Marinade. Drain the chicken pieces and stir-fry for 5 minutes in 1 tablespoon of oil over medium high heat, and garnish with coriander leaves (cilantro).

Red Chicken Curry with Bamboo Shoots

Fresh bamboo shoots (*naw mai*) are a seasonal delicacy in Thailand, and have a sweetness and texture that cannot quite be matched by the canned variety. However, the latter makes an acceptable substitute, providing a firm contrast to the tender chicken in this curry-style dish.

1/2 cup (125 ml) coconut cream
2 tablespoons Red Curry Paste
    (page 158)

12 oz (375 g) boneless chicken
    meat, cut into bite-sized strips
1 1/2 cups (375 ml) thin coconut milk
10 oz (300 g) bamboo shoots, sliced
2 tablespoons fish sauce
1/4 teaspoon salt
1 1/2 teaspoons sugar
5 kaffir lime leaves, halved
1 red finger-length chili, thinly sliced
1/2 cup (20 g) Thai basil leaves
    (*horapa*)

Bring the coconut cream to a boil in a saucepan over medium heat. Reduce to low heat and simmer, stirring constantly, until the surface takes on an oily sheen. Add the Red Curry Paste and chicken, stir well, and add the coconut milk and bamboo shoots.

Continue to simmer over low heat until the chicken is tender, about 10 minutes, then add the fish sauce, salt, sugar, kaffir lime leaves and chili. Remove from the heat and garnish with the basil.

Roast Duck Curry

Seasoned red-roasted duck sold by Chinese restaurants and food stores is the basis for this richly-flavored curry.

1/2 roasted duck (1 1/2 lbs/750 g)
2 tablespoons Red Curry Paste
    (page 158)
1/2 cup (125 ml) coconut cream

1 1/2 cups (375 ml) thin coconut milk
1 large or 2 small tomatoes, cut in
    wedges
1/2 cup (60 g) seedless grapes or
    diced pineapple (optional)
1 cup (150 g) pea-sized eggplants,
    or 1 small eggplant cut into bite-
    sized chunks
3 kaffir lime leaves
2 tablespoons fish sauce
1 teaspoon sugar
1/2 teaspoon salt
10 Thai basil leaves (*horapa*)
2–4 red or green finger-length
    chilies, cut into strips

Remove all bones from the duck and cut the meat into bite-sized pieces.

Place the coconut cream in a saucepan and heat over medium heat. Add the Red Curry Paste, stirring well.

Add the duck and stir well, then add the coconut milk, tomatoes, eggplant, grapes or pineapple (if using), kaffir lime leaves, fish sauce, sugar and salt. Bring to a boil, then remove from heat.

Sprinkle with the basil leaves and red or green chilies. Serve with plain rice.

> The pea-sized eggplants add a slightly crunchy texture to the smooth curry, while the grapes or pineapple add a tangy sweetness. If the tomatoes are sour, you may need to add slightly more sugar to compensate.

Roast Duck Curry

Mussaman Beef Curry

Spices such as cloves, cardamom and cinnamon were brought to Thailand by Muslim traders from Java, India and Sumatra, and dishes using these are referred to as Mussaman (Muslim) curries. This version from southern Thailand uses the basic Mussaman Curry Paste and other spices.

1/2 cup (125 ml) coconut cream
3 tablespoons Mussaman Curry Paste (page 158)
1 teaspoon oil
1 lb (500 g) beef sirloin
2 cups (500 ml) thin coconut milk
5 cardamom seeds, dry-roasted until fragrant
1 cinnamon stick
2 medium potatoes, peeled and cut into chunks
1 heaped tablespoon unsalted peanuts, chopped
5–10 shallots
3 bay leaves
2 tablespoons chopped palm sugar or dark brown sugar
2 tablespoons fish sauce
3 tablespoons Tamarind Juice (page 18)
Sweet and Spicy Pickled Vegetables (page 159)

Heat the coconut cream in a saucepan over medium heat, add the Mussaman Curry Paste, reduce the heat to low and simmer for 5 minutes. Turn off the heat and set aside.

Heat the oil in a large pot or wok, then add the beef and stir-fry for 8–10 minutes, until almost cooked. Add the coconut milk and bring to a boil. Reduce the heat to low and simmer gently for 10 minutes.

Add all the remaining ingredients and cook until the potatoes and meat are tender. Serve accompanied by Sweet and Spicy Pickled Vegetables and rice.

Grilled Beef with Roasted Eggplant

Although freshly grilled beef is delightful when used for this dish, it is also an ideal way to use up any leftover roast or steak.

8 oz (250 g) Asian eggplants
3 tablespoons oil
10 oz (300 g) uncooked or cooked beef steak

Grilled Beef with Roasted Eggplant

3 shallots, sliced
1/2 cup (20 g) mint leaves or coriander leaves (cilantro)

Sauce
2–5 bird's-eye chilies, sliced
2 tablespoons lime juice
1 1/2 tablespoon fish sauce
1 teaspoon sugar

Roast the eggplants under a broiler or on a grill, turning frequently, until the skins are blackened on all sides and the flesh is soft inside. Slice the eggplants in half, scoop out the flesh, discard the skins, and set aside.

If using uncooked beef, add 1 tablespoon of oil to the pan and stir-fry the steak over high heat until brown on both sides, about 3 minutes.

Fry the shallots in a separate pan in 2 tablespoons of oil over medium heat until brown and crisp, about 2 mintues. Drain and set aside.

Thinly slice the beef steak, combine with the eggplant and the Sauce ingredients, and mix well. Top with the fried shallots and serve at room temperature with white rice.

> If Asian eggplants are unavailable, Mediterranean eggplants may be used. Cut the eggplants into bite-sized pieces and stir-fry in 2 tablespoons of oil over high heat in a skillet or wok.

Red Pork Curry

Pork is the most popular meat in Thailand, prepared in many different ways. This is a very simple, quickly prepared curry.

1/2 cup (125 ml) coconut cream
1 tablespoon Red Curry Paste (page 158)
12 oz (375 g) pork tenderloin (pork fillet), cut into bite-sized slices
1/3 cup (90 ml) pea-sized eggplants
1 1/2 cups (375 ml) thin coconut milk
1 1/2 tablespoons fish sauce
1 teaspoon sugar
5 kaffir lime leaves, halved

Red Pork Curry

1 red finger-length chili, thinly sliced
1/2 cup (20 g) Thai basil leaves (*horapa*)

Bring the coconut cream to a boil in a saucepan over medium heat, stirring constantly. Add the Red Curry Paste, pork, eggplant and coconut milk. Stir well and simmer over low heat until done, about 15 minutes.

Add the fish sauce, sugar, kaffir lime leaves and chili. Stir and heat through, then remove from the heat and garnish with the basil.

> If pork tenderloin is not available, use any other lean cut of pork.

Barbecued Chicken

Barbecued Chicken

A northeastern version of a dish now served all over the country.

1 chicken (2¼ lbs/1 kg), cut in serving pieces
1 tablespoon finely sliced ginger

Marinade
10 cloves garlic, minced
1–2 tablespoons black peppercorns, crushed
2 tablespoons soy sauce
2 tablespoons sugar
2 tablespoons brandy or dry sherry
1 teaspoon salt

Sweet Thai Chili Sauce
½ cup (125 ml) distilled white vinegar
½ cup (100 g) sugar
5 cloves garlic, minced
2–3 red finger-lenght chilies, pounded or minced
½ teaspoon salt

Mix the Marinade ingredients in a bowl. Add the chicken and combine thoroughly with the Marinade. Set aside in the refrigerator for 3–4 hours.

Grill the chicken over hot charcoal or under a broiler, turning from time to time until browned on all sides, about 25–30 minutes.

Meanwhile, mix all the Sweet Thai Chili Sauce ingredients in a saucepan, bring to a boil and simmer until the sauce has a thin, syrupy consistency. Set aside to cool.

Serve the chicken and Sweet Thai Chili Sauce accompanied by plain or glutinous rice and Green Papaya Salad (page 160).

Sweet Thai Chilli Sauce is widely available bottled.

Chicken Stir-fried with Chili and Basil

This dish is normally prepared with chicken, but frogs' legs can also be used. Frogs are sometimes euphemistically called "paddy chickens." Their flavor is delicate and similar to chicken.

1 tablespoon oil
10 oz (300 g) boneless chicken thighs, deboned and cut into bite-sized chunks or frogs' legs, cleaned and skinned
1 tablespoon green peppercorns
2–3 red finger-length chilies, sliced lengthwise
3 in (8 cm) young galangal root, very finely sliced
2 teaspoons fish sauce
½ teaspoon chopped palm sugar or dark brown sugar
Large handful Thai basil leaves (*horapa*)

Heat the oil in a wok until very hot. Add the chicken chunks or frogs' legs and peppercorns and stir-fry over high heat for a couple of minutes. Add the chilies, galangal, fish sauce and sugar. Mix well and cook for another minute. Stir in the basil and remove from the heat.

Serve accompanied by rice.

Dry Beef Curry

A southern style of cooking beef, hot and fragrant with typically Indian spices. The use of palm sugar, peanuts and kaffir lime leaves, however, is distinctly Thai.

1 tablespoon coriander seeds and 2 teaspoons cumin seeds, ground in a mortar and pestle or spice grinder
3 tablespoons Mussaman Curry Paste (page 158)
½ cup (125 ml) coconut cream
12 oz (375 g) beef sirloin, cut into thin strips
1½ cups (375 ml) thin coconut milk
½ cup (90 g) roasted peanuts, crushed
1½–2 tablespoons fish sauce
3 tablespoons chopped palm sugar or dark brown sugar
6 kaffir lime leaves, torn in half
1 red finger-length chili, thinly sliced

Mix the ground coriander and cumin with the Mussaman Curry Paste. Heat the coconut cream in a large pot or wok until some of the oil surfaces. Add the curry paste, reduce the heat and slowly bring to a boil, stirring constantly.

Put in the beef strips and cook for 5 minutes, then add the coconut milk and the rest of the ingredients, except for the kaffir lime leaves and chili. Simmer over low heat for 30 minutes, stirring frequently, until the meat is tender, and the oil has come out of the coconut milk.

Add the kaffir lime leaves and chili, remove from the heat and serve with white rice.

Garlic Fried Squid

1 lb (500 g) fresh squid
2 tablespoons oil
½ cup (100 g) minced garlic
1 teaspoon black peppercorns, crushed
1 tablespoon oyster sauce
½ tablespoon soy sauce
1 teaspoon fish sauce
1 teaspoon sugar
Coriander leaves (cilantro)

Remove the tentacles from the squid and cut out and discard the hard beak portion. Remove the skin from the body of the squid. Butterfly the squid by making a lengthwise cut along the body of the squid. Clean the inside and score the flesh by making diagonal criss-cross slits

Dry Beef Curry

across the surface. This allows the squid to cook very quickly inside without becoming rubbery. Slice into bite-sized pieces. Dry thoroughly and set aside.

Heat the oil in a wok over medium heat. Fry the garlic until golden-brown, then add the squid and its tentacles, together with the seasonings.

Stir-fry for 3–4 minutes, stirring constantly until the squid turns white or starts to curl. Do not overcook. Serve hot sprinkled with coriander leaves.

> Be sure to use fresh and not frozen squid, as the latter exudes water when cooked, making it stew rather than fry.

Crabs with Glass Noodles in Claypot

Cooking in a claypot is southern Chinese in origin. One popular version in Thailand uses either crab claws or whole crabs cut into serving pieces. Although slices of pork fat are normally used, bacon improves the flavor of an already tasty dish.

2 whole crabs (about 2 lbs/1kg)
1 tablespoon oil
7 cloves garlic, peeled and left whole
2 slices lean bacon, cut into pieces
2 coriander roots, cut in half
2 in (5 cm) ginger, sliced
1 teaspoon white peppercorns, crushed
8 oz (250 g) dried glass noodles (bean thread or cellophane noodles) soaked in cold water to soften for 5 minutes and drained

1 teaspoon butter
1 tablespoon soy sauce
2 green onions (scallions), cut in lengths
1 sprig coriander leaves (cilantro)

Stock
2 cups (500 ml) Thai Chicken Stock (page 158)
2 tablespoons oyster sauce
1 tablespoon soy sauce
2 teaspoons fish sauce
1 teaspoon sesame oil
2 teaspoons brandy or whisky
2 teaspoons sugar

Place all the Stock ingredients in a pan, bring to a boil and simmer for 5 minutes. Remove from the heat and set aside to cool.

Clean each crab by scrubbing it briskly with a brush. (If still alive, make sure the pincers are tied securely.) Rinse well with cold water. Using a cleaver or a heavy knife, cut the crab in half, then halve it again. Chop off the pincers, crack them and set aside. Remove the shell, scrape it out and set aside any roe.

Heat the oil in a large claypot or heatproof casserole. Stir-fry the garlic over high heat till lightly brown. Add the bacon and stir-fry for one minute. Add the crab, coriander roots, ginger and peppercorns. Stir-fry for 3 minutes.

Add the glass noodles, butter, soy sauce and Chicken Stock. Mix well, cover and cook over high heat for 15–20 minutes or until crabs are cooked. Stir in the green onions and garnish with coriander leaves. Serve hot.

Crabs with Glass Noodles in Claypot

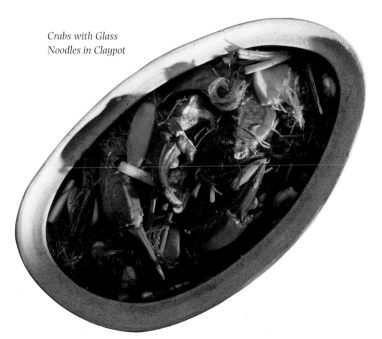

Mussels Steamed with Fragrant Thai Basil

Mussels Steamed with Fragrant Thai Basil

Beautiful orange-fleshed, green-lipped mussels contrast with green basil leaves in this simple but excellent seafood dish.

4 lbs (2 kgs) fresh mussels in their shells, soaked and cleaned well
Large handful of thai basil leaves (*horapa*)

Dipping Sauce
1/2 cup (125 ml) lime juice
2 tablespoons fish sauce
1 teaspoon sugar
2 coriander roots, chopped
2 cloves garlic, crushed
1/2 cup (125 ml) water

Place the mussels in a steamer over boiling water and sprinkle with the basil leaves. Steam for 10 minutes or until all the mussels are cooked and open. Remove from the heat and wait for 2 minutes before opening the steamer.

Mix the Dipping Sauce ingredients together, bring to a boil, then set aside to cool.

Serve the mussels accompanied by the Dipping Sauce.

> Leaving the mussels to sit covered for a couple of minutes after steaming helps the flavor of basil to permeate the mussels.

Fried Fish with Chili Shrimp Paste Sauce

4 cups (1 liter) oil for deep-frying
1 whole fish weighing about 2 lbs (1 kg), or 2 smaller fish

Chili Shrimp Paste Sauce
5–10 dried red chilies, soaked in water, deseeded and chopped
1/2 cup (100 g) minced garlic
1/2 cup (50 g) sliced shallots
1/2 tablespoon dried shrimp paste (*kapee*)
3 tablespoons oil
1 teaspoon fish sauce
1 teaspoon sugar
4–5 kaffir lime leaves, finely sliced

Scale and gut the fish thoroughly, leaving the head on. Make cuts about 1/2 in (1 cm) apart along the back of the fish to give it a decorative appearance.

To make the Chili Shrimp Paste Sauce, heat 3 tablespoons of oil in a wok over high heat and fry the chilies, garlic, shallots and dried shrimp paste until fragrant, then add the fish sauce and sugar. Fry for another 1–2 minutes and set aside.

Dry the fish thoroughly, then deep-fry in very hot oil until cooked. Serve the fish topped with the Chili Shrimp Paste Sauce and sprinkled with shredded kaffir lime leaves.

Grilled Shrimp with Sweet and Sour Sauce

2–3 lbs (1–1$^{1}/_{2}$ kgs) shrimp, crayfish or lobsters
Aluminum foil or banana leaf

Sweet and Sour Sauce
3 tablespoons tamarind pulp
$^{1}/_{2}$ cup (125 ml) water
2–3 tablespoons sugar
Pinch of salt
1–2 tablespoons minced garlic
2–3 bird's-eye chilies or 1–2 red
  finger-length chilies, minced
1–2 teaspoons chopped fresh coriander leaves (cilantro)
1 teaspoon fish sauce
1 teaspoon lime juice (optional)

Prepare the Sweet and Sour Sauce
first. In a bowl, mix the tamarind
pulp with the water, mashing
gently and removing any seeds
and fibers. Transfer to a pan, add
the sugar and bring to a boil.
Lower the heat and simmer, stirring constantly until thick and
syrupy. Turn off the heat, add the
salt and stir well. Remove from the
heat and allow to cool, then strain
the mixture. Add the remaining
ingredients to the strained mixture and mix thoroughly.
  Clean the shrimp or crayfish
and wrap each securely in foil or
banana leaf. Grill over a hot

charcoal fire or under a broiler
for about 12 minutes. Serve
with the Sweet and Sour Sauce.

Stuffed Crabs

Use either mud crabs or blue
swimmer crabs for this dish. The
Stuffing can be prepared in
advance and the crabs stuffed
and deep-fried just before serving.

4 crab shells for stuffing
3 eggs, well beaten
5 cups (1$^{1}/_{4}$ liters) oil
1 tablespoon minced coriander
  leaves (cilantro)
2 red finger-length chilies, to garnish

Stuffing
6 oz (175 g) ground pork
$^{1}/_{2}$ cup (125 g) fresh shrimp, finely
  chopped
$^{1}/_{2}$ cup (60 g) fresh crabmeat
1 tablespoon finely minced onion
1 tablespoon minced green onions
  (scallions)
1 teaspoon ground white pepper
1 teaspoon sugar
$^{1}/_{4}$ teaspoon soy sauce
$^{1}/_{4}$ teaspoon salt

Mix all the Stuffing ingredients
together and fill the crab shells.
  Heat the oil in a deep
saucepan, dip the stuffed crabs
in the beaten egg to coat them
well and then deep-fry for about

10–15 minutes until cooked.
  Remove from the heat and
drain on paper towels. Sprinkle
with coriander leaves (cilantro)
and chilies before serving.

> If using cooked crabs, remove
> the backs carefully and discard
> any spongy matter. Wash the
> backs and set aside. Remove
> the crabmeat from the body,
> legs and claws and measure
> out $^{1}/_{2}$ cup (60 g), keeping the
> rest aside for another dish. If
> using raw crabs, steam first,
> then prepare as directed above.

Clams with Basil and Shrimp Chili Paste

Clams with Basil and Shrimp Chili Paste

Use any type of clams for this
emphatic, quickly prepared dish.
It's worth hunting for Thai basil
(*horapa*), as it makes a definite
difference to the flavor of the
clams.

3 tablespoons oil
2 lbs (1 kg) clams in their shells,
  soaked and cleaned well
2 tablespoons minced garlic
2–3 red finger-length chilies, sliced
  lengthwise
3 tablespoons Shrimp Chili Paste
  (page 158)
2 teaspoons soy sauce
$^{1}/_{2}$ cup (125 ml) Thai Chicken Stock
  (page 158)
Large handful of Thai basil leaves
  (*horapa*)

Heat the oil in a wok over high
heat, add the clams and garlic
and stir-fry for 2–3 minutes
until the clams open slightly.
Add the sliced chilies, Shrimp
Chili Paste and soy sauce, stir
well, then add the Chicken
Stock. Simmer for 5 minutes.
Scoop out the clams and leave
the stock in the wok to simmer
on high heat for 3–5 minutes.
  Add the basil and pour the
sauce over the clams.
  Serve immediately, accompanied by rice.

> Soak the clams in several
> changes of water for $^{1}/_{2}$ hour or
> so before cooking to ensure
> they are thoroughly clean.

Grilled Shrimp with Sweet and Sour Sauce

What Westerners may called desserts are usually eaten between meals as fillers. Rice and tapioca flours, sticky rice, coconut milk, a twist of pan-dan leaf, and palm sugar are indispensable ingredients.

Red Ruby Chestnuts in Sweet Coconut Cream (top), Bananas in Sweet Coconut Milk (bottom)

Bananas in Sweet Coconut Milk

2 cups (500 ml) thin coconut milk
1/2 cup (100 g) sugar
1/4 teaspoon salt
8 small or 4 large ripe bananas, cut diagonally in slices

Pour the coconut milk into a saucepan, then add the sugar and salt. Bring gently to a boil over low heat, stirring constantly to prevent the coconut milk from separating.

Add the bananas, and cook over low heat for 5 minutes. Remove from the heat and serve hot or cold.

Steamed Sweet Pumpkin Custard

A visually intriguing dessert where a rich coconut-milk custard is steamed inside a small pumpkin or acorn squashes.

5 eggs
1 cup (250 ml) coconut cream
1 cup (185 g) chopped palm sugar or dark brown sugar
1 small pumpkin, about 8 in (20 cm) in diameter, or 2 acorn squashes

Beat the eggs with the coconut cream and sugar until the mixture is frothy.

Cut the top off the pumpkin or acorn squashes and carefully scoop out the seeds and any fibers. Pour in the coconut cream mixture, cover with the top of the pumpkin or squashes and place in a steamer. Cover the steamer and place over boiling water.

Steam over medium heat for about 30 minutes or until the mixture has set. Leave to cool (preferably refrigerate) and cut in thick slices to serve.

Duck eggs add richness and a firmer texture to the custard. If using palm sugar, strain the custard through a sieve before pouring into the pumpkin to remove any impurities.

Deep-fried Bananas with Coconut

These bananas are rolled in a mixture of grated coconut and palm sugar before being dipped in batter and deep-fried.

1 cup (100 g) freshly grated coconut
2/3 cup (110 g) chopped palm sugar
14 small ripe finger bananas or 5–6 large ripe bananas, sliced into 2–3 sections
5 cups (1 1/4 liters) oil, for deep-frying

Batter
2 cups (250 g) glutinous rice flour
1 cup (250 ml) thin coconut milk
1/2 cup (125 ml) water
1 egg, lightly beaten
1 tablespoon sesame seeds

Combine the coconut and palm sugar and cook for 15 minutes in a nonstick pan over low heat, stirring frequently. Set aside. Mix the Batter ingredients and let it stand for 3 hours.

Just before serving, heat the oil in a deep saucepan, roll each banana in the coconut-palm sugar mixture, then dip in the Batter and fry in very hot oil until golden brown. Serve hot.

Red Ruby Chestnuts in Sweet Coconut Cream

1 cup (240 g) diced water chestnut morsels
Few drops red food coloring
1/2 cup (60 g) tapioca starch (tapioca flour)
5 cups (1 1/4 liters) water
Crushed ice

Sweet Coconut Milk
1/2 cup (100 g) sugar
3/4 cup (180 ml) water
3/4 cup (180 ml) thick coconut milk

Sprinkle the water chestnut morsels with a few drops of red food coloring and toss until bright red. Put the tapioca starch in a plastic bag, add the water chestnuts and shake until thoroughly coated.

Put the water chestnut morsels and tapioca starch in a colander or sieve and shake until excess flour falls away. Bring 5 cups water to a boil in a pot. Add the water chestnut morsels and simmer for 3 minutes. Drain the water chestnuts and plunge into cold water. Drain again and set aside.

To make the Sweet Coconut Milk, boil the sugar and water in a saucepan over high heat for 3 minutes. Set aside to cool, then add the coconut milk and stir.

To serve, put a little of the water chestnut rubies into dessert dishes and add some of the Sweet Coconut Milk and crushed ice. Additional slices of ripe jackfruit or young coconut may be added if desired.

If you cannot obtain glutinous rice flour, you can make the paste directly from glutinous rice. To make the paste, soak 1 1/2 cups (300 g) uncooked glutinous rice in water for 5 hours. Drain and transfer the rice to a blender. Add 3/4 cup (180 ml) water and grind till a thick liquid mixture forms. Pour the mixture into a fine muslin cloth and drain until the water is gone. Knead the remaining paste to form a dough, adding small amounts of water if needed. You may add canned sweet corn kernels and cooked, colored diced water chestnut (prepared as for Red Ruby Chestnut in Sweet Coconut, page 168) to this dish for a more varied and colorful dessert.

Steamed Sweet Pumpkin Custard

"The land of the Perfume River has been blessed with an astonishing variety of foods from the earth and from the water."

VIETNAM

Not only is Vietnam the site of an economic revival but its great culinary tradition is re-emerging too.

Left: The quiet journey home from market.

Right: A simple but refined meal in Hué, once the political center and today still an important culinary city.

With lengths of unspoiled dramatic coastline, sheltered harbors, well-irrigated lowlands and vast forests, Vietnam is a remarkably beautiful and fertile land, rich in agricultural resources.

It is also a country in the process of change; with the start of a new millenium, a great sense of optimism hangs in the air. The effects of *doi moi*, the economic reform policy allowing small-scale private enterprise, introduced by the communist government in 1986, are becoming more and more evident. The accumulation of personal wealth is now encouraged.

The food markets are a hive of activity: these days produce is trucked in from nearby villages, coastal waters, and the central highlands. Throughout the day, crowds of people fill their baskets from the rows of fresh vegetables and tropical fruits, live fish and game, pickled meats and vegetables, candied fruit, dried and packaged goods, rice, and bottles of pungent *nuoc mam* fish sauce.

The Land and its People

Vietnam is fortunate in being able to grow a diverse variety of vegetables and fruits throughout the country and little food is imported. Rice and seafood are in abundant supply, due in part to its location on the eastern coast of the southeast Asian Indochinese peninsula and a 1600-mile coastline. It boasts countless dykes, canals, and waterways, which include the Red River, the Perfume River, and the Mekong River, one of the longest rivers in Southeast Asia.

Vietnam shares its border with China, Laos, and Cambodia. In the cooler northern region, where undulating limestone hills recall southwest China and where many of Vietnam's ethnic groups have their homes, the cuisine shares distinct similarities with Chinese food.

The center of the country is less agriculturally rich, and in the temperate south, the cuisine more closely resembles that of neighboring Southeast Asian countries, such as Thailand and Malaysia.

The food of the south is more varied and rich than that of Hué or Hanoi, and generously spiced.

The Red River Delta in the north and the Mekong Delta in the south are the two main rice-growing areas, although lush green rice paddies dotted with water buffalo and rows of women with their distinctive conical hats can be seen throughout the country. Sixty percent of arable land in Vietnam is given over to rice production, leaving little pasture for cattle farming. Hence beef, in particular, is a luxury for most Vietnamese, and the famous series of dishes, *bo bay mon* (literally, beef done seven ways), is highly regarded.

In spite of urbanization and increasingly populated cities, roughly 80 percent of the population relies on rice for its livelihood. Rice is used in a diverse range of dishes and in the production of wine and vinegar. The grains are also converted into flour and used to make rice noodles and transformed into rice paper sheets for *goi cuon*, the Vietnamese fresh spring rolls. Glutinous rice cooked overnight, then wrapped into attractive banana leaf parcels, becomes breakfast-time *xoi* or the traditional *banh tay* and *banh chung* eaten during Tet, the Vietnamese Lunar New Year holiday.

The Making of a Cuisine

The Vietnamese people have a history of foreign influences, from neighbors, sojourners and settlers, all of whom have left their mark: Malay, Chinese, Indian, Thai, French, and American. The Chinese offered their use of tofu,

Markets throughout Vietnam sell an extensive variety of fresh herbs and vegetables, which form the basis of the nation's distinctive cuisine.

soy beans, and spices such as star anise. The use of dill in *cha ca*, Hanoi's famous fish dish served at the popular Cha Ca La Vong restaurant, and also in fish congee, could have been a French influence. The Indians left their ground rice pancakes.

At the heart of Vietnamese cuisine is the salty, pale brown fermented fish sauce known as *nuoc mam*. The cuisines of Cambodia, Thailand and Burma use a similar sauce, however, the Vietnamese variety seems to have a particularly pungent flavor. *Nuoc mam* is made by layering fresh anchovies with salt in huge wooden barrels, a process that takes about six months and involves pouring the liquid which drips from the barrel back over the anchovies. Arguably, the best *nuoc mam* comes from the island of Phu Quoc near the Cambodian border.

Nuoc mam cham, the ubiquitous dip made of *nuoc mam* diluted with lime juice, vinegar, water, crushed garlic, and fresh red chilies is used as a dipping sauce at the table, served with dishes like *cha gio* (spring rolls) and *chao tom* (sugar cane shrimp), or simply as a dip for pieces of fish or meat.

What sets Vietnamese cuisine apart from that of other Southeast Asian countries is the pervasive use of fresh leaves and herbs, mak-

ing it lighter and more refreshing than, say, Thai food. Its use of crisp, uncooked vegetables, subtle seasonings, raw herbs and unique flavor combinations—sharp, sweet and fresh and fragrant at the same time—is unforgettable.

While Vietnamese restaurants in other regions of the world rarely manage to offer more than one kind of mint, basil or cilantro, markets throughout Vietnam sell a remarkable array of such herbs, as well as leaves such as the deep-red, spicy perilla leaf, *tia to*, and the pungent saw-leaf herb (long coriander).

Fresh herbs turn up in all sorts of dishes. Soup kitchens serving the glorious noodle soup *pho* also offer a huge plate of raw herbs to be stirred into the steaming soup. The herbs are also served with *ban xeo*, a kind of crêpe enclosing shrimp, pork, mung beans, and bean sprouts, and with spring rolls or grilled meats, and in salads.

Other factors that contribute to the subtlety and uniqueness of Vietnamese food are the refined cooking techniques, the often unusual serving of varying dishes and the combination of flavors.

Imperial Cuisine

Hué, situated on the banks of the tranquil Perfume River, was once an important seat of learning and culture, as well as the imperial seat for nearly 150 years.

To satisfy jaded imperial palates, but lacking in the agricultural diversity of either the north or the south, the imperial kitchens at Hué had to show an enormous amount of ingenuity by refining ordinary dishes until they became something truly special, so that eating could be viewed as art, ritual and sensory pleasure at the same time.

A typical imperial banquet today would include up to a dozen dishes, such as a beautifully fragrant, peppery chicken soup with lotus seeds (*sup ga*), crisp, golden brown spring rolls (*nem ran*), delicate rice flour patties stuffed with minced shrimp (*banh Hué*), grilled pork in rice paper (*thit nuong*) served with a tasty peanut sauce, delicious crab claws stuffed with pork (*cua phich bot*), and the famous minced shrimp wrapped around sugar cane (*cha tom lui mia* or *chao tom*). Main dishes might include fish grilled in banana leaf (*ca nuong la chuoi*), pungent beef in wild betel leaves (*bo la lot*), rice with vegetables (*com Hué*), gently sautéed shrimp with mushrooms (*tom xao hanh nam*), and finally the glutinous rice dessert husband-and-wife cake (*phu the*), which comes in a perfectly formed little box made from pandan leaf.

These dishes are actually variations of those served in other parts of Vietnam, and the ingredients may be vegetables, eggs or fish, rather than exotic sea delicacies or the best cuts of meat. What sets these dishes apart is the sophisticated cooking techniques and the careful presentation.

For example, the favorite *chao tom lui mia* seems so simple—if only! Tiny shrimp are carefully shelled, then marinated in *nuoc mam*. They are then pounded until they form a thick paste, and egg white, onion, garlic, sugar, and pepper added. The mixture is pounded again with a touch of pork fat, and finally wrapped around sugar cane sticks and grilled.

The presentation of food was—and is—very important, not only in the use of color and the arrangement of food on the plate, but also in the manner of serving. Rice, for example, might be draped with an omelet coat, or cooked inside a lotus leaf and further enhanced with the addition of delicate lotus seeds.

Portions are delicate, since perhaps dozens of dishes are served in the course of a meal. All these naturally increased the length of preparation time, with the result that the number of cooks and kitchen staff reached unprecedented heights—a luxury which perfectly befitted the privileged life of an emperor.

The most talented proponents of imperial cuisine today are virtually all women, each of them descended by some route or other from imperial households. Due to its size and relatively small population, Hué today is not a culinary mecca compared with Ho Chi Minh City or Hanoi. There is, however, a renewed interest in the cuisine of Hué, and a number of modern Vietnamese chefs have made it their mission to turn the simple art of cooking into something extraordinary.

The Food of the People

Through the more than four troubled decades of constant struggle and fighting in Vietnam, there was barely enough rice to go around,

let alone interest in what to buy at the market and how to perfect a particular recipe. But since the mid-1980s, a combination of economic upturn and the return of many overseas Vietnamese (encouraged by the government to start new businesses) has resulted in, among other things, the rebirth of a thriving restaurant scene.

Culinary skills are being relearned, courses for the training of professional chefs are being launched and the Vietnamese are once again discovering the joys of cooking. Top-quality, fresh ingredients are widely available.

All over Ho Chi Minh City and, to a slightly lesser extent, in Hanoi, restaurants are built around courtyards in French colonial buildings or designed to resemble old Vietnamese family homes. French restaurants are once again establishing themselves and fashionable Italian restaurants are making an appearance.

Vietnamese cuisine is based on rice, fish, and fresh vegetables. Little oil is used in cooking, except for deep-frying, and salads are lightly dressed. Healthy, invigorating soups such as the tasty *canh chua thom ca loc* are featured on menus, fresh fruit and delicious home-made yogurts are often served for dessert, and drinks like freshly squeezed sugar cane juice are widely available.

Modern Vietnamese cuisine is a marriage of the old and the new. Recipes from past generations are coupled with new dishes created for the increasingly sophisticated and well-traveled local consumer. A good example is *thit kho to*, pork cooked slowly in a claypot, a dish of peasant origins that now appears on restaurant menus alongside *cua rang me*, a fried crab dish richly perfumed with tamarind.

Baguettes at a food stall are a reminder of Vietnam's colonial past.

The sometimes lengthy preparation times and cooking processes required by Vietnamese cuisine can render it something of a luxury for people with busy lives, so many chefs and teachers within Vietnam have begun experimenting with new and innovative methods that preserve the spirit of the cuisine, but allow it to be prepared quickly and simply at home.

As this move towards quicker cooking has been evolving, there has also been a resurgence of interest in the traditional dishes of the Hué court. While more attention is being paid to the presentation of food, very few changes, if any, are made to cater to the tourist trade. What changes are occurring in the recipes are subtle and often imperceptible: *ga bop*, a chicken salad flavored with onion, *rau ram* (*laksa* leaf or polygonum) and a simple seasoning of salt, pepper, and lime juice, has traditionally been made with chicken skin and bones, but new restaurants are preparing it with lean chicken meat.

The Vietnamese Table and Kitchen

Eating in Vietnam is a shared experience, an informal ritual. On the small table that the family has gathered around is a large bowl of steaming rice, a cauldron of aromatic soup, a meat dish, a vegetable dish, and a generous plate of leaves for each diner to wrap around a delicious hand roll and dip into the *nuoc mam cham*. Tea is drunk throughout the meal.

The adage "the fresher the ingredients, the better the food," is especially true of Vietnamese cooking. The various herbs and lettuces are almost always served raw, and salads are never overdressed, so that the full flavors are present. Vegetables and fish in particular, which make up a large part of the Vietnamese diet, are gently cooked and lightly seasoned, allowing the true flavors of the food to come through.

The home and its kitchen are central to Vietnamese culture. A week before *Tet*, the god of the hearth (*Tao Quan*) must be supplicated with a ceremony performed in the kitchen, where offerings of fruit, paper models of luxury consumer goods and a ceremonial costume are placed on the altar.

Traditional Vietnamese cooks generally squat, feet tucked beneath them, preparing much of their food on the floor around the stove on a wet, tiled area, where all utensils, pots, pans, and food items are cleaned before use. Even as incomes gradually increase and some of the modern conveniences (refrigerators, plumbed sinks, built-in work surfaces, and electric rice cookers) are making their way into a number of Vietnamese kitchens, much of the preparation and cooking is still done in the traditional manner.

Most of the cooking is done over an open hearth (ovens are not used), with one member of the family on duty to fan the flames. A wok is still the most versatile implement in any Vietnamese kitchen, usually set over a wood fire. Grilling is another common cooking method. A large pot is standard for soups and stocks, and since rice is the staple, a simple rice cooker with its lid is usually steaming away on a low fire.

As in other countries, food stalls are a popular haunt, both for local gossip and a quick meal, and usually appear on the sidewalks in front of old shophouses. Clusters of tiny chairs and tables surround a steaming hot cauldron of soup set on an open flame, with people huddled over their morning bowl of restorative *pho*. At another streetside restaurant, a team of busy female chefs is busy making open-faced omelets in blackened pans over small charcoal grills. Or it may be vendors with carts filled with baguettes, cheese, sliced pâté, and sausages making sandwiches. It's all in a day's work.

The result of time-consuming preparation is a memorable dining experience.

SUGGESTED MENUS

Family meals

- Fresh Rice Flour Rolls
  (page 177);
- Marinated Grilled Squid
  (page 184)
- Stir- Fried Vegetables with Fish
  Sauce (page 182) and
- Pork Stewed in Coconut Juice
  (page 185) served with rice;
- Pineapple Tartlets (page 187)

Or, lead off with the
- Sweet Sour Fish Soup
  (page 182); followed by
- Shrimp and Green Mango
  Salad (page 179), Tofu with
  Lemongrass and Five Spice
  (page 182) and Grilled Pork
  Meatballs (page 185) served
  with rice;
- Banana Coconut Cake
  (page 187) is a popular way
  to finish.

A dinner party

Most of the recipes in the appetizers section lend themselves readily to dinner-party nibbles, so try serving
- a selection of fried and steamed rice paper rolls (page 177) with a few dipping sauces;
- Cabbage Salad with Chicken and Herbs (page 180)
- Yellow Spinach with Yellow Bean Sauce (page 181), Spicy Jumbo Shrimp (page 183) and a Fragrant Beef Stew (page 186) served with rice;
- Pineapple Tartlets (page 187) and vanilla ice cream.

One-pot meals

The noodle soups of Vietnam deserve honorable mention, so for breakfast, lunch or dinner, do as the locals do and try one of the following:
- Chicken Noodle Soup (page 180);
- Beef Noodle Soup (page 180);
- Grilled Pork Skewers with Rice Noodles (page 185). Very satisfying!

A melting pot menu

- Vegetables Simmered in Dashi and Sake (page 102) from Japan;
- Gung Bao Chicken from China (page 44) and from Vietnam, Whole Fish with Ginger Lemongrass Sauce (page 184), served with rice and a simple salad or stir-fried vegetables;
- freshly sliced seasonal fruits, such as mangoes or pineapple.

THE ESSENTIAL FLAVORS OF VIETNAMESE COOKING

The key to Vietnamese cuisine is freshness, so choose the best of available herbs and leaves for the table salad: **laksa leaf** (*daun kesum*), **lettuces**, **beansprouts**, **basil**, and **cilantro**. These also accompany rice paper rolls. **Chilies** are sliced into **nuoc mam** for dipping sauces. Flavorings widely used include **garlic**, **lemongrass**, **shallots**, and **green onions (scallions)**. **Rice** is a must.

Sweet and Sour Sauce

1 tablespoon oil
3 cloves garlic, minced
2 tablespoons sliced shallot
2 pickled shallots or baby onions, sliced
1 cup (100 g) diced carrot
1 cup (100 g) diced bell pepper
1 finger-length red chili, deseeded and minced
2 tablespoons sugar
1/4 teaspoon salt
1/4 teaspoon ground white pepper
1 teaspoon tomato ketchup
1/4 cup (60 ml) vinegar
1 tablespoon cornstarch mixed with 1 teaspoon of water

Heat the oil in a skillet over medium heat and stir-fry the garlic until golden brown and fragrant, 1 to 2 minutes. Add the shallots, carrot, bell pepper and chili, and continue stir-frying for 1 to 2 minutes. Season with the sugar, salt and pepper, followed by the Tomato Sauce and vinegar. Bring the mixture to a boil and thicken with the cornstarch mixture. Reduce the heat to low, simmer for 1 minute and remove from the heat.

Caramel Syrup

1 cup (250 ml) water
1 cup (185 g) shaved palm sugar or dark brown sugar

Bring the water and sugar slowly to a boil over low heat, then simmer, stirring continuously, until the mixture turns dark brown, about 20 minutes. Remove from the heat and dilute with 2 tablespoons of water.

Carrot and Daikon Radish Pickles

1 tablespoon salt
1 cup (100 g) shredded carrot
1 cup (175 g) sliced daikon radish
2 tablespoons sugar
1/4 cup (60 ml) white vinegar

Rub the salt onto the carrot and daikon, and set aside for 10 minutes, then rinse and drain. Gently squeeze the vegetables until dry. Combine the dried vegetables, sugar and vinegar in a bowl, and toss to mix well. Allow to marinate for at least 2 hours before serving. This pickles is at its best when served chilled.

Fish Sauce Dip

1/4 cup (60 ml) water
1 teaspoon rice vinegar
3 teaspoons sugar
1 finger-length red chili, deseeded and minced
2 cloves garlic, crushed
1 tablespoon lime juice
2 tablespoons fish sauce

Bring the water or coconut juice, vinegar and sugar to a boil in a saucepan. Remove and set aside to cool. Combine with the chili, garlic and lime juice, mix well and stir in the fish sauce. For a variation, add some grated carrot or Carrot and

Peanut Sauce

2 teaspoons oil
1 clove garlic, sliced
4 oz (100 g) pork or chicken livers
1 tablespoon sliced red chili
1/2 cup (125 ml) Yellow Bean Sauce (recipe on this page)
1 stalk lemongrass, tender inner part of bottom third only, sliced
1/4 cup (60 ml) thick coconut milk
1 teaspoon sugar
1 teaspoon salt
2 tablespoons Tamarind Juice (page 18)
1 cup (100 g) ground roasted unsalted peanuts

Heat the oil in a skillet over medium heat and stir-fry the garlic until fragrant, 1 to 2 minutes. Add all the other ingredients and 1/2 of the coconut milk and bring to a boil. Remove from the heat and set aside to cool. Blend the mixture in a blender, adding the remaining coconut milk, until smooth. Transfer to a serving bowl and serve immediately or store in a sealed jar in the refrigerator. Daikon Radish Pickles (recipe on this page) to the dip.

Yellow Bean Sauce

3/4 cup (120 g) dried yellow soy beans, boiled and drained
2 tablespoons thick coconut milk
2 tablespoons ground roasted unsalted peanuts
2 teaspoons sugar
3 cloves garlic
1 finger-length red chili, deseeded
2 tablespoons sliced lemongrass (tender inner part of bottom third only)
1 cup (125 ml) water
2 tablespoons oil

Grind all the ingredients, except the oil, in a blender until smooth. Heat the oil in a skillet over medium heat and stir-fry the mixture until fragrant, then simmer for about 2 minutes and remove from the heat. Store in a sealed jar in the refrigerator.

Shrimp and Pork Salad Rolls

1/2 cup (125 ml) water
2 teaspoons white vinegar
1 tablespoon rice wine or sherry
1/2 teaspoon salt
1 lb (500 g) fresh medium shrimp
2 tablespoons oil
7 oz (200 g) pork loin
12 dried rice paper wrappers (each 8 in/20 cm in diameter)
1/2 small head butter lettuce leaves, washed and separated
1 cup (40 g) Asian basil leaves
1 cup (40 g) mint leaves
2 finger-length red chilies, deseeded and thinly sliced
2 cups (100 g) bean sprouts
1 bunch Asian chives, cut into lengths
Peanut Sauce (recipe on this page)

In a saucepan, bring the water, vinegar, rice wine and salt to a boil over medium heat. Add the shrimp and simmer for 1 to 2 minutes until pink or just cooked. Remove the shrimp. Reserve the stock. Peel and devein the shrimp. Set aside.

If using pork, heat the oil in a wok or skillet over medium heat. Sear the pork for 1 to 2 minutes until lightly browned on all sides. Add the shrimp stock and simmer for about 15 minutes until the pork is tender. Remove from the heat. When cool, thinly slice the pork.

Combine the pork slices and

Pork Rice Paper Rolls (no recipe, bottom) and Shrimp and Pork Salad Rolls (top)

Fresh Rice Flour Rolls

shrimp in a bowl and mix well.

To make the shrimp rolls, briefly dip a rice paper wrapper in a bowl of water until soft. Remove and place on a dry surface, smoothing it with your fingers. Place a lettuce leaf onto the wrapper and top with some basil, mint, chili, bean sprouts and chive, and 2 heaping tablespoons of the pork-shrimp mixture. Fold one end of the wrapper over the filling, then fold the sides and roll up tightly, pressing to seal. Cut the shrimp roll in half and place on a serving platter. Repeat until all the ingredients are used up.

Serve the rolls with a bowl of Peanut Sauce on the side.

Fresh Rice Flour Rolls

The making of fresh rice flour wrappers is actually quite simple and fun, once you master the method. This is another variation on the spring roll, using freshly steamed rice flour wrappers. You may buy ready-made rice paper wrappers if you do not wish to make your own.

Crispy Fried Shallots (page 73)

Filling
2 tablespoons oil
5 to 6 dried wood ear fungus, soaked in water until soft, sliced to yield about 1/2 cup
4 tablespoons minced shallots (about 4–6 shallots)
1 clove garlic, crushed
1 cup (150 g) minced Carrot and Radish Pickles (page 176)

10 oz (300 g) ground pork or shrimp

Dipping Sauce
1 tablespoon sugar
1 tablespoon rice wine vinegar
1/4 cup (60 ml) water
2 tablespoons fish sauce
1 tablespoon lime juice
1 finger-length red chili, deseeded and minced
2 cloves garlic, minced

Fresh Rice Flour Wrappers
1 cup (125 g) rice flour
3 cups (750 ml) water
1/2 teaspoon salt

Make the Filling first by heating the oil in a wok or skillet over medium heat and stir-frying all the ingredients for about 10 minutes until tender and cooked. Remove and set aside.

Combine the Dipping Sauce ingredients in a bowl and mix until the sugar is completely dissolved. Transfer to a serving bowl and set aside.

To make the Fresh Rice Flour Wrappers, mix the ingredients well to form a smooth batter. Fill a steamer with water until 2/3 full and stretch a piece of cheesecloth very tightly over its top, securing it with a string. Bring the water in the steamer to a boil and brush the cheesecloth with a little oil. In a circular motion, spread a small ladleful of the batter onto the cheesecloth, forming a thin, round layer of batter. Cover with a lid and steam the batter until set, 2 to 3 minutes. Remove by carefully lifting the wrapper from the corners with a spatula. Repeat until all the batter is used up.

Place a Fresh Rice Flour Wrapper on a smooth surface and top with 1 heaping tablespoon of the Filling. Wrap into a roll by folding one end of the wrapper over the Filling, then folding the sides and rolling up gently, taking care not to break the wrapper. Repeat until all the Filling is used up.

Sprinkle the rolls with Crispy Fried Shallots. Serve with a bowl of Dipping Sauce on the side.

Crispy Imperial Rolls

These are the classic, deep-fried Vietnamese spring rolls, also referred to as Imperial Rolls.

20 dried rice paper wrappers (each 8 in/20 cm in diameter)
Oil for deep-frying
1 bunch each of Asian basil, coriander leaves (cilantro) and mint leaves to serve
1 small head butter or leafy lettuce leaves, washed and separated
1 cup (50 g) bean sprouts
Carrot and Daikon Radish Pickles (recipe on facing page)
Fish Sauce Dip (recipe on facing page)

Filling
1 lb (500 g) lean ground pork
7 oz (200 g) fresh shrimp or prawns, peeled, deveined and minced
4 oz (100 g) crabmeat
4 tablespoons minced shallots (about 6 shallots)
3 cloves garlic, minced
2 to 3 dried wood ear fungus, soaked in water until soft, diced
2 oz (50 g) dried glass noodles, soaked in water until soft, drained and cut into thirds

1/2 medium carrot, cut into sticks to yield 1 cup
1 egg white
1 tablespoon ground white pepper
1 teaspoon sugar
1/2 teaspoon salt
3 tablespoons fish sauce

Make the Filling first by combining all the ingredients in a large bowl and mixing until well blended. Set aside.

To make the spring rolls, dip a rice paper wrapper in a bowl of water until soft. Remove and place on a dry surface, smoothing it with your fingers. Place 1 heaping tablespoon of the Filling onto the wrapper. Fold one end of the wrapper over the Filling, then fold the sides and roll up tightly, pressing to seal. Repeat until all the ingredients are used up.

Heat the oil in a wok over medium heat until hot. Deep-fry the spring rolls, a few at a time, for about 5 minutes each until golden brown on all sides. Remove with a slotted spoon and drain on paper towels.

Place the spring rolls on a serving platter and serve with the fragrant leaves, lettuce, bean sprouts, Carrot and Radish Pickles and a bowl of Fish Sauce Dip on the side.

Wrap the fragrant leaves and lettuce around the spring rolls before dipping into the sauce and eating them. This is a fun recipe to experiment with. Try using different ingredients such as ground chicken or duck in the Filling.

Crispy Imperial Rolls

Grilled Shrimp on a Sugar Cane Skewer

This is a very important Vietnamese dish, from the imperial capital of Hue. Fresh sticks of sugar cane are used as skewers. The heated cane releases a burst of sweet cane juice when bitten into.

12 fresh medium shrimp (10 oz/
   300 g), peeled and deveined
1 teaspoon sugar
1/2 teaspoon salt
1/2 teaspoon ground white pepper
1/2 cup (80 g) ground chicken
1/2 teaspoon cornstarch
2 tablespoons oil
8 fresh or canned sugar cane sticks
   (each 4 in/10 cm in length)
Sweet and Sour Sauce (page 176)

Grind the shrimp, sugar, salt and pepper to a paste in a food processor, then combine with the ground chicken and cornstarch in a bowl, and mix until well blended.

Lightly grease your hands with a little oil, spoon 1 tablespoon of the shrimp mixture into one hand and wrap it tightly around the middle of a sugar cane stick. Repeat with the remaining shrimp mixture and sugar cane sticks.

Grill on a pan grill or under a preheated broiler for 5 to 10 minutes, turning frequently until crispy and slightly browned on all sides. Serve hot with a bowl of Sweet and Sour Sauce on the side.

*Grilled Shrimp on a
Sugar Cane Skewer*

Grilled Beef Rolls (left) and Hue Spring Rolls (right)

Grilled Beef Rolls

1 lb (500 g) beef flank
10 dried rice paper wrappers (each
   8 in/20 cm in diameter) or 5 fresh
   rice flour wrappers (see recipe for
   Fresh Rice Flour Rolls on page 177)
1 cup (40 g) mint leaves
1 cup (40 g) Asian basil leaves
1/2 small head butter lettuce,
   washed and separated
1 tablespoon sesame seeds, dry-
   roasted until golden brown
2 bunches coriander leaves (cilantro)

Marinade
1 stalk lemongrass, tender inner part
   of bottom third only, minced
1/2 tablespoon dark brown sugar or
   shaved palm sugar
1 tablespoon fish sauce

Dipping Sauce
1/2 cup (125 ml) Yellow Bean Sauce
   (page 176)
2 tablespoons bottled sweet chili
   sauce
1/2 tablespoon ground roasted
   unsalted peanuts

Combine the Marinade ingredients in a bowl and mix well. Place the beef in the Marinade, mix until well coated and allow to marinate for at least 10 minutes or longer if possible.

Combine all the Dipping Sauce ingredients in a serving bowl and mix well. Set aside.

Grill the beef on a pan grill or under a preheated broiler for 2 to 3 minutes on each side, until lightly browned on the outside but still rare inside. Remove and set aside to cool, then thinly slice the grilled beef.

To make the beef rolls, briefly dip a rice paper wrapper in a bowl of water until soft. Remove and place on a dry surface, smoothing it with your fingers. Place a few slices of beef, some mint, basil and lettuce leaves onto the wrapper. Sprinkle with sesame seeds and top with a few sprigs of coriander leaves. Fold one end of the wrapper over the filling and roll up tightly, pressing to seal and leaving the ends open. Repeat until all the ingredients are used up. If using fresh rice flour wrappers, place the filling onto a wrapper and roll up in the same manner.

Place the beef rolls on a serving platter. Serve with a bowl of Dipping Sauce on the side.

Hue Spring Rolls

1 cup (250 ml) water
1/4 teaspoon salt
4 oz (100 g) lean pork
10 fresh medium shrimp (about 8
   oz/ 250 g), heads removed
10 dried rice paper wrappers (each
   8 in/20 cm in diameter) or 5 fresh
   rice flour wrappers (page 177)
10 sprigs water spinach (kangkong)
1/2 cup (20 g) each Asian basil,
   coriander leaves (cilantro) and
   mint leaves
1 medium sweet potato, peeled,
   steamed and thinly sliced
1 oz (25 g) dried glass noodles,
   soaked in water until soft, drained
   and cut into thirds

Shrimp Paste Dip
2 tablespoons oil
2 cloves garlic, minced
1 tablespoon dried shrimp paste or
   belachan, crumbled
1 sweet potato, steamed and mashed
1 tablespoon sugar

Make the Shrimp Paste Dip first by heating the oil in a wok or skillet over medium heat and stir-frying the garlic for 1 to 2 minutes until fragrant and golden brown. Add the shrimp paste, sweet potato and sugar, and stir-fry until well blended, 2 to 3 minutes. Transfer to a serving bowl.

Bring the water and salt to a boil in a saucepan or small pot. Poach the pork over medium low heat for about 5 minutes until cooked. Remove and set aside to cool. Cut the pork into thin slices.

In the same pot of salted water, poach the shrimp in the same manner for 1 to 2 minutes until pink or just cooked. Remove from the heat and set aside.

To make the spring rolls, briefly dip a rice paper wrapper in a bowl of water until soft. Remove and place on a dry surface, smoothing it with your fingers. Place some water spinach, fragrant leaves, sweet potato and glass noodles onto the wrapper. Fold one end of the wrapper over the filling and roll up tightly, pressing to seal and leaving the ends open. Cut the spring roll into 1-in (2^1/2-cm) segments and place them on a serving platter. Repeat until all the ingredients are used up. If using fresh rice flour wrappers, place the filling onto a wrapper and roll up in the same manner.

Top each segment with a slice of pork and a shrimp. Serve with a bowl of Shrimp Paste Dip on the side.

Shrimp and Vegetable Pancake

The Vietnamese version of an open-faced omelet or crêpe, this specialty of many streetside restaurants is also called the "Happy Pancake". The Vietnamese name, *khoai*, comes from the type of pan it is cooked in. *Banh xeo* is the large southern version.

1^1/4 cups (150 g) rice flour
1^1/4 cups (310 ml) water
2 eggs, beaten
^{1}/4 teaspoon salt
1 teaspoon sugar
2 tablespoons oil
^{1}/2 cup (40 g) straw mushrooms, thinly sliced
8 fresh medium shrimp (7 oz/200g), poached for 30 seconds until just cooked, peeled and deveined
5 strips pork or bacon, pan-fried until cooked and thinly sliced
1 cup (50 g) bean sprouts
2 green onions (scallions), sliced
Fish Sauce Dip (page 176)

Mix the rice flour, water, egg, salt and sugar in a bowl until a smooth batter is obtained. Set aside for 10 minutes, then strain to remove any lumps.

Heat 1 tablespoon of the oil in a wok or skillet over high heat, turning to grease the side. Add ^{1}/2 cup of the batter and

turn the wok or skillet to obtain a thin round layer of batter. Top the batter with some sliced mushrooms, then cover the wok or skillet and pan-fry for about 1 minute, taking care not to scorch the bottom. Remove the cover, add some shrimp, pork slices, bean sprouts and green onion on top, and continue to pan-fry the pancake until golden brown and crispy, about 2 minutes. Remove from the heat. Pan-fry all the pancakes in the same manner.

Serve the pancakes hot with a bowl of Fish Sauce Dip on the side and a plate of lettuce leaves and fragrant leaves such as perillas (*shiso*) and Asian basil.

Squid Salad

1 lb (500 g) fresh medium squids, body sacs only
2 cups (500 ml) water
Ice water, for cooling
2 tablespoons lime juice
4 tablespoons rice wine or sherry
3 cloves garlic, crushed
1 teaspoon sesame oil
1 teaspoon sugar
1 teaspoon crushed black peppercorns
^{1}/2 stalk celery (80 g), sliced
^{1}/2 cup (20 g) minced coriander leaves (cilantro)
1 finger-length red chili, deseeded and minced

Shrimp and Vegetable Pancake

^{1}/2 cup (50 g) Carrot and Daikon Radish Pickles (page 176)
2 tablespoons crushed roasted unsalted peanuts
^{1}/4 cup (60 ml) Fish Sauce Dip (page 176)
Rice crackers

Make a lengthwise cut along each body sac. Open and rinse the inside well. Score the flesh with diagonal criss-cross slits across the surface. This allows the squid to cook quickly. Slice into bite-sized pieces.

Bring the water to a boil in a small pot or saucepan over high heat. Poach the squid pieces until just cooked, 30 seconds to 1 minute. Remove and plunge immediately in ice water to cool. Drain and set aside.

Mix the cooked squid with all the other ingredients in a large bowl. Toss until well combined. Transfer to a serving platter.

Serve the squid salad immediately with rice crackers.

Squid becomes rubbery if overcooked. To achieve a soft and velvety texture, barely cook the squid and quickly plunge it in ice water. Squid may be tenderized by soaking it in milk for a day before cooking.

Shrimp and Green Mango Salad

This is essentially a variation on the traditional Vietnamese shrimp salad—using tart, unripe mango instead of lotus root. Green papaya may also be used.

12 fresh shrimp (10 oz/300 g)
1 small carrot, grated
1 green mango (about 5 oz/150 g), peeled and pitted, cut into sticks to yield about 1 cup
1 tablespoon minced Vietnamese mint leaves
^{1}/4 cup (60 ml) Fish Sauce Dip (page 176)
1 finger-length red chili, deseeded and minced
2 tablespoons Crispy Fried Shallots (page 73)
1 bunch Asian chives, cut into lengths

Steam or poach the shrimp until pink and just cooked. When cool, peel and devein.

Combine the cooked shrimp, carrot, mango, polygonum leaves and Fish Sauce Dip in a large bowl and toss to mix well, adjusting the seasoning with more sugar, fish sauce and lime juice if desired. Transfer to a serving platter and sprinkle with chili, Crispy Fried Shallots and chives. Serve immediately.

Cabbage Salad with Chicken and Herbs

This is the classic chicken salad dish found in most restaurants throughout Vietnam. The unique combination of textures and flavors makes for a delightful, refreshing treat.

1 skinless chicken breast (4 oz/ 100 g), steamed or poached until cooked and shredded to yield 1 cup

$1/2$ head cabbage (about 8 oz / 250 g), leaves washed, rolled up and thinly sliced

2 tablespoons minced mint leaves

2 tablespoons minced Vietnamese mint leaves

3 tablespoons fish sauce

$1^1/2$ tablespoons sugar

2 tablespoons freshly squeezed lime juice

$1/2$ teaspoon crushed black peppercorns

2 tablespoons Crispy Fried Shallots (page 73)

2 tablespoons crushed roasted unsalted peanuts

1 finger-length red chili, deseeded and thinly sliced lengthwise

Combine the chicken, cabbage, mint leaves, fish sauce, sugar, lime juice and pepper in a large bowl and toss to mix well, adjusting the seasoning with more fish sauce, sugar and lime juice as needed. Transfer to a serving platter and top with Crispy Fried Shallots and peanuts.

Garnish with red chili and serve immediately.

Cabbage Salad with Chicken and Herbs

Beef Noodle Soup (Pho Bo)

As with most salads, the cabbage leaves should be rinsed and spun dry before slicing. A salad spinner is an easy and effective way to remove the excess water.

Beef Noodle Soup
Pho Bo

You'll find this soup everywhere in Vietnam—from street stalls to fancy restaurants and it is now served in restaurants all over the world. It is practically Vietnam's national dish.

1 whole fresh ginger root (6 in/15 cm), rinsed and bruised

1 large onion, peeled and bruised

10 cups ($2^1/2$ liters) water

2 lbs (1 kg) beef bones

1 lb (500 g) beef brisket

1 teaspoon salt

3 star anise pods

1 cinnamon stick

1 tablespoon fish sauce

1 teaspoon sugar

1 teaspoon salt

1 teaspoon ground white pepper

8 oz (250 g) dried rice vermicelli (*bun*)

1 cup (50 g) bean sprouts, tops and tails removed

1 medium onion, sliced

8 oz (250 g) beef sirloin, very thinly sliced

Ground white pepper

1 green onion (scallion), sliced

$1/2$ cup (20 g) minced saw-leaf herb leaves (*ngo gai*) or Asian basil

Bottled chili sauce

Yellow Bean Sauce (page 176)

Accompaniments

2 finger-length red chilies, deseeded and sliced

2 limes, cut into wedges

Sprigs of saw-leaf herb leaves (*ngo gai*) or Asian basil

Sprigs of mint leaves

Sprigs of coriander leaves (cilantro)

Grill the ginger and onion under the broiler, turning several times or in a skillet until slightly burnt on all sides, about 5 min-

utes. Remove and set aside.

In a pot, bring the water, beef bones and brisket to a boil, skimming off any foam that floats to the surface. Add the grilled ginger and onion, followed by the salt, star anise and cinnamon. Reduce heat to medium and simmer for about 1 hour until the beef is tender. Remove from the heat.

Remove the beef from the stock. Slice the beef into thin slices and set aside. Strain the stock and return the clear soup to the pot. Season with the fish sauce, sugar, salt and pepper, and keep the soup hot over very low heat.

Bring a separate pot of water to a boil. Add the rice noodles and boil until soft, 5 to 7 minutes or longer as needed. Remove and rinse with cold water, then drain.

Place the rice noodles into individual serving bowls and top with the bean sprouts, onion, cooked and raw beef slices. Pour the hot soup into each bowl (the raw beef will partially cook in the boiling soup), sprinkle with pepper and garnish with green onion and saw-leaf herb leaves.

Serve hot with the Accompaniments, and bowls of chili sauce and Yellow Bean Sauce on the side.

Chicken Noodle Soup

This is one of the many warming winter soups that has been popularized in Hanoi.

1 fresh chicken (about 2¹/4 lbs/1 kg)
¹/2 cup (60 g) dried shrimp, rinsed and drained
1 lb (500 g) pork ribs, cut into large pieces
12 cups (3 liters) water, with 1 teaspoon salt added
1 teaspoon sugar
2 tablespoons fish sauce
1 teaspoon ground white pepper
8–10 shallots, diced
4 green onions (scallions), sliced
1 medium onion, sliced
8 oz (250 g) dried rice vermicelli (bun)
1 egg, beaten and pan-fried, cut into strips
4 tablespoons Crispy Fried Shallots (page 73)
10 oz (300 g) Pork sausage, sliced
Ground white pepper
1 green onion (scallion), sliced
Sprigs of coriander leaves (cilantro)
Yellow Bean Sauce (page 176)

Accompaniments
1 lemon or lime, sliced
2 finger-length red chilies, deseeded and sliced
2 cups (100 g) bean sprouts, blanched until cooked
2 green onions (scallions), green part sliced lengthwise into thin strands
Sliced cabbage
Sprigs of Asian basil leaves

In a stockpot, boil the chicken, dried shrimp and pork ribs in the salted water for about 20 minutes, skimming off any foam that floats to the surface. Reduce the heat to medium, season with the sugar, fish sauce and pepper, and simmer covered for about 45 minutes, until the chicken is cooked. Remove the chicken from the stock and set aside to cool. Add the shallots, green onions and onion to the stock, and mix well. Simmer for another 20 minutes, adjusting the seasoning with more sugar or fish sauce if desired. Keep the soup hot over very low heat.

When the chicken is cool enough to handle, shred into thin strips along the grain. Set aside.

Bring a separate pot of water to a boil. Add the rice noodles and boil until soft, 5 to 7 minutes or longer as needed. Remove and rinse with cold water,

then drain. Transfer to individual serving bowls and top with the egg, chicken strips, sausage and Crispy Fried Shallots. Pour the hot soup into each bowl, sprinkle with pepper and garnish with green onion and coriander leaves. Serve hot with the Accompaniments and Yellow Bean Sauce.

Grilled Eggplant with Crabmeat

This recipe is common to Cambodia and southern Vietnam and makes delicious use of eggplant, one of the many vegetables grown in central Vietnam. Shrimp or stir-fried ground pork may be used in place of the crabmeat.

1 lb (500 g) slender Asian eggplants (2 large or 4 small eggplants)
2 tablespoons oil
1¹/2 cups (175 g) cooked crabmeat
2 tablespoons Crispy Fried Shallots (page 73), to garnish
1 tablespoon thinly sliced green onion (scallion), to garnish
Sprigs of coriander leaves (cilantro), to garnish

Dressing
1 finger-length red chili, deseeded and minced
1¹/2 tablespoons crushed roasted unsalted peanuts
1 tablespoon fish sauce
1¹/2 teaspoons sugar or honey
2 tablespoons water

Combine the Dressing ingredients in a small bowl and mix well. Set aside.

Halve each eggplant lengthwise and brush with a little oil. Grill, a few at a time, on a pan grill or under a preheated broiler using medium heat, turning regularly, until the skin turns brown and the flesh is tender, about 10 minutes. Remove from the heat and set aside to cool. Peel off the skin and discard.

Spread the crabmeat along the top of the eggplant halves and pour the Dressing over. Serve immediately, garnished with Crispy Fried Shallots, green onion and coriander leaves.

Water Spinach with Yellow Bean Sauce

Water spinach has hollow, straw-like stems that are crunchy. Bok choy is a good substitute.

1 lb (500 g) water spinach (kangkung) or bok choy
2 tablespoons oil
2 cloves garlic, crushed
2 green onions (scallions), white part thinly sliced
2 tablespoons Yellow Bean Sauce (page 176)
¹/4 teaspoon salt
¹/4 teaspoon ground white pepper

Rinse the water spinach well in water and remove the thick bottom stems. Slice or tear the upper stems and leaves into pieces.

Heat the oil in a wok or skillet over high heat. Stir-fry the garlic and green onions for about 30 seconds until fragrant and tender. Add the spinach and Yellow Bean Sauce, and mix well. Season with the salt and pepper, then remove from the heat.

Transfer to a serving platter and serve hot with steamed rice.

Grilled Eggplant with Crabmeat

Tofu with Lemongrass and Five Spice

1 cup (250 ml) oil
4 cakes pressed tofu (about
    1 1/2 lbs/750 g in total), halved
    and pressed between paper towels
    to remove moisture
2 stalks lemongrass, tender inner
    part of bottom third only, minced
1 finger-length red chili, deseeded
    and minced
2 cloves garlic, minced
1 teaspoon five spice powder
1/2 teaspoon salt
1/2 teaspoon ground white pepper

Heat the oil in a wok or skillet over medium heat until hot. Pan-fry the tofu for about 2 minutes on each side until golden brown and crispy. Remove and drain on paper towels, then arrange on a serving platter.

Drain off all but 1 tablespoon of the oil in the wok or skillet. Reheat the oil over medium heat and stir-fry the minced lemongrass, chili and garlic until fragrant and tender, 1 to 2 minutes. Season with the five spice powder, salt and pepper and remove from the heat. Spread the mixture on top of the fried tofu and serve hot.

Fried tofu is available in many grocery stores, which makes preparing this dish a snap. Heat the fried tofu in a microwave oven or by lightly steaming it before serving with the lemongrass and five spice topping.

Stir-fried Vegetables with Fish Sauce

3 cups (750 ml) water, with 2 tea-
    spoons salt added
1 carrot, thinly sliced
1 cup (100 g) cauliflower florets
1 cup (80 g) baby corn
12 fresh shiitake or dried Chinese
    black mushrooms, stems discarded
1 1/2 cups (7 oz/200 g) tender kale
    or broccoli stems, sliced diagonally
2 tablespoons oil
1 tablespoon rice wine or sake
2 tablespoons fish sauce
2 cloves garlic, crushed
1 teaspoon ground white pepper

Bring the salted water to a boil in a pot and blanch the carrot, cauliflower and baby corn for about 30 seconds. Remove and quickly plunge into cold water, then drain well.

Heat the oil in a wok or skillet over medium heat. Stir-fry the

mushrooms and kale or broccoli stems for 1 to 2 minutes, then add the blanched vegetables, and continue to stir-fry for 2 more minutes, seasoning with the rice wine and fish sauce. Finally add the garlic, season with the pepper and remove from the heat.

Transfer to a serving platter and serve hot with steamed rice.

When blanching, leave the vegetables in the boiling water just long enough to soften slightly, then place in the cold or ice water immediately to ensure a crisp texture. Do not overcook.

Imperial Fried Rice

2 tablespoons oil
3 shallots, minced
1 cup (200 g) diced pork or chicken
8 fresh shrimp (5 oz/150 g), peeled
    and deveined
1 teaspoon salt
1 teaspoon ground white pepper
4 cups (400 g) cooked rice
2 eggs, fried and diced
1 green onion (scallion), sliced

Heat the oil in a wok or skillet over medium heat. Stir-fry the shallots for 1 to 2 minutes until fragrant and translucent.

Increase the heat to high, add the pork or chicken, shrimp, salt and pepper, and stir-fry to mix well, 1 to 2 minutes. Add the rice and fried diced egg, continue to stir-fry until heated through and well blended, about 2 minutes. Remove from the heat and place on a serving platter

Sprinkle the green onion on top of the fried rice and serve hot.

Sweet Sour Fish Soup

Also known as Vietnamese tamarind fish soup, this dish is light and refreshing.

4 cups (1 liter) water
1 lb (500 g) fresh snapper, mullet or
    catfish fillets, cut into pieces
1/2 cup (75 g) pineapple chunks
    (see note)
1 finger-length red chili, deseeded
    and sliced
1/2 cup (60 g) sliced okra
1/2 cup (75 g) sliced celery
1/2 cup (125 ml) Tamarind Juice
    (page 18)
1/4 cup (10 g) bean sprouts
1 ripe tomato, cut into wedges
3 tablespoons fish sauce
1 tablespoon sugar
1 tablespoon Crispy Fried Shallots
    (page 73)
2 tablespoons minced mint leaves
Sprigs of coriander leaves (cilantro),
    to garnish

Bring the water to a boil in a saucepan and poach the fish for 3 to 5 minutes until just cooked. Remove from the heat and transfer the fish to a large serving bowl. Strain the fish stock.

Return the clear fish stock to the pan and bring to a boil again over high heat. Add the pineapple, chili, okra and taro stems or celery, and mix well. Reduce the heat to medium and simmer for 3 to 4 minutes. Add the Tamarind Juice, bean sprouts and tomato, and bring the mixture to a boil again, skimming off any foam that floats to the surface. Season the soup with the fish sauce and sugar, and remove from the heat.

Pour the hot soup over the fish and top with Crispy Fried Shallots, mint leaves and coriander leaves (cilantro). Serve hot.

If using canned pineapple, drain the syrup and reduce the amount of sugar used.

Tofu with Lemongrass and Five Spice (bottom) and Stir-fried Vegetables with Fish Sauce (top)

Crabs Simmered in Beer

4 lbs (2 kgs) fresh crabs
2 tablespoons oil
1 clove garlic, crushed
1 teaspoon sesame oil
1 tablespoon oyster sauce
1/2 teaspoon salt
1/2 teaspoon ground white pepper
1 large onion, cut into wedges
1 ripe tomato, cut into wedges
1 finger-length red chili, deseeded
  and sliced
1 cup (250 ml) beer
Crispy Fried Shallots (page 73)
Sprigs of watercress

Scrub and rinse the crabs thoroughly. Detach the claws from each crab. Lift off the carapace and discard. Scrape any roe and discard the gills. Rinse well, halve the crabs with a cleaver and crack the claws with a mallet.

Heat the oil in a wok over medium heat and stir-fry the garlic until golden brown and fragrant, 1 to 2 minutes. Increase the heat to high, add the crabs and stir-fry for about 5 minutes, seasoning with the sesame oil, oyster sauce, salt and pepper. Add the onion, tomato and chili, and mix well. Reduce the heat to medium, add the beer, cover the wok and simmer for about 10 minutes until the crabs are cooked. Remove from the heat.

Transfer to a serving platter, sprinkle with Crispy Fried Shallots and garnish with watercress. Serve hot.

Crabs with Tamarind and Rice Wine

Crabs Simmered in Beer

Crabs with Tamarind and Rice Wine

4 lbs (2 kgs) fresh crabs
Oil for deep-frying
1 tablespoon tamarind pulp
1/2 cup (125 ml) rice wine or sherry
4 cloves garlic, minced
2 tablespoons fish sauce
1 teaspoon ground white pepper
2 green onions (scallions), cut into
  lengths
1/4 cup (60 ml) water

Scrub and rinse the crabs thoroughly. Detach the claws from each crab. Lift off the carapace and discard. Scrape out any roe and discard the gills. Rinse well, halve the crabs with a cleaver and crack the claws with a mallet. Pat dry with paper towels.

Heat the oil in a wok until very hot. Deep-fry the crabs for about 30 seconds, until the color changes. Remove and drain on paper towels.

Mix the tamarind pulp with rice wine in a bowl. Mash well and strain. Discard the seeds and fibers. Set aside.

Heat 2 tablespoons of the oil in a wok over medium heat. Stir-fry the garlic for 1 to 2 minutes until fragrant and golden brown. Increase the heat to high, add the deep-fried crabs and stir-fry for 2 to 3 minutes, seasoning with the tamarind mixture, fish sauce and pepper. Reduce the heat to low and stir-fry for 2 more minutes. Finally add the green onions and water, mix well and remove from the heat. Serve immediately with steamed rice.

A large wire strainer with a handle is very useful for lifting the crabs out of the wok. Or if you have a deep-fryer, this makes the cooking easier. You can substitute freshly ground black pepper for white pepper although the latter is preferred by Vietnamese cooks.

Spicy Jumbo Shrimp

This is a southern Vietnamese recipe that calls for jumbo shrimp, which are often almost as big as lobsters.

1 tablespoon oil
3 cloves garlic, minced
1 finger-length red chili, deseeded
  and minced
1 teaspoon crushed black peppercorns
11/2 tablespoons sugar
3 tablespoons fish sauce
1/2 cup (125 ml) water
6 fresh jumbo shrimp (about
  11/2 lbs/750 g in total)
4 tablespoons minced coriander
  leaves (cilantro)

Heat the oil in a wok or skillet over medium heat. Stir-fry the garlic and chili until fragrant and soft, 1 to 2 minutes. Add the black peppercorns, sugar, fish sauce and water, and mix well. Add the shrimp and simmer uncovered for 7 to 10 minutes, basting frequently with the sauce, until the shrimp turn pink and are just cooked. Remove the shrimp and arrange them on a serving platter.

Reduce the heat to low and continue to simmer the sauce until it thickens, 3 to 5 minutes. Remove from the heat and pour the sauce over the shrimp and garnish with coriander leaves. Serve hot.

Marinated Grilled Squid

1 lb (500 g) fresh medium squids,
   body sacs only
1/2 tablespoon salt
Sprigs of coriander leaves (cilantro)
Fish Sauce Dip (page 176)

Marinade
1/2 teaspoon ground white pepper
2 cloves garlic, crushed
2 tablespoons oil
1 teaspoon five spice powder
1 teaspoon curry powder
1 tablespoon minced lemongrass
   (tender inner part of bottom third
   only)
1 tablespoon dark soy sauce
1 teaspoon sesame oil
1 tablespoon lime juice
1 teaspoon sugar

Make a lengthwise cut along
each squid body sac. Open up
and rinse the inside well. Score
the flesh by making diagonal
criss-cross slits across the surface. This allows the squid to
cook very quickly. Slice into
bite-sized pieces.

Rub the salt onto the squid
pieces. Set aside for about 15
minutes, then rinse and drain.

Combine the Marinade
ingredients in a bowl and mix
well. Place the squid pieces in
the Marinade. Mix well and let it
stand for at least 1 hour.

Grill the marinated squid
pieces on a pan grill or under a
preheated broiler using high
heat until just cooked, about
2 minutes on each side.

Arrange the grilled squid on
a serving platter and garnish
with coriander leaves. Serve hot
with a bowl of Fish Sauce Dip
on the side.

Fish Stew with Dill and Tomato

6 cups (1 1/2 liters) chicken stock
1 lb (500 g) freshwater fish fillets,
   cut into chunks
2 ripe tomatoes, cut into wedges
1 tablespoon minced dill
1 teaspoon salt
1/2 teaspoon ground white pepper
Fresh dill, to garnish

Bring the Chicken Stock to a
boil in a pot. Add the fish and
simmer for about 5 minutes,
skimming off any foam that floats

to the surface, then add the
tomato and chopped dill, seasoning with the salt and pepper.
Simmer for another 2 to 3 minutes and remove from the heat.

Serve hot in individual
bowls. Garnish with fresh dill.

Braised Fish Fillets with Galangal Sauce

3 tablespoons oil
6 fish steaks (halibut, swordfish or
   carp, each about 4 oz/100 g)
1 1/2 in (4 cm) fresh galangal root,
   peeled and cut into thin strips
2 tablespoons fish sauce
1 tablespoon Caramel Syrup
   (page 176)
1/2 cup (125 ml) water

Heat the oil in a wok or skillet
over medium heat. Stir-fry the
galangal until golden brown
and fragrant, about 1–2 minutes. Add the fish steaks and
pan-fry for 2–3 minutes on each
side. Add the fish sauce,
Caramel Syrup and water, and
braise the fish uncovered until
cooked, about 5 minutes.
Remove from the heat.

Arrange on a serving platter
and serve hot with steamed rice.

Whole Fish with Ginger Lemongrass Sauce

1 fresh grouper, snapper or sea bass
   (about 1 1/2 lbs/750 g)
1/4 teaspoon salt
1/2 teaspoon ground white pepper
1 tablespoon oil
1 tablespoon sliced green onion
   (scallion)

Sauce
1 tablespoon oil
3 fresh shiitake mushrooms, stems
   discarded, caps thinly sliced
1 1/2 in (4 cm) fresh ginger root,
   peeled and cut into thin shreds
1 tablespoon minced lemongrass
   (tender inner part of bottom third
   only)
1 finger-length red chili, deseeded
   and cut into thin strips
1 teaspoon soy sauce
2 tablespoons fish sauce
1/2 cup (125 ml) water

Clean and pat the fish dry with
paper towels. Rub the salt and
pepper onto the fish and brush
with a little oil. Grill the fish on
a pan grill or under a preheated
broiler using medium heat for
about 7 minutes on each side,
until the fish is cooked.

Alternatively, you can shallow-fry
the fish in a wok or skillet using
4 tablespoons of oil for 3–5 minutes on each side until crispy
and cooked. Remove and transfer the fish to a serving platter.

Combine the Sauce ingredients in a saucepan and simmer
over low heat for about 5 minutes. Remove and pour the
Sauce over the fish.

Garnish the fish with green
onion and serve hot.

Pork Stewed in Coconut Juice

2 lbs (1 kg) boneless pork loin, cut
   into chunks
1 tablespoon oil
2 cups (500 ml) young coconut
   juice (from 1 young coconut)
5 eggs, hard-boiled and shelled

Marinade
4 cloves garlic, minced
1 tablespoon shaved palm sugar
6 tablespoons fish sauce

Make the Marinade by combining all the ingredients in a bowl.
Place the pork in the Marinade,
mix until well coated and allow
to marinate for at least 1 hour.

Whole Fish with Ginger Lemongrass Sauce (left) and Braised Fish Fillets with Galangal Sauce (right)

Pork Stewed in Coconut Juice

Heat the oil in a wok or skillet over medium high heat until hot. Sear the marinated pork for 2 minutes on each side, until lightly browned. Add the coconut juice and bring to a boil. Reduce the heat to low and simmer uncovered for 30 to 45 minutes, skimming off any foam that floats to the surface, until the pork is tender. Add the eggs (if using) and simmer for another 15 minutes before removing from the heat.

Serve hot with fresh vegetables and steamed rice.

Grilled Pork Meatballs

1 lb (500 g) ground pork
1/2 teaspoon salt
7 oz (200 g) pork fatback
2 tablespoons sugar
2 cloves garlic, minced
2 red finger-length chilies, deseeded and minced
1 teaspoon salt
3/4 tablespoon ground white pepper
12 bamboo skewers, soaked in water for 1 hour before using
2 tablespoons ground roasted unsalted peanuts (optional)
Fish Sauce Dip (page 176), for dipping

Accompaniments
1 cup (50 g) beansprouts
1 starfruit, washed and thinly sliced
2 medium unripe bananas, peeled and thinly sliced
1/2 small cucumber, halved and thinly sliced

Combine the ground pork and salt in a bowl and mix well. Set aside.

Pan-fry the pork fatback in a skillet over medium heat for about 8 minutes. Remove and set aside to cool, then slice into very thin strips. Season the pork strips with the sugar, garlic, chilies, salt and pepper, and set aside for at least 5 minutes, then combine with the ground pork and mix well.

Wet your hands, spoon 1 heaping tablespoon of the pork mixture and shape it into a bowl. Repeat until all the pork mixture is used up.

Thread the meatballs onto bamboo skewers. Grill the meatballs, a few skewers at a time, on a pan grill or under a preheated broiler using medium heat for about 5 minutes each, turning frequently until cooked.

Sprinkle the grilled meatballs with ground peanuts and serve with the Accompaniments and a bowl of Fish Sauce Dip on the side.

Grilled Pork Skewers with Rice Noodles

1 lb (500 g) pork shoulder, cubed
7 oz (200 g) dried rice vermicelli (bun)
1 green onion (scallion), green parts only, thinly sliced
15 bamboo skewers, soaked in water for 1 hour before using
Sprigs of Asian basil leaves
2 cups Carrot and Radish Pickles (page 176)
Peanut Sauce (page 176)

Marinade
1 teaspoon minced garlic
2 baby leeks or green onions (scallions), sliced
3 tablespoons fish sauce
1/2 teaspoon ground white pepper
1 tablespoon sugar

Combine the Marinade ingredients in a large bowl and mix well. Place the pork cubes in the Marinade and mix until well coated. Set aside to marinate for at least 20 minutes.

Bring a pot of water to a boil. Add the rice noodles and boil until soft, about 5–7 minutes. Remove and rinse with cold water, then drain. Transfer to individual serving bowls and sprinkle the noodles with green onion. Set aside.

Thread the marinated pork onto bamboo skewers. Grill the skewers, a few at a time, on a pan grill or under a preheated broiler using medium heat, turning and basting frequently with the Marinade, for about 5 minutes each, until the pork is cooked through and evenly browned on all sides.

Arrange the grilled pork skewers on a serving platter and garnish with basil leaves. Serve with the rice noodles, Carrot and Radish Pickles (if using) and a bowl of Peanut Sauce.

Grilled Pork Meatballs(left) and Grilled Pork Skewers with Rice Noodles (right)

Honey Roasted Chicken

Honey Roasted Chicken

2 tablespoons sugar
2 teaspoons sesame oil
2 teaspoons salt
2 teaspoons ground white pepper
1 fresh chicken (about 3 lbs/ 1¹/2 kgs)
Cucumber and tomato slices

Honey Glaze
3 tablespoons honey
2 tablespoons sweet black soy sauce
1 tablespoon annatto seed oil
   (see recipe for Fragrant Beef Stew
   on this page)
1 tablespoon lime juice
1 teaspoon sesame oil

Combine the sugar, sesame oil, salt and pepper in a bowl, and mix well. Rub the mixture onto the outside and inside of the chicken. Seal the cavity with a skewer and set aside for 1 hour. Preheat the oven to 375°F (190°C). Combine the Honey Glaze ingredients in a bowl and mix well.

Place the chicken on a roasting pan and spread ¹/2 of the Honey Glaze over the chicken. Roast the chicken in the oven for about 40 minutes, basting with the remaining Honey Glaze every 10 to 15 minutes, until golden brown and well cooked.

Cut the chicken into pieces and serve hot with cucumber and tomato slices.

Fragrant Beef Stew

3 tablespoons oil
2 tablespoons annatto seeds
5 cloves garlic, minced
1 large onion, diced
2 tablespoons sugar
2 lbs (1 kg) top round (top-side)
   beef, cut into chunks
1 tablespoon salt
1 tablespoon curry powder
1 cup (250 ml) beer or water
1 stalk lemongrass, tender inner part
   of bottom third only, bruised
3 star anise pods
1 cinnamon stick
1 carrot, sliced diagonally
1 lime, sliced, to serve
1 cup (40 g) mint leaves
Salt, Pepper and Lime Mix (page 176)

Heat the oil in a wok or skillet over medium heat. Briefly stir-fry the annatto seeds until the oil turns reddish-brown. Remove from the heat, strain the oil and discard the seeds.

Fragrant Beef Stew

Combine ¹/2 of the annatto flavored oil, ¹/2 of the garlic, the onion, sugar and salt in a large bowl. Add the beef chunks and mix well. Allow to marinate for at least 30 minutes.

Heat the remaining annatto flavored oil over medium heat. Stir-fry the remaining garlic until fragrant and golden brown, 1 to 2 minutes. Add the curry powder, beer or water and marinated beef, and mix well. Bring the mixture to a boil, then add a little water, lemongrass, star anise and cinnamon, and stir well. Reduce the heat to low and braise the beef uncovered for about 45 minutes until tender. Add the carrot and simmer for another 10 minutes until cooked. Remove from the heat.

Serve the beef stew with lime, mint leaves and a bowl of Salt, Pepper and Lime Mix on the side.

Steamed Rice Flour and Mung Bean Cakes

1¹/2 cups (200 g) rice flour
1¹/3 cups (250 g) sugar
1 teaspoon pandanus or vanilla
   essence mixed with 2¹/2 cups (625
   ml) water
²/3 cup (150 g) dried yellow mung
   beans, soaked in water overnight
   to soften
1 tablespoon vanilla essence
15 banana leaf pieces (each 8 x 6
   in/20 x 15 cm), soaked in hot
   water to soften, for wrapping

Steamed Rice Flour and Mung Bean Cakes (left)

2 tablespoons oil, for greasing the
banana leaves
Toothpicks, for fastening
1 1/2 cups (375 ml) thick coconut milk
3 tablespoons sugar
1/2 teaspoon salt
1/2 tablespoon cornstarch
2 tablespoons roasted sesame seeds

Combine the rice flour, 2/3 cup
(130 g) of the sugar and 2 cups
(500 ml) of the pandanus juice
in a saucepan. Heat over low
heat, stirring constantly, until
the mixture thickens to a paste,
about 20 minutes. Remove from
the heat.

Heat the mung beans, re-
maining sugar and vanilla
essence in a saucepan over low
heat, stirring constantly, until
the mixture thickens to a similar
consistency as the rice flour
paste, about 5 minutes. Remove
and set aside to cool. Wet your
hands and roll the mung bean
paste into 15 small balls.

Lightly grease a piece of the
banana leaf with a little oil.
Spread 1 tablespoon of the rice
flour paste in the middle of the
leaf and place a mung bean ball
on top, then cover the mung
bean ball with more rice flour
paste. Fold one of the longer
ends of the banana leaf over the
filling, then the other longer
side over it tightly. Tuck both
sides of the leaf underneath and

secure the packet with toothpicks. Repeat until all the ingredients are used up. Steam the
rice cakes for about 20 minutes
until cooked.

Heat the remaining pandanus
juice, coconut milk, sugar, salt
and cornstarch in a saucepan
over medium heat, stirring
occasionally, until the sugar is
dissolved and the mixture is thick,
about 10 minutes. Remove and
transfer to a serving bowl.

To serve, unwrap the rice
cakes. Sprinkle some sesame
seeds on top and spread the
coconut sauce over them.

Banana Coconut Cake

1 3/4 lbs (800 g) ripe bananas (about
5 bananas), peeled and thinly
sliced lengthwise
1 cup (200 g) sugar
3/4 cup (185 ml) coconut cream
1/2 teaspoon vanilla essence
8 slices sandwich bread
2 tablespoons melted butter
Vanilla ice cream

Sprinkle the banana slices with
1/2 of the sugar.

In a small pot, heat the
remaining sugar and coconut
cream over medium heat until
the sugar is dissolved. Add the
vanilla essence and mix well.
Remove from the heat.

Remove and discard the
crusts from the bread. Briefly
soak the bread in the sweetened
coconut cream and transfer to a
plate. Set aside.

Preheat the oven to 350°F
(180°C). Grease a cake pan (12
in/30 cm in diameter) with
some butter. Arrange a layer of
the banana slices on the base of
the pan, then top with a layer of
the bread. Repeat to lay alternate layers of banana and bread
in the pan and finish the top
layer with the banana slices.
Drizzle the remaining butter
over the top. Cover with aluminum foil and bake in the oven
for about 1 hour. Remove from
the heat and set aside for 12
hours before slicing.

Serve the banana cake with
vanilla ice cream (if using).

*Banana Coconut Cake (left)
and Pineapple Tartlets (right)*

Pineapple Tartlets

24 tartlet molds (each 2 in/5 cm in
diameter)

Dough
1 cup (225 g) soft salted butter
1/4 cup (50 g) sugar
1/2 cup (125 ml) fresh milk
4 cups (600 g) flour
2 eggs, beaten

Filling
1 large or 2 small pineapples (about
3 lbs/1 1/4 kg in total) peeled,
cored, minced or chopped
1 cup (200 g) sugar
2 drops vanilla essence

Make the Dough first by combining the butter, sugar and
milk in a mixing bowl and beating until well blended. Fold in
the flour and continue beating
until a smooth dough is formed.
Flour your hands and using a
rolling pin, roll the Dough on a
floured surface to 1/8 in (3 mm)
thick. Cut out circles large
enough to line the tartlet molds.
Lightly flour each mold and line
with a Dough circle. Cut the
remaining Dough into thin strips.

Preheat the oven to 300°F
(150°C). To make the Filling, heat
the pineapple and sugar in a
saucepan over low heat for about
45 minutes, stirring continuously,
until the mixture is thickened.
Add the vanilla essence, mix well
and remove from the heat. Fill
each mold with the Filling and
lay the Dough strips to form a
criss-cross pattern on top. Brush
with the beaten egg and bake
in the oven for 30 minutes
until golden brown.

MEASUREMENTS AND CONVERSION TABLES

Measurements in this book are given in volume as far as possible. Teaspoon, tablespoon and cup measurements should be level, not heaped, unless otherwise indicated. Australian readers please note that the standard Australian measuring spoon is larger than the UK or American spoon by 5 ml, so use only $3/4$ tablespoon when following the recipes.

LIQUID CONVERSIONS

Imperial	Metric	US cups
$1/2$ fl oz	15 ml	1 tablespoon
1 fl oz	30 ml	$1/8$ cup
2 fl oz	60 ml	$1/4$ cup
4 fl oz	125 ml	$1/2$ cup
5 fl oz ($1/4$ pint)	150 ml	$2/3$ cup
6 fl oz	175 ml	$3/4$ cup
8 fl oz	250 ml	1 cup
12 fl oz	375 ml	$11/2$ cups
16 fl oz	500 ml	2 cups

Note:
   1 UK pint = 20 fl oz
   1 US pint = 16 fl oz

SOLID WEIGHT CONVERSIONS

Imperial	Metric
$1/2$ oz	15 g
1 oz	30g
$11/2$ oz	50 g
2 oz	60 g
3 oz	90 g
$31/2$ oz	100 g
4 oz ($1/4$ lb)	125 g
5 oz	150 g
6 oz	185 g
7 oz	200 g
8 oz ($1/2$ lb)	250 g
9 oz	280 g
10 oz	300 g
16 oz (1 lb)	500 g (0.5 kg)
32 oz (2 lb)	1 kg

OVEN TEMPERATURES

Heat	Fahrenheit	Centigrade/Celsius	British Gas Mark
Very cool	225	110	$1/4$
Cool or slow	275–300	135–150	1–2
Moderate	350	175	4
Hot	425	220	7
Very hot	450	230	8

INDEX